Pakistan in Regional and Global Politics

Pakistan in Regional and Global Politics

Editor
Rajshree Jetly

Routledge
Taylor & Francis Group

LONDON AND NEW YORK

First published 2009 by Routledge

2 Park Square, Milton Park, Abingdon, Oxfordshire OX14 4RN
711 Third Avenue, New York, NY 10017

Routledge is an imprint of the Taylor & Francis Group, an informa business

First issued in paperback 2018

Typeset by
Star Compugraphics Private Limited
D–156, Second Floor
Sector 7, Noida 201 301

British Library Cataloguing-in-Publication Data
A catalogue record of this book is available from the British Library

ISBN: 978-0-415-48141-0 (hbk)
ISBN: 978-1-138-38421-7 (pbk)

Contents

List of Tables   vii
List of Figures   ix
Preface   xi

Introduction   xiii
  Rajshree Jetly

1. Musharraf and Pakistan's Crisis   1
   Amin Saikal

2. Global Terrorism: US Policy After 9/11 and Its Impact
   on the Domestic Politics and Foreign Relations
   of Pakistan   20
   Selig S. Harrison

3. Nuclear Issue: Current Developments and Future
   Challenges for Pakistan   45
   Pervaiz Iqbal Cheema

4. Managing Ambivalence: Pakistan's Relations with
   the United States and China since 2001   63
   Kanti Bajpai

5. The Progress of Détente in India–Pakistan Relations:
   New Chapter or Strategic Charade?   98
   Robert G. Wirsing

6. Pakistan's Relations with Central Asia   125
   C. Christine Fair

7. The Spectre of Islamic Fundamentalism over Pakistan
   (1947–2007)   150
   Ishtiaq Ahmed

8. Civil–Military Relations in Pakistan   181
   Mohammad Waseem

9. Resurgence of the Baluch Movement in Pakistan:
   Emerging Perspectives and Challenges   212
   Rajshree Jetly

10. Pakistan: Political Economy and Post-2000
    Developments   235
    Imran Ali

11. Analyzing Pakistan's Economic Prospects in an
    Increasingly Integrated World: External Constraints
    on Sustainable Growth   262
    Arslan Razmi

12. The Puzzle of Pakistan's Social Sector Development:
    Finally on Track?   311
    S. Akbar Zaidi

Bibliography   333
About the Editor   350
Notes on Contributors   351

Index   357

List of Tables

5.1 Hydel Potential of India's Major River Basins/
Systems   111
5.2 Status of Hydroelectric Potential Development in
India, 2006   111
5.3 State-wise Status of 50,000 MW Hydel Initiatives   112

8.1 Patterns of Civilian and Military Rule
in Pakistan, 1947–2009   187

11.1 Sources of Aggregate Demand (%),
1975–2003   264
11.2 Pakistan's Tariffs on Non-Agricultural and
Non-Fuel Imports   267
11.3 Pakistan's External Accounts (US$ mn.),
1976–2005   270
11.4 Composition of Pakistani Imports and Exports
by Origin and Destination (%)   273
11.5 SITC2-Wise Classification of Pakistan's Exports   274
11.6 SITC2-Wise Classification of Pakistan's Imports   275
11.7 Broad Economic Categories (BEC) Classification
of Pakistan's Exports (US$ mn. and %)   276
11.8 Broad Economic Categories (BEC) Classification
of Pakistan's Imports (US$ mn. and %)   277
11.9 Percentage of High-Technology Products in Each
Developing Country's Total Exports   278
11.10 Concentration of Pakistan's Exports Relative
to Other Developing Countries   282
11.11 A Comparison of Intra-Group Trade within
SAARC and Other Regional Trade
Groupings (US$ mn. and %)   284

12.1 Growth Rates (%)   314
12.2 Trends in Growth, Poverty and Income Distribution   317
12.3 International Comparison of the Social Sectors   323
12.4 Pakistan's Human Development Index, 1975–2004   328

List of Figures

5.1 Shares of Exports and Imports in South Asia, 2005   104
5.2 SAARC Two-Way Trade, 1998–2006   105

11.1 Contribution of Various Sectors to Value-Added
(% of Total Value Added)   265
11.2 Evolution of the Fiscal Balance and Government
Revenue as a Proportion of GDP, 1953–2005   266
11.3 Evolution of Pakistan's Trade as a Proportion of GDP
(left-hand scale) and Taxes on International Trade as
Percentage of Total Revenues (right-hand scale)   268
11.4 Current Account, Financial Account, and Official
Reserves (US$ bn.), 1976–2004   268
11.5 The Persistent Savings–Investment Gap, 1976–2004   272
11.6 The SITC Category-Wise Composition of
Developing Country Exports, 1984–2004   279
11.7 The Technology Composition of Pakistan's Trade
Structure in Comparative Terms   280
   (a) Growth Rates of Manufacturing Value-Added,
     1980–2000   280
   (b) Share of Manufactured Exports by Technology,
     1976–2000   280
   (c) Value of Pakistani Exports by Technology
     (US$ mn.)   281
   (d) Comparative Export Structures by Technology,
     1981–2000   281
11.8 Free Market Price of Pakistani Cotton
(Pakistan Sindh/Punjab, SG Afzal, 1–1/32",
CIF North Europe [¢/lb.])   283
11.9 Composition of Merchandise Exports from
Developing Countries by Major Product Group,
1980–2003   291
11.10 Pakistan's Real Exchange Rate with Respect
to Developed and Developing Countries,
Respectively, 1984–2004   294

11.11 Recent Evolution of Net Barter Terms of Trade
for Different Groups of Developing Countries   295
11.12 Worker Remittances as a Percentage of GDP,
Official Development Assistance (ODA) as a
Percentage of GDP, and Pakistan's Share of Total
ODA Destined for Developing Countries   297
11.13 Remittances, Official Development Assistance
(ODA), and Debt Servicing Obligations (US$ mn.)   297
11.14 Time Plots of Worker Remittances as a Percentage
of GDP (left-hand scale) and Real GDP Growth
Rate (right-hand scale)   299

Preface

This book arose out of a conference held in May 2007 under the aegis of the Institute of South Asian Studies, an autonomous research institute at the National University of Singapore. The conference was conceived at a time when Pakistan was relatively stable, albeit under military rule, and was a key player in the global war on terrorism. Nevertheless, signs were emerging that Pakistan's political future was in trouble, as the state was already at the centre of several conflicting tensions. There was a growing movement against General Musharraf with calls for return to civilian democratic rule. Rising Islamic militancy within Pakistan was targeting not just the Western powers but the Pakistani state itself. In February 2008, Pakistan returned to democratic rule and in August 2008, Musharraf stepped down as the President of Pakistan. Unfortunately Pakistan remains mired in crisis as the two leading democratic parties in the ruling coalition, namely the PPP and PML-N, have since parted ways over a number of issues. As this book goes to Press, the leader of the PPP, Asif Ali Zardari has been elected President of Pakistan.

The period that is the focus of this collection of essays is between the events of 11 September 2001 and the return to democratic elections in February 2008. This is a period marked by heightened international concern for security and the rule of Pakistan by a military dictator. The various chapters in this book analyze Pakistan's political, social and economic developments in the context of a country that is grappling with democratization, religious fundamentalism, domestic ethnic conflict and international terrorism. The authors who were invited to contribute the various chapters were selected both for their special expertise and for their diversity in terms of scholarly and expert views, thus providing an objective evaluation of the subject matter.

Many people have contributed to the production of this volume. First of all, I would like to acknowledge the generous funding and support of the Institute of South Asian Studies under the Chairmanship of Mr Gopinath Pillai and the leadership of the Director, Prof Tan Tai Yong. I would especially like to thank Prof Tan Tai Yong for entrusting this project to me and for his constant encouragement and guidance. I am also grateful to the Head of Research, Dr Narayan, for his support. Thanks are also due to the administrative team, led by Mr Hernaikh Singh for their efficiency and their patience in dealing with the numerous organizational matters surrounding the conference which generated this book. The book benefitted considerably from the intellectual stimulation provided by my fellow researchers, especially Prof Ishtiaq Ahmed whose valuable insights of Pakistan were most helpful.

I would like to take this opportunity to recognize all the contributors for their scholarly work and their patience and cooperation in finalizing the chapters for publication. I would also like to express my gratitude to the team at Routledge especially Mr Prabir Bhambal and Dr Nilanjan Sarkar as well as the anonymous referee for the helpful comments that greatly improved the final product. Finally, and on a personal note, I would like to acknowledge the love and support of my husband, Kumaralingam, and our two sons, Krishiv and Ishan, the latter of whom was born just two months before the conference on which this book is based.

Rajshree Jetly

8 September 2008

Introduction

Rajshree Jetly

Pakistan is once again at a critical juncture in its political history as it undertakes an uncertain journey towards democratization. The key question Pakistan faces today is whether it will be able to put in place a new stable democratic order, or whether it will slip further into a political turmoil that has characterized most of its history. The world is watching because the present situation has ramifications far beyond Pakistan, affecting the region and the globe in an era forever changed by the events of 9/11. Given Pakistan's difficult journey so far, it is not an easy task to make projections for its future, but what is clear is that its future would lie as much in the political processes and structures that evolve now as in the inherited legacies of its difficult past.

Three factors deserve attention in this regard. First, Pakistan has been under military rule for more than half the years of its existence, including the preceding decade. The country has witnessed three coup d'états — at almost regular intervals in 1958, 1977 and 1999 — and celebrated its 60th anniversary in 2007 under the shadow of military rule. The military in Pakistan has come to exercise a formidable influence, both 'direct' and 'indirect', in all spheres of the Pakistani polity, be it political, economic or social. Second, Pakistan has been plagued by exceptional political turbulence since its inception and has had a poor record of democracy. Its political scene has, over the years, been characterized by weak party systems and organizational structures. More important, the major political parties have indulged in personal rivalries and petty politicking, often placing self-interest ahead of long-term national interests, and have made little effort to sustain a durable framework of participatory processes and institutions. Third, and possibly of the greatest significance, is the equilibrium that has come to characterize civil–military relations in Pakistan. Notwithstanding the oft-repeated promises of successive military leaderships to work for a quick return to democracy and the political spectrum's firm commitment to establish a stable democratic framework, the situation on the ground remains strikingly different. In reality, the military rulers, while seeking political legitimacy, have steadily entrenched their control over key sectors of the Pakistani polity. On the other hand, successive democratic dispensations in Pakistan, while seeking to curtail the power of the military, have inevitably hobnobbed with it to remain in political power. This has led to a vicious cycle, which has become an integral part of Pakistan's political realities, and remains crucial to understanding Pakistan's continuing political paradox.

This book makes a broad assessment of Pakistan in the context of regional and global politics, delineating the major strategic, political and economic trends in its polity in the last decade. General Pervez Musharraf's assumption of power in 1999 in a bloodless coup signalled the end of a decade of turbulent civilian democracy and the return of military rule in Pakistan. More important, it coincided with the momentous fallout of 9/11, which had significant implications for Pakistan's domestic and foreign policy concerns. Several key factors marked the post-9/11 period as a critical one for Pakistan. First, it witnessed the advent of global terrorism, fuelled by growing religious fundamentalism with its epicentre remaining in and around Pakistan. Pakistan had to project itself as a moderate Islamic state that could engage both the Islamic bloc and the Western world in the altered geopolitical environment. Second, this period also saw the nuclear coming of age for India and Pakistan, both of which tested their nuclear weapons in 1998, with far-reaching implications for Pakistan's regional and global security perspectives. Third, this period marked the most dangerous period for Pakistan's internal stability as growing ethnic conflict and religious radicalism challenged the state to its very foundation.

▓ Musharraf's Rise to Power

After ousting the democratically elected government of Nawaz Sharif and assuming charge in 1999, Musharraf made the routine declarations about introducing 'real democracy' in Pakistan and restoring the democratic processes through free and fair elections. However, once in power, he behaved exactly in the same manner as the preceding military governments under General Ayub Khan and General Zia-ul-Haq. He set about systematically consolidating his own power base by declaring a state of emergency and suspending the Constitution, and further ensured by a special decree that his actions could not be challenged by a special court. In 2002, he sought political legitimacy through a controversial referendum and secured a mandate for five years in office as President. Secure in his new position, he effected a key constitutional change, restoring the power to the President for dismissing the National Assembly. Simultaneously, he also put in place a military dominated National Security Council, which gave the military an unprecedented institutional role in the country's governance. In the event, the new civilian government that came to power following the 2002 elections remained intrinsically impotent, as President Musharraf continued to exercise formidable power while holding the dual offices of President and Army Chief.

Musharraf's consolidation of power and concurrent occupation of the post of the Army Chief and President rankled the major opposition parties. This led to a political deadlock with both the secular opposition and the newly formed Muttahida Majlis-e-Amal (MMA), comprising the Islamist parties, opposing the constitutional changes and his continuation as Army Chief. Musharraf countered this by springing a surprise in making a surreptitious deal with the Islamist opposition by agreeing to bring the constitutional changes before the Parliament and to give up the office of Army Chief before 2004 end. Although the non-Islamist parties unified under the banner of ARD (Alliance for Restoration of Democracy) and continued their struggle against Musharraf, it was clear that Musharraf had no intention to relinquish the post of Army Chief as promised, and was hoping instead to ride out the political storm through clever political manipulations.

To some extent, Musharraf was able to derive some political mileage by focusing on his economic performance, which had resulted in a visible improvement in Pakistan's economy under his leadership. The country was in a dire economic crisis when he assumed power, with a consistent drop in its GDP and rising government debts. However, Pakistan witnessed a positive upturn in its macroeconomic indicators after 2001, as a result of the infusion of a massive dose of foreign aid following 9/11. Subsequently, Musharraf was able to push through with his macroeconomic and administrative reforms, which resulted in greater productivity and an improved growth rate in Pakistan. Its total liquid reserves rose to about $13.7 billion in 2007, registering a staggering five-fold increase from its dismal showing in 1999. More important, Pakistan was also able to stabilize its external debt, which had reached dangerous levels in 2000. Foreign remittances grew from US$ 1 billion in 2001 to over US$ 4 billion in 2003. Industrial and service sectors grew substantially, resulting in a steady increase in Pakistan's real GDP. Poverty rates in Pakistan dropped substantially from 34 per cent to 24 per cent. Notwithstanding some persisting negatives — lagging growth of the agricultural sector, high rates of domestic inflation, undue dependence on foreign aid and lending and fiscal deficits — Pakistan's economic environment improved considerably under Musharraf. This created a feel-good factor that won him support from large sections of the populace who had derived benefits from a revitalized economy, and helped him, to some extent, to offset his increasingly negative political image.

Another area where Musharraf was able to score was in his dextrous management of Pakistan's foreign policy concerns and its relations with the external world. 9/11 and the United States' declaration of a global war on terrorism brought Pakistan into sharp focus as an important strategic player in the regional and geopolitical security environment. The three biggest challenges that emerged on the global scene were fundamentalist terrorism, nuclear stability, and regional security. Pakistan was in some ways integral to all of them: as a nuclear power, which shared borders with two other nuclear weapon states in Asia, namely India and China; as a front-line state in the US-led war on terror; and as an Islamic gateway to the strategic regions in Central Asia and West Asia. Cognizant of the fact that Pakistan had been pushed to the centre stage as an important strategic player in the altered geo-strategic context, Musharraf moved deftly to work out a delicate balance in its external relations, particularly with the United States, China and India.

▣ Strategic and Foreign Policy Perspectives

The foremost foreign policy concern for Musharraf was to structure Pakistan's relationship with the United States as its key ally in the global crusade against international terrorism. Pakistan–US relations, it may be mentioned here, have been generally marked by a broad strategic convergence on regional and global security issues: Pakistan sought close relations with the United States as a countervailing power to Indian pre-eminence in South Asia; the United States, on its part, found Pakistan a valuable ally in its wider regional and global security agenda. Inevitably, the frequent ups and downs in the state of relations between the two countries became a function of Pakistan's relevance in the United States' security interests and priorities.

On assuming power, Musharraf's key foreign policy concern was how to deal with the pressures of a lukewarm relationship with the United States, whose changed strategic priorities in the post-Cold War had put Pakistan on the backburner of its security calculations. Pak-US relations remained strained on a number of issues, the most important being the unceremonious siphoning off of US aid and Islamabad's defiant consolidation of its nuclear weapons programme and indulgence in a game of brinksmanship with India. The US' imposition of sanctions on Pakistan soon after its nuclear tests in 1998 and its military coup in 1999 made for a new low in Pak-US relations.

Things however changed dramatically post-9/11 with Pakistan once again becoming important to the United States' vital regional and global interests. Its emergence as a front-line state initiated for Islamabad a new phase of close relations with the United States, even as it had to renege on its Afghanistan policy and dump the Taliban unceremoniously. President Musharraf publicly maintained that Pakistan had very little choice but to give in to intense US pressure and threats of strong reprisals, including bombing of Pakistan. The other side of the story, equally important, albeit unspoken, was that Musharraf had his own stakes in taking up the offer. First, it helped him to significantly shore up his personal position and further tighten the army's grip on political power. Second, it allowed Pakistan to gain access to much needed economic and military assistance, which would help it to pursue its long-term strategic and economic goals. Third, it gave Pakistan a certain manoeuvrability to hold out on two crucial areas of its foreign policy concerns: its nuclear weapons programme and Kashmir.

As expected, benefits flowed fast for the government of Pervez Musharraf. His government gained international legitimacy as the agenda for the restoration of democracy took a back seat in US calculations. All the US sanctions against Pakistan were quickly waived, paving the way for a massive aid package for Pakistan's support to the US-led war on terror. Furthermore, in 2004, Pakistan was designated a major non-NATO ally of the United States and received in US sales and grants, a wide array of military equipment, including military transport aircrafts, surveillance radars, air traffic control systems, patrol aircraft and anti-armour missiles, giving a tremendous boost to its military capabilities. This was an important gain for Pakistan given its quest for military parity with India, its traditional adversary.

The picture, however, was not all that rosy for Pakistan. It continued to remain wary of the United States' growing strategic dialogue with India as an independent centre of power. It also had serious apprehensions about the proposed Indo-US nuclear deal, which it felt would adversely change the balance of power in South Asia. The United States' pointed rebuff to Pakistan on seeking a similar agreement by its statement that India was a responsible nuclear power and the Indo-US deal was a 'stand-alone' agreement was an obvious setback to Pakistan's policy calculations.

The United States on its part remained wary of Pakistan's continued nuclear weapons programme. The A.Q. Khan controversy brought to the fore Pakistan's dubious record in the proliferation of nuclear weapons. Notwithstanding Pakistan's repeated denials, the United States had worried about Pakistan's quest for building a stockpile of weapons and procuring warheads and delivery systems, which it feared, could trigger a nuclear race between India and Pakistan, and in the process, effectively derail its larger security agenda in South Asia.

Musharraf's failure to fulfil his commitment to end the use of Pakistan as a safe haven and base for terrorism, and the unbridled growth of anti-US sentiments in Pakistan also remained worrisome for the United States. In the initial stages, Musharraf had acted promptly: he banned several militant organizations, detained thousands of extremists and cooperated with the US military and law enforcement agencies to flush out and apprehend several Al-Qaeda and Taliban terrorists. However, Musharraf's inability to curb militancy in the Federally Administered Tribal Areas (FATA) along the Pakistan–Afghanistan border, and his vacillating policies towards Islamic militancy and extremism in the region, raised growing doubts regarding Musharraf's capabilities and Pakistan's projected role in the US-led war on terror.

On balance, Musharraf was able to leverage on Pakistan's newly gained status in US strategic calculations to both his and Pakistan's advantage. He was able to project himself as the only trustworthy and effective bulwark against the growing tide of Islamic radicalism, making it worthwhile for the United States to continue seeking close relations with Pakistan for furthering its security agenda on the war on terrorism.

Another important foreign policy concern for Musharraf was to further strengthen Pakistan's ties with China, which had remained its most staunch ally and strategic partner, regardless of the external circumstances, unlike the United States, which has shown itself to be less consistent. Sino-Pak friendship had withstood the test of time and proved to be of great value to both the countries in furthering their geopolitical and strategic objectives. Pakistan needed China for augmenting its defence and nuclear capabilities as well as to counter Indian pre-eminence in the region. This has also ensured for Pakistan that it would not be left diplomatically isolated in the region whenever its relations with the United States hit a rough patch. China, on the other hand, had a clear strategic interest in Pakistan as a counter to India's growing strength and the US' global dominance in the context of changing strategic alignments in South Asia. China also had an interest in leveraging Pakistan's geo-strategic location as a gateway to the energy-rich West and Central Asian regions for its own interests.

Over the years, China emerged as Pakistan's largest benefactor in the defence and economic spheres, which effectively bolstered its strategic capabilities. The defence cooperation between the two countries was strengthened by China's extensive investment in Pakistan's military industrial segment in the field of defence industries, aeronautical complexes, ordinance factories, shipyards, power plants and communication infrastructure. More important, China's significant nuclear assistance to Pakistan's nuclear programme was critical to its emergence as a nuclear weapons power in 1998. China has also played a major role in the development of Pakistani civilian nuclear power plants, which though essentially for civilian nuclear use, could easily be diverted for military use.

Given Pakistan's stake in a continued strategic alliance with China, Musharraf invested a great deal in publicly projecting Sino-Pak friendship as a model of a shared vision on key regional and global issues. Pakistan signed a landmark 'Treaty of Friendship, Cooperation and Good-neighbourly relations' with China in January 2005 underlining the 'all-weather friendship' and 'all direction cooperation' between the two countries. The treaty stipulated that 'neither party will join any alliance or bloc which infringes upon the sovereignty, security, and territorial integrity of the other side' and bound both countries to 'not conclude treaties of this nature with any third party'.

Pakistan also secured China's support in the development of its nuclear energy. In May 2004, just before it joined the NSG, China signed an agreement to build a second nuclear power plant (Chashma 2).

During his visit to China in February 2006, following the proposed Indo-US nuclear deal, Musharraf was able to arrive at an understanding with China for enhancing cooperation in the peaceful application of nuclear energy. This was particularly reassuring for Pakistan, which had been publicly rebuffed by the United States when it had asked for a similar deal for itself.

Another important dimension of Sino-Pak relations was the growing partnership between the two countries on the issue of energy security. China provided extensive financial and technical support to Pakistan to build the deep sea port at Gwadar and its connecting links with the existing infrastructure, which would help it to emerge as a trade and energy hub for the entire region.

Fully cognizant of its need for China's strategic support, Pakistan went out of its way to allay China's concerns on Pakistan's role in the US' strategic designs in the region, as well as Pakistan's role in the rise of insurgency in the Chinese Xinjiang province. According to some reports, the 'Treaty of Friendship, Cooperation and Good-neighbourly relations' was concluded to reassure China that Pakistan's strategic relationship with the United States was in no way going to affect the close Sino-Pak ties. As for China's concerns regarding the support from fundamentalist groups in Pakistan to separatist militants in Xinjiang, Musharraf in his 2001 visit to China, expressed full support for the Chinese campaign against the Uyghur separatists in Xinjiang. Pakistan also signed a Cooperation Agreement in 2005 with China on combating the 'three forces' — Terrorism, Separatism and Extremism. Musharraf's decisive action in targeting Uyghur settlements in Pakistan, and expelling them from its madrasas, underlined Pakistan's desire to keep on the right side of China for its long-term strategic interest.

A central concern for Pakistan has been to achieve a degree of parity with its traditional rival, India, and counter its natural dominance in the region. Pakistan's relations with India have been adversarial since 1947, laden with historical animosities and continuing conflict that acquired a critical nuclear dimension in 1998. The two neighbours, who have fought three wars and a bitter and short conflict in Kargil, have failed to resolve their differences on Kashmir, which has historically remained the most visible symbol of their mutual antagonism. The growth of militancy in Kashmir, since the 1980s, had effectively stalled any worthwhile progress in putting a substantive Indo-Pak dialogue in place.

Musharraf's efforts to engage with India in a much-publicized peace process failed to make any headway given India's repeated demands for cessation of Pakistani-sponsored cross-border terrorism. Pakistan, on its part, vehemently denied the allegations and claimed that it was only providing moral support to the freedom fighters in their just struggle for emancipation from Indian rule in Kashmir. The situation took a turn for the worse when terrorist attacks by suicide bombers on the Indian Parliament in 2001 and the subsequent attack on the Kaluchak army camp in 2002 brought Pakistan–India relations to a new low. India maintained that the suicide bombers were linked to ISI-supported militant organizations, an allegation denied by Pakistan, which swiftly moved its troops in substantive strength along the entire border in Pakistan, including the LOC in Kashmir. Pakistan's countermoves on its own borders brought the two countries virtually to the brink of war. The situation eased only after Pakistan, under intense pressure from the United States, took action against militant organizations such as the Lashkar-e-Taiba and the Jaish-e Muhammad. Later, in a speech to the nation in January 2002, Musharraf declared that no internal extremism would be tolerated and no safe havens for terrorists operating along Pakistani borders would be allowed. At the same time, however, he pointedly reserved the right to support the Kashmiri brethren morally and politically; the implications of which were not lost on India. Clearly, Musharraf was finding it difficult to reconcile his international obligations as a front-line ally of the United States against terrorism and the domestic compulsions of not making any radical shift on Pakistan's support for the jihadi groups in Kashmir. Nevertheless, notwithstanding the seeming ambivalence in its stand, the mood had imperceptibly changed in Pakistan. This was reflected in its unilateral declaration of a ceasefire in November 2003, which helped to considerably ease the situation on the ground. Subsequently, in January 2004, President Musharraf and Indian Prime Minister Vajpayee issued a joint statement emphasizing the need for a sustained and productive dialogue between the two countries. This gave a visible push to the India–Pakistan Composite dialogue that had begun in 1998 but had been in limbo since.

A key area of mutual concern, which remained high on the agenda of Indo-Pak discussions, was ensuring peace and security on the borders and averting a possible conflict, which could end in a nuclear showdown. On 1 January 2006, the two countries finally exchanged a list of each other's nuclear facilities in terms of the 1988 accord that prohibited attacking each other's nuclear facilities and installations. There were also clear signs of a gradual change in the atmospherics between the two countries. This came about from the visible easing of visa restrictions and stepped-up people-to-people contacts. A number of new transportation links were also opened between the two countries, which helped the countries to connect with each other in some measure.

For Pakistan, Kashmir continued to occupy its undivided attention. In October 2004, Musharraf identified seven regions in Jammu and Kashmir on both sides of the border along religious, ethnic and geopolitical lines. He raised the prospect of demilitarization and suggested various governance options for the region including independence, joint Indo-Pak control and UN supervision. Later in 2006, Musharraf came out with yet another proposal where he spoke of autonomy and self-governance for Kashmir, and appeared to drop the call for independence and UN supervision. However, without responding to the specific proposal, Indian Prime Minister Manmohan Singh made an encouraging statement about exploring all avenues for Kashmir except the redrawing of boundaries. He offered, on his part, a treaty of 'Peace, Security and Friendship' with Pakistan to put in place a larger framework of cooperative relationship between the two countries.

The leadership in both countries were clearly ready to display a greater sense of realism in taking stock of the situation on the ground and were willing to do business with each other in a more dispassionate manner. This was so for a number of reasons. First, India was more confident to look at Kashmir in a new framework and engage with whichever government was in power in Pakistan. Pakistan, on its part, was cognizant of the high cost of indefinitely sustaining state-sponsored terrorism in view of the rising tide of sectarianism and violence within its own borders. Second, both countries were mindful of the serious repercussions of the long-term implications of their status as nuclear powers and were thus inclined to explore all avenues for a peaceful and negotiated settlement on Kashmir. Third, and equally important, the US's unequivocal interest in pursuing a balanced policy between India and Pakistan, evident since 9/11, albeit in pursuance of its own regional agenda, created an atmosphere that made mutual confrontation unsustainable and counter productive for both the countries. Having said that, it bears reiteration that, given the burden of the past legacies, the road ahead remains uncertain, and a dramatic breakthrough in Pakistan–India ties may not be on the cards any time soon.

▨ Islamic Fundamentalism: A Growing Internal Challenge

Pakistan's foreign policy imperatives have been inextricably linked with its domestic agenda and compulsions. While Pakistan was able to draw a great deal of mileage from its renewed importance as a strategic player to make a credible showing in its external relations, it remained embroiled in a prolonged and bitter civil conflict, which cast an ominous shadow on its long-term stability. During this period, the rise of Islamic militancy posed the most virulent threat to Pakistan's internal stability, shaking the country to its very foundations. Although Pakistan was created as a state in the name of Islam, it wasn't until 1977, when General Zia-ul-Haq proclaimed the goal of making Pakistan a truly Islamic state that a steady growth of Islamization of both the state and society was witnessed in Pakistan. Islamic fundamentalism insidiously spread its tentacles as evidenced by an unchecked growth of madrasas and increasing incidence of sectarian conflicts across the country. Following the Soviet intervention in Afghanistan in 1979, Islamic militancy received a visible fillip when the ISI became actively involved in recruiting and training the jihadis to wage a war against Soviet occupation. Some of these jihadi outfits, such as Lashkar-e-Taiba and Jaish-e-Muhammad, shifted their activities to Kashmir and remained actively involved in fomenting militancy there. Pakistan's active support to the Taliban–Al-Qaeda nexus to gain control of Afghanistan after the Soviet withdrawal, firmly entrenched extremism along its borders, making the whole area a bastion of Islamic militancy.

In the wake of 9/11, and under considerable US pressure, Musharraf declared that he would put an end to the use of Pakistan as a base for terrorism. He detained many extremist elements and clamped down on many madrasas that were seen as breeding ground for terrorism. However, religious extremism by now had become so potent and prevalent in the country that the state found itself increasingly ill-equipped to deal with the terrorist menace. In any event, the banned groups simply resurfaced under new names and continued their terrorist activities in FATA, a traditionally autonomous area along the Pakistan–Afghanistan border. In 2003, Pakistani troops moved into FATA, which had now become a safe haven for Al-Qaeda and the Taliban. Notwithstanding continued battles between the militants and Pakistani forces from 2004 to 2006, which led to heavy civilian casualties, Musharraf was unable to achieve any significant victory in weeding out the militants. Recognising the failure of the military option, Islamabad also pursued diplomatic options and brokered peace deals with pro-Taliban elements in South and North Waziristan. Pakistani forces suspended military operations in return for an assurance by the tribal leaders that they would make efforts to prevent the use of FATA by the Taliban. However, far from bringing peace, the deals seemed to have only strengthened the Taliban, and Islamic militancy reached an all-time high in the troubled region, fundamentally exposing Islamabad's weakness in dealing with this grave problem.

The government's failure to contain Islamic militancy was again highlighted in July 2007, when the siege of the Lal Masjid by religious extremists posed the biggest challenge to the Musharraf government in its own backyard. The siege was led by two brothers, Abdul Aziz and Abdul Rashid Ghazi, who had close links with Al-Qaeda and the Taliban. By late 2006 and early 2007, their followers were engaged in street battles with the security forces, openly challenging the state by trying to establish a state within a state, based on sharia law, in the heart of Pakistan. With his back to the wall, President Musharraf ordered a crackdown on the heavily armed Islamists, killing hundreds of people, including a large number of civilians, in the crossfire. The incident was a grim reminder of how far the tentacles of Islamic radicalism had spread in Pakistan and how ineffective the writ of the state had become in exercising its control.

▣ Ramifications of Ethnic Conflict

The resurgence of the Baluch movement in 2004 brought to the fore once again the deep ethnic cleavages in Pakistan. Ethnic conflict has presented a formidable challenge to Pakistan since its inception, leading to two civil wars and the secession of the country's most populous province of East Pakistan in 1971. The ruling elites' failure to provide mechanisms for power-sharing and equitable distribution of economic benefits, and the centralized character of its federal structure, dominated by the Punjabis, has marginalized minorities such as the Baluch, the Sindhis and the Pashtuns from the mainstream and led to widespread discontent across the country at different points in time in Pakistan's history.

The root cause of the Baluch problem lies in Islamabad's continued marginalization of the Baluchi people and the exploitation of Baluchistan's resources, particularly its vast gas reserves, to Islamabad's own advantage. Baluchistan remained the most backward and underdeveloped province in Pakistan, despite its rich natural resources, and this gradually led to a groundswell of discontent. Post 9/11, the Baluch were also resentful of the increased presence of the military, which the Baluch saw as a deliberate move by the military to consolidate its presence in the province. Amidst growing frustration, Baluch guerrillas resorted to attacking military and government installations all through 2004, which was countered by the federal government with full force resulting in high casualties on both sides. The confrontation reached its peak in 2006 when a key Baluch leader Akbar Khan Bugti was killed, which plunged the whole province into continued anarchy, forcing the government to deploy substantial military troops in the province. Prolonged insurgency in the province could have serious consequences for Pakistan's internal stability, as tensions in Baluchistan could spill over to neighbouring Sindh and NWFP, and trigger a chain of ethnic disturbance. Furthermore, with the Al-Qaeda/Taliban base shifting to Baluchistan, there is a danger of the Baluch cooperating with Al-Qaeda/Taliban forces for strategic reasons, which would further compound the problem of fundamentalist terrorism in Pakistan.

▣ Unravelling of Musharraf's Power

2007 was an eventful year for both Musharraf and Pakistan. For Musharraf, it marked the beginning of the end of his absolute political power; for Pakistan, it brought to the fore the critical issues of de-militarization of the government, restoration of democracy and open elections, as well as respect for the rule of law and independence of the judiciary. Musharraf's troubles began with the dismissal of the Chief Justice, Iftikhar Chowdhry, in March 2007 — a move that ultimately proved to be his undoing. Instead of rectifying the situation at the start, Musharraf got himself into a deeper quagmire. He engineered his re-election as President by the outgoing national assembles in a questionable election in October 2007, just beating the deadline when his term as President was about to end. This led to a chain of events that went far beyond his calculations. His re-election was challenged in court, but instead of waiting for the Supreme Court to deliver its verdict, Musharraf imposed emergency rule on 3 November 2007 and dismissed the Chief Justice and other senior judges of the Supreme Court to prevent a ruling that would most certainly have gone against him. He justified his actions on the grounds that the judiciary was working at cross-purposes with the executive and the legislature to check extremism — a charge that few believed was at the heart of the dismissal. Under emergency rule, he imprisoned a large number of political and civil society activists, and clamped restrictions on the media.

▣ Role of Civil Society

Musharraf's relentless assaults on the Constitution, the judiciary, the press, political leaders and individual activists created a wave of popular discontent. More important, it underscored the strength of civil society in Pakistan and its power to initiate political change through mobilization. The first dismissal of the Chief Justice in March 2007 had galvanized lawyers into an unprecedented move to push for the reinstatement of the independence of the judiciary. The Chief Justice's refusal to accept his dismissal meekly served as a catalyst for a grassroots movement, which blossomed from supporting the Chief Justice to rallying against Musharraf. There were protests in Lahore and Karachi to support the Chief Justice, leading to riots amidst a confrontation between the Muttahida Qaumi Movement (MQM) — (supporters of Musharraf) — and the Pakistan People's Party, which aligned itself with the supporters of the Chief Justice. The ensuing media crackdown by the government further inflamed the situation and paradoxically, exposed the government's vulnerability, as it appeared to be acting in desperation. The lawyers' movement snowballed into a bigger civil society movement as it was joined by human rights activists, media persons and political cadres, and became a catalyst for the nationwide demand for the ouster of Musharraf and for democratic reform.

The galvanization of civil society was in some ways a defining moment. It may be noted here that Pakistan has had a history of civil society movements, but these movements have generally been short-lived. This was partly due to the reactive nature of these movements and the fact that the civil society agencies were usually poorly resourced, poorly coordinated and fragmented. At a broader level, the failure of Pakistan's civil society can also be attributed to political repression and a lack of democracy in the country.

Civil society movements are generally activated when two things happen: one, the government acts in an absolutist manner and tramples upon individual and collective rights, and two, the institutions entrusted with checking such government excesses are rendered ineffective. Both these factors were present in Pakistan's recent crisis with the military controlling the legislature and the executive, and emergency rule emasculating the judiciary. This helped to unleash the forces of civil society, which acted as a catalyst in hastening the end of the military rule of Musharraf. In this context, the recent revival of democracy in Pakistan was in some ways a victory for its civil society movement, which had long been pressing for political change and empowerment of the masses.

▧ The Way Ahead

The 2008 election results gave an overwhelming mandate to the democratic parties, led by the Pakistan People's Party (PPP) and the Pakistan Muslim League (Nawaz) or the PML-N, which formed a coalition government at the centre. The newly created coalition remained on rather shaky grounds; the most important question being whether the lure of power and a common anti-Musharraf platform was enough to bind these democratic parties together for long. It was a fragile coalition in which neither was a junior partner and, as was feared, the two parties soon fell apart under the weight of past rivalries and dissensions. Historically, the PPP and the PML-N have been bitter rivals with competing ideologies and agendas; changing sides to achieve their tactical ends is not new to them. It is pertinent to recall here that during the years 1988–99, the former Prime Ministers — the late Benazir Bhutto and Nawaz Sharif — alternated power twice, each parlaying with the military to undo the other for short-term political gains. The military on its part did not hesitate to get rid of both the civilian governments, as Benazir Bhutto and Nawaz Sharif eventually discovered to their dismay. How these political parties conduct themselves will have significant implications for Pakistan's political future. In the end, Pakistan's long-term political stability will depend on the speed and sincerity with which its political elite are able to initiate processes of durable change in all spheres of its polity. If democracy has to find firm roots in Pakistan, the political leadership has to display the requisite courage to evolve a new framework of political dialogue and consensus. Failure to do so would only push Pakistan back into political chaos and endemic instability. Equally important will be the role that the military will choose to play in the unfolding political scenario. History has shown that the army has not hesitated to strike quickly to protect its own professional and corporate interests. Would the army in Pakistan ever be prepared to voluntarily move away from the centre stage that it has occupied in Pakistan's polity for so long? In this connection, the growing military-mullah axis and the role of the United States in backing a strong army in Pakistan will remain crucial factors in the emerging civil–military equations in the country.

Faced with mounting domestic and international pressures, Pakistan is presently in the midst of one of the most challenging phases of its history. Catapulted to the international strategic stage following 9/11, Pakistan finds itself increasingly on the horns of a dilemma. On the one hand, as a key ally on the global war on terrorism, it is committed to fight Islamist terrorism; on the other hand, it faces severe domestic constraints to do so. In the long term, Pakistan's future lies in the attainment of three inter-related goals: arresting Islamic fundamentalism and ethnic conflict; removing the military from the centre stage of politics and governance; and restoring democracy through viable political structures and effective leaders. Pakistan clearly has a long way to go on all these fronts before it enters an era of political stability and democratic governance. Meanwhile, the last thing that the region and the world would want is to see Pakistan fail.

▨ Overview of the Chapters

This volume makes a critical assessment of Pakistan in the context of domestic, regional and global politics under Musharraf's rule and focuses on the post-9/11 period, which in more ways than one, marked a defining moment for Pakistan's domestic and international politics. The chapters bring together diverse perspectives and deal with three broad inter-related areas: international security and foreign policy, national identity and politics, and economic perspectives.

The first three chapters deal with issues of global security and their impact on Pakistan. Amin Saikal, in the opening chapter, analyzes how 9/11 dramatically changed Musharraf's domestic and foreign policy strategies and provided the golden opportunity for him to manipulate the US-Pak alliance for consolidating his own position and also considerably improving Pakistan's international image, which had been severely tarnished by its militant adventurism in Afghanistan and Kashmir. However, as Saikal argues, notwithstanding the public posturing, Musharraf ensured that his foreign policy actions remained in line with the interest of the military and the ISI, and did not invoke a serious backlash from conservative fundamentalist forces in Pakistan. Saikal maintains that the measures Musharraf took were the bare minimum needed to keep Washington on his side; there was no real willingness to return to democracy, no reduction of the role of the ISI and army and significantly no real reforms with respect to curtailing extremism and cross-border insurgency. He concludes that recent developments in Pakistan in 2007 have once again served to underline that Pakistan can ill-afford to muddle through by drifting between poles of authoritarianism and quasi-democracy, Islamism and secularism, exploitation and double-edged postures, in its regional and international relations, without raising serious questions about its survival as a viable state.

Selig S. Harrison in the next chapter deals with global terrorism and US policy after 9/11 and their impact on Pakistan's domestic and foreign policy. He argues that US support to Musharraf's regime had paradoxically magnified the threat of terrorism in terms of strengthening the Islamist elements and radicalizing the sensitive Afghan border areas where Al-Qaeda and Taliban forces were concentrated. Harrison puts forth the view that the United States on its part, had not received much from Pakistan in return for the massive aid that it had pumped into Pakistan. The US forces were still being shut out of operating within Pakistani territory and little had been done by the Pakistani authorities to move decisively against the Al-Qaeda and the Taliban. In fact, the Musharraf regime, Harrison maintains, had tended to look the other way when Islamic groups, allied with the 'rogue' ISI elements, had helped the Taliban. Harrison also points to the danger of growing radicalization of the Pashtun areas across the Pakistan–Afghanistan border since 9/11, which could complicate the already difficult ethnic picture of Pakistan. Intensification of Islamic fervour and Pashtun nationalism and the rekindling of the demand for an independent Pashtunistan, he warns, could have serious repercussions for Pakistan's long-term stability and jeopardize the very prospects of Pakistan's survival in its present form.

The third chapter by Pervaiz Iqbal Cheema looks at Pakistan's options in the face of a changing security environment in the region where both Pakistan and India are nuclear-armed states. Cheema argues that while India's quest for nuclear weapons power was 'status oriented', that of Pakistan was 'security driven', to reduce nuclear imbalance and establish deterrence for national security. Cheema notes that notwithstanding fears in the international community regarding the possible destabilization of South Asia after 1998, both Pakistan and India had been able to put in place a credible strategy of minimum nuclear deterrence as well as a series of confidence-building measures to reduce the risk of any accidental nuclear confrontation. Cheema is, however, critical of the proposed Indo-US nuclear deal, which he contends is discriminatory in as much as it would enable India to divert its indigenously produced fissile material to its military programme while attaining fuel for its civilian reactors from the Nuclear Security Group (NSG). The deal could also tilt the balance in India's favour and spur a new arms race between India and Pakistan. Finally, Cheema looks at the prospects of Iran's emergence as a nuclear power and its impact on Pakistan's wider regional security interests. He concludes that it was difficult enough for Pakistan to live under the shadow of a nuclearized India, but to be sandwiched between two nuclear neighbours would place it in an unenviable situation.

The next two chapters deal with Pakistan's foreign policy perspectives. Providing a broad overview of Pakistan's relations with China and the United States, Kanti Bajpai argues in Chapter four that the strategic attention of both the United States and China had shifted away from Pakistan, albeit in varying degrees, after the Cold War. This became evident from the United States' growing criticism of Pakistan's external and internal policies, including Pakistan's nu-clear weapons programme, and its role in Kashmir, as also the rise of Islamic fundamentalism and erosion of democratic structures in the country. China, on its part, had also showed visible signs of seeking rapprochement with its traditional adversary, India, and adopting a more balanced stand on Kashmir. The events of 9/11, however, changed all this. Both China and United States now came to view Pakistan simultaneously as a strategic danger and a strategic opportunity. It was thus that notwithstanding the new US-Pak axis, the United States had continued to be worried about Pakistan's ambivalence to growing Islamic extremism, its failure to curb anti-Americanism and its dubious record on proliferation. Similarly, China, although cognizant of Pakistan's role in counterbalancing

India and its geo-strategic importance as its entry point to the energy-rich areas, remained uneasy about Pakistan's resurrection as a front-line state, presence of US troops and growth of Islamic fundamentalism. The major challenge for Islamabad, Bajpai concludes, would be to manage the strategic ambivalence of both China and the United States and take advantage of the opportunities that become available as a result of their reappraisal of Pakistan's importance. In this context, Pakistan would have reasons to worry about the attitude of the United States and China towards India, its traditional adversary.

Chapter Five is by Robert G. Wirsing who examines the key trends in India–Pakistan relations under Musharraf's leadership. The thrust of his chapter is that India–Pakistan relations have come a long way and are based on a variety of issues and not solely, or even predominantly, on Kashmir as has been often thought to be the case. Although Kashmir would continue to be played up by both sides for strategic reasons, the Kashmir dispute, he argues, has lost most of its centrality in Indo-Pak relations as there was for all practical purposes a de facto settlement on Kashmir. Wirsing maintains that the relationship would now be driven by other issues, including rivalry over natural resources (especially hydrocarbons), energy supplies and river waters, which would make for intense competition and rivalry between the two countries in the high-stake contest for energy resources and markets. Wirsing opines that given these new dynamics, a noticeable movement in Indo-Pak dialogue would not guarantee a positive transformation of the relationship as a whole. The road ahead for India and Pakistan, he concludes, could go in any direction, including intensified rivalry and conflict.

Christine Fair discusses Pakistan's Central Asia strategy in Chapter Six. She argues that while Pakistan remains reluctant to embrace a Central Asia strategy publicly, it has had little option but to remain engaged with the region. Fair argues that Islamabad was pursuing two objectives with respect to Central Asia: to discourage its neighbours from providing India with any leverage which it could use against Pakistan; and to seek enhanced commercial access to the region with respect to hydrocarbon and hydroelectric resources. However, Pakistan's fiscal weaknesses as well as domestic instability in key areas such as Gwadar and Karachi presented substantial hurdles to achieving the above objectives. In addition, India's growing relations with Iran, Afghanistan and Central Asia, could also pose a challenge to Pakistan's geo-strategic calculations in the region.

Chapters seven, eight and nine of the volume deal with Pakistan's domestic politics, focusing on the pressing issues of the rise of Islamic fundamentalism, civil–military relations and ethnic conflict in Pakistan. Ishtiaq Ahmed, in his chapter, traces the rise of Islamic fundamentalism in Pakistan from 1947 until 2007 to understand its genesis and its present hold over the country. Ahmed argues that despite efforts by the modernist elite in 1947 to accommodate Islamic precepts in the constitutional process of Pakistan to make the country both Islamic and democratic, the former gained prominence over the latter, especially after the 1980s when Pakistan became a front-line state against Soviet intervention in Afghanistan. This gave a boost to jihadi forces that worked in tandem with the state. However, post 9/11, the dynamics changed and Pakistan, under Musharraf, came into direct conflict with the fundamentalists. Ahmed concludes that Islamic fundamentalism is incompatible with a pluralist, democratic and human rights-friendly social and political order; it is also violence prone and therefore amenable to terrorist activities. Unless Islamic fundamentalism was brought under control, he concludes, there could be no return to peace and stability within and outside Pakistani borders.

Mohammad Waseem analyzes the civil–military relations that have been at the core of the Pakistani state since its inception, focusing on three major aspects of civil–military relations in Pakistan: state formation, genesis of military politics and constitutional engineering. Waseem argues that the function of safeguarding the socioeconomic and political order in Pakistan was assumed by the army in the background of structural discontinuity that occurred at the time of Partition. The migrant-led state put in place an institutional apparatus and a tradition of constitutional thinking and practice which, at least by default, prepared the ground for military takeover.

Waseem argues that the insecurity syndrome relating to state building at home in the context of regional security complex has kept the military establishment from letting the political initiative go out of its hands, even when it was not in government. Confrontation with India increased the insecurity of the army and the ruling elite; in the event, as the army got politicized, politics became militarized in the sense that national policies and priorities were increasingly set by the army. In course of time, the army was able to infiltrate all aspects of Pakistani life, including the elite, the civil bureaucracy, professionals, the business community and the religious leaders. Finally Waseem shows how the army developed a set of constitutional preferences and priorities relating to the form of government, distribution of power between various institutions of the state both horizontally and vertically as well as parliamentary sovereignty.

He concludes that despite the recent developments in Pakistan, including the formation of a new civilian government, the army was too well-ensconced in the political, administrative and commercial spheres of public life to be completely ousted from the centre stage of politics.

In the next chapter, Rajshree Jetly examines the resurgent Baluch movement, which has posed a considerable challenge to Pakistan's internal security. The Baluch movement, dormant for many years, was reignited in 2004 following a series of events, which culminated in an all-out military assault by the Pakistan army on Baluch strongholds. Jetly compares the current insurgency with the previous one in the 1970s and demonstrates that similar factors had come to underpin both insurgencies. These included a deep sense of Baluch alienation from the economic and political mainstream, which has been compounded by their perceived deprivation vis-à-vis other ethnic groups in Pakistan, particularly the Punjabi ruling elites at the centre. The Baluch were also resentful of the fact that despite being rich in natural resources, particularly the gas reserves, Baluchistan had remained the poorest and the most underdeveloped province of Pakistan. However, Jetly concludes, the present volatile geopolitical realities are very different from those prevailing in the 1970s and 1980s, and therefore prolonged instability in Baluchistan would have far more dangerous implications for Pakistan's internal and regional stability.

The remaining three chapters deal with issues of economic development in Pakistan. Imran Ali makes a broad overview of Pakistan's economic structures and processes and points out that by 2001, Pakistan's economy had taken a complete nosedive. Conceding that the post-9/11 period had brought about a massive infusion of foreign aid giving a substantial fillip to Pakistan's economy, Ali, however, argues that the economic benefits Pakistan had obtained were a mere pittance compared to the strategic contribution that it was called upon to make. Ali maintains that the real dynamics behind the turnaround of Pakistan's economy were mainly the inflow of money in the form of remittances by the expatriate Pakistanis, and the investment funds from Arab oil economies. He further argues that despite the substantial economic progress made by Pakistan in recent years, Pakistan would need to make more efforts to sustain its economic performance, particularly in terms of reducing economic inequities, and focusing on human development and social sectors. Ali concludes that the visible slowing down of the economic momentum in recent months had only confirmed the oft-repeated fears that the post-2001 economic growth was not based on strong fundamentals. In this context, the anti-Musharraf vote in Pakistan was as much a rejection of his political manipulations as his economic failures.

Chapter Eleven by Arslan Razmi surveys some recent developments in Pakistan's economy focusing on international trade, current account and finance regimes. Like Ali, Razmi maintains that the impressive improvement in some macroeconomic growth indicators in recent years rests on shaky foundations and is reflective of the impact of benign external conditions than any improvement in the basic fundamentals of Pakistan's economy. He argues that Pakistan's rapid growth from exports, which has remained concentrated in the narrow sectors of textile and clothing, may not be sustainable in the emerging international environment for trade in apparel and textiles. Neither is SAFTA expected to lead to dramatic benefits for most countries in the SAARC region or Pakistan. Razmi further cautions that the short-term gains that had accrued from the post-9/11 financial aid, debt write-offs and a spike in remittances, would not translate into long-term benefits without sound management and policies. Sustained long-term growth would, in particular, require targeted investment in the segments of the economy that create human capital, an area that has received scant attention in Pakistan so far.

Finally, Akbar Zaidi looks at the human development outcome of Pakistan's economic growth. Zaidi notes that different patterns and processes have been at work in Pakistan in different periods. From 1947–77, economic growth (either high or low) did not reflect the same trend in the social and human sectors; but from 1977–2007, there seemed to be a trend in human development that was reflected in the trends in economic growth. Zaidi argues that a key difference between the two periods in terms of social development related to the extent of state involvement and privatization of services. Pakistan's adoption of a far more open and market-based delivery mechanism for social services after 1977 witnessed a closer relationship between growth and human development. Looking at the impact of development expenditure and public policy, he maintains that in the 1971–77 period, there was active intervention in social sectors as well as increased spending despite low growth. In the 1999–2005 period, however, despite the fact that development expenditure was very low, since private incomes were rising, the market-based model was more responsive to peoples' incomes than development expenditure, resulting in improved human development indicators. He concludes that as human development outcomes are increasingly determined by the pace of economic growth and rise in incomes, economic growth remained critical for better human and social development. Any slowing down of Pakistan's economy, which was already resting on shaky foundations, would therefore have a deleterious impact on social and human development outcomes. This could prove costly to Pakistan in the long run.

※

1

Musharraf and Pakistan's Crisis

Amin Saikal

The interplay between the internal settings and the external environment of a state is critical to determining its place in world politics. While Pakistan is no exception, there are two features that set it apart from many others. One is the country's reputation as a state that has shuttled painfully between quasi-democratic rule and military dictatorship at a fluctuating pace and intensity, with Islam as a central reference of national identity and unity. The other is the terrifying dichotomy — of the country's position as *both* a source of ideological extremism, aiding and spawning various terrorist groups, as well as a central player in fighting these phenomena. The first feature has dominated Pakistan's history ever since its creation in 1947, whilst the second one has become the country's modus operandi since the early 1980s and, more specifically, since the tragic events of 11 September 2001.

No Pakistani leader has exploited these two features as skilfully as President Pervez Musharraf to ensure the continuity of his thinly concealed military rule and to solidify a critical role for Pakistan in regional and international politics. In the process, he generated important opportunities and major challenges for Pakistan at regional and wider levels. The fear of what an extremist Pakistan can produce was played upon to perpetuate Musharraf's rule and maintain international support for it. The counter-terrorism card was played to promote the country as a pivotal force in shaping the regional geopolitical landscape in interaction with changing world politics.

This chapter has three specific objectives:

First, assess Musharraf's main policy postures against the backdrop of what has transpired in regional and world politics since his seizure of power in 1999.

Second, examine how Musharraf was able to shape and manage his domestic needs in an interactively manipulative manner with the changing dynamics of Pakistan's wider environment.

Third, investigate some of the major possible scenarios for Pakistan in the medium to long term.

▨ Policy Postures

Musharraf's seizure of power through a coup on 12 October 1999 came against the backdrop of a number of important internal and external developments:

First, Pakistan, since the death of President General Zia-ul-Haq in a mysterious air crash in August 1988, had not progressed beyond a quasi-democracy under Prime Ministers Benazir Bhutto and Nawaz Sharif. The military, and more specifically its Inter-Services Intelligence (ISI) — which had grown to the position of almost a government-within-the government — had continued to act as the main determinant in Pakistani politics.[1]

Second, Pakistan was in the grip of an economic crisis as well as social divisions and sectarian strife, threatening the unity and possibly even the very survival of Pakistan. Between 1997 and 2001, Pakistan's GDP dropped from US\$ 75.3 billion to US\$ 71.5 billion and by 2001, government debt was 82 per cent of its GDP. Over one-third of the government's revenue was spent on interest payments on the national debt.[2] In the meantime, the country suffered from growing ethno-linguistic hostilities, sectarian violence, rampant corruption and administrative malpractices.

Third, Pakistan's transformation into a source of Islamic extremism was nurtured and deployed as a foreign policy tool to boost the country's national cohesion and regional position within an approach that aimed at creating and exploiting a favourable external environment whenever possible.[3] In this respect, the ISI had scored important successes in relation to Afghanistan, where it had raised and backed the medievalist Islamic Taliban from late 1994 to take over the country, and in the Indian-held Jammu and Kashmir, where it had supported a separatist movement through an array of radical Islamic groups. It had also managed to forge a mutually supportive relationship between these groups and the Taliban. The ISI's efforts in Afghanistan had resulted in the country becoming a hub for international terrorism, based on an alliance between the Taliban and the Al-Qaeda under its patronage. ISI activities amounted to a 'creeping invasion' of the country, causing a bloody conflict between the Taliban and the anti-Taliban forces, led by the legendary Afghan commander Ahmed Shah Massoud, who had also successfully resisted the Soviet occupation of Afghanistan in the 1980s.[4] In Kashmir, the ISI's activities had led to increased strife and bloodshed. Its interventionism had substantially contributed to the Indo-Pakistan Kargil mini-war of early 1999, which according to many analysts had brought the two sides to the brink of a nuclear clash. Although the antagonists had pulled back from the brink under intense pressure from a number of major powers, especially the United States, their ensuing relation can only be described as an uneasy truce.[5]

Fourth, Pakistan and India came to be officially confirmed as nuclear powers. In 1998, India had carried out a series of nuclear tests and Pakistan had followed suit in response. These actions had evoked international condemnation for both sides, but had placed Pakistan, more so than India, under difficult military and economic sanctions, given Pakistan's position as the weaker of the two countries in terms of its capacity to cope with the sanctions.

Fifth, the US presence in the region started waning in the wake of the defeat of Soviet communism on the one hand, and a concurrent growth of Pakistan as a bastion for Islamic militancy on the other. Washington had become especially concerned about Pakistan's backing of the Taliban and the Taliban–Al-Qaeda alliance, as well as a number of other Pakistan-based radical Islamic groups, such as the Lashkar-e-Taiba and the Harkat-ul-Ansar cum Harkat-ul-Mujahideen in support of its Kashmir policy. Originally, Islamabad had quite successfully marketed the Taliban to Washington on the grounds that the militia was a Sunni outfit, capable of bringing stability to Afghanistan, checking Iranian influence and opening up Afghanistan as a direct corridor to the newly emerged, resource-rich region of Central Asia. However, the situation had changed following the bombing of the US embassies in Kenya and Tanzania by the Al-Qaeda in August 1998. The administration of President Clinton had embarked on a drive to punish the Al-Qaeda and review its attitude towards the Taliban; it had carried out a cruise missile attack on the Al-Qaeda training camps in Afghanistan. It had also mounted a concerted effort to coordinate an anti-terrorism policy with India, which had bitterly complained about cross-border terrorism from Pakistan for years, and with Russia, which had viewed the Taliban–Al-Qaeda's support of Chechen separatists and certain radical Islamic groups in Central Asia with increasing alarm. Further, it had engaged in a diplomatic offensive against the Taliban, resulting in a number of incremental UN (United Nations) sanctions against the militia. The US official who played a key role in all this was the then Under-Secretary of State, Thomas Pickering.[6] Even so, Washington had remained remarkably reluctant to do anything that could tip the balance of power in favour of the anti-Taliban forces in Afghanistan, or exert enough pressure on Islamabad to drop its support for the Taliban and other radical Islamic forces as a foreign policy instrument. This was largely because Washington had reasoned that it needed Pakistan's cooperation for the success of its anti-terrorism measures, and that it wanted to refrain from taking any policy action that could possibly accentuate Pakistan's domestic problems and cause the country to implode, with a possibility of its nuclear arsenals falling in the wrong hands.

Sixth, Washington had grown concerned about the rising power of China, confronting it with the question of how to contain the communist power. Pakistan had historically developed close strategic ties with China, based partly on a common anti-Indian position ever since the Indo-Chinese border war of 1962. Although Washington had ample opportunities in the past to forge close ties with democratic India, it had not done so partly because of its aversion to New Delhi's determination to pursue an independent course of foreign policy. Washington's off-and-on alliance with Pakistan from the early 1950s had taken on a dimension of realpolitik, but was void of any lasting principles.[7] In this context, after many years of coolness, the US–Pakistan alliance had been revived in the wake of the decade-long Soviet occupation of Afghanistan in the 1980s, which Pakistan firmly opposed. At the same time, New Delhi's adoption of a rather support-ive position on the occupation had irritated Washington. Although by late 1999, Indo-US relations had warmed up, so had also to some extent ties between India and China. This could not encourage Washington to court India to the degree that was necessary to use an 'India card' in formulating a policy that could put pressure on both China and Pakistan. As a result, Islamabad remained in a position to use its strategic ties with China not only to maintain a source of pressure on India, but also to caution the United States against pressuring Pakistan over its role in the post-Soviet environment in the region.

When Musharraf seized power, these developments confronted him with serious dilemmas and set the limits for the kind of foreign policy priorities he could pursue. He had personally been involved in most of the developments in one way or another. He was Army Chief of Staff under Nawaz Sharif, who served as Pakistan's elected prime minister for the second time from 1997 until his overthrow by Musharraf in 1999; he was also an active participant in all of the major policy decisions, including Pakistan's Afghan and Kashmir adventures. In other words, he could not be exonerated of his role in the circumstances that had befallen Pakistan. He now had to deal with those circumstances from a position of leadership in ways that could help him consolidate his military rule on the one hand, and assuage the concerns of the international community (especially the United States, India, and many of its democratic allies within the Commonwealth) who had expressed deep concern over the 'end of democracy' in Pakistan, on the other. Initially, he could not but act within very limited policy options.

While relying necessarily on the military, the ISI and the ISI-linked Islamic groups as well as on the public's disillusionment with Sharif's government, Musharraf promised to return Pakistan to 'genuine democracy' as soon as possible, but signalled no major foreign policy changes. He found it imperative to defend Pakistan's nuclear status, and to pursue Pakistan's Afghan and Kashmir policies more or less in the same manner that had previously been constructed.

In relation to Afghanistan, Musharraf stood firm on Pakistan's support of the Taliban (and by implication of the Taliban–Al-Qaeda alliance), describing it as a 'national security imperative'[8] for Pakistan. He pleaded repeatedly to the international community to recognize the Taliban as the legitimate government of Afghanistan, as Pakistan and two of its close Arab friends — Saudi Arabia and the United Arab Emirates (UAE) — had done. He shared the military and ISI view of Afghanistan as a source of 'strategic depth' in the event of a confrontation with India, and as an important corridor for Pakistan's access to the former Soviet Central Asian Muslim republics, partly to promote a wider regional economic and strategic role for Pakistan, and partly to deny India and Iran an opportunity to enhance their influence in the region.

With regard to Iran, he could count on the support of a number of Arab countries — especially Saudi Arabia and the UAE — and the United States, for several reasons. Saudi Arabia championed the cause of Sunni Islam and a close friendship with the United States, which locked it in serious sectarian and political rivalry with Iran's Shiite Islamic regime. As for the UAE, it was a close partner of Saudi Arabia in the Gulf Cooperation Council (GCC), which was formed in 1981 as a response to the call by Ayatollah Khomeini (the founder of the Iranian Islamic regime in the wake of the Iranian revolution of 1978/79) for the export of the Iranian revolution to the region. The UAE also had a major territorial dispute with Iran. The dispute was over three strategic islands — Abu Musa and Greater and Lesser Tumbs in the Gulf — which the Sharjah emirate of the UAE claimed, but which had been taken over in 1971 by Iran under the Shah. Iran's refusal to return them had caused tension in Iran–UAE relations, which remains unresolved to the present day. Abu Dhabi was in search of means and ways to pressurize Tehran over the issue, and this also partly explained its support for the Taliban as a means to do so. Meanwhile, the United States was keen to reinforce its policy of containment of the Iranian regime, which it had pursued since the rise of Khomeini's Islamic government to power and the famous hostage crisis, which had emanated from the Iranian detention of about 52 US embassy staff members from 4 November 1979–21 January 1981 and had caused much humiliation for the United States.[9] This could only give Musharraf confidence that despite the growing aversion of the United States to the Taliban and to Pakistan's support of the militia, Washington could not but remain lenient towards Pakistan.

In the case of Kashmir, Musharraf reiterated Pakistan's historical support for the right of the Kashmiri people to self-determination, and as an extension of this, for the ISI's continued backing of groups that had engaged in cross-border violence and linkages between these groups and the Taliban and their Al-Qaeda allies. Although the cross-border violations had reduced in both intensity and frequency since the Kargil conflict, they were still at a level that had prevented Islamabad and New Delhi from reducing tension in their relations and moving faster towards a rapprochement.

However, this is not to claim that there was no tension between Musharraf's public stand and what he privately harboured. Although presenting himself as committed to the religion of Islam, he essentially wanted to pursue secular politics. As he points out in his autobiography, *In the Line of Fire*, he had all along been deeply impressed by the secularist founder of modern Turkey, Mustafa Kemal Ataturk, and entertained a wish to style himself after him as a military-cum-civilian reformer.[10] As a result, he could not feel very comfortable with Pakistan's support of radical Islamism as a major ideological strand in its politics. Yet the prevailing circumstances under which he had come to power had severely impaired his legitimacy and ability to manoeuvre easily against the situation. While he was personally languishing as a pariah in world politics and Pakistan was struggling under the growing weight of political, economic and social stagnation, Musharraf was confronted with serious policy confusions and dilemmas. He was badly in need of an external stimulus to enable him to break the circuit.

▨ Domestic and Foreign Policy Interplay

That stimulus came with the events of 11 September 2001 (henceforth to be referred to as 9/11). The Al-Qaeda's attacks, which were masterminded from Afghanistan, proved to be almost a godsend to Musharraf. They presented him with an unexpected but necessary opportunity to prove his worth as a clever military politician, to shore up his own position as the leader of the country, and to transform Pakistan from being a producer of extremism and terrorism to becoming an actor without whose cooperation the United States and its allies could not combat the phenomenon. Musharraf could now engage, with more vigour and assumed credibility than ever before, to combine politics of opportunism with that of regime preservation within an approach that would interface his own political survival with that of Pakistan. In other words, he was enabled to promote the claim that what was good for him was also good for Pakistan. He would become indispensable to what was required to save Pakistan and Pakistan would become critical to what was needed to defeat international terrorism. This was very much similar to the way that the Soviet invasion of Afghanistan had enabled one of his military predecessors, General Zia-ul-Haq, to revive his fortunes two decades earlier and renew Pakistan's strategic importance to the United States as a front-line state against 'Soviet expansionism'.

In the face of an ultimatum from the Bush Administration either to join the United States or to side with the Al-Qaeda's terrorism and its harbourers — the Taliban, and 'be bombed back to the Stone Age', Musharraf shrewdly threw in his lot with Washington.[11] In declaring Pakistan as a partner of the United States in what President Bush called the 'war on terror', commencing with the 'Enduring Freedom Operation' in Afghanistan in October 2001, he forged a new and robust alliance with them. He changed certain basic elements of Pakistan's foreign policy posture almost overnight, with considerable impact on the country's domestic political dynamics. He found it both imperative and expedient to turn his back on Pakistan's clients — the Taliban regime and its Al-Qaeda allies — and to moderate Pakistan's support for cross-border violence in Kashmir, with a commitment to do everything possible to lead Pakistan on a policy-path free of religious extremism.

However, he knew from the start that this new alliance was based on politics of mutual vulnerability and leverage, which if carefully and craftily managed could be highly advantageous to his regime and Pakistan. He needed Washington's partnership to help him consolidate power and lead Pakistan out of the dire predicaments in which it was placed. On the other hand, the Bush Administration needed Pakistan as a key state for not only toppling the Taliban and redirecting Afghanistan, but also successfully executing its war on terror strategy with wider aims than what it wanted to achieve in Afghanistan. The benefits that Musharraf was able to extract from the new alliance proved to be more than anybody could have originally anticipated. By presenting himself as a champion ready to fight extremism and terrorism, he was able to rapidly build an externally driven basis of legitimacy for his military rule and to gain a degree of international acceptability that would otherwise not have been within his reach.

Musharraf thus was no longer a pariah, but was courted as a trusted and much needed ally by the United States and its allies, which rapidly dropped all sanctions against Pakistan. While exalting him to a position of a close and trusted friend — a position that was once reserved for the Shah of Iran (1953–79) in the region — the Bush Administration found it politically and strategically expedient to shower Musharraf's regime with massive economic and military assistance. For example, in the three years following the events of 11 September 2001, the US military aid alone to Pakistan soared to $4.2 billion, compared to $9.1 million in the three years before the events. The total US military, economic and development assistance to Pakistan since the 2001 attacks has to date amounted to more than $10 billion. Most of the money has come from the US Defence Department programme called the 'Coalition Support Fund'.[12] Meanwhile, US–Pakistan relations reached such a level of closeness in 2005 that Washington elevated Pakistan to the position of a major non-NATO ally, reflecting Musharraf's personal friendship with President Bush to the extent that few of the United States' traditional allies could dream of enjoying.

Musharraf could use US aid not only to strengthen the military and the ISI as the main pillars of his rule, but also to generate a level of economic activity that could win him support from those secularist elites and segments of the population that would mostly benefit from the development. As a result, Pakistan's real GDP suddenly grew by 5.1 per cent during 2002–04, with all economic sectors — from agriculture to industry — registering healthy growth, giving rise to a degree of economic and social activity that Pakistan had not experienced for many years.[13] Meanwhile, Musharraf found himself in a position to push for extra political and economic leverage for the military. He further formalized and expanded the role of the military in the political and economic life of Pakistan by enlarging its share in the National Security Council of Pakistan and allowing many influential military personnel to buy vast tracts of land, especially in the province of Baluchistan, at very low prices, and to secure an even greater stake in the country's new economic life.

Musharraf was suddenly placed in such a comfort zone that he could now act more in terms of what he saw fit for Pakistan under his rule than what the United States' 'war-on-terror' interests dictated. He was no longer required to keep his original promise of returning Pakistan to democracy soon, or to take the necessary steps to lead Pakistan on any other path than that of concealed military authoritarianism. Nor did he find it compelling to come totally clean on Pakistan's meddling in Afghanistan and Kashmir. Whatever measures he adopted in the name of democratization, they ultimately amounted to surface rather than structural changes. He managed these changes in ways that could enable him to increase his personal powers, to marginalize internal opposition and to neutralize foreign critics. In foreign affairs, he engaged in a public campaign that projected his regime and Pakistan as the repository of 'enlightened Islam' and defender of public good against the evils of extremism and terrorism. He refused to take any responsibility for what had transpired in Afghanistan and in Kashmir as a result of Pakistan's past policy actions. Musharraf repeatedly blamed Afghanistan as being the cradle for extremism and terrorism, and lambasted India for not doing enough to address the root causes of the Kashmir problem. He rapidly projected an image of himself as a very worthy ally of Washington, capable of not only democratizing Pakistan without changing his military uniform, but also assuming a central role in protecting US interests during the difficult phase of the war on terror in world politics. Concurrently, he ensured that Pakistan remained as much of a vital regional player in the post-9/11 scenario as it was before it, but of course now in different regional and international settings. In the process, he poised himself to give Washington what was needed to retain its favours, but not more, even if at times that meant Washington's interests were not truly served. This was so to the extent that he could get away with action as serious as nuclear proliferation, in which Pakistan's chief atomic scientist, A.Q. Khan, had engaged. Musharraf was able to override the whole episode without any public recrimination from the Bush Administration.

In this context, Musharraf skilfully, though in the eyes of many analysts also manipulatively, focused on achieving a number of subtly self-serving foreign policy priorities and objectives.

He declared full support for the US-backed government of Hamid Karzai in Afghanistan and extended (apparently) full security and intelligence cooperation to the US-led 'war on terror'. In this regard, he made a remarkable public display of what he called Pakistan's brotherly contributions to the reconstruction of Afghanistan and national resolve to fight the Al-Qaeda and the Taliban at all levels, and prevent them from receiving any aid from Pakistan for cross-border operations. To this end, from time to time, Islamabad captured and handed over to the United States certain Al-Qaeda operatives as 'high value targets' in a blaze of publicity. In 2005, it even announced the deployment of 80,000 troops on the border with Afghanistan, resulting in fighting with a number of tribal and foreign supporters of the Taliban and the Al-Qaeda in the free tribal areas of Pakistan, especially in north Waziristan, over which no Pakistani government had full control in the past. Similarly, in relation to the Kashmir dispute, he scaled down Pakistan's support for cross-border violence, agreed to a number of confidence-building measures with India and proposed ostensibly bold initiatives to secure an enduring resolution of the Kashmir problem.

Beyond these, Islamabad declared a campaign to reform religious education, especially in Pakistani madrasas (which had been widely viewed as a source of Islamic extremism), quietly supported the US-led invasion of Iraq (although declining to send troops there for fear of public backlash), and secretly expressed solidarity with Washington in its hostilities with the Iranian Islamic regime. Further, it assured Washington that Pakistan's historical friendship with China should not be a source of any concern, given Pakistan's growing commitment to the new alliance with the United States.

Yet, Musharraf never failed to press for his vision of a Pakistan whose politics must be conducted on the basis of what was conducive to his interests. While maintaining his domestic reforms largely at a non-structural level, he made sure that his foreign policy actions were in line with maintaining the support of the military and the ISI as his real power base and was careful not to invite a serious backlash from conservative Islamic forces. This meant that he found it imperative to sustain continuity between Pakistan's pre- and post-9/11 foreign policy postures. Hence, his strenuous efforts to walk a tightrope on Afghanistan, Kashmir and Pakistan's wider regional relations within an approach of one step forward and one step backward, requiring the Bush Administration to play its regional politics more in tune with Musharraf's priorities than according to US needs. The strong lobby group that he established in Washington constantly reminded the Bush Administration and the Congress that if the United States failed to remain sensitive to the complexity of Pakistan's position under Musharraf, Pakistan could easily fall prey to serious instability. This, they maintained, could result not only in undermining the US operations in Afghanistan and its wider war on terror, but also in confronting Washington with an even greater nightmare — a collapse of Musharraf's regime and Pakistan's implosion.

In this context, the Musharraf regime successfully pushed for four policy objectives:

First, while publicly backing the Karzai government, Islamabad privately demanded that Karzai give his ethnic Pashtuns, to which the Taliban also belong, the largest share in the post-Taliban power structure and rid his government of the influence of those non-Pashtuns who had formed the bulk of the anti-Taliban resistance within the United Front or the so-called Northern Alliance, and who had played a critical role in the US-led ground war that had toppled the Taliban regime. To reinforce this position, Musharraf in September 2006 went so far as to claim (inaccurately) that in Afghanistan the Pashtuns constituted almost 60 per cent of the population and that the Tajiks formed a mere 5–7 per cent minority.[14] Yet historically, the Pashtuns have never accounted for more than 42 per cent of the Afghan population, followed by ethnic Tajiks as the second largest group with 25–30 per cent of the population and other minorities making up the rest.

However, the Pashtuns had traditionally dominated the Afghan political and military leaderships ever since the emergence of modern Afghanistan as an identifiable political unit in the mid-eighteenth century. Islamabad essentially called for the restoration of this situation as a necessary foundation for creating the conditions of stability in Afghanistan, and for avoiding the kind of developments in Pakistan that could adversely affect the United States' regional interests and operations. Yet, in this, Islamabad chose to ignore the fact that the conflicts following the seizure of power by a cluster of pro-Soviet communists in Kabul in April 1978 had profoundly changed the Afghan political and social landscapes, empowering the non-Pashtun segments of the population to resist any return to past Pashtun supremacy. Islamabad nonetheless persisted with its reasoning as part of an approach essentially designed to pressure the Karzai government and its international supporters to incorporate the Taliban in the government, and as a consequence enable Pakistan to regain some of its past influence in Afghan politics. It seems to have reasoned that the foreign forces will eventually leave Afghanistan (as the Soviet Union ultimately did) and that the prospects for Afghanistan's transformation do not look bright. As such, Pakistan seemed to be in a position to safeguard its interests against any adverse developments in Afghanistan and the region. Hence, Pakistan's continued support for the Taliban in terms of provision of both sanctuary and material assistance, despite a demand by the United States and its allies that all such support be stopped. Musharraf did admit to a certain level of Pakistani support, but denied his government's role in it.

All the anti-Taliban measures that he announced — ranging from deploying troops along the border with Afghanistan, and fighting both the foreign and tribal backers of the Taliban on the Pakistani side of the border to fencing parts of the Afghan-Pakistan border and closely cooperating with the US-led coalition and NATO forces for enhancing border security — amounted to little more than impressing Washington that he remained a committed partner in the war on terror. Yet, the bitter fact was that Musharraf's alliance with the US had rested primarily on the Afghan conflict and the war on terror. Therefore, a continuation of the two was clearly in his interests.

The second was the Musharraf regime's stand on relations with India exhibited a degree of double-speak that complemented to a large extent its position on Afghanistan and the war on terror. While urged by Washington to improve relations with India, the regime only took measures that were expedient to its domestic needs and capabilities, and did what minimum it was required to do to please Washington. There was certainly an improvement in Indo-Pakistan bilateral relations, based on a number of confidence-building measures since 2004, but Islamabad was not able to build on this by cutting off all links with Kashmiri separatists and negotiating to turn the 'Line of Control' into a de jure border with India. This is not to deny that Musharraf did not come up with some unprecedented proposals for a resolution of the Kashmir issue. In October 2004, he proposed that India and Pakistan should identify 'regions' of Kashmir on both sides of the Line of Control, demilitarize them and grant them the status of independence — joint control or under UN mandate.[15] The proposal was publicized enough to generate some optimism, but it was ultimately designed to soothe Washington's quest for action. As New Delhi expectedly gave the proposal an initially cold reaction, Islamabad followed it up in 2006[16] by nothing bolder that could bring New Delhi to the negotiating table. Two factors hampered Musharraf's efforts in this respect. One is that the entire Kashmir problem has been closely knotted to Pakistani domestic politics, as is also the case in relation to India. It has suited Islamabad, whenever needed, to use it to highlight Pakistan's Islamic credentials, but it has also served diversionary purposes. Another is that, given its nature, Musharraf's regime was not able to rely on a public mandate to do what was required to secure a resolution of the Kashmir problem. Instead, it found it easier to deflect the need for a resolution by making its usual claim that any degree of US pressure on Pakistan to do more would endanger Pakistan's internal stability and hurt the success of the war on terror.

The third was to maintain and strengthen Pakistan's position, despite its misdeeds, as a central player on the regional and international scenes. For this, the Musharraf regime again pursued a double-edged approach. On the one hand, it emphasized the regime's normative commitment to expunging Pakistan of Islamic extremism by reforming religious teaching and schools, and bringing them under government control, and de-linking Pakistan from Islamic extremist groups in the region and beyond. On the other, it concurrently sought to promote an image of Pakistan as a closely Arab-linked and potentially Sunni bulwark against the predominantly Shiite and anti-US Iran and other hostile forces as part of a policy of safeguarding Pakistani and US interests in the region. While announcing some measures to control Islamic extremism at home, it balanced this by constantly prompting Washington to remain content with the fact that Pakistan needs to maintain its Sunni Muslim status as a means to retaining its close ties with the United States' oil-rich Arab allies in the Gulf and mainly Sunni-profiled friends in Central Asia. It intimated that without such a status Pakistan would be unable to help the United States in containing possible Iranian predatory actions in Afghanistan and the Central Asian republics.

The fourth objective focused on carving a critical niche for Pakistan in relation to a drive by the Karzai government and its international supporters to capitalize on Afghanistan's strategic position to strengthen the country's reconstruction and security on the basis of promoting economic cooperation and integration between Central Asia and South Asia.[17] The Musharraf regime was careful to make sure that this drive did not result in either an emergence of a strong Afghanistan or extra leverages for India that could possibly limit Pakistan's role as a central regional player. While conscious of Kabul's close ties with New Delhi as a counter to Pakistan, and of Afghanistan's entry into the South Asian Association for Regional Cooperation (SAARC), the regime endeavoured that whatever economic and infrastructural networks and facilities were built, they were conducive to two things. One was that they lead only to the kinds of linkages between Afghanistan, the Central Asian republics and India that would not limit Pakistan's manoeuvrability as a pivotal actor in the process. The other was that Pakistan remained in a position to obstruct such linkages whenever it deemed it necessary. As a result, on the one hand, the Musharraf regime made sure to be seen as a strong supporter of regional economic cooperation; on the other hand, it sought to shape this cooperation in a way that proved to be quite frustrating for Kabul and New Delhi. Again, in the context of its alliance with the United States, it was able not only to make the Bush Administration tolerate its double-edged attitude, but even to demand that Washington help it in directing the regional cooperation in a manner that would make Afghanistan essentially an extension of Pakistan. This was firmly reflected in a series of talking points that Pakistani lobbyists circulated to officials of the Bush Administration and the Congress in January 2007.[18] The main message was that an economic integration of Afghanistan into Pakistan was the best way to stabilize Afghanistan and to strengthen Pakistan as a foundation for enabling the United States to succeed in the war on terror and protect its interests in the region against a rising Iran, Russia and China.

However, by 2007 the tide turned against Musharraf and his US supporters. A majority of the Pakistani people evidently grew very impatient with his politics of deception. Meanwhile, the sham parliament that he had created and which had endorsed the continuation of his military rule for another term five years ago, was to end in November 2007. But he wanted that parliament to elect him for another term before it wrapped up. To achieve this goal, he doubled his efforts from early in the year to silence his critics and create a national political environment conducive to his purposes. His actions included: an attempt to dismiss Chief Justice Iftikhar Ahmad Chowdhry; measures to marginalize the two main opposition parties, the Pakistan People's Party (PPP) and the Muslim League, and keep their respective leaders Benazir Bhutto and Nawaz Sharif in exile; the use of maximum force to violently suppress a challenge by a radical Muslim group in the Red Mosque in Islamabad in early July 2007; and moves to clamp down on nationalist opponents, especially in Baluchistan and the North West Frontier Provinces.

However, none of his actions paid off; if anything, they backfired. They helped the growth of Muslim extremism and the Talibanization of Pakistan's 'free tribal belt' on the border with Afghanistan, and united diverse groups against his rule — many of which would otherwise have had little in common ideologically or politically. While in July, the Supreme Court reinstated Chowdhry, who had emerged as a credible opposition figure and who doubted the constitutionality of Musharraf's move to secure himself another term as president without shedding his military uniform before being re-elected, his military assaults on the Red Mosque in the same month unleashed a sustained wave of violent retaliatory actions by Islamic militants across the country. As a substantial cross-section of the Pakistani population grew very discontented and frustrated with Musharraf,[19] the latter reached a position where he could no longer sustain his rule as before.

By the same token, his relations with the Bush Administration reached a critical point. The two sides became a liability for one another — many Pakistanis viewed Musharraf as a US puppet and Washington could not reliably depend upon Musharraf for maintaining its 'war on terror' or regional interests. The two countries faced a serious dilemma about how to salvage the situation. Of the few policy options open to them, two deserve attention as more likely than the others:

One was for Musharraf to impose a state of emergency, to suspend the parliament, to postpone elections and to rule by decree as he did when he first seized power. He was on the verge of declaring such a measure in mid-August 2007, but Washington advised him against it, for two main reasons — it would sink Pakistan into deeper instability, and it would make a mockery of the Bush Administration's stand for democracy. The US Secretary of State, Condoleeza Rice, urged him to stay on course with elections.

The second option was for Musharraf to hang on to power, but on the basis of reaching a power-sharing agreement with one of the main civilian political parties — either Benazir Bhutto's PPP or Nawaz Sharif's Muslim League — or both to enable him to put an acceptable civilian face on his rule. Washington was keen to see this option materializing as the most viable one. However, Nawaz Sharif's refusal to reach any accommodation with Musharraf and the latter's immediate deportation of the former upon his return to Islamabad in September 2007 to participate in the forthcoming parliamentary elections narrowed Musharraf's option to a considerable extent. The PPP was left as the obvious choice. Bhutto was not only politically ambitious but also amenable to the United States, given her strong public stand against terrorism. Although a partnership with Musharraf would have benefited Musharraf more than Bhutto, given the military's pervasive control of power and politics, Bhutto's interest in status rather than policy drove her to return to Pakistan in October 2007, based on an understanding that Musharraf would drop corruption charges against her to allow her to contest the parliamentary election and she would support Musharraf to become a civilian president for another term.

None of these options was very attractive in terms of putting Pakistan on a path of enduring stability and viability, but in the end Musharraf was compelled to follow both. Given the circumstances he faced, Musharraf at first embraced the second option as Washington's preferred one. However, he did so reluctantly, and feared that the Supreme Court under Chowdhry would not declare his October parliamentary re-election as constitutional. This proved instrumental in Musharraf resorting to the first option by declaring a state of emergency in November 2007 to save his rule. He appointed a new Supreme Court bench that immediately endorsed his presidency for a further term. It was only then that he shed his military uniform and appointed one of his loyalists, General Kayani, as Army Chief of Staff, without necessarily weakening his firm grip on the military and the ISI.

As he came under mounting domestic and international criticism, he found it imperative to lift the state of emergency in mid-December and set 8 January 2008 as the new date for parliamentary elections, while still keeping hundreds of judges and political activists in prison and severely restricting media activities. Bhutto agreed to this with much trepidation, but was assassinated on 27 December.

Although Musharraf blamed the Islamic extremists for Bhutto's death, fingers were also pointed at him. Bhutto's killing removed a major challenge to Musharraf, prompting Washington to rally once again behind Musharraf as one of its most important allies in the so-called war on terror. Despite the fact that Musharraf rescheduled the elections for 18 February 2008, with a promise to bring genuine democracy to Pakistan, few inside or outside Pakistan believed that the elections would meet international standards. Even so, when the elections were held, they were won by the opposition parties, with the PPP gaining the largest number of seats and Nawaz Sharif's Muslim League (PML-N) coming second. Initially, the two parties formed a coalition government, with a commitment to unseating Musharraf. Under threat of parliamentary impeachment, Musharraf finally resigned on 18 August 2008. However, the PPP–PML-N alliance also could not survive because of their differences, leaving the PPP to govern with the help of minor parties, but on a highly unstable basis.

▧ Conclusion

Pakistan and the US–Pakistan alliance are now in a serious crisis. Pakistan cannot afford to muddle through for much longer, drifting between the poles of authoritarianism and quasi-democracy, Islamism and secularism in its domestic politics, with exploitative and double-edged postures in its regional and international relations, as it has done up to this point. It is badly in need of enduring foundations that can consolidate its position as a stable, secure and responsible actor in world politics. It requires institutionalized processes of change and development, and publicly mandated governments, without the military acting as the real power either overtly or covertly.

The United States and its allies bear a special responsibility in this respect. Instead of manipulating Pakistan to realize their short-term goals, they need to work out a long-term strategy whereby the Pakistanis could develop an inclusive, participatory system of governance on an enduring basis. It is now in no one's interest to see a nuclear-armed Pakistan either becoming a weak state or disintegrating — both scenarios would have far-reaching consequences for world politics. The sooner Pakistan is moved on the path of solid democratic transformation, the better. The emphasis should not be on whether or not the 'war on terror' is successful, but rather on what is imperative to transform Pakistan into a viable state. The best way forward is for the military and the ISI to be placed under democratic control, and this requires serious constitutional and political changes in Pakistan.

▦ Notes

1. For background analysis, see Mary A. Weaver, *Pakistan: In the Shadow of Jihad and Afghanistan* (New York: Farrar, Straus and Giroux, 2003), pp. 11–44.
2. Ministry of Finance, 'Accelerating Economic Growth and Reducing Poverty: The Road Ahead Poverty Reduction Strategy Paper' (Islamabad: Ministry of Finance, Government of Pakistan, December 2003), p. 21; for a detailed background analysis, see Christophe Jaffrelot (ed.), *A History of Pakistan and Its Origins*, trans. Gillian Berumont (London: Anthem Press, 2004), pp. 163–90; Syed Mubashir Ali and Faisal Bari, 'At the Millennium: Macro Economic Performance and Prospects', in Charles H. Kennedy and Craig Baxter (eds), *Pakistan 2000* (New York: Lexington Books, 2000), pp. 25–44.
3. For a detailed discussion, see Stephen Cohen, *The Idea of Pakistan* (Washington, DC: Brookings Institution Press, 2004), pp. 161–200.
4. William Maley, *The Afghanistan Wars* (London: Palgrave, 2002), pp. 218–50.
5. Mary A. Weaver, *Pakistan*, pp. 249–74; Devine T. Hagerty, 'Kashmir and the Nuclear Question Revisited', in *Pakistan 2000*, pp. 81–106.
6. Amin Saikal, *Modern Afghanistan: A History of Struggle and Survival* (London: I.B. Tauris, 2006), pp. 209–30.
7. For details, see Dennis Kux, *The United States and Pakistan, 1947–2000: Disenchanted Allies* (Washington, DC: Woodrow Wilson Center Press, 2001).
8. Owen Bennett-Jones, 'US and Pakistan in Talks', *BBC Monitoring South Asia–Political*, 26 May 2000, http://news.bbc.co.uk/2/hi/south_asia/764518.stm (accessed 21 July 2008); 'Jon Stewart Interviews Gen. Musharraf', *The Daily Show*, 26 September 2001, http://www.thedailyshow.com/video/index.jhtml?videoId=114685&title=pervez-musharraf-pt-1 (accessed 21 July 2008); Amin Saikal, 'The Role of Outside Actors in Afghanistan', *The Middle East Policy*, October 2000, 7(4), pp. 50–57.
9. For background, see Amin Saikal, *The Rise and Fall of the Shah: Iran from Autocracy to Religious Rule* (Princeton, NJ: Princeton University Press, 2009), pp. 135–208.

10. Pervez Musharraf, *In the Line of Fire* (London: Simon & Schuster, 2006), p. 19.
11. Ibid., p. 201.
12. Nathaniel Heller, Sarah Fort and Marina Walker Guevara, 'Pakistan's $4.2 Billion "Blank Check" for U.S. Military Aid', *The Center for Public Integrity*, 27 March 2007, http://www.publicintegrity.org/news/entry/218/ (accessed 21 July 2008).
13. 'Accelerating Economic Growth and Reducing Poverty: The Road Ahead', Poverty Reduction Strategy Paper: Government of Pakistan, http://siteresources.worldbank.org/PAKISTANEXTN/Resources/PRSP.pdf (accessed 21 July 2008).
14. 'A Conversation with Pervez Musharraf', Council on Foreign Relations (New York), 25 September 2006, http://www.cfr.org/publication/11576/conversation_with_pervez_musharraf_video.html (accessed 21 July 2008).
15. *BBC News*, 'India Cool on Kashmir Proposals', 26 October 2004, http://news.bbc.co.uk/2/hi/south_asia/3953417.stm (accessed 21 July 2008).
16. *BBC News*, 'Musharraf Pushes Kashmir Proposal', 5 December 2006, http://news.bbc.co.uk/2/hi/south_asia/6208660.stm (accessed 21 July 2008).
17. See Afghan-American Chamber of Commerce, 'Afghanistan Compact of 31 January 2006', http://www.ands.gov.af/admin/ands/ands_docs/upload/UploadFolder/The%20Afghnistan%20Compact%20-%20Final%20English.pdf (accessed 21 July 2008).
18. Pakistan's lobby team in Washington has included Dr Herbert Davis and Ms Espernanza Gomez, the former and present Executive Director of US–Pakistan Business Council. Also, see Amin Saikal, 'Bid to Integrate Afghanistan will not Bring Democracy', *The Age*, 26 March 2006, http://www.theage.com.au/news/world/bid-to-integrate-afghanistan-will-not-bring-democracy/2007/03/16/1173722749140.html (accessed 21 July 2008); 'Briefing by U.S. Administration Highlights Proposed Re-construction Opportunity Zones (ROZs) for Afghanistan and Pakistan', Afghan-American Chamber of Commerce, http://www.a acc.org/docs/ROZ_Press_Release_march_2007.pdf (accessed 21 July 2008).
19. Ahmed Rashid, 'A Distraction from Washington's Grand Design', *Daily Telegraph*, 11 September 2007, http://www.telegraph.co.uk/news/worldnews/1562832/A-distraction-from-Washington%27s-grand-design.html (accessed 21 July 2008).

❋

2

Global Terrorism: US Policy After 9/11 and Its Impact on the Domestic Politics and Foreign Relations of Pakistan

Selig S. Harrison

Historians assessing the impact of the World Trade Center attack on 11 September 2001, will confront one central question: Did the nature of the US response to the tragedy inadvertently magnify the challenge of terrorism?

The provisional answer to this question is clearly yes. The Bush Administration's concept of a 'war on terror' has focused all too narrowly on developing an operational response to identifiable terrorist groups such as the Al-Qaeda. No effort has been made to assess the motivations or mindset of the terrorists and to modify US foreign policies and defence policies on the basis of this assessment. On the contrary, until recently, to suggest that the terrorists were motivated in part by opposition to the US military presence in the Persian Gulf and the Middle East, and to the unconditional US support given to Israel on the issue of a Palestinian state, has been treated as heresy, at best, and treason at worst.

Almost seven years after 9/11, it has at last become intellectually respectable to discuss the conceptual flaws in the concept of the 'war on terror' and the self-defeating impact of the US policies based on this concept, which have strengthened the indigenous forces in many countries sympathetic to the Al-Qaeda and other Islamic terrorist groups.

The first significant overt challenge to the 'war on terror' orthodoxy came in a September 2006, *Foreign Affairs* article declaring that the entire US response to 9/11 has been 'overblown', that it was 'probably a one-time event that cannot be repeated, and that the threat from terrorist groups within the United States itself is almost non-existent'.[1]

Soon afterwards, a *New York Review of Books* article concluded that 'the mental construct that framed the administration's reaction to September 11 as a "war" is beginning to fall apart'.[2] This was followed by a *Wall Street Journal* commentary and a book in which the influential billionaire financier, George Soros, wrote that 'the war on terror is a false metaphor that has led to counterproductive and self-defeating policies. Five years after 9/11, a misleading figure of speech applied literally has unleashed a real war fought on several fronts — Iraq, Gaza, Lebanon, Afghanistan, Somalia — a war that has killed thousands of innocent civilians and enraged millions around the world. Yet Al-Qaeda has not been subdued.'[3] Then on 11 December 2006, the British Foreign Office said that it would no longer use the term 'war on terror' because 'Islamist extremists find it easier to recruit followers when Western governments speak of a war on terrorists, by suggesting that it is actually a war against Islam.'[4]

That there is a widespread Muslim perception of the 'war on terror' as a war on Islam was emphasized by Prime Minister Abdullah Badawi of Malaysia, chairman of the 57-nation Organization of the Islamic Conference, who told the *Financial Times* that Muslims throughout the world have been 'radicalized by western policies in the Middle East, including the failure to resolve the conflict between Israel and the Palestinians, and the invasion of Iraq. Trying to resolve terrorism without examining its root causes is like trying to fertilize the fruits and not the roots.'[5] Similarly, Zbigniew Brzezinski, who served as National Security Advisor to US President Jimmy Carter, has warned that 'the war on terror has gravely damaged the US internationally. For Muslims, the similarity between the rough treatment of Iraqi civilians by the US military and of the Palestinians by the Israelis has prompted a widespread sense of hostility toward the United States in general. It's not the war on terror that angers Muslims watching the news on television. It's the victimization of Arab civilians.'[6]

▣ Subsidizing Musharraf: A Bad Bargain

An examination of the impact of US policies since 2001 on the domestic politics and foreign relations of Pakistan dramatically illustrates that the United States has indeed inadvertently magnified the challenge of terrorism. By providing unconditional support on a massive scale to the military regime of Pervez Musharraf, the United States strengthened the Islamist elements in both the armed forces and the Pakistani civilian polity on whom his regime depends; undermined secular political forces; radicalized the Afghan border areas where Al-Qaeda and Taliban forces are concentrated; rekindled

Pashtun support on both sides of the border for an independent 'Pashtunistan' that could become a terrorist haven, and encouraged Pakistani Islamist groups to employ terrorist tactics in supporting the Kashmiri insurgency in India.

The direct and indirect cost of Musharraf's nominal cooperation with the United States had reached a staggering $27.5 billion by 2007.

Direct, overt economic and military aid to Pakistan has totalled $4.5 billion. But the United States also provides disguised subsidies for the Pakistani armed forces — set to reach $7.5 billion in 2008 — that are papered over in Pentagon statistics and have received little Congressional scrutiny. What Pakistan gets, nominally as reimbursement for the cost of its counter-terrorism operations, is lumped together statistically with other counter-terrorism funding. These payments continue to flow whether or not Pakistani forces come out of their barracks in Afghan border areas in a given month.[7]

In addition to these direct forms of aid, the Bush Administration has given Pakistan various forms of indirect financial support. For example, the United States authorized the Pakistan Air Force to buy F-16 fighter jets under the US Foreign Military Sales (FMS) programme. If the Air Force gets its way in internal Pakistani budgetary battles, these purchases could eventually total $5 billion. These are nominally commercial purchases from private US manufacturers, but it is much easier to get private financing for them under the government-approved FMS programme than it would otherwise be. More importantly, after 9/11, the United States orchestrated the postponement of debt repayments to aid donor countries totalling another $13.5 billion, which prevented what would otherwise have been an economic collapse. This is what made possible the Musharraf regime's purchasing of F-16s and other military hardware out of 'Pakistani' funds.

A lower estimate of the cost in a Centre for Strategic and International Studies analysis — $10 billion — includes the counter-terrorism subsidies to the armed forces but excludes the indirect costs cited in the $27.5 billion figure: $13.5 billion in rescheduled debt repayments and up to $5 billion in FMS-authorized F-16 purchases.[8]

What did the United States receive in return for this profusion of direct and indirect economic and military aid to the Musharraf regime?

In his memoirs, Musharraf recalls that the US Secretary of State, Colin Powell had telephoned him on 12 September 2001, to warn him bluntly, 'you are either with us or against us'. On the same day, the US Deputy Secretary of State, Richard Armitage told the ISI Director General, then visiting Washington, that 'if we chose the terrorists, then we should be prepared to be bombed back to the Stone Age'.[9] On the next day, Musharraf said that the US Ambassador in Islamabad had presented to him, in writing, seven specific demands for Pakistani help:

1. Stop Al-Qaeda operatives at your borders, intercept arms shipments through Pakistan, and end all logistical support for Bin Laden.
2. Provide the United States with blanket over flight and landing rights to conduct all necessary military and intelligence operations.
3. Provide territorial access to the United States, and allied military intelligence as needed and other personnel, to conduct all necessary operations against the perpetrators of terrorism and those that harbour them, including the use of Pakistan's naval ports, air bases, and strategic locations on borders.
4. Provide the United States immediately with intelligence, immigration information and databases, internal security, and information, to help prevent and respond to terrorist acts perpetrated against the United States, its friends, or its allies.
5. Continue to publicly condemn the terrorist acts of 11 September and any other terrorist acts against the United States or its friends and allies, and curb all domestic expressions of support (for terrorism) against the United States, its friends, or its allies.
6. Cut off all shipments of field to the Taliban and any other items and recruits, including volunteers en route to Afghanistan, who can be used in a military offensive capacity or to abet a terrorist threat.
7. Should the evidence strongly implicate Osama bin Laden and the Al-Qaeda network in Afghanistan and should Afghanistan and the Taliban continue to harbour him and his network, Pakistan will break diplomatic relations with the Taliban government, end support for the Taliban, and assist the United States in the aforementioned way to destroy Osama bin Laden and his Al-Qaeda network.[10]

'We just could not support demands two and three', writes Musharraf. 'How could we allow the United States "blanket over flight and landing rights" without jeopardizing our strategic assets? I offered only a narrow flight corridor that was far from any sensitive area. Neither could we give the United States "use of Pakistan's naval ports or fighter aircraft bases." We allowed the United States only two bases — Shamsi in Baluchistan and Jacobabad in Sindh — and only for logistics and aircraft recovery. No attack could be launched from there. We gave no "blanket permission" for anything.'[11]

General Tommy Franks, US Army (retd.) in his own memoirs, refers to 'basing, staging and over flight support' formalized in 'a detailed list of 74 basing and staging activities to be conducted in Pakistan'. But he cites specifically only combat search and rescue, communications relay sites, and medical evacuation points near the Afghan border.[12] Franks was accentuating the positive aspect to stay in tune with the Bush Administration policy, just as Musharraf was sensitive to his domestic political audience in Pakistan.

What is clear in both accounts, and most important militarily, is that the United States could not use bases in Pakistan for combat missions and that access to the bases at Shamsi and Jacobabad was limited to logistics and aircraft recovery. The combat aircrafts used in Afghanistan were based on US aircraft carriers deployed in the Arabian Sea or in bases in Afghanistan itself.

In subsequent US and NATO operations against insurgent Taliban forces opposed to the United States-backed Kabul regime of President Hamid Karzai, no US air or ground operations have been permitted on the Pakistan side of the Durand Line — the de facto boundary between Pakistan and Afghanistan — either in the border areas of Pakistan's Baluchistan province, directly administered by Islamabad, or in the Federally Administered Tribal Areas (FATA) that are nominally part of Pakistan but have in reality been an autonomous No Man's Land since the days of the British Raj.

However, Pakistani forces, with the cooperation of US intelligence agencies, have carried out operations of their own in FATA and the border areas of Baluchistan designed to root out Al-Qaeda and Taliban forces. In the United States' eyes, Pakistan's role has been woefully inadequate, while in Pakistan's eyes, as this essay will elaborate, American pressure has forced the Pakistani forces to conduct politically self-defeating offensives in FATA that have radicalized the populace and made it more hospitable to the Al-Qaeda and the Taliban than it was previously.

Although Pakistan's value to the United States since 9/11 in the military sphere has been limited, it has played a noteworthy role in partnership with the FBI and US intelligence agencies in capturing Al-Qaeda operatives. In the most important of such cases, Khalid Sheikh Mohammed, the third-ranking Al-Qaeda leader, was captured on 1 March 2003, after the FBI confronted Pakistani officials with intercepted communications, pinpointing his hideout in the Rawalpindi home of a leader of the Islamic extremist Jamaat-e-Islami Party. Two other Al-Qaeda leaders captured by Pakistan were Ramzi bin al-Sheikh and Abu Zubaydah, both key lieutenants of Osama bin Laden. Except for these and several lesser cases, the Musharraf regime had shown little initiative of its own in finding and breaking up either Al-Qaeda networks, or the networks of sympathetic Islamic extremist groups that give sanctuary and help to Al-Qaeda.

▣ The Taliban Connection

Popular support for Islamic extremism has grown steadily in Pakistan as a result of the unpopular US policies in the Middle East and the Persian Gulf cited earlier, especially the unconditional US support for Israel on the issue of the Palestinian statehood and the large-scale civilian casualties inflicted by US forces in Iraq and Afghanistan. A leading Pakistani secular political figure, Mushahid Hussain, Secretary General of the pro-Musharraf Muslim League, emphasized the Israel–Palestinian issue in an address during a US visit, declaring that 'the failure to push through the road map on Palestine has been disastrous for the US image. There is no legitimacy to the war on terror because it is perceived as part of an anti-Muslim US posture.'[13]

While making proforma statements in his memoirs, denouncing terrorism and professing support for a moderate form of Islam, Musharraf explains his decision to back the United States after 9/11 not in terms of moral solidarity with Washington but as an unavoidable response to the threats made by Powell and Armitage. Pakistan had no choice but to accede to US pressures, he says, because of its 'military weakness as compared with the strength of the United States', its economic weakness and above all its 'social weakness. We lack the homogeneity to galvanize the entire nation into an active confrontation. The United States undoubtedly would have taken the opportunity of an invasion to destroy the Pakistani nuclear arsenal' he said, 'and India, needless to say, would have loved to assist the United States to the hilt.'[14]

To win public acceptance of his alignment with Washington and reassure Pakistanis who sympathized with the Al-Qaeda and the Taliban, Musharraf made a revealing TV address in the Urdu language, not intended for American ears, on 19 September 2001. Sprinkling in citations from the Quran, he drew a lengthy analogy between the situation then facing Pakistan and the opportunist alliance that the Prophet Muhammad made with the Jewish tribes of Medina to defeat his enemies. After six years of fighting against non-believers in Mecca who challenged his claim to be the Prophet, Muhammad made a deal with them and ditched the Jews. Mecca became the headquarters of the new religion.

Although veiled, Musharraf's message, as widely interpreted in the Urdu media, was unmistakable: The alliance with the Americans is only temporary. He directed special words of reassurance to Taliban sympathizers, reminding them, 'I have done everything for Afghanistan and the Taliban when the whole world was against them. We are trying our best to come out of this critical situation without any damage to (them).'[15]

Pakistan had supported the Taliban while it was in power, he writes 'for geo-strategic reasons. If we had broken with them, that would have created a new enemy on our western border, or a vacuum of power there into which might have stepped the Northern Alliance, comprising anti-Pakistan elements. The Northern Alliance was supported by Russia, India and Iran.'[16]

For the same geo-strategic reasons, the Musharraf regime had done its best since 9/11 not only to 'come out of this critical situation without any damage' to the Taliban but also to give direct and in-direct support to its operations in Afghanistan. Another reason not stated by Musharraf is the Pakistani fear that the Pashtun ethnic majority in Afghanistan will join with the Pashtuns in adjacent areas of Pakistan to revive the movement for an independent 'Pashtunistan' that Afghanistan had sponsored with Indian and Soviet support in earlier decades. Although the Taliban is itself Pashtun-based, Pakistan hopes that its Islamic ideological fervour will dilute the appeal of Pashtun nationalism and make it a reliable Afghan surrogate. But the possibility of a revival of the 'Pashtunistan' movement is taken seriously by Pakistan against the background of the British imposition of an Afghan-Pakistan boundary — the

Durand Line — which Afghanistan has never accepted. When the Taliban was in power in Kabul, it refused to recognize the Durand Line and to give up the long-standing Afghan claim to the Pashtun areas of Pakistan's North West Frontier Province (NWFP) that were annexed by the British Raj in 1893 and handed over to Pakistan when it was created in 1947.

How much direct support is given by Pakistani government agencies to the Taliban remains unclear. *New York Times* correspondent Carlotta Gall, visiting the border towns of Quetta and Chaman, found 'signs that Pakistani authorities are encouraging the insurgents, if not sponsoring them.'[17] In any case, the US Defence Secretary, Robert Gates said after a Kabul visit in February 2007, that 'there are more Taliban attacks coming across the border', and it is clear that the Musharraf regime looks the other way when Islamic extremist groups allied with 'rogue' ISI elements help the Taliban. Zahid Hussain, a respected Pakistani journalist, cited evidence that two former ISI directors, General Hamid Gul and General Javad Nasir, have 'remained actively involved' with Islamic radical movements linked to the Al-Qaeda and the Taliban.[18] Hussain reported that Chaman is 'the main base' for the Taliban, and that several madrasas, or religious seminaries in the Pashtunabad slum area of Quetta 'not only provide the Taliban with ideological training but with extended material help'. The rise to power of Islamic groups in the province of Baluchistan, where Quetta and Chaman are located, 'gave a tremendous boost to the Taliban's efforts to regroup', Hussain wrote, and 'many of the provincial ministers and members of Parliament belonging to the ruling MMA (Muttahida Majlis-e-Amal) alliance became actively involved with the Afghan rebels, using the region as their base. Many Pakistanis belonging to the ruling group also joined the Taliban.'[19]

Musharraf contributed directly to the MMA election victory in the two key Afghan border provinces in the 2002 elections. Apart from the covert ISI role in undermining its rivals, Musharraf openly supported the MMA by rewriting a key provision of the electoral law relating to educational qualifications. To be a candidate for the provincial assembly, his government ruled, it was necessary to have a college degree, with one important exception: a certificate of graduation from a madrasa or a religious seminary would also suffice. The requirement for a college degree barred many candidates from the secular parties, just as the less demanding madrasa provision helped the MMA. Musharraf backed the MMA at the provincial level because he needed its support to win a National Assembly majority for the Legal Framework Order that sanctioned his military overthrow of the elected Nawaz Sharif government. The MMA helped to secure the approval of the Assembly for his military coup, in exchange for his promise to step down as the Army Chief of Staff, a promise he took a while in honouring.

▣ The Rise of the Islamists

In helping the MMA to win power in the two border provinces, Musharraf was acceding to the political reality that the Islamic parties have been steadily strengthened by not only unpopular US policies in the Gulf and the Middle East but also the reckless use of US airpower closer to home in Afghanistan, which has led to large-scale civilian casualties. According to one authoritative study, civilian casualties in Afghanistan had reached 4,643 by October 2006, primarily in the Pashtun tribal areas adjacent to Pakistan. [20]

Faced with an anti-US political climate, the popularity of the Islamic parties and his own lack of a significant political base, Musharraf had been reluctant, and in many cases unable, to move forcefully against the Islamic extremist groups allied with the Al-Qaeda and the Taliban, as the Bush Administration has repeatedly demanded, and to shut down the madrasas used by these groups to incubate jihadis.

When Musharraf took over, Islamic extremist activities were already well organized in Pakistan, centered primarily in three groups that had been nurtured by the ISI for missions in Afghanistan during the Soviet occupation and in the Indian-held sector of Kashmir — Lashkar-e-Taiba, Jaish-e-Muhammad and Harkat-ul-Mujahideen. These groups, together with the anti-Shia Sepahe Sahaba, became increasingly active, and increasingly radicalized, after Musharraf joined hands with the US. The Jaish-e-Muhammad had 'a substantial following among soldiers and lower-ranking military officials', Zahid Hussain found. Despite Musharraf's orders to shut down its main training camp at Kotli in Pakistan's Azad Kashmir, the Jaish-e-Muhammad expanded the camp, and was so entrenched in the Air Force that it was able to organize a clandestine cell of two dozen Air Force officers at the Chaklala air base in Rawalpindi. It was this Chaklala cell, meeting regularly, undetected, with jihadist leaders, that planned the 14 December 2003 attempt to kill Musharraf by blowing up a bridge over which his presidential cavalcade passed. A high-tech jamming device in the President's car delayed the destruction of the bridge just long enough to allow him to cross the bridge safely. One of those who planted the explosives, Mushtaq Ahmed, was captured, imprisoned at the Chaklala base and sentenced to death, but jihadist penetration of the base was so extensive that he mysteriously escaped.[21] Musharraf's narrow escape from death led to tightened security protection for him and an escalation of his anti-extremist rhetoric, but not to a meaningful crackdown on extremist groups, whose leaders have been periodically put under house arrest in response to US demands for action against them and then released quietly several months later, usually after the names of their organizations have been changed.

The unchecked growth of madrasas directly linked to jihadi groups is striking evidence that the US embrace of Musharraf has increased and not diminished, extremist Islamic influence in Pakistan. To be sure, many madrasas have no jihadi links, but some of the most important ones make no secret of their orientation.

In Karachi, the Jamia Binoria, with some 10,000 students enrolled in eight affiliated madrasas, displays a banner at its main gate, urging Muslims to join the Taliban. Some of the other madrasas in the city have been used as safe havens by international terrorist networks. When the police raided the Jamia Abu Bakr Islamia Madrasa, after an FBI tip that it harboured Al-Qaeda sleeper cells, they found that a student enrolled under the name of Ahmed Madi was actually Gun Rusaman Gunawaji, a leading activist of Indonesia's Jemmah Islamiya, which staged the 2002 bombing of a Bali resort, and was a brother of its leader, Mambali. Lashkar-e-Taiba runs another Karachi madrasa, Jamia Darasitul Islamia, where several Southeast Asian students were arrested on suspicion of Al-Qaeda links. One of the suicide bombers involved in the July 2005, terror attacks in London, Shehzad Tanweer, spent a week at the Manzoor ul Islamia madrasa in Lahore, run by Jaish-e-Muhammad, during a 2004 visit to Pakistan.[22]

The most detailed, authoritative study of Pakistani madrasas, published by the International Crisis Group in March 2007, notes the absence of any rigorous or systematic system of madrasa registration, and the resulting difficulty in making a firm estimate of how many there are. The report notes the official countrywide registration figure of 12,006 and makes its own 'well-founded' nationwide estimate of 'up to' 20,000, with more than 1,000 in Karachi. No attempt is made to estimate the number of those most directly linked to jihadi activity, but many are named. The central Jamia Binoria madrasa, known as the Binoria Town madrasa, is the 'fountainhead' of jihadi militancy nationwide, said the report, and a generation of its former students have 'spread a web of similar jihadi madrasas across Karachi and beyond that pay allegiance to the Binori Town madrasa and seek guidance and support from its leader, Nizamuddin Shanzai.' The report specifically pointed to Binori Town graduates and leaders as the organizers of Jaish-e-Muhammad, Harkat-ul-Mujahideen and Sepahe Sahaba. Madrasa officials quoted in the report insist that the seminaries do not permit weapons to be stored on their premises, and that students cannot take part in jihadi activities while they are studying, but 'can do so after completing their studies'. Even those madrasas 'without direct links to violence', the Crisis Group study declared, 'promote an ideology that provides religious justification for such attacks'.[23]

The Pakistani government has yet to take any of the 'overdue and necessary steps to control religious extremism in Karachi and the rest of the country', the Crisis Group concluded, and 'Musharraf's periodic declarations of tough action, given in response to international events and pressure, are invariably followed by retreat'. His failure to confront the extremist forces is attributed primarily to his dependence on the religious right. The report emphasized particularly his coalition partner in the Baluchistan government, MMA, dominated as it is by the Jamiat Ulema-e-Islam, which has the largest network of madrasas. The report urges 21 specific steps, specifically the establishment of a national Madrasa Regulatory Authority, headed by the Interior Minister, operating under parliamentary oversight, with enough power to bar jihadi and violent sectarian teaching from madrasa syllabi and establish controls over foreign and domestic financing from both foreign and domestic sources. Indirectly criticizing Musharraf's 2002 electoral decree, which barred candidates who did not have a college degree but permitted the candidacy of madrasa graduates, the report recommended that madrasa certificates 'should not be treated as the equivalent of degrees issued by recognized boards of education and universities'.[24]

▨ Will Pakistan Survive?

In addition to strengthening the very forces of Islamic extremism that sponsor terrorism, the unconditional US embrace of Musharraf runs counter to the professed long-term US commitment to promote a democratic Pakistan. Sensitive to international public opinion, Musharraf had attempted to project a moderate image, permitting high-profile journalists and English-language publications with an international reputation to report with relative freedom on many issues, so long as they did not expose corruption in his regime or delve into sensitive religious and ethnic issues, especially issues relating to the Afghan border areas. Behind this façade of moderation, however, the Musharraf regime had become increasingly repressive in the face of growing opposition. The Human Rights Commission of Pakistan has estimated that at least 400 critics of Musharraf's government had been abducted and detained in secret by the ISI and other intelligence agencies, with no charges filed against them, and their whereabouts undisclosed to their families. The largest number of these 'disappearances' occurred in two disaffected ethnic minority provinces, Baluchistan and Sindh.

The central political problem facing Pakistan, largely shielded from international attention by the 'War on Terror', is how to deal with the deep ethnic tensions between the Punjabi majority, which controls the armed forces, and Baluch, Sindhi and Pashtun minorities that have been denied a fair share of economic and political power. For the government, satisfying US concerns about the Al-Qaeda and the Taliban is much less important than dealing with ethnic unrest: in the short term, suppressing a Baluch insurgency allied with a nascent, less unified Sindhi insurgency; and in the longer term, preventing the rebirth of the movement for an independent 'Pashtunistan' that would unite the Pashtuns on both sides of the Afghan-Pakistan border.

If history is a reliable guide, the prospects for the survival of the Pakistani state in its present form, with its existing configuration of constituent ethno-linguistic groups, cannot be taken for granted. There is no precedent in the history of South Asia for a state consisting of the five ethno-linguistic regions that made up Pakistan as originally constituted in 1947, or even for the truncated Pakistan, consisting of the four regions that remained after Bangladesh seceded in 1971. The ideologians of Pakistani nationalism exalt the historical memory of Akbar and Aurangzeb as the symbols of a lost Islamic grandeur in South Asia. By contrast, for the Baluch, Sindhis and Pashtuns, the Moghuls are remembered primarily as the symbols of past oppression.

Given its ethnic divisions, democratization in Pakistan would have to include a return to the 1973 Constitution, which recognizes the identity of the minorities and guarantees their autonomy in specified spheres. The nullification of the 1973 charter had been one of the Army's central objectives.

The ethnic arithmetic of Pakistan is a subject of bitter controversy. In the most recent census, in 1998, speakers of Punjabi constituted 44.15 per cent of the population (73.2 million); Seraiki, 10.53 per cent (17.5 million); Sindhi, 14.1 per cent (23.4 million); Pashtu, 15.42 per cent (25.6 million), and Baluchi, 3.57 per cent (5.9 million).[25] In political terms, the distinction between Punjabi and its Seraiki variant is not a meaningful one, especially in the eyes of the Baluch, Pashtuns, and Sindhis, who view Punjabi and Seraiki speakers as a single bloc. More important, with the notable exception of the Sindh region, the minorities emphasize the alliance between the Punjabis and the elite elements of the Urdu-speaking refugees (Muhajirs), numbering 7.6 per cent (12.6 million) people, who migrated to Pakistan from India after the partition. Baluch, Sindhi and Pashtun leaders all accuse the government of manipulating the statistics for political reasons. It is noteworthy that although the Baluch, Sindhis, and Pashtuns comprise less than 30 per cent of the population, they identify themselves historically with ethnic homelands that constitute 72 per cent of Pakistan's territory. To proponents of Pakistani nationalism, it is galling that the minorities should advance proprietary claims over such large areas of the country despite their numerical inferiority, and Islamabad deliberately seeks to stamp out regional and ethnic identities in order to push modernization programmes addressed to what is viewed as the greatest good for the greatest number of Pakistanis. But to most members of the minorities, the disparity between their population and their territorial claims is irrelevant, since they equate 'Pakistan' with the Punjabis and Muhajirs, who are perceived as having occupied and annexed their territories forcibly as an imperial power.

▣ The Shadow of Pashtunistan

The Baluch and Sindhis feel much more alienated from the Punjabi-Muhajir establishment than the Pashtuns. The Baluch perception is that the Punjabis view them with condescension and contempt as 'primitive', in contrast to a more favourable Punjabi attitude toward the Pashtuns, especially toward the Pashtun aristocracy. More important, the Baluch have been almost completely shut out of the economic and political power structure in Pakistan, whereas the Pashtuns, albeit bitter over Punjabi-Muhajir dominance, do not feel a comparable sense of complete exclusion. During British rule, Pashtuns from the more aristocratic, urbanized families were given powerful posts in the army and bureaucracy. Pashtun officers constituted a significant bloc in the upper ranks of the army following the partition, until many of them were pushed out in the late 1950s, when the Punjabis increased their power. Even today, however, there is still a significant number of Pashtuns in high places in Pakistan, and the expansion of Punjabi influence in the military and the bureaucracy has for the most part not been at the expense of Pashtun members of the establishment.

Geographically, the Pashtun areas are not as cut off from other parts of Pakistan as the Baluch areas, which partly explains why the Pashtun areas are better integrated within the overall Pakistani economy than the Baluch areas are. In Pashtun eyes, this integration has its disadvantages, in that it brings what is seen as excessive dependence on the Punjab province and makes the Pashtun areas vulnerable to exploitation by big-business interests centered in Karachi and Lahore. Pashtun antagonism towards Punjabi domination focuses, in large part, on alleged economic discrimination against the NWFP in allocations of development expenditures both in industry and agriculture.

Among the standard charges levelled by Pashtun leaders is that Islamabad deliberately holds back on electrification of the Pashtun areas because it does not want them to become industrialized — that even the electricity produced there goes primarily to the Punjab province, and that most of the tobacco and cotton grown in the NWFP is used to supply cigarette and textile factories located in other provinces. Islamabad even discriminates against the Pashtuns in agricultural development, Pashtun spokesmen argue, channelling funds for the expansion of irrigation primarily to Punjab or to areas in other provinces where Punjabi settlers will benefit most.

Pashtun dissatisfaction also focuses on the role of Punjabi civil servants in provincial administration and Islamabad's resistance to the use of the Pashtu language as the medium of instruction in education. At present, Urdu is the medium in public schools, with Pashtu taught as an optional subject up to the eighth grade. Pashtun children not only must attend classes conducted in Urdu but must also use textbooks written in Urdu, though English is permitted in civil service examinations and in university and graduate school entrance examinations. The language issue is important in Baluchistan, Sindh, and the NWFP alike, but it is more important in the Sindhi and Pashtun areas than in Baluchistan, because Sindhi and Pashtu are more standardized and better developed as literary languages than Baluchi and thus more readily adaptable for educational purposes.

Political scientist Hamida Khuhro, a Sindhi, once told me that 'basically, the Pashtuns want a bigger share of the cake', while the Baluch and the Sindhis want something more — identity, self-respect, real autonomy. This distinction is valid, but it does not necessarily follow that the possibility of a resurgent Pashtun separatism can be dismissed, especially against the background of the turmoil in the Pashtun areas on both sides of the Durand Line since 9/11. On the Pakistan side, Islamabad, pressed by Washington for action against Al-Qaeda and Taliban forces, has run roughshod over the traditional autonomy of the FATA tribes, both politically and militarily, arousing deep resentment. On the Afghan side, the large-scale civilian casualties resulting from the reckless use of US airpower against suspected Taliban hideouts has intensified Pashtun alienation from the US-backed Kabul government. In the eyes of many Pashtuns, the US alliance in 2001 with the Tajik leaders of the Northern Alliance to oust the Taliban regime has led to disproportionate Tajik influence in the Afghan intelligence, police and military apparatus at the expense of Pashtun interests.

Pakistan has worked single-mindedly to stifle Pashtun impulses for an independent Pashtunistan, both during and after the Soviet occupation of Afghanistan. During the occupation, the ISI channelled US aid to the Islamist resistance groups under its tutelage, denying significant aid and weaponry to resistance groups oriented to former King Zahir Shah, who had supported the Pashtunistan movement during the monarchy. When the Soviet forces left, the ISI initially sought to install Afghan surrogates regarded as compliant on the Pashtunistan issue. When these groups proved unable to consolidate power, Islamabad turned to the Taliban, which had a Pashtun base but was dominated by clerical leaders with a pan-Islamic ideology who had no previous identification with the Pashtunistan movement. Significantly, however, as noted earlier, when the Taliban came to power, it did not recognize the Durand Line despite Pakistani pressures to do so.

The Pashtun refugees who poured into the NWFP from Afghanistan after the departure of the Soviet forces, uprooted from their tribal moorings, have provided a fertile recruiting ground for the Jamaat-e-Islami, Jamiat Ulema-e-Islam and other Islamist groups. Strengthened by its alliance with Musharraf, the Islamist MMA coalition has eclipsed secular Pashtun political forces in the NWFP, centred in the National Awami Party, founded by the late Khan Abdul Ghaffar Khan, which does not subordinate ethnic Pashtun identity to Islamic identity. Nevertheless, Islamist and secular Pashtuns alike share a common desire to escape from the domination of Islamabad. Both share Pashtun traditions and historical memories with the Pashtuns in Afghanistan. The Pashtunistan movement is dormant, but not dead, and its re-emergence cannot be ruled out in the context of the growing instability and disintegrative tendencies in both Pakistan and Afghanistan.

▧ Afghanistan and Pashtun Identity

Just as the Baluch blame their absorption by the British Raj for their failure to achieve national identity, the Pashtuns too feel that colonialism robbed them of their birthright. Until the Raj, the Pashtuns were politically united for nearly a century under the banner of an Afghan empire that stretched eastwards as far as the Indus River. It was traumatic for the Pashtuns when the British seized 40,000 square miles of ancestral Pashtun territory between the Indus and the Khyber Pass, embracing half of the Pashtun population, and then imposed the Durand Line, formalizing their conquest. When they subsequently handed over this territory to the new, Punjabi-dominated government of Pakistan in 1947, the British bequeathed an explosive irredentist issue that has perennially dominated the rhetoric of Pashtun-dominated Afghan regimes and has poisoned relations between Afghanistan and Pakistan. At various times, Zahir Shah's monarchy, Muhammad Daoud's republic, and post-1978 Communist governments in Kabul have all challenged Pakistan's right to rule over its Pashtun areas, alternatively espousing the goal of an autonomous Pashtun state within Pakistan — an independent

'Pashtunistan' to be carved out of Pakistan or a 'Greater Afghanistan' directly annexing the lost territories.

The Pashtuns today gloss over the internecine strife within the newly established Afghan monarchy, which opened the way for the intervention of the British and their allies in the early nineteenth century. Surveying the broad picture, however, there is more than enough evidence in the historical record to account for the emotive power of Pashtun nationalism. Long before the British arrived on the scene, the Pashtuns were struggling to preserve their identity against the onslaught of advancing Moghul emperors, who ruled tenuously over the areas west of the Indus, from their capital in Delhi.

Pashtuns on both sides of the Durand Line share an ancient social and cultural identity dating back at least to the Pakti kingdom mentioned in the writings of Herodotus and possibly earlier. When a Punjabi critic asked him in 1975 whether he was 'a Muslim, a Pakistani, or a Pashtun first', Wali Khan, the National Awami Party leader, gave a much-quoted reply that he was 'a six-thousand-year-old Pashtun, a thousand-year-old Muslim, and a 27-year-old Pakistani'.[26] Eighth-century inscriptions have been found in a precursor of the Pashtu language. By the eleventh and twelfth centuries, Rahman Baba and other poets were writing Pashtu folk ballads that are still popular today, and by the mid-seventeenth century, Khushal Khan Khattak had begun to develop what is now treasured as the classic style of Pashtun poetry.

The size of the Pashtun population in Afghanistan is disputed and no definitive census data exists in Afghanistan. The CIA World Factbook estimates that the Afghanistan population was 31.05 million in 2006, of which 13 million were Pashtuns. In Pakistan, census data cited earlier indicated 25.6 million Pashtu speakers. To this must be added some 2.5 million Pashtun refugees in Pakistan. These figures suggest a total Pashtun population in both countries of 41 million.

There are two to three dozen Pashtun tribes, depending on how one classifies them, generally divided into four major groupings: the Durranis and Ghilzais, concentrated in Afghanistan; the so-called independent tribes, straddling the Durand Line, and several tribes, such as the Khattaks and Bannuchis, centered in the NWFP of Pakistan. As Richard Tapper wrote, 'In spite of the endemic conflict among different Pashtun groups, the notion of the ethnic and cultural unity of all Pashtuns has long been familiar to them as a symbolic complex of great potential for political unity.' Of all the tribal groups in Iran or Afghanistan, the Pashtuns have had, perhaps, the most pervasive and explicit segmentary lineage ideology on the classic pattern expressed not only in written genealogies but in territorial distribution.[27]

However, in contrast to Baluch society, with its hierarchical structures and its all-powerful Sardars, Pashtun culture has an egalitarian mystique epitomized by the role of the Jirga (assembly). Moreover, as Akbar Ahmed has observed, although the tribal *malik* (village headman) is the most powerful single figure in tribal affairs per se, the *malik* shares local power with the *mullah* in a complex, symbiotic relationship.

The Afghan state that Ahmad Shah Durrani forged in 1747 was frankly Pashtun in character. It was a Pashtun tribal confederacy, established for the purpose of uniting the Pashtuns and shielding their interests and integrity against non-Pashtun rivals. To be sure, even at its inception, the new state was not entirely homogenous ethnically, but Afghanistan had an overwhelming Pashtun majority in the early nineteenth century. By contrast, the loss of the trans-Durand territories in 1823 and the consequent division of the Pashtuns left a truncated Afghanistan with a more tenuous ethnic balance. As the 'great game' between Britain and Russia developed during the nineteenth century, the British egged on successive Afghan rulers, who gradually pushed the border of Afghanistan northwards to the Oxus river. The British goal was to make Afghanistan a buffer state, and the Pashtun rulers in Kabul had imperialist ambitions of their own. Extensive areas populated by Hazaras, Tajiks, Uzbeks, and other non-Pashtun ethnic groups were annexed by Kabul after long and costly struggles that left a legacy of built-in ethnic conflict.

Non-Pashtuns constituted at least 35 per cent — possibly as much as 45 per cent — of the population of Afghanistan during the decades preceding the Soviet occupation, and their relative strength has grown in the wake of the large-scale Pashtun refugee movement to Pakistan. As the ethnic balance has changed, the Pashtuns in Afghanistan have intermittently attempted to forge some form of political unity with the Pashtuns in Pakistan that would make possible a restoration of unchallenged Pashtun dominance in Kabul. By the same token, given the responsibility of the British for the division of the Pashtuns, it is not surprising that anti-British sentiment during the 1920s and the 1930s sparked the emergence of a Pashtun nationalist movement on what was to become the

Pakistan side of the Durand Line — Ghaffar Khan's 'Red Shirts' — which called explicitly on the eve of partition for an independent Pashtunistan. In Ghaffar Khan's Bannu Declaration of 22 June 1947, he demanded that the Pashtuns be given a choice between joining Pakistan or establishing an independent Pashtunistan, rather than a choice limited to Pakistan or India.

The Red Shirts boycotted the referendum that was used by the departing British as their legal rationale for handing over the NWFP and the adjacent tribal areas to the new Pakistani state. As a consequence, when it fit their purposes, Ghaffar Khan and Wali Khan were able to cast doubt on the legitimacy of the incorporation of these Pashtun-majority areas into Pakistan. For their part, Pakistani leaders, questioning protestations of loyalty to Pakistan by Ghaffar Khan and Wali Khan, have frequently cited the Bannu Declaration.

Even though the National Awami Party has reformulated the Pashtunistan demand since 1947 as a demand for provincial autonomy within Pakistan, Islamabad has continued to doubt its allegiance to Pakistan. This distrust is rooted not only in suspicions of collusion with Afghanistan but also in the fact that Ghaffar Khan was openly opposed to the very idea of Pakistan and was actively identified with the Indian National Congress in its struggle against the British. Driven by its fear of Pashtun demands for provincial autonomy or, worse still, for Pashtunistan, the Punjabi-dominated regime in Islamabad has been seeking to resettle as many Afghan refugees and other Pashtuns as possible in Baluchistan, hoping to vitiate the strength of Baluch and Pashtun separatism at one stroke.

▧ The Taliban and Pashtun Nationalism

With Pashtuns outnumbering Baluch in parts of northern Baluchistan, a US Institute of Peace study noted, Pashtun nationalists now propose restructuring the Pakistani state to unite all Pashtun regions in FATA, the NWFP. and northern Baluchistan in a new province of Pakhtoonkhwa that would seek greater autonomy than Pakistani provinces now have.[28]

The inclusion of FATA in the Pashtun nationalist vision is a significant development that conflicts directly with the US-backed Pakistani development plans designed to bring the vast, hitherto-autonomous tribal tract under the control of the central government. Until recently, there was little popular political consciousness in

FATA, but the use of the areas as a sanctuary and staging area by the Al-Qaeda and Taliban forces since 9/11, leading to Pakistani military incursions in response to US pressure, has led to unprecedented inter-tribal contacts and to a polarization of increasingly well-organized Pashtun nationalist and Islamist forces.

In July 2002, the Pakistan army sent a division of troops into FATA, focusing on areas believed to be transit points in and out of Afghanistan for Al-Qaeda and Taliban forces. Pressed by Washington for action, Pakistani forces, using helicopter gunships and heavy artillery, launched operations in October 2003, and the first three months of 2004 that displaced some 50,000 people, according to the Human Rights Commission of Pakistan, inflicting heavy civilian casualties. 'The use of indiscriminate, excessive force undermined the military's local standing and alienated the locals', reported the International Crisis Group. A Pashtun former Federal Law Minister reported 'seething anger' throughout FATA.[29] Musharraf concluded that further military pressure would make FATA ungovernable and authorized peace agreements with tribal leaders in Waziristan, bitterly criticized by the US, in which Pakistani forces suspended military operations in return for efforts by tribal leaders to prevent the use of FATA by the Taliban as a staging area for Afghanistan. But the damage was already done, and the FATA populace is now politicized and radicalized more than ever.

The architect of the peace deal was a retired Pashtun Army Lieutenant General, Jan Orakzai, Governor of the NWFP. In October 2006, Gen. Orakzai was quietly negotiating a similar deal in the Bajaur area of FATA, but many Pakistanis suspect that the US intelligence got the wind of it. Precisely what happened next has not been clearly established, but on 30 October 2006, 83 students at a madrasa in the Bajaur village of Chenagai were killed in a missile attack. *The News* of Karachi reported eyewitnesses as saying that the missiles were fired from a pilotless US Predator drone aircraft that had circled overhead for hours.[30] However, the Pakistan Army claimed credit for the attack, and the US and Pakistani spokesmen said that the seminary was an Al-Qaeda training facility. Whatever the truth, the raid led to massive protests, especially in FATA, and retaliatory suicide bombings in the Malakand tribal district.

The radicalization of the Pashtun areas straddling the Pakistan–Afghanistan border has intensified both Islamist zealotry and Pashtun nationalism. In conventional wisdom, one or the other, that is either

Islamist or Pashtun identity, will eventually triumph, but an equally plausible possibility is that the result could be what Hussain Haqqani has called an 'Islamic Pashtunistan'.[31] At a Washington seminar on 1 March 2007, at the Pakistan embassy, the Pakistani Ambassador, Major General (Retd.) Mahmud Ali Durrani, a Pashtun, commented that 'I hope the Taliban and Pashtun nationalism don't merge. If that happens, we've had it, and we're on the verge of that.'

▨ The Impact of 9/11

The destabilizing impact of post-9/11 US policy on Pakistan's domestic politics, spelled out here, has been largely obscured by the focus of the international media on the Pakistani posture towards the Al-Qaeda and the Taliban. By contrast, the deterioration in Pakistan's relations with its immediate neighbours, Afghanistan, India and Iran, is better known and requires less elaboration.

The tensions between Musharraf and the US-backed Hamid Karzai regime in Kabul were dramatically displayed in public during the joint meeting of the two leaders arranged by President Bush at the White House on 27 September 2006. Karzai has repeatedly accused Pakistan of complicity with the Taliban. During one of their meetings, he handed Musharraf a list of Taliban bases and safe houses in Pakistan, complete with addresses and telephone numbers. Musharraf, in turn, flatly denying the accusations, has consistently alleged that Karzai's own failure of leadership explains the continuing growth of Taliban strength.

Given its long-standing desire for a client regime in Kabul to offset the perceived threat of India to the East, Pakistan might well have had uneasy relations with Afghanistan even if there had been no 9/11 and the Taliban had remained in power with Al-Qaeda financial support. Afghanistan's refusal to recognize the Durand Line, noted earlier, was only one of the indications that it did not intend to be a subservient client. 'After the Taliban came to power', Musharraf said in his memoirs, 'we lost much of the leverage we had had with them.'[32] Still, the advent of a US-backed Kabul regime with close links to the anti-Pakistan Tajik ethnic minority in Afghanistan, clearly strengthened Pakistan's dependence on the Taliban as its sole vehicle for influencing future internal power struggles in Afghanistan. The overall impact of 9/11 on Pakistan–Afghanistan relations has been to intensify built-in tensions. The strong support given by India to

Karzai, accompanied by the reopening of Indian consulates in Jalalabad and Kandahar, close to the Pakistan border, has added to these tensions.

India had offered unlimited support to the US in countering terrorism after 9/11, including military bases, but the Bush Administration gave only perfunctory recognition to these offers. The US response to 9/11 nominally condemned all terrorist acts but focused in operational policy terms on terrorism against the United States and its allies. Thus, the Bush Administration addressed its response to 9/11 in South Asia narrowly to Pakistan, making no effort to condition economic and military aid to Musharraf on verifiable Pakistani measures to rein in anti-Indian terrorist activity, especially in Indian-held areas of Kashmir.

Less than a month after 9/11, the Lashkar-e-Taiba staged an attack on the Kashmir Assembly, killing 36. This was followed on 13 December 2001, by an attack on the Indian Parliament, blamed by New Delhi on Islamic extremists linked to both Lashkar-e-Taiba and Jaish-e-Muhammad. The attack on Parliament prompted India to launch 'Operation Parakaram (Valour)', the biggest Indian troop mobilization since the 1971 Bangladesh war, which led Pakistan to counter with its own build-up. With nearly 1 million troops facing each other, the United States pushed Musharraf to take action against Lashkar-e-Taiba and Jaish-e-Muhammad. But his ban on the two groups and a tough speech on 12 January 2002 proved to be 'insufficient' to stop anti-Indian jihadi activities, as Zahid Hussain has observed. 'The ban was not applied to Pakistan-controlled Kashmir', he has noted, 'or to the semi-autonomous tribal areas bordering Afghanistan, which enabled militant organizations to shift their infrastructure and cadres to these regions.'[33] On 14 May 2002, Islamic militants staged a string of suicide attacks on a bus in the residential quarters of an Indian Army camp in Kashmir. Despite continuing tensions however, India and Pakistan pulled their forces back from the border, partly in response to international pressure and partly because the spectre of a full-scale war had deterred the foreign business investment that both countries now actively seek.

In Indian eyes, the most important aspect of the US policy in South Asia since 9/11 has been an influx of large-scale military aid to Pakistan that has affected the India–Pakistan military balance. India understandably asks what value nuclear-capable F-16s will have for the Pakistan Air Force for countering the Al-Qaeda and the Taliban. Like past US military aid received by Islamabad during the Cold War and in the campaign to oust Soviet forces from Afghanistan, the military aid received by Islamabad for its cooperation since 9/11 has been frankly intended to strengthen its military position against India. This is the reason that 9/11 and its aftermath have 'changed the entire regional security scenario and triggered a rapid downslide in India–Pakistan relations'.[34]

Although Pakistan, with its large Shia population, has attempted to keep relations with Iran on an even keel, tensions have boiled beneath the surface. Teheran has repeatedly charged that Musharraf permits US Special Forces units and CIA agents to use Pakistani Baluchistan, which borders Iranian Baluchistan, as a staging area for covert actions designed to spy on the Iranian nuclear programme and to smuggle military aid to rebellious Baluch, Azeri, Khuzestani Arab and Kurdish ethnic minorities seeking to destabilize the Ahmadinejad regime in Teheran. These allegations are denied by Islamabad, but reports by Seymour Hersh[35] and my own contacts with Baluch sources make these allegations credible.

On the surface, it might seem that close Pakistani relations with the United States will offset the damage to Pakistan's security resulting from its estranged relations with its neighbours, and that continued US support will assure the economic and political survival of Pakistan for the indefinite future. However, as domestic opposition to military rule grows; as ethnic conflicts intensify; as 9/11 recedes in memory; as US staying power in Afghanistan ebbs, and as political alignments change in Washington and Islamabad alike, the nature of US relations with Pakistan could well undergo dramatic changes and the very existence of the Pakistani state in its present form could become increasingly uncertain.

▨ Notes

1. John Mueller, 'Is There Still a Terrorist Threat? : The Myth of the Omnipresent Enemy', *Foreign Affairs* (September/October 2006), 85(5), pp. 2–8. See also Anataol Lieven, 'A State of Terror', review of *Overblown: How Politicians and the Terrorism Industry Inflate National Security Threats, and Why We Believe Them* by John Mueller, *New York Times Book Review*, 18 February 2007, p. 23.
2. Max Rodenbeck, 'How Terrible Is It?', *New York Review of Books*, 19–30 November 2006, p. 33.

3. George Soros, 'A Self-Defeating War', *The Wall Street Journal*, 17 November 2006. See also George Soros, *The Age of Fallibility: Consequences of the War on Terror* (New York: Public Affairs, 2006).

4. John Semmens, 'Britain to Drop "War on Terror" Terminology', *The Arizona Conservative*, 11 December 2007.

5. Quentin Peel, 'Malaysian PM urges battle against 'roots of terror', not symptoms', *Financial Times*, 29 January 2007.

6. Zbigniew Brzezinski, 'Terrorized by "War on Terror"', *The Washington Post*, 25 March 2007, p. B1

7. K. Alan Kronstadt, Specialist on Asian Affairs, Congressional Research Service, e-mail to author, 29 January 2007. See also Nathaniel Meller 'Pakistan's $4.2 Billion "Blank Check" for US Military Aid', report, Center for Public Integrity, 27 March 2007.

8. Craig Cohen and Derek Chollet, 'When $10 Billion Is Not Enough: Rethinking US Strategy Toward Pakistan', *The Washington Quarterly* (Spring 2007), pp. 11–14.

9. Pervez Musharraf, *In the Line of Fire*: A *Memoir* (London: Simon & Schuster, 2006 and New York: Free Press, 2006), p. 201.

10. Ibid., p. 205.

11. Ibid., p. 206.

12. Tommy Franks, *American Soldier* (New York: Harper Collins, 2004), p. 256, cited in Hussain Haqqani, *Pakistan between Moscow and Military* (Washington, DC: Carnegie Endowment for International Peace, 2005), p. 302.

13. Address at the School of Advanced International Studies, Johns Hopkins University, Washington, DC, 25 January 2007.

14. Musharraf, *In the Line of Fire*, p. 202.

15. Selig S. Harrison, 'Bush Needs to Attach Strings to US Aid', *USA Today*, 24 June 2003, p. 8.

16. Musharraf, *In the Line of Fire*, p. 203.

17. Carlotta Gall, 'At Border, Signs of Pakistani Role in Taliban Surge', *New York Times*, 21 January 2007, p. 1.

18. Zahid Hussain, *Frontline Pakistan: The Struggle with Militant Islam* (New York: Columbia University Press, 2007), p. 21.

19. Ibid., p. 87.

20. Marc W. Herold, Professor of Economics Development, University of New Hampshire, in 'A Dossier of Civilian Victims of United States Bombing in Afghanistan: A Comprehensive Accounting', December 2001, cites 3,742. Subsequently, in 'The Daily Casualty Count of Afghan Civilians Killed by US Bombing' Herold has updated his count, which had reached 4,643 on 1 October 2006.

21. Hussain, *Frontline Pakistan*, pp. 68–70.

22. Ibid., p. 83.

23. *Pakistan: Karachi's Madrasas and Violent Extremism*, Asia Report No. 130, International Crisis Group, Islamabad/Brussels, 29 March 2007, pp. 5–8.
24. Ibid. See also Appendix B, pp. i, 24.
25. Population Census Organization, Statistical Division, Ministry of Economic Affairs and Statistics, Government of Pakistan, *Demographic Indicators in 1998*. For 1961 data, covering the areas then constituting West Pakistan, see *Census of Pakistan: Population 1961* (Karachi: Ministry of Home and Kashmir Affairs, 1961), Statement 7-B, p. IV–46. See also, *Main Finding of 1981 Population Census* (Islamabad: Population Census Organization, Statistics Division, Government of Pakistan, 6 December 1983), p. 13, Table 4(c).
26. Affidavit of the Supreme Court of Pakistan, 1975, p. 133.
27. Richard Tapper, 'Tribal Society and its Enemies', *Royal Anthropological Institute News*, London, October 1979, p. 6.
28. Barnett R. Rubin and Abubakar Siddique, 'Resolving the Pakistan–Afghanistan Stalemate', Special Report 176, United States Institute of Peace, Washington, October 2006, p. 14.
29. *Pakistan's Tribal Areas: Appeasing the Militants*, International Crisis Group Asia Report No. 125, Islamabad/Brussels, 11 December 2006, Section A(2), p. 12.
30. Cited in B. Raman, 'The Bajaur Air Strike',South Asia Analysis Group, Paper No. 2008, Chennai, 10 November 2006, p. 1. (The news article was filed from Nawagai in the Bajaur Agency, signed by Rahimullah Yusufzai.)
31. Conversation with the author, Washington, 16 October 2006.
32. Musharraf, *In the Line of Fire*, p. 203.
33. Hussain, *Frontline Pakistan*, p. 108.
34. Ibid., p. 106.
35. Seymour M. Hersh, in 'Annals of National Security: The Iran Plans', *The New Yorker*, 17 April 2006, p. 33, quotes a Pentagon consultant involved as saying that since late 2005, Special Forces units had been 'studying the terrain, giving away walking around money to ethnic tribes, and recruiting scouts for local tribes and shepherds. The goal, said the consultant, is to "encourage ethnic tensions" and undermine the Teheran regime.'

✳

3

Nuclear Issue: Current Developments and Future Challenges for Pakistan

Pervaiz Iqbal Cheema

Since the nuclear testing by India and Pakistan in May 1998, many countries have expressed the need for introducing an effective restraint regime in South Asia. The continuing conflict over Kashmir was seen as a potential flashpoint that could cause a nuclear exchange between the two countries. Unable to convince India and Pakistan to sign the Nuclear Non-Proliferation Treaty (NPT), many Western countries began to describe South Asia as an unstable region, which could witness the first nuclear war between the two countries. This may have been an important strategy to pressurize the two countries into signing the treaty, or, possibly, to warn them of the impending doomsday. While it is difficult to deny the risks involved in acquiring and maintaining nuclear weapons, to insinuate that both India and Pakistan were irresponsible nations was more than a little unreasonable.

In such a scenario, serious efforts need to be made to make a comprehensive assessment of the situation and find ways to minimize the risks involved. Both India and Pakistan have already taken steps in that direction: they have not only introduced many confidence-building measures (CBMs) to improve the atmosphere between them but have also been seriously engaged in finding ways and means to reduce the risks associated, initially with the acquisition, and later, with the maintenance of nuclear weapons. The recently concluded nuclear risk reduction agreement clearly reflects the desire of the two countries to put safeguards on their nuclear assets and make the region safer.

This article discusses the strategies and policies adopted by Pakistan prior to and after the acquisition of nuclear weapons in order to address its security concerns in an uncertain South Asian environment; it also focuses on the new nuclear environment and Pakistan's future strategies in dealing with security issues, including its role in strengthening international security measures.

◙ Pakistan's Policy Prior to the Acquisition of N-Weapons

India tested its first nuclear device in 1974. From then onwards, until the second set of nuclear tests by both India and Pakistan in 1998, the two countries maintained a deceptive nuclear posture, by practising what was often referred to as a deliberately contrived strategy of ambiguity. Neither of them was prepared to give up the nuclear option; to justify this policy, both countries advanced various support arguments. One common argument that was repeatedly put forward was that of security requirements.

Here, we need to look at the scenario in a broader context. No country admits that it wants another nation to be insecure, yet it always favours the creation of an equilibrium, or rather disequilibrium, tilted in its favour in order to acquire the maximum security. Most countries adopt this policy out of national interest.

Various programmes, often contradictory in nature, ranging from absolute deterrence to total disarmament, from complete isolation to world leadership, from non-alignment to military alliances, from economic self-sufficiency to free trade are rationalized in order to acquire greater security than other nations. Security — essentially a negative term — implies the absence of real or perceived threats, to certain coveted values, stemming from external or internal sources or inherent economic weaknesses, disparities and inequalities. To cope with such threats, nations tend to seek power, hoping that power would generate the desired level of security. Insecurity often compels nations to strive for greater power in order to tilt the scales in their favour. Such a process can not only trigger a regional arms race, it invariably also invites extra-regional actors into the conflict. While the outsiders enter the region in pursuit of their own strategic interests, they often find themselves drawn into the regional conflicts and, at times, forced to play the role of the equalizer.

Coming back to our main discussion, the strategy of designed ambiguity in nuclear policies played out by India and Pakistan prior to 1998 was either adopted deliberately or arrived at due to compulsions generated by the then operative circumstantial forces. India adopted the posture after the Chinese nuclear tests of 1964 and Pakistan opted for such a strategy in the mid-1980s.[1] Both India and Pakistan played this game of hide and seek with considerable mastery, which implied repressing or revealing, as the case may be, sensitive information, in tandem with a well-planned design. For example, despite the existence of a regular communication channel of the Directorate General of Military Operations (DGMO), the supply of information to the adversary was often faulty and distorted, giving the impression that honouring the spirit of an agreement was not as sacrosanct in South Asia as it was in other parts of the world.[2]

The greatest advantages of this strategy for both India and Pakistan were being able to hold on to the nuclear option while keeping the adversary in a state of doubt. The strategy also proved to be useful in buying time and pacifying both the hawks and the doves simultaneously within the two countries. While there is difference of opinion on what influenced the two countries to finally abandon the strategy of ambiguity and decide on nuclear testing in 1998, there is no doubt that it enabled them to acquire the necessary lead time to master the techniques.

With the passage of time, the American resolve on strengthening the NPT restraint regime had been considerably weakened. This enabled the two countries to continue perfecting their systems, especially the missiles, and improve their nuclear arsenal. To maintain the effectiveness of the strategy of ambiguity, it was necessary to keep the warheads away from the missile sites or silos: if the silos or missile sites were maintained considerably away from the adversary's border, it would lengthen the flight time. This charade was aimed at making the opponent uncertain about the operational aspects of the nuclear weapons. Moreover, it might create doubts in the minds of observers as to whether or not a clear operational policy even existed. By keeping the adversary guessing, any kind of conclusive assessment would be made difficult to achieve.

Another important aspect of this approach was to repeatedly stress the defensive aspect of the nuclear weapons. The then Indian Prime Minister A.B. Vajpayee, for example, remarked in the Lok Sabha on 15 March 1999 that the nuclear weapons were not offensive but defensive weapons that helped to preserve peace.[3]

The Nuclear Explosions of May 1998

For years, both India and Pakistan maintained their strategies of ambiguity, while continuing to gather scientific momentum for their nuclear expertise. Each incremental improvization took them closer to the status of a nuclear weapon state. What made the two countries finally give the green light to their respective scientists? Many arguments have been advanced in this respect. Among the factors that influenced India was its quest for Great Power status, the operative security environment, the bloody engagement in Kashmir, the existing world order, and the Bharatiya Janata Party's (BJP) commitment to acquiring nuclear weapons. Similarly, the factors that motivated Pakistan to go nuclear included security considerations for its survival, ineffective sanctions imposed on India, mounting domestic pressures and threatening statements issued by some BJP leaders.

The international community responded swiftly by condemning the tests. Most European countries, along with Japan and the United States criticized the tests as being a major setback for peace and arms control. What is interesting, however, is that while most countries followed the lead of the five permanent members of the Security Council in condemning the nuclear tests, only a few states followed the American and Japanese examples in imposing sanctions. The European Community collectively expressed its dismay over the tests and the German foreign minister forcefully stated that it was ridiculous that countries like India and Pakistan, which were unable to feed their own people, were indulging in the luxury of testing nuclear devices. The European Union (EU) passed a resolution in Strasbourg calling its members to prevent the export of nuclear materials and technology to India and Pakistan.[4]

Although many interpretations of the nuclear tests were advanced in the West, almost all of them viewed it as an adverse development. Nuclearization of Pakistan and India was generally seen as a great blow to the operative international trends, and a failure of the US policies of nuclear restraint, which could ultimately lead to regional instability, a likely regional arms race, and increased regional tension.

Following the May 1998 explosions, many significant developments took place — among them were the imposition of economic sanctions on both India and Pakistan, moratorium on further testing, internationalization of the Kashmir dispute, resumption of India–Pakistan dialogue, the Lahore Declaration, the Kargil clashes, the troops confrontation of 2001–02, successful 12th SAARC Summit and initiation of the current peace process.

▨ Pakistan's Policy after the Acquisition of N-Weapons

Overall, the Western assessments were probably too alarmist. As a case in point, the International Institute for Strategic Studies (IISS) thought that the nuclear arms race between India and Pakistan could lead to devastating political and economic consequences. IISS further argued that the 1998 nuclear tests had sent shivers through the international community and had upset the stability of an already unsettled region.[5] Realistically speaking, however, nothing could have been farther from the truth. Such statements merely reflected the inability to influence the South Asians to walk on the path chalked out by their former Western masters. Both India and Pakistan had now moved away from the strategy of ambiguity to a strategy of deterrence, though both stressed the need for minimum deterrence. Both Islamabad and New Delhi now recognized that they could inflict unacceptable damage on the adversary, which served, in many ways, to strengthen the mutual minimum deterrent relationship.

As a result, the inherent dangers of the strategy of ambiguity were effectively removed. Both countries came to recognize that neither of them was in possession of what was often termed as an impregnable air defence system. Indeed the advent of nuclear weapons had, in many ways, taken a toll on their conventional superiority (although India is equipped with formidable conventional military capabilities). Compared to India, Pakistan's nuclear weapons capability is small but in nuclear deterrence relationships, numbers don't really play a significant role. As a matter of fact, the mutual deterrence strategy had been operative between the two countries even prior to the acquisition of nuclear weapons, with some people calling it non-weaponized deterrence and others looking at it as deterrence based on anticipated capabilities. Dangerously loaded situations of 1986–87 (Brasstacks), the crisis of 1990 (Kashmir Crisis), the Kargil clashes, and the 2002 confrontation of troops, did not lead to an outbreak of a fully-fledged war primarily because of the existence of nuclear capabilities. If deterrence worked with the strategy of ambiguity, it is only logical to assume that operative deterrence would be further stabilized with overt nuclear weaponization.

Compared to Indian nuclear policy pursuits, which announced its draft nuclear doctrine, only to be modified later, Pakistan did not formally announce its nuclear doctrine but pursued a policy of minimum nuclear deterrence. Not only are Pakistan's security policies largely determined by Indian threats, but Pakistan is highly sceptical of Indian assertions of 'No First Use'. Living under the shadow of an Indian threat, Pakistan's strategic policy is directly linked with the Indian nuclear policy. Past experience has taught the Pakistanis that the employment of 'No First Use' merely implies that the involved state is working towards the acquisition of a second strike capability, just like the Soviets and the Chinese in the past.

While Pakistan has not yet clearly stated its nuclear doctrine specifically by outlining the eventuality in which the deployment of nuclear weapons would become imperative, an Italian writer quoting an interview with the Director General of Strategic Plans Division (DGSPD) described certain contingencies in which the use of nuclear weapons could be seriously considered. Among these eventualities were included Indian conquest of large parts of Pakistani territory, large-scale destruction of Pakistan's land and air forces, pursuit of policies leading to Pakistan's effective economic strangulation, successful push for Pakistan's political destabilization and creation of large-scale internal subversions.[6] It needs to be mentioned here that the DGSPD later denied these eventualities.[7]

Pakistan has consistently apprehended a looming threat from India; as a result, the main determinant for its defence policy and foreign policy has always been Indian policy pursuits. 'Its fundamental objective is deterring rather than fighting a war with India. Other objectives of Pakistani nuclear doctrine in dealing with the perceived threat from India are to maintain an overall strategic equilibrium, to neutralize conventional military asymmetries against India and to maintain its territorial integrity and political sovereignty'.[8]

Pakistani decision-makers are quite wary of India's continuous enlargement of its conventional capabilities. Pakistan has repeatedly stated that it is not and does not intend to be involved in any kind of an arms race with India. However, that does not imply that it would in any way lower its guards; it indicates that it would defend its interests as best as it can with its own means. For obvious reasons, Pakistan is vigilant about its increasing gap with India in conventional weapons. Being aware of the significant role played by the threat of nuclear confrontation in some of the past crises such as Brasstacks, the Kargil episode and the India-Pak border mobilization of troops, Pakistan is likely to further improve its delivery capabilities. This explains its focus on perfecting its missile systems.

In this scenario, it is imperative that the Western powers make concerted efforts to resolve the underlying causes of insecurity and conflict between the two countries in order to make the region stable, safe and peaceful. They should avoid all measures that can lead to increased asymmetry. Without the resolution of the ongoing Kashmir dispute, the quest for narrowing the gap is going to remain a major preoccupation of the weaker party to redress its insecurity.

Security concerns are country-specific and dynamic in nature. Whenever a change in the military balance occurs or moderate leaders emerge, the security environment is altered. Pakistan's threat perceptions are based on its geographical characteristics, an unsettled and lingering dispute over Kashmir, the capabilities and intentions of a hostile neighbour, and its inability to maintain an acceptable conventional military balance with India due to resource constraints. The subcontinent of South Asia has witnessed continuous turmoil, conflicts, and wars in the last 60 years. India and Pakistan have had one of the longest adversarial relationships that this period has ever known. It is not surprising then that when India shocked the world by carrying out three underground atomic tests on 11 May 1998 and two more tests on 13 May 1998 — 24 years after its first explosion at Pokhran — 150 kilometres from the Pakistan border, Pakistan retaliated soon after by carrying out five nuclear tests on 28 May 1998, followed by one more on 30 May 1998.

▨ The New Nuclear Environment: Developments and Challenges

With the end of the Cold War and the tragic events of 9/11, the global environment underwent a radical transformation. Not only did a new world order emerge, but its impact on various regions also posed fresh challenges and opportunities. The post-Cold War New World Order is, however, still in the process of evolution and its shape has yet to concretize. The New World Order followed by the 9/11 tragedy is marked by uncertainty, confusion and contradictory tendencies. Both integrative and disintegrative forces are at work in the world. The end of dominance of ideologies has given way to the rise of sub-nationalism based on primordial loyalties like ethnicity, religion, race and language, making the world much less safe as compared to the past and posing new threats to the International Political System.

The tragic events of 9/11 further impacted upon the world system. These events not only focused the spotlight on terrorism and the consequent formation of international coalitions against terrorism, but also caused a US-led war against Afghanistan initially and later another war against Iraq. An aim to stamp out the Al-Qaeda led to the invasion of Afghanistan, and the removal of Saddam Hussein on allegations of making Weapons of Mass Destruction (WMD) provided the excuse for the invasion of Iraq. The situation has not stabilized in either of these countries; in fact a sizable number of forces are engaged even now in both countries.

Since 9/11, the debate over exact definitions of terrorism and its different categories, the somewhat neglected differentiation between terrorism and freedom struggles, and a mechanism on how to counter the problem of terrorism is raging among almost all countries. Although the debate has remained inconclusive in many ways, Western countries that were keen on initiating some form of action to counter what they perceive as terrorist activities, have not waited for any consensus to develop. Instead, they have undertaken selective punitive actions against the target countries. While the debate rages, developments of far-reaching consequences have influenced many countries, including Pakistan.

▨ Changing Environment and Pakistan's Policy

As mentioned earlier, the most important development that changed the strategic environment in South Asia was the nuclearization of both India and Pakistan in May 1998. Since then, other significant developments have also taken place. In Southwest Asia, Iran, a close neighbour of Pakistan, is trying to develop its nuclear programme, ostensibly peaceful at this stage. President Mahmoud Ahmadinejad dismissed on 23 December the United Nations Security Council (UNSC) 2006 sanctions on his country as a mere 'scrap of paper'.[9] He added that 'whether the West likes it or not Iran is a nuclear country and it is in their (West) interest to live alongside Iran.'[10]

It is anticipated by most Western sources, that in a few years, Iran could also emerge as a new entrant to the nuclear club (besides Israel, which is known to have already acquired nuclear weapons capability). Indeed, Iran's acquisition of nuclear weapon capability could complicate the prevailing security environment in the region and pose new challenges. While Iran's acquisition of nuclear arsenals could be an indigenous decision, the push factor comes from the US policies, and especially the December 2006 Indo-US civil nuclear deal. The deal has provided incentives, removed inhibitions and dealt a strong blow to the non-proliferation regime, whose major exponent had been the United States.

In the Far East, North Korea has claimed to have acquired a nuclear device. It is often alleged that the Americans mishandled the North Korean situation. In October 1994, the United States and North Korea worked out an Agreed Framework under which North Korea agreed to dismantle its reactors, remain in NPT and observe full IAEA (International Atomic Energy Agency) safeguards. This was in return for US economic oil supplies and construction of two light water reactors, as well as a move towards normalization of economic and political relations. By the year 2002, the Agreed Framework broke down not only because North Korea was suspected of cheating but also because the United States did not fulfil its part of the bargain by delaying construction of the light water reactors and utterly failing to start the process of normalization between the two countries.[11]

▣ Pakistan and the Indo-US Civil Nuclear Deal

The Manmohan Singh–George Bush Joint Statement of 18 July 2005 on Indo-US nuclear cooperation resulted in signing of the Agreement in March 2006, and followed by legislation later that year under which the United States would supply nuclear fuel to India. Not surprisingly, the new US Act has ignited considerable debate within the Indian and the Pakistani strategic community.[12]

The India–US nuclear agreement was signed in March 2006 in New Delhi, following President Bush's visit to India. After hard lobbying and debate, the bill[13] was overwhelmingly passed by the US Congress and became a law in December 2006. It has been described as an historic and 'unique agreement with a unique country'. It stood to reverse the US policy towards India that had lasted till July 2005, when the latter had opposed nuclear cooperation with that country for developing nuclear weapons in contravention of the Nonproliferation treaty.

Under the US–India nuclear deal, India was to be given access to civilian nuclear technology in return for placing its 14 civilian atomic reactors under global safeguards. The United States rationalized the passage of the Act by terming it as a 'stand-alone' agreement. An important State Department official, who played a key role in negotiations observed that, 'unlike some of their neighbours, the Indians, have been very responsible' and 'have protected their nuclear technology.'[14] Moreover, it was put forward that the deal was a US 'exemption' and an exception to the laws, due to India's special energy needs, as it is a major contributor to global warming and air pollution, and dependent on the Middle East oil.[15] Former US President Jimmy Carter referred to India being treated as a special case as a dangerous deal.[16]

It would not be out of order to mention here that Pakistan also faced a similar energy dilemma but the United States was unwilling to consider helping Pakistan on the same lines as India. Compared to Pakistan, Washington considers India a responsible nuclear power as the latter has not indulged in nuclear commerce. Despite the fact that it has been internationally recognized that the state of Pakistan was not involved in or even in the know of A.Q. Khan's activities with regard to nuclear commerce, the United States was not at all sympathetic to Pakistani request.[17] Though A.Q. Khan did not break any of Pakistan's international legal obligations, the government of Pakistan awarded a harsh penalty to him and also passed a legislation making nuclear commerce a punishable offence.[18] However, when the West put strong pressure on Pakistan to gain direct access to A.Q. Khan for interrogation, the demand was rejected outright by the Pakistani government.

▣ Impact on Pakistan

While the proposed Indo-US nuclear deal still does not recognize India as a nuclear weapon state, it will enable 14 of its 22 nuclear facilities to come under international inspections. The US and other nuclear supplier nations will provide fuel and technology to build the Indian civil nuclear programme. It is believed in some quarters that this reward compensates India for a possible strategic role against international terrorism and acts as a counterweight to China.

However, it is increasingly being felt that the deal would upset the strategic balance in South Asia and make India more obdurate in the resolution of disputes with its neighbours. Already, India is seen to be dragging its feet on the India–Pakistan peace process, and has been non-responsive to many peace proposals put up by President Musharraf for resolution of the Kashmir dispute.

The deal could also motivate India to enter into similar nuclear commerce arrangements and conventional arms deals with other countries, thus drastically tilting the military balance in its favour. This could spur a new arms race, leading to instability and tension in South Asia. There is also a feeling in Pakistan that through this deal, India aspires to acquire a global power status. This seems like a stepping-stone for its eventual recognition as a fully-fledged nuclear power. The development can also be seen as strengthening India's case for a permanent membership in the UNSC. In addition, the deal could also help India develop economically at a much faster pace.

It bears reiteration that had India not gone for nuclear detonation in 1998, Pakistan would not have carried out its nuclear test and the subcontinent might have been spared the nuclearization: many critics of the Indo-US deal therefore see it as 'rewarding' proliferators.

Not only is the Act discriminatory, but it would also enable India to divert its indigenous produced fissile material to its military programme, while obtaining fuel for its civilian reactors from the Nuclear Suppliers Group (NSG). India wants to invest $100 billion for expanding its nuclear energy programme over the next 10 years, in which the US companies shall be getting major contracts. There is, however, growing anxiety in Pakistan that any diversion of military fissile material towards production of greater nuclear weapons would create a nuclear imbalance in the region and might lead to military adventures by a 'big neighbour'.

India's self-imposed moratorium on nuclear testing can be violated at any time on pleas of national security; moreover, since it has not defined any upper limits for its deterrence capability, it could easily engage in vertical proliferation by liberating its existing unsafeguarded fissile material. As Indian Prime Minister Manmohan Singh categorically stated in the Upper House of Indian Parliament, India was not bound on nuclear testing by a foreign legislature.[19] It is argued by some that in case the proposed FMCT (Fissile Material Cut-off Treaty) treaty is finalized, and India becomes a party to it, it would not be able to produce missile material in future. However, it is important to remember that the existing un-safeguarded fissile material would continue to cause deep concern to Pakistan.[20] Besides, India's commitment to the IAEA safeguards and Additional Protocol is 'voluntary', so, it can withdraw any time, if it feels that its national interests are threatened. Furthermore, if India is accommodated as an exception by the NSG, it would contravene its own guidelines which would not only reduce its effectiveness but would set precedents for future exceptions by other nations.[21]

▩ Iran's Nuclearization and Its Impact on Pakistan

Iran has categorically stated that, notwithstanding US sanctions, it would continue to build its nuclear enrichment facilities for peaceful purposes, and would be installing 3,000 centrifuges at Nantanz nuclear plant immediately at 'full speed'. President Ahmadinejad had stated that 'Iran is a *nuclear* country' whether the West likes it or not, and the nation would celebrate its 'nuclearization' by March 2007.[22] Meanwhile, the Iranian Majlis passed a bill demanding a 'review' for cooperation with IAEA, and, if possible, curtailment of access and inspections to its nuclear facilities.

Some Pakistanis feel that Iran becoming a nuclear weapon state should not create any major problems for Pakistan. Both are friendly Muslim neighbours with historical and cultural affinities and with no major dispute per se. Their relations have been traditionally friendly, albeit with some degree of cooling off that occurred during the Taliban period. These relations, however, have reverted to normalcy since 9/11, when both countries supported the ouster of the Taliban regime in Afghanistan.

There are others who feel that for Pakistan it is bad enough to live under the shadow of a large nuclear country, but to be sandwiched between two nuclear neighbours would indeed be an unenviable situation. No wonder, the nuclear-related US–Iran 'war of words' over the last few years was of great interest and concern to Pakistan. The Pakistani government's reaction to the UN Resolution 1737 imposing sanctions was that trade with Iran and its improvement in the Iran–Pakistan India (IPI) pipeline plan would remain unaffected.[23]

In the last three years of the US–Iran standoff, Pakistan could do precious little, except to persuade Iran to follow IAEA rules, and dissuade the United States from resorting to any use of force. At the same time, Pakistan desires that Iran should cooperate with the international community on the nuclear issue.[24] Earlier in May 2006, the then Prime Minister of Pakistan, Shaukat Aziz, while attending the D-8 conference in Bali, stated that Iran's 'nuclear issue was a very complex issue', and, while Iran had the right to generate nuclear energy, it should not make nuclear weapons or go for proliferation in the region.[25] Further, he stated that Pakistan has already paid a 'big price' due to the US-led war in neighbouring Afghanistan and did not want instability on its borders with Iran.[26]

One school of thought says that nuclear Iran would lead to some kind of strategic parity in the Middle East, presently dominated by a hegemonic nuclear Israel. According to this line of reasoning, Iran's acquiring of nuclear weapons could usher normalcy in the region by inducing counter-deterrence towards Israel.[27] Also, the Palestinian issue could get resolved with a new configuration of balance of power in the Middle East.[28]

However, should Iran become aggressive and act as a strong competitor, it could be perceived as a threat in the region. Pakistan has had traditionally friendly ties with the Arab world, which it would not wish to disturb. But in the event of Iran's belligerent policies, some deterioration in Pak-Iran relations could follow. However, the Iranians have tried to allay these fears by offering to share technologies with its Arab neighbours. There are also fears in some quarters that Pakistan's alleged connections with Iran's nuclear programme[29] could be resurrected by the United States to put pressure on Pakistan. Pakistan, on its part, has always made strong denials on this charge.

In the event of an American or Israeli military strike against Iran, albeit a decreasing possibility, a strong domestic backlash could occur in Pakistan as it is a multi-sectarian society and prone to sectarian conflicts.

In the event of strikes against Iran's nuclear installations, environmental effects could follow along with the inflow of refugees into Pakistan's bordering areas. Notwithstanding Pakistan government's assurances, the prospect of Iran–Pakistan and Iran–Pakistan–India pipeline could be jeopardized further, if not abandoned. Above all, Pakistan would be placed in a difficult situation as to whether to support its immediate neighbour, Iran, or go along with the United States and close Arab friends such as Saudi Arabia and the Gulf states.

The acquired nuclear clout by Iran could tempt it to exert pressures on smaller Gulf neighbours. Its support for Islamic groups, such as Hezbollah, Hamas and the Islamic jihad is well known, and, could possibly increase. Besides, Iran's nuclear preponderance may make many Arab states friendly to Pakistan quite vulnerable. Pakistan's economic interests in the Gulf and the broader Middle East could also suffer, if Iran tries to export its brand of ideology and influence. The Shiite populations of Iraq, Bahrain, and, to some extent, of Kuwait, UAE and eastern Saudi Arabia, could turn more militant. In short, an ideological Iran, laced with nuclear weapons, could become a difficult actor to deal with in the region.

While Pakistan's relations with the United States, as a major non-NATO (North Atlantic Treaty Organization) ally, and 'front-line state' are generally durable, its relations with a post-nuclear Iran might take time to settle down, as the latter's nuclear doctrine matures. For, in a period of nuclear transition, there are greater chances of nuclear powers undertaking risks, which could be avoided through risk reduction measures and CBMs. Pakistan desires that the United States, through a policy of deterrence and incentives, should engage with Iran.[30] It seems that sanctions could at best only delay, but not prevent Iran from going nuclear. Meanwhile, any contemplated military strikes by the United States or Israel would have minimum chances of success. In any case, the United States could only keep Iran under pressure while the Gulf States opt for nuclear options to develop alternative sources of energy.

▣ Conclusion

Despite a radically altered environment, Pakistan remains deeply committed to the NPT regime and is maintaining what is known as the 'minimum deterrence'. Pakistan, since 1947, had consistently offered India different proposals to avoid the advent of nuclear weapons in the region, including the establishment of a Nuclear Weapons Free Zone (NWFZ). India not only opposed these proposals but also even refused to talk to Pakistan on the subject. In addition to the NWFZ proposal, Pakistan had also floated other proposals in various national and international platforms with a view to check the horizontal nuclear proliferation in South Asia.[31] Even after becoming a nuclear weapon state, Pakistan not only imposed a moratorium on further testing but continued to support the operative NPT regime. In recent times, Pakistan accepted the UNSC Resolution (on 28 April 2004) 1540 to prevent the proliferation of WMD to the non-state actors and terrorist groups.[32] Pakistan's ambassador to the UN, Munir Akram, recently reiterated that Pakistan had established effective command and control of its assets, sites and materials.[33] At the same time, he maintained that Pakistan would not accept any demand for access, much less inspections, of its nuclear and strategic assets, materials and facilities.[34]

In South Asia, Pakistan–India rapprochement has come about due to a configuration of forces: series of crises, role of the United States as an intermediary, risk reduction measures and track-two diplomacy efforts. Presently, the India–Pakistan peace process is proceeding well, albeit with some attendant problems. It is also heartening to note that given the recent pricing agreement and the recent encouraging statements of both Pakistani and India leaders at the time of the 14th SAARC Summit at New Delhi, the chances of materialization of the IPI gas pipeline project with Iran have somewhat brightened.

Occupying as it does, a strategic location, lying at the tri-junction of South, Southwest and Central Asia, Pakistan has emerged as a major non-NATO ally and a 'front-line' state allied with the United States in the war against global terrorism. Notwithstanding the upward turn in Pak-US relations, Pakistan, however, remains worried about the Indo-US nuclear deal in the context of American intentions in South Asia. A number of questions have been raised in this context. Is India being made a regional hegemon? Why are the Americans putting all their eggs in the Indian basket? What about the Indian assertion that if it chooses to conduct another nuclear explosion, it would be a national decision and no outsider would have any right to question it? The prevalent belief is that while India may not allow itself to be exploited by the United States, it will maximize its gains from the American association.

Nuclearization, it bears pointing out, is not a panacea to problems of historical underdevelopment and poverty. While nuclear weapons have some positive value to act as a deterrent against some 'predatory' and 'hegemonic' neighbours, the nation-state system is redefining its paradigm of security, with greater emphasis on human security. Greater threats now seem to emanate from within countries than from without. Globalization is adding to internal and external pressures. Nuclear weapons can address only a specific *nature and type* of military threat, that is, in preventing nuclear blackmail and pre-emptive strikes.

In terms of security requirements, Pakistan is likely to continue with its current policy of maintaining the minimum credible deterrence. Given its increasing energy needs, it is likely that Pakistan would wish to establish a greater number of nuclear power plants. In this context, it is reassuring for Pakistan that China is already involved in Pakistan's nuclear plants such as Chashma I (which is operational) and Chashma II (which is under construction). However, it needs to be understood that acquiring nuclear energy is not the major focus for Pakistan. Instead, efforts to secure energy sources of supply through IPI (Iran–Pakistan–India pipeline) or TAP (Turkmenistan–Afghanistan–Pakistan line) or getting electricity from Central Asian Republics such as Kyrgyzstan and Tajikistan may receive greater attention from Islamabad in the days ahead. In this regard, it may be noted that Iran has already agreed to supply 1000 MW to Pakistan.[35]

◙ Notes

1. For a detailed analysis, see Stephen Philip Cohen, *Nuclear Proliferation in South Asia: The Prospect of Arms Control* (Boulder, CO: Westview Press, 1991), pp. 338–58.
2. See Michael Krepon, 'A Time of Trouble, A Time of Need', in Michael Krepon and Amit Sevak (eds), *Crisis Prevention, Confidence Building and Reconstruction in South Asia* (New York: St. Martin's Press, 1995), pp. 1–10.
3. See T. Jayaraman, 'Deterrence and Other Myths', *Frontline*, vol. 16, 8–21 May 1999.
4. *Dawn*, 19 June 1998.
5. See *Strategic Survey, 1998–99* (London: International Institute for Strategic Studies, 1999), pp. 199, 222–32.
6. Quoted in Zafar Iqbal Cheema, 'The Role of Nuclear Weapons in Pakistan's Defense Strategy', *Islamabad Policy Research Institute (IPRI) Journal*, Summer 2004, iv (2), pp. 59–80.
7. Ibid.
8. Ibid.
9. See 'Tehran Refuses to Bow to N-plans', *Dawn* (Islamabad), 25 December 2006, p. 1.
10. Ibid.
11. See Scott D. Sagan, 'How to Keep the Bomb from Iran', *Foreign Affairs*, September–October 2006, vol. 85, pp. 45–59.
12. For a sample of this debate, see *The Debate on Indo-U.S. Nuclear Cooperation* (New Delhi: New Policy Group, 2006).
13. This bill was known as Henry J. Hyde United States–India Peaceful Atomic Energy Cooperation Act of 2006.
14. As cited in, 'China not to Oppose Nuclear Deal: US', *Dawn*, 20 December 2006, p. 7.
15. Ibid.
16. See Jimmy Carter, 'A Dangerous Deal', *Daily Times*, 30 March 2006.
17. See 'America's New Strategic Partner', *Foreign Affairs*, July–August 2006, 85 (4), pp. 33–44.
18. See Shireen Mazari, 'When will we ever learn', *The News*, 9 May 2007. Also see Rabia Akhtar, 'IISS Dossier and A.Q. Khan Network', *The News*, 13 May 2007 and *Nuclear Black Markets: Pakistan, A. Q. Khan*

and the Rise of Proliferation Network; A Net Assessment (London: International Institute for Strategic Studies, May 2007), p. 102.

19. Michael Krepon, 'Update on the US–India Nuclear Cooperation Agreement', Henry Stimson Center, Washington, DC, 21 August 2006, http://www.stimson.org/pub.cfm?id=322 (accessed 31 July 2008).

20. See M. Qasim Mustafa, 'Indo-US Civilian Nuclear Cooperation Agreement: Implications for International Nuclear Non-Proliferation Regime', *Strategic Studies*, Quarterly Journal of the Institute of Strategic Studies, Islamabad, Summer 2006, XXVI (4), p. 150.

21. Ibid.

22. *The News*, 25 December 2006.

23. 'IPI pipeline to be…' op. cit.; also see PML chief's remarks on the pipeline as quoted in Ahmed Hassan, 'Shujaat met Benazir in Dubai, says Mushahid', *Dawn*, 27 December 2006, p. 16.

24. Ibid.

25. As cited in 'More Co-operation among D-8 Urged', *Dawn*, 13 May 2006, pp. 1, 3.

26. As reported in *Daily Times* (Islamabad), 21 April 2006.

27. M.P. Bhandhara articulates this view. See his 'Nuclear Option for Peace in Mid-East', *Dawn*, 24 December 2006, p. 6.

28. Ibid.

29. For a factual denial, see 'Pakistan, Iran Blast Nuclear Cooperation Accusations', *The AFP*, 29 August 2003; also see Iran's admission of European help in its nuclear enrichment programme in Joby Warrrick, 'Iran Admits Foreign Help in Nuclear Facility', *The Washington Post*, 17 August 2003.

30. George Perkovich, 'Why Engaging Iran is a Good Idea', *Daily Times*, 15 December 2006, p. 12.

31. Some of these proposals were as follows: (1) Setting up of a NWFZ in 1974. (2) Pakistan repeated the NWFZ proposals to India in 1976, 1987, 1990. (3) On 4 May 2003 Pakistan asked India to jointly sign the NPT and bilateral/joint agreements to full-scope safeguards or inspections, in November–December 1984, June 1985, and July 1987. (4) India rejected all these overtures and continued to call for a universal general and complete nuclear disarmament and non-discriminatory NPT. (5) Pakistan called for the renunciation of acquisition and development of nuclear weapons in 1978. (6) It also called for accession by both India and Pakistan to the NPT regime in 1979. (7) Bilateral acceptance of full IAEA safeguards in 1979. (8) A mutual inspection of each other's nuclear facilities in 1979. (9) In 1981, Pakistan offered a No War Pact to India that was not accepted by New Delhi. (10) Bilateral signing of a treaty banning all types of nuclear tests in 1987. (11) Proposed to India not to manufacture and to explode nuclear weapons in 1987 and

1991 but India did not reply to these proposals. (12) Convening of a conference on the issue of nuclear non-proliferation in South Asia, which should be attended by Russia, USA, China, India and Pakistan, in 1992. (13) An idea of South Asian Zero-Missile Zone was again suggested in 1994.

32. Peter Heinlein, 'UN Security Council Adopts Resolution to Prevent WMD Transfer to Terrorists', http://www.payvand.com/news/04/apr/1191.html, p. 1 (accessed 31 July 2008).

33. *UN Security Council Press Release SC/8070*, p. 7, http://www.un.org/News/Press/docs/2004/sc8070.doc.htm (accessed 31 July 2008).

34. Ibid.

35. *Dawn*, 9 April 2007.

❋

4

Managing Ambivalence: Pakistan's Relations with the United States and China since 2001

Kanti Bajpai

Pakistan's relations with India consume a great deal of its foreign policy energies. However, its relations with the United States and China, allies at various times in its history, are almost as demanding, if not more so. This chapter traces Pakistan's relations with both these great powers in the wake of 11 September 2001 (9/11).

Before 9/11 and the war on terrorism, Pakistan's relations with the United States were on a downward slide. Relations with China, also, were problematic. After 9/11, Pakistan resumed its importance in the strategic thinking of both countries: it came to be seen by both powers as a strategic danger as well as a strategic opportunity.

Managing the strategic ambivalence of these two powers and taking advantage of the opportunities that became available as a result of the reappraisal of the importance of Pakistan has been a major challenge for Islamabad. In both cases, Pakistani leaders have had to manage the domestic realm as well. Historically, managing ambivalence in relation to the United States and China is not new for Pakistan. Yet, this period has been full of dangers and worries for Islamabad. Inevitably, part of Pakistan's anxiousness arises from the attitude of the United States and China towards India — its perennial concern.

▨ Pakistan's Relations with the United States and China before 2001

Before 9/11, Pakistan's relations with the United States and China were marked by a waning of interest in it on the part of both the major powers and a rise in criticism of its policies and postures, both external and internal. Both powers also showed a growing interest in India — Pakistan's perennial concern. Pakistan's leaders had to present the country as a state that continued to be important to both powers and to ward off criticism of its domestic and external policies and postures.

It is ironic that Pakistan should have fallen off the map strategically after the Cold War. The country had been a 'front-line' state in the war in Afghanistan against the Soviet Union. As a base for mujahideen operations and as a funnel for US and Chinese aid to the Afghan resistance, Pakistan had indeed played a pivotal role. Hundreds of thousands of Afghan refugees, escaping their war-ravaged and conquered land, moved to Pakistan and lived there for a decade. Pakistan received considerable international assistance to look after the Afghan refugees. When the Soviet Union finally decided to move its troops out of Afghanistan and later as the Soviet empire crumbled, Pakistanis congratulated themselves on not only having defeated Soviet aggression but also in having helped unravel the Soviet Union itself.[1]

Pakistani people and leaders could be forgiven for thinking that they would feature in the strategic calculations of the great powers, and in particular the United States and China — allies for the better part of the Cold War and collaborators in the defeat of Soviet forces in Afghanistan. Instead, Pakistan seemed to fall off the strategic map. Washington and Beijing shifted their gaze to other parts of the world. Worse, both capitals began to perceive Pakistan as a source of some degree of worry: strategic issues that had been earlier ignored in relations with Islamabad gradually became more significant.

▣ Pakistan–US Relations

With the Cold War consigned to the back burner, and the great rival having abdicated from the competition, the grand strategic focus of the United States changed. Managing the end of the Cold War and the consequences of the break-up of the Soviet Union, such as the future of Soviet nuclear weapons, the collapse of the old communist regimes and the redrawing of maps in Europe and Asia, were substantial concerns. The violence and deprivations in Africa rose in importance. Above all, however, it was the rise of China that captured the attention of US strategic analysts. Pakistan might have mattered here except that, since the 1960s, Washington was aware that Islamabad would not be a front-line state or partner against the Chinese. Its role as a via media, exercised by Henry Kissinger in 1971, was over. The United States had extensive direct links to China and did not need the good offices of an intermediary.

The declining interest of the United States in its alliance with Pakistan manifested itself in respect to Afghanistan and the Afghan refugees.

Washington, in Islamabad's view, having used the mujahideen to fight the Soviets, washed its hands of the various groups and forces after 1989. US aid for the Afghans dried up, and Pakistan was left to cope with the political instability in the new Afghanistan, the economic burden of the refugees, the social conflicts engendered by the presence of Afghans in Pakistan, the massive supply of drugs and small arms, and the growing religious extremism of those who had fought the Soviets. That these groups were increasingly anti-American was another worry for Pakistan's leaders. The more the United States ignored the Afghans, Afghanistan, and Pakistan, the more it fuelled anti-American forces including amongst Pakistanis.[2]

The United States' concerns over Pakistan's nuclear programme resurged after 1989. During the Cold War, successive US administrations chose to either look the other way or to pursue non-proliferation goals in terms of a global or South Asian concern and to subsume Pakistan within a larger effort at controlling nuclear weapons. Washington was aware of Islamabad's desire for nuclear weapons against a nuclearizing India and the growing sophistication of its nuclear science. The role of A.Q. Khan, the head of Pakistan's nuclear programme, in stealing nuclear secrets from Holland and in reaching out to China in particular to advance the Pakistani programme was well understood in the United States. However, with Pakistan in the front line against the Soviets in Afghanistan, the United States' nuclear proliferation concerns had necessarily to be held in abeyance lest Islamabad become unhelpful in the fight against communism.[3]

With the withdrawal of Soviet troops from Afghanistan, the United States' worries about Pakistan's nuclear weapons became more relevant. Domestic critics in the United States were emboldened by the end of the Cold War. The United States was forced to slap sanctions on Pakistan and curtail arms sales. US administrations, particularly the Clinton Administration, which was at the forefront of post Cold War non-proliferation efforts, were openly critical of Pakistan's nuclear policies. Islamabad came under pressure to sign the Nuclear Non-Proliferation Treaty (NPT) as well as the Comprehensive Test Ban Treaty (CTBT). When Pakistan matched India's five nuclear weapons tests in 1998 with six tests of its own, Washington, after failing to stop the tests, slapped sanctions on both India and Pakistan. Islamabad could scarcely have expected anything else given US laws and opinion at the time. Nevertheless, it was aggrieved over the hypocrisy of the United States with respect to nuclear weapons and the fact that sanctions would hurt Pakistan more than India. The United States increasingly criticized Chinese involvement in the Pakistani nuclear and missile programme and the A.Q. Khan network that was proliferating technologies to other non-nuclear countries.[4]

The United States' criticism of Pakistan was wide-ranging after the Cold War. It was not just Pakistan's nuclear programme that drew Washington's disapproval. It was also Pakistan's external and internal policies. Externally, partly in relation to nuclear proliferation, Washington was critical of Islamabad's role in the Kashmir Valley and Pakistan's relations with India. US officials now openly accused Pakistan of helping the militants in the Valley, if not sponsoring them, and thus creating conditions for a confrontation with India that might end in a nuclear showdown. Internally, Pakistan's politics caught Washington's eye. As the late Benazir Bhutto and Nawaz Sharif alternated in power, with the military pulling the strings, the United States indicated its unhappiness with the political instability and the tampering with democracy. The rise of Islamic extremism also worried the United States. Washington saw a link between Afghanistan, the mujahideen, the rise of the Taliban, Kashmir, and the rise of Islamic militants and fundamentalists in Pakistan. While these forces had been part of the jihad against communism in Afghanistan, they became at the same time a source of worry for the United States and the other Western powers. Their anti-Americanism was open and their general distaste for Western values was hardly a secret. US decision-makers understood that they could not continue to operate as openly as they did without the Pakistani army's approval. Washington's criticism of Pakistan's internal situation did not end there. Pakistan was a major transit point for narcotics, much of which ended up in the US market. It was also a virtual supply depot for arms — small arms in particular — at least partly left over from the war in Afghanistan. Many of these arms were American, given to the Pakistani government for the mujahideen. The United States was worried that arms were finding their way to and fuelling extremist violence both within Pakistan and outside it.[5]

Finally, the United States, from 1989 onwards was clearly edging closer to India. Through the Cold War, these two 'estranged democracies' had intermittent periods of warmth, but more often than not, found themselves supporting causes and countries that the other found unpalatable.[6] The United States was critical of many Indian policies in this period. Ironically, rather similar issues were involved: nuclear proliferation, Kashmir, India's internal violence and human rights record (in Punjab, Kashmir, over the Babri Masjid), among others. With the Indian nuclear tests in 1998, the criticism of India climaxed. In the ensuing two years however, India–US relations warmed perceptibly. The United States sided with India in the Kargil war in the summer of 1999.[7] It began the longest and perhaps the most intense strategic US–India dialogue in recent history, when Strobe Talbott, the former US Undersecretary of State, engaged in several months of talks with Jaswant Singh, India's former Foreign Minister. This was followed by President Clinton's visit, for over five days, to India — the first US president to come to India since Jimmy Carter in 1976. That the five-day trip to India was followed by a five-hour trip to Pakistan, only underlined the growing distance between US–Pakistan relations and US–India relations, in the short span of a decade.[8]

Having said that the United States' interest in Pakistan was flagging and interest in India was growing, there was at the same time a recognition in the United States that the relationship with Islamabad should not be allowed to wither altogether. Pakistan's size, location, military strength, religion, and willingness to ally itself with the United States were attributes that had always attracted American attention. Washington could not ignore the eighth biggest country in the world. Pakistan's location next to Afghanistan, China, India, and Iran made it an actor in several theatres — Central Asia, South Asia, and the oil-rich Gulf. It was a potential beachhead if US forces had to intervene in the region. Its large, well-trained and well-equipped armed forces made it a potential asset for regional operations. Notwithstanding the growth of extremism, Pakistan was regarded as a relatively moderate Islamic country amongst the more influential ones in the region, stretching eastwards from Jordan, and was a useful bridge therefore to the Muslim world. Finally, Pakistan had been an ally at the beginning and end of the Cold War and in 1970–71 when it helped President Nixon to establish relations with China. US leaders, politicians, and military officers felt comfortable with Pakistan in a way that was unmatched outside the NATO brotherhood.[9]

⊞ Pakistan–China Relations

Pakistan's relations with China after 1989 also underwent change. China too showed a declining interest in Pakistan. For one thing, China's great northern neighbour — the Soviet Union — had been defeated in Afghanistan. In addition, it was unravelling politically and was no longer the threat it was perceived to have been since the mid-1950s. Beijing's strategic focus turned elsewhere — to East and Southeast Asia and the emerging Central Asian republics and to the United States. In East Asia, growing Taiwanese and Japanese power, and a progressing Korean peninsula were crucial areas of concern. In Southeast Asia, the emergence of the Southeast Asian Nations (ASEAN) was seen as both a threat and an opportunity. The Spratley Island territorial dispute between China and several Southeast Asian states was also on Beijing's strategic radar screen. In addition, China saw threats and opportunities in Central Asia, where, freed from Soviet control, a new region in effect had emerged right on China's doorstep with implications for its western borderlands.

China's attitude to Pakistan therefore mirrored the US attitude in a way: it no longer considered Pakistan a front-line state, strategically speaking. There were a number of other front lines to worry about. Indeed, for China, the front line was increasingly drawn in relation to the United States, not the Soviet Union. Here East Asia, Southeast Asia, and Central Asia mattered more, as the United States was a massive presence in East Asia and Southeast Asia and was looking to enter Central Asia.

China, like the United States, continued to be interested in Pakistan on nuclear matters. The Chinese had helped with the design of Pakistan's weapon technology and were committed to building reactors for peaceful purposes as well. Through the 1990s, it became apparent that China had also transferred missile technology to Pakistan via North Korea. On both counts, Beijing was under international scrutiny. India, increasingly the United States, and the Western countries publicly criticized China's role. China's motives were thought to be its desire to build Pakistan up against India. However, China's involvement with Pakistan on nuclear issues was based on more complex motives than that. After all, China's nuclear and conventional strengths were such that Beijing was quite capable of handling India militarily by itself.

Beijing's investments in Pakistan's nuclear programme were driven by a number of factors. This is a grey area and evidence is scarce, but it would not be incorrect to suggest that Beijing was driven to help Pakistan for reasons that included keeping Pakistan out of the US camp, encouraging moderation in the Pakistani military (particularly on the issue of separatism in Xinjiang), accessing US weapon systems in the Pakistani armoury, and assessing Pakistani nuclear technology — particularly its uranium enrichment methodology.[10]

These factors for nuclear cooperation with Pakistan had to be balanced against the growing international criticism of China as a proliferator. They also had to be balanced against China's own worries about Pakistani nuclear weapons, a point that is rarely noted. Pakistan with nuclear weapons, for one thing, would be more independent of Beijing. It might also become more aggressive in its differences with China — for instance, over the links between Uyghur militants and extremists based in Pakistan. Like the United States, China had cause to worry about the possibility that Pakistani nuclear weapons could pass into the hands of extremists within the Pakistan armed forces or jihadists of one stripe or another.

Pakistan's internal policies and postures were also of concern to the Chinese, as they were to the United States. While China had worked with Pakistan in encouraging and arming the mujahideen in Afghanistan, it too feared the extremism of the fighters in Afghanistan and Pakistan. The Uyghur problem in Xinjiang province, where Muslim separatists have fought for independence from China, had festered for years. During the war against Soviet occupation, the Chinese had subdued their concerns over Pakistan's role in training and tolerating these forces. With the departure of the Soviet Union from Afghanistan, the mujahideen might become free to link up with and support Uyghur militants. Disaffected Uyghurs were turning to violence, and there was evidence that they obtained support from Pakistan-based Islamic groups.[11]

After 1989, China began to repair its relations with India. On Kashmir, China's stand was balanced. Beijing emphasized the need to arrive at a bilateral solution. In 1999, during the Kargil war, Chinese officials insisted that the Line of Control should be respected and that both parties should maintain peace — the word 'both' seemingly gesturing at a more even-handed judgement about the war.[12] The boundary talks with New Delhi were more regular. A series of confidence-building measures were instituted so as to maintain 'peace and tranquility' along the border. Indian and Chinese leaders met more often than ever before. Even after the 1998 nuclear tests and the Indian defence of the tests in relation to the rivalry with China, Beijing was surprisingly calm, asking India to 'untie the knot' that it had 'tied' with the public comments about the Chinese threat. Finally, rather ominously for Pakistan, there was the rapidly growing economic relationship between China and India. Bilateral trade between the two countries rose from hundreds of millions of dollars annually to several billions in the course of a decade.[13]

China, like the United States, was ambivalent towards Pakistan. On the one hand, Pakistan was less important strategically and was a possible threat. On the other, just as for the United States, Pakistan could not be ignored: Chinese thinking here probably paralleled the United States' thinking. (It is necessary to say 'probably' here because Chinese strategic calculations are never very open.) Yet, it seems safe to suggest that, for Beijing as much as for Washington, Pakistan's size, location, military strength, and willingness to be an ally were attractions that it could not ignore.

▣ Pakistan and the United States since 9/11

Pakistani foreign policy towards the United States was tuned to the ambivalences described above: declining interest in Pakistan as a strategic ally mirrored by increasing interest in India, and at the same time, worry about Pakistan as a strategic problem because of its nuclear weapons and Islamic extremism. The events of 11 September 2001 changed this view of Pakistan in one major respect. Interest in Pakistan as a strategic ally resurged massively. It was once again a front-line state, this time in the 'war on terrorism' that was about to open up in Afghanistan. It was also the front lines literally, since terrorism resided in and was tolerated or encouraged within Pakistan. Pakistan continued to be a worry because of its nuclear weapons, which might fall into the hands of terrorists, and its Islamic extremists who were not just destabilizing Pakistani democracy and the region — Afghanistan and India — but were also a danger to democracies elsewhere and to regional spaces far away. In particular, nuclear weapons and extremism were now a direct threat to the United States. In sum, the ambivalence of the United States towards Pakistan grew manifold with the events of 9/11. Pakistan soon became for the United States its most important non-NATO ally — a base for intelligence and military operations. At the same time, it became for the United States an object of the greatest social and political worry as its internal disorder and conflict threatened to further the interests of extremists.

How has Pakistan coped with this greatly magnified sense of strategic ambivalence on the part of the United States? First of all, Pakistan has accepted its role as a front-line state once again. Second, it has tried to suggest that Pakistan is a moderate Islamic state. Third, it has attempted to reassure the United States on its nuclear weapons programme. Fourth, in return for its role in the war on terrorism, it has leveraged its position as a front-line state to get military and economic aid from the United States and other Western donors.

Front-line State

On 13 September 2001, two days after the tumultuous events of 11 September, the United States apparently made at least seven demands on Pakistan:

1. Stop Al-Qaeda operations at your [i.e. Pakistani] borders, intercept arms shipments through Pakistan, and end all logistical support for Osama bin Laden.
2. Provide the United States with blanket over flight and landing rights to conduct all necessary military and intelligence operations.
3. Provide territorial access to the United States and allied military intelligence as needed, and other personnel to conduct all necessary operations against the perpetrators of terrorism and those that harbour them, including the use of Pakistan's naval bases, air bases and strategic locations on borders.
4. Provide the United States immediately with intelligence, immigration information and data bases, and internal security information, to help prevent and respond to terrorist acts perpetrated against the United States, its friends, or its allies.
5. Continue to publicly condemn the terrorist acts of 11 September and any other terrorist acts against the United States or its friends and allies, and curb all domestic expressions of support for terrorism against the United States, its friends, or its allies.
6. Cut off all shipments of fuel to the Taliban and any other items and recruits, including volunteers en route to Afghanistan, who can be used in a military offensive capacity or to abet a terrorist threat.

7. Should the evidence strongly implicate Osama bin Laden and the Al-Qaeda network in Afghanistan and should Afghanistan and the Taliban continue to harbour him and his network, Pakistan will break diplomatic relations with the Taliban government, end support for the Taliban, and assist the United States in the aforementioned ways to destroy Osama bin Laden and his Al-Qaeda network.[14]

To the surprise of Pakistanis, including within the inner sanctums of military decision-making, General Musharraf accepted the United States' conditions with alacrity. However, Musharraf states that Pakistan did not grant items 2 and 3 on the list. Islamabad offered the United States only a 'narrow corridor' for flights that were 'far away from sensitive areas'. Musharraf also refused to give access to all bases and ports. The United States was given access to Shamsi and Jacobabad only. Even here there were conditions. The United States was allowed to use the bases for 'logistics and recovery', not to launch attacks. Also, Pakistan did not give the United States blanket permission for 'anything'.[15] The United States itself changed its mind on the break of diplomatic relations, fearing that this would tip Washington's hand in respect of the impending attack on the Taliban. The story of the events leading up to the US demand and Pakistan's acceptance has been told elsewhere. Of interest here is Musharraf's reasoning, namely, that he had no choice but to accept the terms if he was to save Pakistan's nuclear weapons, keep alive Pakistan's claims to Kashmir, and preserve its economic infrastructure, which could not have withstood US hostility.[16]

There is considerable controversy about exactly how threatening the United States was in its demands in the aftermath of 9/11. Whether or not the United States threatened to attack Pakistan's nuclear assets — its nuclear weapons and reactors — is unknown. Musharraf, at the time, suggested that the United States had threatened to go that far. He feared, in addition, that Pakistan's support of the Kashmir struggle would be jeopardized if he did not sign on to the war on terrorism. It is unclear what Washington had threatened to do if Pakistan had refused to accede to its demands. One possibility is that the United States would have thrown its diplomatic support behind India, especially on the Kashmir issue.[17] Declaring Pakistan a terrorist state was probably another option.[18]

Despite these threats, Pakistan was able, right from the beginning, to deflect or modify some of the US demands. President Zia-ul-Haq, back in the 1980s, in the front-line days against the Soviet Union, had cooperated with the United States and its allies and had maintained a degree of control over the terms of the relationship. For instance, all military equipment was given to the mujahideen by Pakistani officials. No Americans were allowed direct contact with Afghan forces.[19] The 9/11 strikes, directly on the US homeland, meant that Washington was in no mood to negotiate with Islamabad over military and other arrangements. Yet General Musharraf was able to modify the original US terms and exert a modicum of control for Pakistan. The United States was forced to accede to some of Musharraf's conditions because, without active support from Pakistani leaders, military access to Afghanistan would have been quite impossible. Also, Musharraf's survival might have been at stake. Musharraf was regarded as the most moderate and cooperative Pakistani leader; riding roughshod over him could well have led to a rebellion within the Pakistani Army and a confrontation with the United States.[20]

While Musharraf was able to resist the United States to a degree, it is clear that Pakistan's front-line status from 2001 onwards has been much more demanding than it was in the 1980s. Indeed, Pakistan, in all probability, accepted more US demands than are listed in Musharraf's autobiography. For instance, there are persistent reports that US ground troops have operated in Pakistan, in the border areas with Afghanistan. US air force personnel were rumoured to be stationed at three Pakistani air bases near Afghanistan, in addition to the air base at Jacobabad in Sindh.[21] There have been suggestions that US and Pakistani troops conducted joint operations in the border areas near Afghanistan. What is certain is that Pakistan has handed over many suspected Islamic militants to the US authorities for interrogation and internment at Guantanomo Bay. In addition, Pakistani forces have carried out strikes against militant hideouts based on information and requests from the United States.[22]

With time, the United States came to question Pakistan's commitment to and cooperation in the war on terrorism. Pakistani officials have reiterated that US ground troops do not operate in Pakistan. While it is not certain whether this statement is true, the public airing of the issue does indicate that there is public resistance to a large US military presence in the country. US officials have complained that Pakistani forces have not been aggressive enough in curbing the movement of Taliban and Al-Qaeda militants out of Afghanistan and into Pakistan. Washington has also criticized Islamabad for not persisting with attacks on militants within Pakistan. The recent Waziristan peace accord, between Islamabad and the local chiefs and tribes, by which Pakistani troops end their operations and the tribes refuse refuge and support to the Taliban, did not make Washington happy. The United States saw this as something of a surrender to the militants.[23]

Washington has also not been happy with the intelligence co-operation from Pakistan. At the very least, it fears that there are rogue operations outside the control of the Pakistani government that are undermining the war on terror. Elements in Pakistani intelligence agencies may be tipping militants off about impending US and Pakistani attacks and may also be continuing to supply them with arms and money.[24] Quite what the role of Pakistani intelligence was in the killing of Daniel Pearl, the American *Wall Street Journal* reporter, is still unknown. Omar Sheikh, who was involved in his abduction, was arrested in Pakistan but was not handed over to the United States. Most importantly however, US officials have repeatedly insisted that Osama bin Laden and Mullah Omar are in Pakistan, most likely in the area near Quetta. Pakistani officials and leaders, and especially President Musharraf most vehemently, have denied this. Either Pakistani intelligence is not aware of his whereabouts, which is worrying for the United States, or it is hiding information, which is equally worrying.

Even more troubling from the US point of view is that Pakistan has not done enough to curb anti-American sentiments in Pakistan and threats of jihad and terrorism against the United States and its friends and allies. In January 2002, partly in response to the massive mobilization of Indian troops along the border, Musharraf had proscribed certain groups and had promised to end all support to terrorism — a promise that no one took very seriously. The extremist groups changed their names, opened front organizations, moved their funds, and so on.[25] After a brief spell of control and circumspection, extremist groups once again became active and continue to be effective, within and outside Pakistan. The rise of Islamic extremist forces in Pakistan and the retreat of the Pakistani government on several domestic issues in the face of Islamic protests and demands have worried US officials. In Baluchistan and the North West Frontier Province, local groups are aggressively implementing exceedingly conservative rules and laws that they claim are in consonance with the sharia.[26] The central government either does not wish to or is unable to stop this. US officials suspect that there are times when Pakistan allows a certain amount of radicalism to flourish to protect its leaders from US pressures. It is also true that the writ of the central government does not run much beyond the major cities, particularly beyond Punjab, and that federal forces do not have the capacity to stop radicals.

Moderate Pakistan

One of Pakistan's responses to the United States' doubts about its commitment to the war on terror after 9/11 has been to emphasize its moderate Islamic credentials. Washington, traditionally, has regarded Pakistan in exactly this way — an Islamic country, to be sure, but one that was moderate and therefore an example to other Muslim countries. Pakistan was also regarded as a gateway to the Muslim world for the United States (as it was to China in 1971). After 9/11, it has been harder for Pakistan to convince US officials of this idea, but it has persisted in doing so. The United States has continued, at least publicly, to tout Pakistan as a moderate Islamic ally, as an example, and as a gateway.

After 9/11, Pakistan has made significant efforts to emphasize that it is a moderate Islamic state and society. There are a number of themes and policies that Pakistani leaders have touted as evidence of the country's moderate outlook. President Musharraf's autobiography, released in 2006, details these and his belief in the essential moderation of Pakistan. One important premise that he advances is that Pakistan's brand of Islam is antithetical to extremism:

> At our core, the people of Pakistan are religious and moderate. Pakistan is an Islamic state created for the Muslims of the subcontinent. Only a small fringe of the population is extremist. This fringe holds rigid, orthodox, even obscurantist and intolerant views about religion. A problem arises when it wants to impose its rigid, dogmatic views on others. This fringe not only is militant and aggressive but also can be indoctrinated into terrorism.[27]

According to Musharraf, extremism and terrorism came about in Pakistan under unusual circumstances, mostly as a result of the actions and mistakes of others. The Soviets invaded Afghanistan and laid the conditions for the jihad that radicalized both Afghanistan and Pakistan and Muslims from other parts of the world, many of whom fought in Afghanistan and stayed on in South Asia. The United States first encouraged the extremists in the jihad against the Soviets. Then, it turned its back on these groups and indeed on Pakistan. Other Islamic countries that had contributed to the struggle against the Soviets also failed the mujahideen and other extremists. For instance, Musharraf notes that all the Islamic countries (except for Pakistan) refused to recognize the Taliban-led Afghan government. They thus lost the opportunity to influence the Taliban who became increasingly extreme and violent.

India also contributed to the problem of extremism and terrorism by its mishandling of Kashmir, arousing Muslim anger and militancy. It gave the foreign militants in Afghanistan, as well as many Pakistanis and Kashmiris from India a new cause to enlist in after the war in Afghanistan subsided in 1989. The foreign militants in Afghanistan, according to Musharraf, were the biggest source of extremism and terrorism. Worse than the Taliban was the Al-Qaeda, and the Al-Qaeda consisted mostly of Muslims from other parts of the world, not South Asia. They penetrated Pakistani organizations and radicalized them.[28]

In sum, Musharraf laments, Pakistan has been more victim than victimizer: 'In 2001 it was just as natural for us to join the war against terrorism because Pakistan had been a victim of sectarian and external terrorism for years, and certainly had no desire to be "Talibanized".'[29] Even when Musharraf points the finger closer home, he points not at broader trends in Pakistan or to any one institution, but rather to an individual, specifically, General Zia-ul-Haq, who nurtured Islamic orthodoxy: 'The entire decade of the 1980s saw religious extremism rise, encouraged by Zia.... Actually, Zia, for his own personal and political reasons, embraced the hardline religious lobby as his constituency throughout Pakistan and well beyond, to the exclusion of the huge majority of moderate Pakistanis.'[30]

Musharraf notes that when he went public with his reasons for joining the US in the war on terrorism, it did not lead to any significant disturbances. He briefed his cabinet and the corps commanders: 'I answered every question until all doubts were removed and everyone was on board.' He then went on national television and radio to address the people: 'As I had thought, the reaction was limited and controllable.' At the time, Musharraf had calculated that only in the NWFP and parts of Karachi would there be any significant opposition to his decision, led by the radicals. Crucially, Punjab, 'the heart of Pakistan', would be calm because 'Punjabis are very pragmatic people.'[31] To Musharraf, these were signs of the moderation of the ordinary Pakistani.

The moderation of Pakistanis, according to Musharraf, is also borne out by their response to his post-9/11 policies. Islamabad proscribed extremist organizations, stopped the funding of these groups, banned hate materials, changed the school curriculum to rid it of sectarian and religious hatred, placed controls on the street broadcasts of mosques, and intervened in the teachings of the madrasas, among other things. In the educational sector, the government instituted a reform of the curriculum in schools, of the examination system, and teacher training. State schools and textbooks were made free in Punjab. In higher education, there was to be an emphasis on research, particularly in science and engineering. Most importantly, though, the government opened up a dialogue with the madrasas, forced all madrasas to register themselves with the government and persuaded them to teach 'normal subjects specified by the board of education', and funded only those madrasas that complied with these rules. Musharraf reports that most madrasas accepted these reforms. He notes: 'It bears repeating that among Pakistan's 150 million Muslims, only a small fraction are extremists.'[32]

Musharraf also lists a series of reforms relating to the empowerment and treatment of women. These include the establishment of a women's political school (to train women for political office), the institution of various commissions on the status of women, micro credit for women, training facilities, a Women's Chamber of Commerce and Industry, and legislation banning 'honour killings', repeal of the Hudood laws, and the opening of facilities for women facing violence (crisis centres, shelters, and complaint telephone lines). 'Women themselves', he writes, 'have risen to fight for their rights, and many men now realize that they cannot, and should not try to, stop the process.'[33]

A most important part of the positioning of Pakistan as a moderate state has been the Pakistan government's offer to initiate a dialogue between Islamic and Western civilizations. Pakistani leaders have urged the United States to start communicating with

Islamic countries. Islamabad has argued that unless the feelings of hurt, anger, and injustice that Muslims experience are addressed worldwide, from Palestine to Kashmir, there will continue to be extremism and terror.[34] At the same time, Pakistan has attempted to promote the idea of 'enlightened moderation' among Islamic countries. Thus, at the Islamic Summit in 2004 in Malaysia, Pakistan's proposals on the subject were adopted by the conference. Musharraf reports that Pakistan's proposals aimed at 'restructuring' the Organization of Islamic Conference (OIC) leading to the formation of an eminent persons group (EPG) was adopted at the conference. At the Special Ka'aba Summit in Mecca in December 2005, the EPG was told to revise the OIC charter.[35]

Beyond this, Pakistan has argued that solutions to the Palestine and Kashmir problems are the key to peace between Islam and other religions. Islamabad has urged the United States to use its power to bring about a solution in Palestine and in Kashmir. In addition, Pakistan has projected itself as a peacemaker. For instance, while maintaining its support for the creation of an independent Palestinian state, it has publicly stated that 'Pakistan now accepts Israel as a Jewish state and a de facto reality'. It has promised that if Israel makes progress towards the establishment of a 'viable' Palestinian state, Islamabad will recognize Israel.[36] Through the good offices of Turkey, the Pakistani foreign minister met his Israeli counterpart in Istanbul in September 2005.[37] Later that month, Musharraf spoke to leaders of the American Jewish community in New York.[38] On Kashmir, Pakistan has suggested that it has taken the initiative to resolve issues with India. In particular, Islamabad has said that President Musharraf's four-point plan for Kashmir (consisting of a firm commitment to India–Pakistan negotiations, acceptance of Kashmir as the central problem between the two countries, rejection of solutions to the Kashmir dispute that are unacceptable to India, Pakistan, and Kashmiris, and the search for a win-win solution for both India and Pakistan) still awaits an Indian response.[39]

Pakistan and Nuclear Proliferation

With the events of 9/11, the United States' worries about Pakistan's nuclear programme only became magnified. There has in fact been considerable speculation about the US–Pakistan nuclear relationship since 9/11. It has been suggested that the United States has taken over Pakistan's nuclear weapons and has them in custody. This is almost certainly untrue. It is improbable how the United States could have taken control and why Pakistan would have given up its nuclear assets. What is true is that Pakistan has certainly taken some steps to curb the A.Q. Khan proliferation network in the wake of the 9/11 revelations.

President Musharraf lists a number of steps that Pakistan had taken during his tenure to curb proliferation. In his account, he suggests that as Director General of Military Operations (DGMO), he had become suspicious of Khan as early as 1998. Later, as Chief of Army, under Prime Minister Nawaz Sharif, he had tried to bring the army more centrally into nuclear decision-making and control. After assuming power in 1999, Musharraf took a number of further steps to restrict Khan's movements and activities — with mixed success. Musharraf's position has been that it was not simply the events of 9/11 and US pressure that caused Pakistan to move against Khan.[40]

Nonetheless, it is clear that US pressures finally pushed Musharraf to retire Khan from the nuclear programme, place him under virtual house arrest, and to work with US intelligence to follow the Khan trail. The most important point to emerge from the investigations that Musharraf launched in 2002 is that the Khan network certainly helped Iran and North Korea who got centrifuges from Pakistan. Khan also helped Libya. While these revelations are useful, they are hardly revolutionary. Over the years, a good deal had been conjectured and revealed about Khan's activities. Musharraf's investigations confirm the suspicions that Khan proliferated widely.[41]

Musharraf's assertion that Khan was taken out of the nuclear programme, that no Pakistani leader knew of Khan's activities, and that the Pakistan Army was ignorant of and not implicated in his decisions are, by contrast, questionable. The United States had asked for permission to interrogate Khan, but Musharraf had refused, and so Washington has been unable to determine whether or not Khan's network has been terminated, how much government connivance existed, and the role of the Pakistani military in it. There is worry even now that elements of the Khan network continue to be active.[42] If so, it can hardly be without the knowledge of the military. How much the United States knows and how far Washington is willing to go to confront Islamabad are unclear. Certainly, the United States no longer makes any very public criticism of the Pakistani government on this score. In spite of the United States' fears of Pakistani proliferation, it did not impose sanctions on Pakistan.[43]

Having laid bare the nuclear activities of Khan, Pakistan has attempted to reassure the United States that its nuclear weapons are secure from terrorists or from unauthorized use. Islamabad has apparently briefed Washington on its command and control system and asked for help in making the arsenal even safer.[44]

The India–US nuclear deal, in the works since 2005, predictably enough has made Pakistan uneasy. Islamabad has worked hard in the United States to lobby against it. There are rumours that it has even allied with Israel lobbyists who have worked against the deal because the United States has not been terribly helpful in legitimizing Israel's nuclear programme. Pakistan has accused the United States of discrimination against an Islamic nation. It has suggested that while its past record in nuclear matters has been 'poor and indefensible', the United States should cooperate with Pakistan's civilian nuclear programme.[45] The United States' reply to this has been rather tart, saying that Pakistan did not warrant the same treatment. The India–US nuclear deal is still in the making, and increasingly there are doubts that the Bush Administration or the Manmohan Singh government can bridge the differences between Washington and New Delhi. If so, Pakistan will be relieved. Pakistan did hint that it would turn to China if the US–India deal went through. However, Beijing has been fairly circumspect on the issue. Pakistan had apparently asked China to give it 'complete power reactors' but there is no indication that Beijing has agreed.[46] China continues to help Pakistan with the Chashma nuclear plant, but it has not made any definitive offers to Pakistan beyond this.

In the meantime, the Pakistanis are pushing ahead with a heavy water plant at Khushab, which has attracted US concern. Khushab, according to US analysts, is a 1000-megawatt reactor and could give Pakistan up to 200 kilograms of weapons-grade plutonium per year, sufficient for 50 bombs.[47] The prospects of a nuclear arms race in South Asia, including China, worry the United States: as Pakistan and India increase the production of fissile material, China may well respond by speeding up its own production, which by all accounts it has slowed down since the end of the Cold War.

Military and Economic Aid for Pakistan

Pakistan has leveraged its participation in the war on terrorism into military and economic aid, primarily from the United States. Musharraf, in his autobiography, records that in his calculations about whether or not to accept the United States' demands, he counted up the benefits to Pakistan. Among the key benefits was access to US military and economic assistance.[48]

In this, Pakistan has been successful. In the wake of 9/11, virtually all sanctions were lifted, including those related to the military coup that brought General Musharraf to power as well as proliferation-related sanctions. As time went on, bills that sought to link Pakistani actions against terrorism and proliferation were set aside by the Senate. Freed from the possibility of sanctions, US assistance to Pakistan began to flow. The Congressional Research Service (CRS) records that between 1947 and 2005, Pakistan received $15 billion in US military and economic assistance. In June 2003, the United States promised to give Pakistan $3 billion over the next five years. CRS reports that the United States also pays 'billions of dollars' to 'reimburse Pakistan for its support of US-led counterterrorism operations'. Between January 2002 and August 2005, $3.6 billion had been paid out, representing one-quarter of Pakistan's total military expenditure over the roughly three-year period. In 2007, the United States estimates that it will pay out another $900 million in reimbursements to Pakistan.[49]

US military transfers to Pakistan began in 2002. Pakistan was finally able to get parts for some of its old F-16 fighter aircrafts. In March 2005, the United States once again agreed to sell new F-16s to Islamabad. Other sales have included C-130 military transport aircrafts, Cobra attack helicopters, surveillance radars, air traffic control systems, military radio systems, Harpoon anti-ship missiles, Phalanx guns, anti-armour missiles, and maritime patrol aircrafts. In addition, discussions are on for the sale of air-to-air missiles and self-propelled howitzers. The most controversial issue was the sale of F-16s. The US Congress was concerned that these were intended for hostilities with India, rather than for combating terrorism. There was also worry that Pakistan might pass on the technology to China. Nevertheless, in September 2006, the United States and Pakistan signed a multi-billion dollar deal for the sale of the F-16s.[50]

US assistance has extended to military and police training. The United States has promised to train Pakistani air assault teams to fight terrorists. The United States has helped to train the security personnel protecting the Pakistani President, has funded a Diplomatic Security Unit, and has provided equipment and training for Pakistan's internal police forces.[51]

▓ Pakistan and China since 9/11

China is Pakistan's 'all-weather' friend and reportedly its most consistent ally. This is mostly a great strategic myth, at least in so far as Beijing has never come meaningfully to the rescue of Pakistan in its confrontations with India. Nor has Beijing's support been unequivocal. Until the mid-1950s, Pakistan was an enemy to China because it had aligned with the West in the fight against communism. Since the late 1970s, as Beijing and New Delhi set about repairing their relationship, China has been far more balanced between the two South Asian rivals. In addition, as we noted earlier, China has had its own worries about Pakistan, particularly relating to Islamabad's tolerance of and encouragement of Islamic rebels and militants in Xinjiang.

After 9/11, China's ambivalent view of Pakistan, like the United States' view, grew more ambivalent. Pakistan's resurrection as a front-line state, the presence of US troops in Afghanistan, massive US aid to Pakistan, and the growth of Islamic extremism in its neighbour worried Beijing. At the same time, Pakistan is something of a strategic complication for India; it is seen as an entry into the Islamic world for China; and it is a physical asset in respect of the Gulf, particularly with the commissioning of the Gwadar port (built with Chinese help) and the completion of the Karakoram highway (also built by China), which allows Chinese goods to go by land to the Arabian Sea.

Pakistan's multi-pronged responses to China's ambivalence have included reassuring China about its strategic ties with the United States, curtailing Islamic militants along China's borders, and expanding military and economic ties with China.

Reassuring China

In the wake of the war on terrorism, Pakistan has had to explain its new front-line status to China. Islamabad is not new to this game. In the 1950s and 1960s, it was allied to both the United States and China (in this sense its status was exactly the obverse of India's non-alignment). Then again, in the 1980s, in Afghanistan, it worked closely with both powers against the Soviets. After 9/11, whereas the United States and China had a common interest in containing Islamic extremism and violence, the presence of US troops and US influence in Pakistan was worrying to China. Through Pakistan and Afghanistan, the United States would have an opening into Central Asia.

China would therefore confront the United States not only in East Asia and Southeast Asia but also in Central Asia. With US influence on the rise in Pakistan and also in India, Chinese analysts were worried that for the first time Washington would have strong strategic ties with both South Asian countries — Pakistan as the United States' 'major non-NATO ally'; and India as its 'natural ally'.[52]

In response to the new strategic situation, Pakistan and China increased bilateral contacts at the highest level.[53] Inclusive of the three visits Musharraf made to China during the India–Pakistan crisis of 2001–02, the two sides had at least 22 meetings between December 2001 and April 2007 at the level of Presidents, Premiers, Foreign Ministers, and other senior political leaders. With a view to reassuring China and increasing its bargaining power with the United States, Pakistan has gone to considerable lengths to underline the importance of its relationship with China. Thus, just prior to President Bush's visit to Pakistan in March 2006, President Musharraf was in Beijing from 19 to 24 February.[54]

The two sides have also invested in a fair degree of symbolic fanfare. During Musharraf's visit to China, the 55th anniversary of formal diplomatic relations between the two countries was marked by China by releasing a special postage stamp to commemorate Musharraf's visit and the anniversary. That this is no particular landmark — the 50th anniversary is a more 'logical' landmark — is evident enough. Seven months later, in November 2006, President Hu Jintao was in Pakistan to sign a free trade agreement and to receive Pakistan's highest award, the Nishan-e-Pakistan.[55]

As relations with the United States have gone through many ups and downs, Pakistan has sought out the Chinese even more. During Musharraf's visit to Beijing, on 23 February 2006, Pakistan's Information Minister, Sheikh Rashid Ahmad declared on Chinese television that Pakistan would stand by China if the United States ever chose to 'besiege' its great northern neighbour. There was no comment by Pakistani officials in the wake of this very public statement about the United States.[56] In April 2005, as part of its efforts to reassure the Chinese, Pakistan signed a 'Treaty of Friendship, Cooperation, and Good-Neighbourly Relations', which among other things, states that 'neither party will join any alliance or bloc which infringes upon the sovereignty, security and territorial integrity' of either country. The treaty also prohibits the two states from entering into a similar treaty with a third party.[57]

Pakistan evidently has explained its relations with the United States fairly convincingly because China has never criticized Pakistan's front-line status and its relationship with the United States. At the same time, China has tried to limit US influence and to draw Pakistan into its sphere of influence in Central Asia. It invited Pakistan to be an observer at the Shanghai Cooperation Organization (SCO) whose members are China and the major Central Asian states. The United States is conspicuously not part of the organization.

Curtailing Islamic Extremism

China's problems in Xinjiang with ethnic Uyghur restiveness and violence have been a source of discomfort in its relationship with Pakistan. The decade between 1987 and 1997 probably was the most unstable in the province. As Islamic extremism grew in Afghanistan and Pakistan, Beijing's anxieties grew.

It is unclear how important the issue remains for China. There appears to have been a decrease in Uyghur restiveness. The Hanification of Xinjiang (the Han are the majority population of China) seems to be proceeding apace, both in terms of Han migration as well as cultural inroads. Beijing's development policies have also helped quell unrest. The communist party patronizes 'official' Muslim clerics and therefore attempts to control Uyghur communities through religious leaders. Beijing has also used force to deal with the 'splittists' and separatists. It has, in addition, warned its Central Asian neighbours to shut down support for separatists to the extent that they operate from these countries. The formation of the Shanghai Cooperation Organization (SCO) has to be seen in part from this perspective. In June 2001, months before the terrorist attacks of 9/11, the five original members of the SCO plus Uzbekistan signed the Shanghai Convention on the Fight Against Terrorism, Separatism, and Extremism.[58] China has followed a similar policy of Hanification, development, official religion, force, and international cooperation in neighbouring Tibet, thereby communicating to the Uyghurs that it means business.

China has also, over the years, held discussions with Pakistan on the activities of groups operating from Pakistani soil that have helped the Uyghurs and on the presence of Uyghur separatists in Pakistan. Most recently, China and Pakistan have signed an agreement on the 'three forces' problem — terrorism, separatism, and extremism. During his state visit to China in 2003, President

Musharraf promised to 'oppose' terrorism and in this context publicly mentioned the East Turkestan Islamic Movement, one of the leading groups in Xinjiang.[59]

On the whole, China seems far more comfortable with the situation in Xinjiang than in the 1990s, though it is hard to be sure just how concerned the Chinese are about Pakistani behaviour since officially the issue scarcely ever features in communiqués and statements.[60] Perhaps a greater worry is the fate of Chinese workers in Pakistan. Since May 2004, there have been three attacks on Chinese personnel. In May 2004, Chinese engineers working at Gwadar port were killed in a car explosion. In October 2004, two engineers were kidnapped and one died in the subsequent rescue attempt. Then on 15 February 2006, Baluch rebels killed three Chinese engineers. Baluch rebels have promised to continue targeting Chinese personnel because of Beijing's support to Islamabad.[61]

Nonetheless, the issue of Islamic extremism, as a bilateral irritant, should not be exaggerated. The two governments have been fairly adept at keeping the matter private. In 2003, in response to one of the few questions on terrorism in Xinjiang and the presence of terrorist training camps in Pakistan, the Chinese foreign ministry spokesperson complimented Pakistan. The spokesperson noted that Pakistan had taken 'a series of measures to fight religious extremists and terrorism in recent years ... China has good relations with Pakistan. China has lots of help and assistance from Pakistan in fighting the "three forces" and safeguarding the integrity of territory and sovereignty. The Chinese side is satisfied with that and will continue its cooperation with Pakistan.'[62] The fact that Uyghur restiveness has reduced, partly as a result of Chinese policies, has of course helped the cause of Pakistan–China relations.[63]

In any case, China has evidently concluded that its strategic interests in Pakistan were such that this issue could not be allowed to harm the relationship. Thus, China reacted publicly and, in relation to its traditional policy, rather sharply in 2004 when its engineers were killed but noted that its strategic interests in Pakistan were vital. State Councillor Tang Jiaxuan on 18 October 2004 during a goodwill visit to Pakistan carried a verbal message from President Hu Jintao that foregrounded China's larger strategic concerns: 'the Chinese side values the cooperation and friendship with the Pakistani side and we also value the life and safety of every Chinese citizen. It is our hope that Pakistan will take more effective measures to guarantee the security of Chinese workers in Pakistan.... the Chinese Government has all along viewed China–Pakistan relationship from a strategic plane and attached importance to the cooperation between the two countries. China is willing to work with Pakistan to surmount difficulties and challenges....'[64]

Expanding Military and Economic Ties

After 9/11, military and economic issues have become even more important than in the past. Pakistan has been one of the major beneficiaries of Chinese defence sales since the 1960s. Nevertheless, over the past five years, as Chinese equipment has become more sophisticated and also, ironically, as US sales to Pakistan have resumed, Islamabad has sought and Beijing has acquiesced in the speeding up of defence deals. Pakistan's economic relations with China have also surged. Over the past fifty years, the economic relationship has not been a prominent feature of the involvement between the two countries. However, this has changed rapidly.

Pakistan sees China as a reliable supplier of military equipment, more so than the United States, which has periodically shut off supplies — either in the event of hostilities with India or over nuclear proliferation and, most lately, over nuclear testing.[65] China, on the other hand, has been a regular source of arms. In the coming years, China will sell Pakistan the F-7 fighter, the T-96 main battle tank, and is helping build four frigates for the Pakistani navy. Pakistan has also shown an interest in buying the new FC-12 fighter and the JF-17 Thunder. The FC-1 may enter Pakistani service by 2009. Islamabad is interested in buying 150 of the FC-1s, which it will co-produce. Pakistan might also buy the Chengdu F-10, depending on how many F-16s it gets from the United States. The J-10 may eventually be comparable to the F-16s and to the Sukhoi-30 MK1 that India possesses.[66] China will also reportedly supply Pakistan with an AWACS (Airborne Warning Control System).[67]

Pakistan and China have embarked on a new economic relationship. This has been fuelled by several factors including China's economic growth and the growing attraction of its products and services, its search for markets, its desire to strengthen Pakistan's development in a bid to limit extremism and terrorism, and its desire to retain its influence in Pakistan after 9/11. The Karakoram highway and the improved transportation links between northern Pakistan and Xinjiang are also factors in promoting trade. The centrepiece of this surge in economic interactions was the idea of setting up a free trade area, which emerged in 2004.

The trade relationship between Pakistan and China is an unequal one, with China enjoying a considerable trade surplus. Pakistan's main export is cotton, accounting in 2004 for 70 per cent of its total exports. Annual trade between the two countries is small but growing rapidly, indeed at 30–40 per cent, per annum. Eleven per cent of Pakistan's imports were from China. Total bilateral trade currently stands at $4.5 billion annually. Chinese investments in Pakistan are small. There are only 60 Chinese companies operating in Pakistan, about one-eighth of all foreign companies in the country. These are mostly in the public utilities sector and in mining, telecommunications, and energy. White goods companies are also entering Pakistan as are consumer manufacturers, more generally. Chinese companies are attracted to low-cost labour and the possibility that Pakistan can serve the Central Asian markets. Pakistani decision-makers are quite explicit about the security implications of a free trade area. Tariq Ikram, Minister of State and Chairman of the Export Promotion Bureau of Pakistan notes, that an FTA will cement their 'all-weather friendship' and will be the 'key to social stability in the cross-border area because economic growth can significantly reduce violence and separatism in this area'.[68]

In November 2006, the two countries finally signed a free trade agreement. Trade between the two could rise as high as $15 billion by 2011. They also signed an accord on a five-year development programme and a joint investment company. President Hu Jintao told a press conference after the signing that 'This [agreement] serves the fundamental interests of our two peoples and is also conducive to the peace and development of our region.'[69] President Musharraf has promised to set up special industrial zones as well, exclusively for Chinese companies.[70] While there is some worry among Pakistani business interests as Chinese goods flood into the country and harm small- and medium-sized producers, there is no sign that the Pakistani government will change course on the FTA.[71]

Pakistan and China's economic cooperation goes beyond trade though. Energy is also a major area of possible cooperation. A memorandum signed in 2006 envisages the building of an energy corridor, with China constructing pipelines directly all the way to

Karachi or Gwadar from where presumably Gulf oil and gas would be unloaded. The Karakoram highway would help here as well, but Pakistan envisages the creation of 'the ninth and tenth wonders [of the world] by establishing energy pipelines and railway linkages between the two fast growing economies'.[72] China is to help Pakistan with oil and gas exploration in Pakistan and the exploitation of Pakistan's coal, lignite, and renewable energy.[73]

All this is to be supplemented by Chinese help in Pakistan's infrastructure. The Karakoram highway, the eighth wonder of the world, according to President Musharraf, is already open. There is talk of joining the highway up to Russian railway systems. Phase I of the Gwadar port project has also been completed. Gwadar will likely give the Chinese naval access to the Arabian Sea, allow it to monitor US ships and signals, and keep an eye on the Indian Navy. Gwadar may also be turned into a free trade zone with special privileges for Chinese companies, which would help the local economy.[74]

▩ Conclusion

Prior to the events of 9/11, as Islamabad viewed the emerging strategic picture, it could see the assembling of an India–US partnership and an India–China rapprochement. Pakistan's strategic importance, at the same time, appeared to be in decline. While both the United States and China have often suggested that their relations with India and Pakistan are not zero-sum — that good relations with India or Pakistan are not necessarily at the expense of the other South Asian states — this argument has not found easy acceptance in New Delhi and Islamabad. After 9/11, the United States and China seem to have more or less achieved a balance in their relations with the two subcontinental neighbours. Pakistan has once again become a highly valued strategic asset for both the United States and China; and both Washington and Beijing are building better relationships with India. From the point of view of India and Pakistan, one could say that India has strengthened its ties with the United States and China while Pakistan has arrested its strategic decline.

The United States and China continue to have a rather ambivalent relationship with Pakistan. Pakistan remains a concern particularly for the United States over its role in the war on terrorism, its nuclear weapons, its relations with India, and the influence of extremists within the country. Pakistan also remains a concern for China, as a possible outpost of US influence and power. China worries that Pakistan's relations with India could worsen and that Beijing would be drawn into the hostilities. In such a situation, the United States, perhaps also Russia could be sucked into the conflict, with unpredictable consequences for China.

While India–US relations have deepened since 2001, the events of 9/11 headed off an India–US strategic partnership that seemed imminent when President Bush came into office. The India–US nuclear deal is rather telling in this respect. After lengthy negotiations, it is far from certain that the deal will go through. The India–US strategic partnership is largely a grand strategic convergence around issues such as terrorism, the rise of China, the importance of democracy in building world order, and the virtues of the market for prosperity. There is no real operational depth to the relationship beyond that, except for some intelligence sharing and some rather modest military exercises. The India–China relationship has continued to deepen, but a border settlement is still not visible. The leaders of the two countries meet more often, and economic relations are burgeoning. There is nevertheless a latent, subdued competition for status and influence between the two giants of Asia. This is good news for Pakistan, which has gained strategic ground with both powers in the meantime.

The US–Pakistan and China–Pakistan relationship after 9/11 has helped stabilize South Asia. Pakistan, under not only US pressure but also under pressure from China, has taken steps to reduce the activities of Islamic extremists both inside and outside Pakistan. This has had some effect in Kashmir. Pakistan has also kept up talks with India. In short, the US–China–India–Pakistan quadrilateral is well balanced, with better relations between all the major parties including the United States and China over the past six years.

Pakistan's deepening relations with the United States and China, and the eviction of the Taliban government and fight against the Al-Qaeda in Afghanistan, have helped reduce extremist Islamist influences in Central Asia. As India's relations with Pakistan have improved, and as New Delhi has engaged the United States and China since 9/11, it has become more venturesome in Asia. What is not yet clear however is how India conceives its overall role in Asia. Nevertheless, a greater Indian presence in East Asia and Southeast Asia will add to the balance in these regions, where China, Japan, and the United States are already big players.

On the whole then, Pakistan's relations with the United States and China since 9/11 have been positive for South Asia and Central Asia, and even, looking to the long term, in the rest of Asia as India and China engage each other in various parts of the continent.

While Pakistan's relations with the United States and China since 9/11 have been positive for South and Central Asia, in the years to come much will depend on (i) Pakistan's internal politics and how long it is able to prosecute the war on terrorism, (ii) the Afghanistan situation and how much control allied forces are able to exert against a resurgent Taliban and Al-Qaeda, and (iii) the India–Pakistan dialogue, particularly on Kashmir and peace and security.

First of all, with the assassination of Benazir Bhutto in December 2007, the stability of Pakistan has received a massive blow. The general elections were held under rather extraordinary circumstances. While the results indicate that there is considerable public feeling against President Musharraf and against Islamic extremists in Pakistan, it is not certain that Bhutto's Pakistan People's Party (PPP) and Nawaz Sharif's Pakistan Muslim League (PML-N) can work together to bring stability to Pakistan, or to give it good governance. As for the war on terrorism, neither the PPP nor the PML-N is likely to confront the extremists, in spite of Benazir's assassination. The Taliban, for its part, has stated that it would like to enter into discussions with the PPP and PML-N.

If Pakistan does not stabilize, indeed if matters get worse and the extremists gain ground, if the relatively liberal, constitutional forces are pitted against each other or are rendered rudderless by means of assassination, then the consequences for South Asia, for the United States, and for China, will be grave. The safety of nuclear weapons in Pakistan will only add to the dangers. Nuclear scientists in Pakistan have made contact with the extremists. Pakistan has stated that its arsenal is protected against internal subversion and theft, but given that there are radicals in both the scientific and military establishment, and given the possibility of massive internal unrest in the coming months and years, there are reasons for worry about the command and control of nuclear weapons.

Second, the Afghanistan situation continues to be worrisome for Pakistan, China, and the United States. The Taliban is growing in strength and influence, and the violence in the countryside has not subsided. Outside Kabul, the writ of the government does not run far. Increasingly, there are attacks on the government and on foreigners within Kabul. A number of US allies are talking about withdrawing their forces, sooner or later. The resurgence of the Taliban has meant that Pakistan's tribal areas are being convulsed by a mix of violence and religious fundamentalism. Al-Qaeda is almost certainly operating out of and recruiting in these troubled areas. Pakistani military operations have not had great success, and so there is little prospect of change. Combined with instability in Pakistan, the Talibanization of Afghanistan and of the northern areas of Pakistan could cause the entire zone to become even more volatile. The United States continues to both support and upbraid the Pakistan government in relation to the extremist menace, but there is little sign that the government or the army are willing to go much further in confronting the threat even though both continue to be targets of extremist violence.

Finally, the India–Pakistan dialogue is for the time being stalled. The UPA government in India, under Manmohan Singh, has attempted to take the dialogue forward, but its own preoccupations as well as the instabilities in Pakistan over the past few years have combined to stall the Kashmir talks. Musharraf has repeated his famous four-point formula for a Kashmir solution, and Manmohan Singh continues to insist that South Asian borders cannot be redrawn. The talks between the two governments have evidently gone beyond these public pronouncements, but it is clear that the Kashmir negotiations are on the backburner. Pakistan's internal disarray suggests that it will be quite a long time before discussions get serious again. In addition, given India's own internal preoccupations and turbulence, it is unlikely that the Indian government will give relations with Pakistan great priority even though there is worry over Pakistan's future and even though Indians recognize that progress on Kashmir would be helpful in isolating Pakistani extremists.

If India and Pakistan get into another confrontation, the United States and China will find themselves in a very uncomfortable position: both countries need Pakistan's help, both have stakes in good relations with India, and both need stability in South Asia. They would like to see progress on Kashmir, but given the disarray in Pakistan and the countdown to elections in India, there is not much likelihood of serious bilateral discussions in South Asia. The most positive thing that can be said about Kashmir is that violence on the Indian side has been reduced, but this could well change if New Delhi does not use the opportunity to find a more lasting settlement of the dispute and overcome the alienation of Kashmiris.

In the months and years after 9/11, Pakistan managed its relations with the United States and China with deftness. Particularly in dealing with the United States, Islamabad took a number of risks. Looking ahead, Pakistan must manage its internal relations and its relations with neighbouring countries — Afghanistan and India — with equal felicity if it is to cope with the challenges in its domestic and international politics. This will test the will and creativity of Pakistan's rulers to the limit.

▨ Notes

1. On Pakistan's role as a front-line state under General Zia-ul-Haq, see Hassan Abbas, *Pakistan's Drift into Extremism: Allah, the Army, and America's War on Terror* (New Delhi: Pentagon Press, 2007), pp. 89–132.
2. For a typical Pakistani view along these lines, see Zahid Hussain, *Frontline Pakistan: The Struggle with Militant Islam* (New Delhi: Penguin Books India, 2007), p. 22; Hussain Haqqani, *Pakistan: Between Mosque and Military* (Lahore: Vanguard Books, 2005), p. 282 on the post-Cold War period and the way in which the US withdrew from the Afghanistan situation as well as US pressures on Pakistan over Islamabad's nuclear programme. On the US role in creating the jihad and of Islamic militancy, see Benazir Bhutto's statement quoted in Mary Ann Weaver, *Pakistan: In the Shadow of Jihad and Afghanistan* (New York: Farrar, Straus, and Giroux, 2002), p. 203.
3. On Pakistan's nuclear programme and US knowledge of it, see the damning analysis and documentation by Adrian Levy and Catherine Scott-Clark, *Deception: Pakistan, the United States, and the Global Nuclear Weapons Conspiracy* (New Delhi: Penguin Books India, 2007).
4. See Levy and Scott-Clark, *Deception*.
5. Hussain, *Frontline Pakistan*, pp. 26–27.
6. The term 'estranged democracies' to refer to India–US relations is the title of the fine study of the relationship by Dennis Kux. See Dennis Kux, *Estranged Democracies: India and the United States, 1941–1991* (New Delhi: Sage Publications, 1994).
7. Strobe Talbott, *Engaging India: Diplomacy, Democracy, and the Bomb* (Washington, DC: Brookings Institution Press, 2004), p. 158 and Haqqani, *Pakistan*, pp. 251–54.
8. On the strategic talks between India and the US, see Talbott, *Engaging India*.
9. For an overview of US views of Pakistan, see Haqqani, *Pakistan*, pp. 29–36, 152–53, 162–63, and 256–57. Haqqani notes that 'Pakistan's military has successfully used its contacts with Central Command officers to promote a more positive view of itself' (p. 323).

10. I explore these issues at greater length in my essay, 'Strategic Threats and Nuclear Weapons: India, China, and Pakistan', in M.V. Ramana and C. Rammanohar Reddy (eds), *Prisoners of the Nuclear Dream* (New Delhi: Orient Longman, 2003), pp. 27–52.
11. On the Uyghur problem in Pakistan–China relations, see Ziad Haider, 'Sino-Pakistan Relations and Xinjiang's Uyghurs: Politics, Trade, and Islam along the Karakoram Highway', *Asian Survey*, July–August 2005, XLV(4), pp. 522–45.
12. See Haqqani, *Pakistan*, p. 251 on how the US and China supported India's stand on the Kargil war.
13. In 2002, bilateral trade was $5 billion. At the end of 2005, it had reached $18.7 billion. In 2006, it was expected to be over $20 billion. See B. Raman, 'India, China Trade: Still Miles to Go', *Rediff.news*, 30 November 2006, http://www.rediff.com/money/nov/30raman.htm (accessed 3 August 2008).
14. *In the Line of Fire: A Memoir* (New York: Free Press, 2006), pp. 204–05.
15. Ibid., p. 206.
16. Ibid., p. 202. Hussain, *Frontline Pakistan*, p. 41 records Musharraf's reasoning as being somewhat different, namely, 'to save the country's strategic assets, safeguard the cause of Kashmir and prevent Pakistan from declared a terrorist state.'
17. Musharraf, *In the Line of Fire*, p. 202.
18. Hussain, *Frontline Pakistan*, p. 41.
19. Ibid., p. 50 on how Musharraf also did not allow the US to make contact directly with local tribal leaders.
20. Ibid., p. 41 on how some of Musharraf's top commanders were against Pakistan's support to the US in the days after 9/11.
21. Ibid., pp. 43–44.
22. See, for instance, Weaver, *Pakistan,* pp. 214–48; Hussain, *Frontline Pakistan*, p. 50 on Pakistan's worry about the US' request to deploy combat troops in the tribal areas, and Haqqani, *Pakistan*, pp. 304–06.
23. On US warnings to Pakistan about the situation in Waziristan and the tribal areas, see David E. Sanger, 'Cheney Warns Pakistan to Act Against Terrorism', *The New York Times*, 27 February 2007, http://nytimes.com/2007/02/27/world/asia/27cheney.html (accessed 3 August 2008) and 'Cheney Concerned that Al-Qaeda Regrouping, Taliban Preparing Offensive', *USA Today*, 26 February 2007, http://www.usatoday.com/news/world/2007-02-26-cheney-pakistan_x.htm (accessed 4 August 2008). On Waziristan, see Hussain, *Frontline Pakistan*, pp. 141–53.
24. Haqqani, *Pakistan*, p. 307 on Pakistani intelligence working with Islamic militants and against US interests.
25. See Hussain, *Frontline Pakistan*, pp. 72, 85–86, 99 on how Islamic militants regrouped and carried on operating in Pakistan.

26. Ibid., pp. 181-84, 190–91.
27. Musharraf, *In the Line of Fire*, p. 277.
28. Ibid., p. 278.
29. Ibid., pp. 222–23.
30. Ibid., p. 275.
31. Ibid., pp. 203–04.
32. See ibid., pp. 308–11 on these various reforms. The quote is from p. 310.
33. Ibid., pp. 312–17. The quote is from p. 317.
34. Ministry of Foreign Affairs, Islamabad, 'US Congressional Delegations Call on the President', P. R. No. 97/107, 3 April 2007, http://www.mofa.gov.pk/Press_Releases/2007/April /PR_97_07.htm, (accessed on 22 July 2008) on the necessity of resolving the Palestine issue. See also Salim Bokhari, 'US Must Help Facilitate Kashmir, Palestine Solutions: Aziz', *The News International*, 19 January 2006, http://www.jang.com.pk and Musharraf, *In the Line of Fire*, p. 296.
35. Musharaff, *In the Line of Fire*, p. 296.
36. Ibid., pp. 304–05.
37. Ibid., p. 296.
38. Ibid., p. 296.
39. Ibid., p. 302.
40. Ibid., pp. 286–89.
41. Ibid., pp. 286–94 on A. Q. Khan and Pakistan's nuclear programme.
42. Levy and Scott-Clark, *Deception*, pp. 442–49.
43. K. Alan Kronstadt, *Pakistan–US Relations*, CRS Report for Congress, updated 26 October 2006, p. 16.
44. Ibid., p. 1 reports that Lt. Gen. Khalid Kidwai of Pakistan's Strategic Plans Division, visited the US on 24 October 2006 and briefed US officials on Pakistan's command and control system. Musharraf reports that the US was also most likely briefed in the wake of 9/11. See also Musharraf, *In the Line of Fire*, p. 289 and Jehangir Karamat, 'The Future of Pakistan–US Relations', *Los Angeles World Affairs Council*, 10 March 2005, p. 3, http://www.lawac.org/speech/2004-05/Karamat%202005.pdf (accessed 22 July 2008).
45. Ibid., p. 1.
46. Ibid., p. 9.
47. Ibid., p. 16.
48. Musharraf, *In the Line of Fire*, p. 203.
49. Kronstadt, *Pakistan–US Relations*, CRS Report for Congress, pp. 26–27.
50. Ibid., pp. 14–15.
51. Ibid., p. 15.
52. For Chinese assessments of US policy towards South Asia, see Zhang Guihong, 'US Security Policy Towards South Asia After September 11

and Its Implications for China: A Chinese Perspective', *Strategic Analysis*, April–June 2003, 27(2), pp. 145–71.

53. President Musharraf made trips to China in December 2001, within months of 9/11, a month later in January 2002, and yet again in August 2002. These were however against the background of the India–Pakistan military standoff after the attack on the Indian Parliament in December 2001 and not related to the US factor. The Pakistani President may have taken advantage of the visits to explain his country's new relationship with the US. The visits are noted in J. Mohan Malik, 'The China Factor in the India-Pakistan Conflict', *Parameters*, Spring 2003, p. 37.

54. On the timing of the visit, see Urvashi Aneja, 'Pakistan-China Relations: Recent Developments (Jan–May 2006)', IPCS Special Report No. 26, June 2006, pp. 2–3, http://www.ipcs.org/IPCS-Special-Report_26.pdf (accessed 22 July 2008).

55. 'Pakistan, China Sign Free Trade Deal', *Arab News*, 25 November 2006, http://www.arabnews.com/?page=4&section=0&article=89160&d=25&m=11&y=2006 (accessed 22 July 2008) and Nasim Zehra, 'The Rock Solid Partnership', *Mediamonitors.net*, 25 November 2006, http://world.mediamonitors.net/content/view/full/38075 (accessed 22 July 2008) on the conferral of the award. Hu's visit was the first by a Chinese President in a decade. The last Chinese President to visit Pakistan was Jiang Zemin in 1996.

56. Richard Fisher, 'Musharraf Visits China: Current Issues in Pakistan–China Relations', International Assessment and Strategy Center, 25 February 2006, http://www.strategycenter.net/research/pubID.92/pub_detail.asp (accessed 22 July 2008).

57. These treaty provisions are noted in Aneja, 'Pakistan–China Relations', p. 2. The treaty is referred to in the 'Joint Statement between the People's Republic of China and the Islamic Republic of Pakistan', 26 November 2006, http://pk.china-embassy.org/eng/svhjt/t282202.htm. (accessed 22 July 2008).

58. Rizwan Zeb, 'Pakistan and the Shanghai Cooperation Organization', *China and Eurasian Forum Quarterly*, 2006, 4(4), p. 53, http://www.silkroadstudies.org/new/docs/CEF/Quarterly/November_2006/Zeb.pdf (accessed 22 July 2008).

59. See Tim Luard, 'China Keeps Pakistan Guessing', *BBC News*, 4 November 2003, http://news.bbc.co.uk/1/world/asia-pacific/3236683f.stm (accessed 22 July 2008). Luard reports that in September 2003, the Xinjiang Communist Party secretary had stated that the East Turkestan Islamic Movement had trained in Pakistan and had links to Al-Qaeda.

60. Ghulam Ali, 'Fifty-Fifth Anniversary of Sino-Pakistan Relations: An Appraisal', p. 18, http://cfcc.nthu.edu.tw/~chinastudies/fellowship

symposium/Ali's%20 Paper%20CfCC.doc. (accessed 4 August 2008). Ali notes though that 'eminent opinion leaders in Beijing did not hesitate to register their displeasure over what they saw as the export of Islamic fundamentalism to the Muslim majority Chinese province of Xinjiang … Their real concern, however, was that the government of Pakistan had done nothing to stop it.' See Ghulam Ali, 'Fifty-fifth anniversary', p. 17.

61. These incidents are reported in Fisher, 'Musharraf Visits China'.
62. 'Spokesperson's Remarks on Report of Terrorists' Training Camp in Pakistan', Ministry of Foreign Affairs, People's Republic of China, 16 September 2003, http://fmprc.gov.cn.eng (accessed 22 July 2008).
63. A recent conference on South Asia organized by CERI-Sciences Po (Paris) and the Brookings Institution made scarcely any reference to China's Xinjiang problem. The conference report notes that the group felt that 'China has solved its Islamic problem'. See *Strategic Dialogue on South Asia Conference Report*, an international conference organized jointly by CERI-Sciences Po (Paris) and the Brookings Institution (Washington, DC), Paris, 29–30 June 2006, http://www.brookings.edu/~/media/Files/events/2006/0629south%20asia/20060629.pdf. (accessed 22 July 2008).
64. 'Pakistani President Pervez Musharraf Meets with State Councillor H. E. Tang Jiaxuan', Ministry of Foreign Affairs, People's Republic of China, 18 October 2004. Also on the incidents, see 'Li Zhaoxing Holds a Phone Conversation with Pakistani Foreign Minister', Ministry of Foreign Affairs, People's Republic of China, 14 October 2004, 'Li Zhaoxing Talks Over Phones with His Pakistani Counterpart', 10 October 2004, http://www.fmprc.gov.cn/eng/zxxx/t164428.htm (accessed 4 August 2008) and 'Foreign Minister Li Zhaoxing Holds a Phone Conversation with His Pakistani Counterpart', Ministry of Foreign Affairs, People's Republic of China, 4 May 2004, http://ie.china-embassy.org/eng/NewsPress/t165241.htm (accessed 4 August 2008).
65. For a typical statement of US unreliability and Chinese reliability, see Ghulam Ali, 'Fifty-Fifth Anniversary of Sino-Pakistan Relations', p. 14.
66. Fisher, 'Musharraf Visits China: Current Issues in Pakistan–China Relations', International Assessment and Strategy Center, 25 February 2006.
67. 'Pakistan, China Sign Free Trade Area', *Arab News*, 25 November 2006.
68. On the free trade area and the quote from Tariq Ikram, see 'Pakistan, China to Set Up Free Trade Area', *China Business Weekly*, 26 December 2004, http://www.chinadaily.com.cn/english/doc/2004-12/26/content_403376.htm (accessed 4 August 2008).On Pakistan's imports from Pakistan, see Aneja, 'Pakistan–China Relations', p. 6.
69. 'Pakistan, China Sign Free Trade Deal', *Arab News*, 25 November 2006.
70. Aneja, 'Pakistan–China Relations', p. 6.

71. Ejaz Haider, 'Pakistan and the "Alliance Maze"', *Himal*, 2006, http://www.himalmag.com/2006/september/coverstory_2.htm (accessed 2 December 2007) notes the concern of Pakistani businesses.
72. This is a quote from President Musharraf, cited in Aneja, 'Pakistan–China Relations', p. 7.
73. Ibid., p. 7.
74. Ibid., pp. 7–9. Gwadar will eventually be able to receive oil tankers with a capacity of 200,000 tonnes. See Esther Pan, 'China and Pakistan: A Deepening Bond', Council on Foreign Relations, 8 March 2006, p. 4, http://www.cfr.org/publication/10070/china-and-pakistan.html (accessed 22 July 2008).

✳

5

The Progress of Détente in India–Pakistan Relations: New Chapter or Strategic Charade?

Robert G. Wirsing

▓ Introduction*

This chapter argues that the long-running dispute between India and Pakistan over Kashmir, understood conventionally to be a conflict over territorial possession, has in recent years shown multiple and serious signs of diminished intensity. The two sides have shown an increasing propensity to negotiate agreements that are slowly, steadily, and very likely permanently, draining the dispute of its traditionally intractable character. Although the Kashmir dispute is yet far from a resolution in the formal sense, it has already lost most of its centrality in India–Pakistan relations. For all intents and purposes, it has arrived at a de facto settlement.

Paradoxically, this change does not indicate — indeed it provides no guarantee at all — that a positive transformation of the relationship as a whole is in the cards. On the contrary, the change now in progress in India–Pakistan relations is entirely compatible with a future as turbulent and inclined to conflict as ever in the past. This is because the relationship between India and Pakistan is driven by far more than the Kashmir dispute; and some of the other drivers of this relationship, including some relatively new ones, are virtually bound to present formidable obstacles to friendly relations. Foremost among these other drivers is a rapidly mounting regional rivalry over natural resources, specifically over hydrocarbon (petroleum and natural gas) energy supplies and river water. These drivers, I shall be arguing, are not strongly counterbalanced by existing cooperative tendencies, neither in regard to energy and water resources themselves nor in regard to regional integration and economic trade.

---

* The views expressed in this paper are those of the author and do not necessarily reflect the official policy or position of the Asia-Pacific Center for Security Studies, the US Pacific Command, the US Department of Defense, or the US government.

The argument of this chapter is obviously not going to meet with approval in all quarters. Indeed, commentaries in recent years on Pakistan's evolving relationship with its Indian neighbour have been anything but uniform in their assessment of its prospects. At one end of the spectrum of opinion, well illustrated in a paper presented in June 2006 to a conference at the University of Leiden by geographer Joseph E. Schwartzberg, we encounter unadulterated optimism about the likelihood of progress in the relationship. Schwartzberg began his paper with the observation that there existed 'a wide range of factors that now contribute to an improved climate for conflict resolution, a climate better than has existed at any time since the early 1950s'.[1] He enumerated a number of reasons for his optimism, including:

- substantial external pressures on both India and Pakistan to settle their differences over Kashmir;
- awareness on both sides of the border that Kashmir cannot be settled by force;
- recognition that the Kashmir problem's resolution will enhance the prospects of foreign investment and trade, as well as cooperation in securing energy supplies;
- genuine commitment of Indian and Pakistani leaders to the promotion of peace in South Asia, and their evident willingness to modify formerly inflexible positions on Kashmir;
- the 'de-demonization' of one another by Indians and Pakistanis — a fundamental change in mutual perceptions brought on by the work of peace-oriented NGOs, international conferences, athletic and cultural exchanges, the opening of cross-LOC bus service, and the support rendered by India to the Pakistani victims of the October 2005 earthquake; and
- the 'craving of ordinary people', especially on the Indian side, for peace and security and their weariness with strife and indignity.

All of these developments, Schwartzberg concluded, 'hold out the promise … of an enduring set of peace accords on Kashmir within the coming decade'.

At the other end of the spectrum is the deeply pessimistic vision of Sumit Ganguly, who holds the Rabindranath Tagore Chair of Indian Cultures and Civilizations at Indiana University. In an article published in Summer 2006 in *Foreign Affairs*, Ganguly argued that while Kashmir so far had not prevented India's rise, 'the prospects that the two sides will reach a settlement on their own are dim'.[2] His reasons included:

- neither government has seriously moderated its claims;
- despite a decline in the rates of infiltration from Pakistan-controlled Kashmir into Indian-controlled Kashmir and a corresponding decline in the level of violence, the insurgency has not ended;
- almost all proposed solutions — from regional plebiscites to autonomy to independence — are lacking in political feasibility; and
- uncritical support of Pakistan's military regime by the United States forecloses the possibility of serious rapprochement between India and Pakistan.

The thrust of Ganguly's argument is that there will be no meaningful progress on Kashmir until and unless there is a fundamental change in the US policy towards Pakistan.

Confronted with these two opposed interpretations of the India–Pakistan equation, some observers, including the eminent diplomat-turned-diplomatic historian Dennis Kux, simply confess their bafflement. 'As 2006 begins', he disappointingly concludes his excellent review of India–Pakistan negotiating behaviour with, 'the outlook is unclear'.[3]

The task I've set for myself in this article is to weigh the prospects of the current détente in India–Pakistan relations without falling prey to the seductive arguments served up by either the optimistic or pessimistic schools of analysis, but at the same time making a sincere effort to avoid concluding on a note of complete bafflement.

▨ Kashmir: The Virtual Dispute

First in order of business is to discard the timeworn cliché that India–Pakistan relations are hostage to Kashmir — that the hostility in their relationship is due almost solely to the unsettled nature of the Kashmir dispute and, by the same token, that to resolve the Kashmir dispute is tantamount to launching the India–Pakistan bilateral relationship on a new, firm and positive trajectory. This notion, which has achieved near hallowed status among subcontinent watchers, was never an entirely satisfactory statement of the relationship; it is today without any merit at all.

This isn't the first time I've made this argument. In a book about Kashmir published over a decade ago, I wrote that the Kashmir dispute had evolved over time in ways that had resulted in its fundamental transformation. The traditional (territorial) dispute's parameters had become a convenient 'cover story' or metaphor, I insisted, for a conflicted relationship that bore less and less kinship, as the years passed and circumstances changed, to what it had been in the immediate post-Partition era. 'For the most part', I said then in introducing the book, 'the "Kashmir dispute" is not about Kashmir. It is at least not *mainly* about Kashmir. The phrase long ago mutated into an inclusive metaphor or "cover story" for the multifaceted interstate power struggle between India and Pakistan.'

'Put in a slightly different way', I added, 'the Kashmir dispute is as much a symptom, as a cause, of India–Pakistan rivalry. The rivalry is not Kashmir-dependent. This is disheartening since it means that "the Kashmir dispute" is extremely complicated. It is about far more than a contested piece of territory.'[4]

Thinking about Kashmir in this way, whether as metaphor or symptom, requires a good bit of mental spring-cleaning. Today, for instance, Pakistan can no longer be fairly described as a 'revisionist' state, bent upon the irredentist mission of reclaiming the lost land of Kashmir. Not that we can't find Pakistanis nowadays who still cling to this vision; but their numbers have unquestionably thinned out in the higher reaches of the government and the military. Both sides in the dispute over Kashmir — India by choice, Pakistan by necessity — accept the territorial status quo, even if they are reluctant to say so, and even if they wish it could be otherwise. President Musharraf has been unequivocal in acknowledging publicly and repeatedly since he first brought the idea to the surface in October 2004, his acceptance of the new order — an order in which there is little if any room left for aggressive territorial expansion, however much disguised. His four-point scheme for resolving the dispute, which appears 'to finally bury the argument that Jammu & Kashmir should be a part of the Islamic state of Pakistan by virtue of its overwhelming Muslim majority',[5] leaves little room for doubt that Pakistan has for all intents and purposes abandoned its irredentist aspirations.

While Musharraf's apparent conversion to a more benign view of Kashmir has been widely welcomed around the world, it would be a mistake to read too much into it. It does not mean that Musharraf no longer detects any grounds for conflict between India and Pakistan.

It doesn't mean that at all. The positive steps in India–Pakistan relations today in regard to Kashmir owe much to Kashmir's decline in importance, and not to a change of heart, among the leaders of these two traditional adversaries. Kashmir is being 'settled', so to speak, because neither side expects to advance its national interest by keeping it alive. Both sides in fact, are now quite in agreement that keeping the issue alive mainly runs counter to their national interests. I hasten to reemphasize that the de facto settlement of the territorial dimension of the dispute should not be taken as a huge leap forward in India–Pakistan relations. What these two countries are currently in the process of 'settling' have long since been greatly diminished in importance. As much as anything, the two sides are clearing away a half a century's worth of accumulated rhetorical debris. This is a positive development as far as it goes; were it accompanied by major positive developments across the board in their relationship, we would be justified in speaking of an historic breakthrough: Nothing of this sort is currently apparent.

▦ The Limits of Cooperation

There are a number of bilateral and multilateral frameworks in South Asia designed to bolster interstate cooperation, including cooperation between India and Pakistan. At the bilateral level, Indian and Pakistani delegations have completed four rounds of the so-called Composite Dialogue, a formula developed by mutual agreement for sustained multi-level, multi-phase talks on a number of contentious issues in India–Pakistan relations. The idea for a Composite Dialogue was initially raised in June 1997 in a meeting of the Foreign Secretaries of the two countries. The Joint Statement issued following their meeting spoke of the need for establishing a mechanism, including working groups at appropriate levels, to discuss, in a composite dialogue, eight specific subjects, including Jammu & Kashmir. The idea went unsupported at the time, but it was revived in February 1999 at the Lahore Summit — an historic meeting between Indian Prime Minister Atal Bihari Vajpayee and Pakistani Prime Minister Nawaz Sharif that laid the groundwork for a series of cooperation-aimed diplomatic initiatives that have continued, off and on, to this day. Of particular importance was the agreement then struck to move beyond traditional stated positions on Kashmir.[6]

The Composite Dialogue process has endured in spite of several major setbacks, including the Kargil war in Spring 1999, the massive mobilization of Indian and Pakistani forces in the wake of the near-catastrophic terrorist attack on Parliament House in New Delhi in December 2001, and the general bitterness between the two neighbours that persisted up until the end of 2003. The process has resulted in a host of minor agreements and concessions. To date, however, no major agreement has been struck. Pakistani officials complain that India is dragging its feet; Indian officials insist that little progress can be made until and unless Pakistan effectively terminates the violent activities in Kashmir of militant (jihadi) groups that are based in Pakistan.

At the multilateral level, the most conspicuous achievement has been the signing by the region's (then) seven-member grouping[†] — the South Asian Association of Regional Cooperation (SAARC) — of the South Asian Free Trade Agreement (SAFTA). Formally agreed upon in 2004, SAFTA went into effect on 1 July 2006. If it lives up to its promoters' expectations of rapid growth in intra-regional two-way trade, then the economies of India and its neighbours could be major beneficiaries.

There are, however, huge impediments to living up to expectations. As can be seen in Figures 5.1 and 5.2, two-way trade among SAARC members is in most cases miniscule; and set against the dramatic increases in two-way trade visible between these states and the European Union, the United States, Japan, the Middle East, and China in the first half of the present decade, the snail's pace visible in their intra-regional trade relationships is far from encouraging. South Asia is, in economic terms, one of the most weakly integrated regions in the world. Intra-regional trade, according to one recent study, 'is only 2 per cent of GDP, compared with 37 per cent in NAFTA, 63 per cent in the European Union, and 38 per cent in ASEAN'.[7]

Recently, strong arguments have been made about the potential for substantial growth, particularly in India–Pakistan trade. For instance, in a carefully formulated World Bank-supported study, the author, Nisha Taneja, maintains that 'there is a vast untapped trade potential between the two countries' — that two-way trade between them could be about ten times its present size.[8] Taneja carefully

---

[†] Afghanistan was officially added as the eighth member of SAARC at the 14th SAARC Summit in early April 2007.

Figure 5.1: Share of Exports (EX) and Imports (IM) in South Asia, 2005

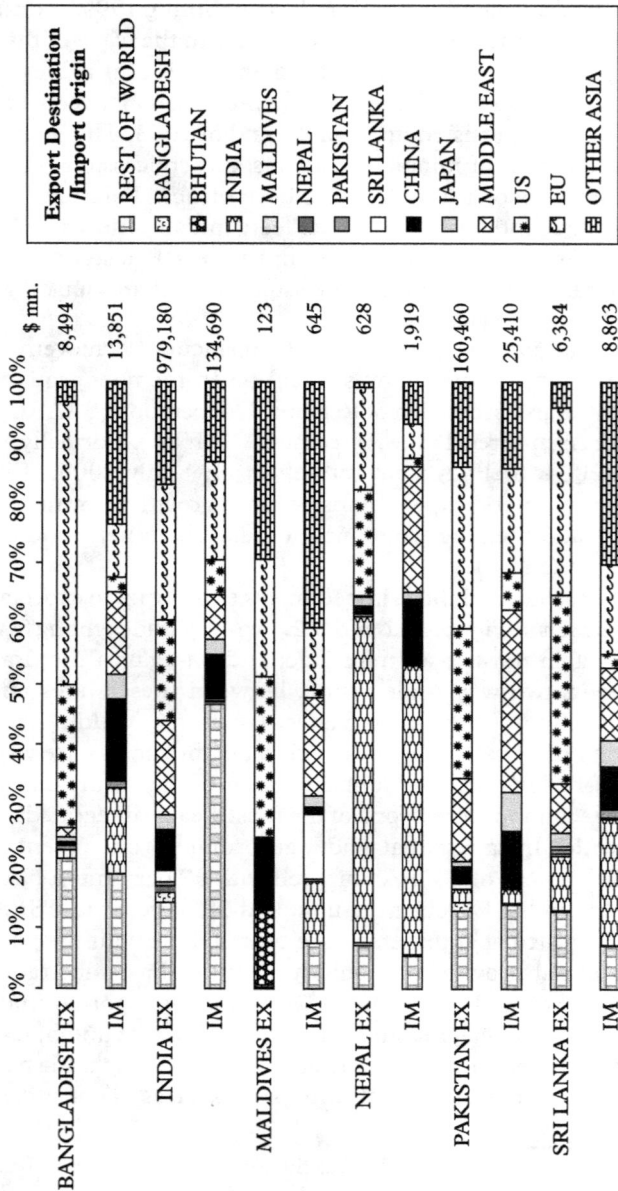

Export Destination /Import Origin

- REST OF WORLD
- BANGLADESH
- BHUTAN
- INDIA
- MALDIVES
- NEPAL
- PAKISTAN
- SRI LANKA
- CHINA
- JAPAN
- MIDDLE EAST
- US
- EU
- OTHER ASIA

	$ mn.
BANGLADESH EX	8,494
IM	13,851
INDIA EX	979,180
IM	134,690
MALDIVES EX	123
IM	645
NEPAL EX	628
IM	1,919
PAKISTAN EX	160,460
IM	25,410
SRI LANKA EX	6,384
IM	8,863

Source: International Monetary Fund, *Direction of Trade Statistics Yearbook, 2006.*

Figure 5.2: SAARC Two-Way Trade, 1998–2006

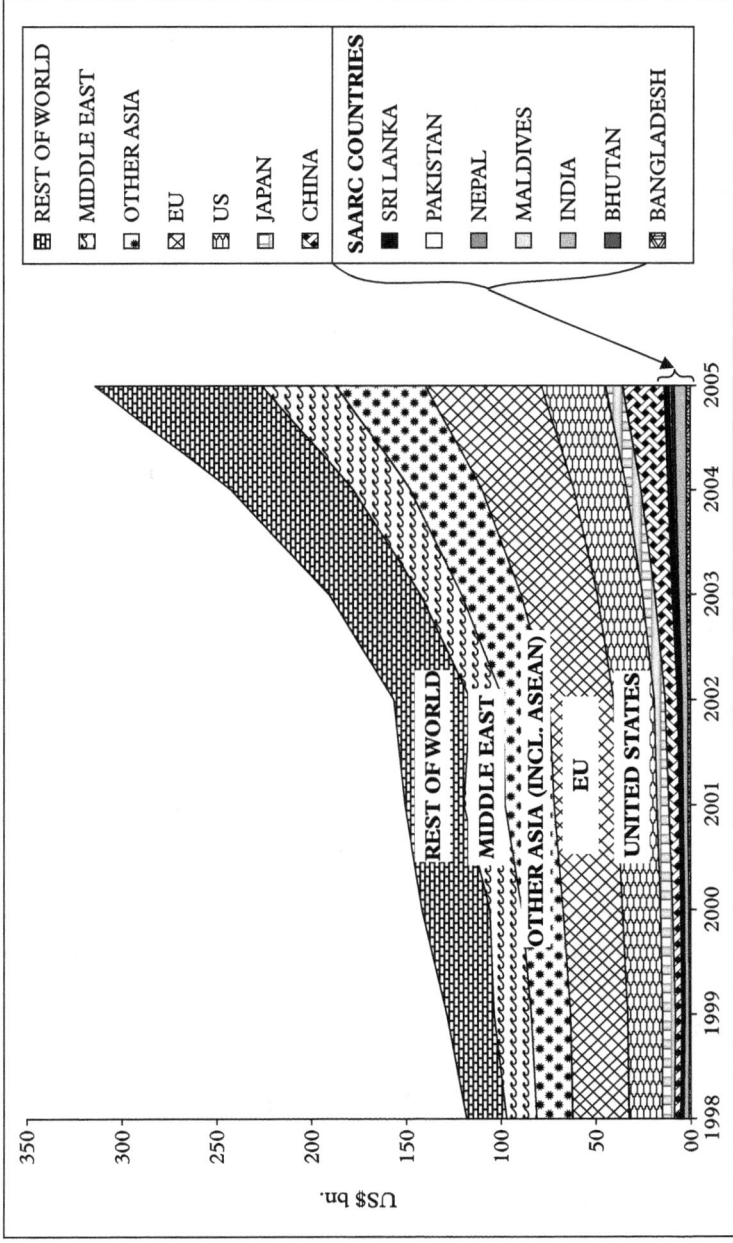

	REST OF WORLD
	MIDDLE EAST
	OTHER ASIA
	EU
	US
	JAPAN
	CHINA

SAARC COUNTRIES

	SRI LANKA
	PAKISTAN
	NEPAL
	MALDIVES
	INDIA
	BHUTAN
	BANGLADESH

US$ bn.

REST OF WORLD

MIDDLE EAST

OTHER ASIA (INCL. ASEAN)

EU

UNITED STATES

Source: International Monetary Fund, *Direction of Trade Statistics Yearbook, 2006.*

examines areas of trade interest and areas of possible joint ventures where greater cooperation could be sought. Alongside a detailed array of existing formal and informal barriers to trade, she provides a list of policy suggestions for enhancing India–Pakistan trade. None of these suggestions — which include Pakistan's grant of MFN status to India, information exchange, opening of new transport routes, elimination of transport bottlenecks, greater efficiency and transparency in banking transactions, and removal of non-tariff barriers to lower costs — appear impractical or impossible to achieve if the will exists on both sides of the border. Generating that will is at the heart of the problem. Needed for its generation, for one thing, is the conviction in Indian and Pakistani leaders that their historic rivalry is indeed a thing of their past, but not of their future. For another, they need also to be convinced that a dramatic increase in two-way trade between them would, in fact, work to their mutual advantage. Such convictions are hard to propagate successfully in an environment where the economies are both conspicuously asymmetric and largely non-complementary, and, moreover, where signs of continued rivalry are still everywhere to be seen. In the mounting competition in the region over natural (energy and water) resources, signs of this latter sort are especially abundant.

▣ The Rise of Natural Resource Rivalry

In the contemporary geopolitical environment in which India and Pakistan are located, scrambling for access to and control over natural (energy and water) resources almost everywhere trumps interstate cooperation in regard to these resources.[9] The reason for this is not hard to find: the South Asian neighbourhood is confronted nowadays by the powerful twin drivers — on the one hand, of sharply increasing natural resource *scarcities*, and, on the other, of no less sharply increasing *demands* for these resources. The policy imperatives accompanying this potentially alarming feature crowd the domestic and international agendas of both countries. In the absence of well-developed and reliable bilateral or multilateral institutional frameworks for addressing these imperatives, India and Pakistan necessarily fall back upon unilateral measures. Their conspicuous self-help measures act, in turn, to reinforce existing distrust, increase tensions, and stall efforts at interstate management of resource problems. How this works can readily be seen in the context of river resource rivalry.

River Resource Rivalry[#]

On 12 February 2007, there occurred an event bearing considerable importance, symbolic if not material, for the river resource futures of India and Pakistan. The event, given little notice in the international media, was the turning over to the governments of India and Pakistan the final and binding decision of a World Bank-appointed neutral expert in regard to the Baglihar Hydroelectric Plant, under construction since 2002 on the Chenab River (a tributary of the Indus) in Jammu & Kashmir. Bearing the title *Expert Determination on Points of Difference Referred by the Government of Pakistan under the Provisions of the Indus Waters Treaty*, the decision brought to an end an arbitration proceeding triggered over two years earlier, on 15 January 2005, by a Pakistani request that the World Bank appoint a neutral expert, under Article IX (2) of the Indus Waters Treaty (IWT), to consider 'differences' that had arisen between Pakistan and India over the Baglihar project.[10] (The dispute and the verdict are discussed in detail a little later.) The two countries had quickly agreed upon the appointment of the Swiss civil engineer Raymond Lafitte as the neutral expert. He was appointed on 12 May 2005. Over the next twenty months, his labours included a site visit in October 2005 to the unfinished Baglihar project, a total of six intensive meetings with delegations of the two countries, and examination of multiple written arguments and counter-arguments prepared by the country teams and their hired consultants.

Lafitte's verdict, though it clearly found India's design of the Baglihar Dam to be in some respects in violation of the IWT, received a far warmer reception on the Indian side than on the Pakistani side. While public statements on the decision by Pakistani officials affirmed the government's general satisfaction with the results of the vigorously contested proceeding, private comments to the author by several members of the Pakistani team revealed deep disappointment with Lafitte's verdict.[11] Some of the disappointment could no doubt be traced to the inevitable letdown Pakistanis would feel at having been significantly bested — in a legal contest initiated by

---

[#] As used here, river resources are defined broadly to include water for navigation, fisheries, irrigation, hydroelectric power generation, ecological balance and biodiversity, domestic and industrial uses. Hydropower qualifies also, of course, as an *energy* resource.

themselves and in which they apparently felt at some advantage — by their long-standing rival India. Some of it, however, I believe could be traced to the Pakistani team's conviction that the first-ever test of the painstakingly-detailed conflict prevention provisions of the IWT had resulted not in the treaty's strengthening but in its dilution; and, perhaps worse, that in the manner in which the determination had been reached an opportunity had been squandered for putting the treaty to work as a positive instrument for promoting greater cooperation between India and Pakistan in future management of Indus river resources.

Pakistan had referred three 'points of difference' for arbitration — one concerning the basic design of the dam, including, in particular, the size and position of gated spillways; a second concerning the amount of pondage or live storage; and a third concerning the height of intake tunnels serving the plant's power turbines. Without going into the technical details of the matter, it is clear that the Pakistanis, virtually from the outset of the dispute, were disturbed primarily by the number, size, and elevation of the eight-gated spillways specified in the dam's design — three of them chute (crest-level) spillways, five of them (the most unacceptable from the Pakistani perspective) 10.5 meters high sluice (submerged orifice) spillways. With their gate sills positioned well beneath the so-called 'dead storage' level of backed-up waters (the level beneath which stored waters are not utilized in power production), the five sluice spillways enabled the Indian side to control the flood discharge of water on a scale, the Pakistani team argued, that the IWT had deliberately sought to preclude.

In defence of their position, the Pakistani team pointed to Annexure D-Part 3: New Run-of-River Plants, Paragraph 8 (e) of the IWT, which reads as follows:

> If the conditions at the site of a Plant make a gated spillway necessary, *the bottom level of the gates in normal closed position shall be located at the highest level consistent with sound and economical design and satisfactory construction and operation of the works.*[12]

In their rebuttal, the Indian side contended that the spillway design of the dam was necessary to ensure safe passing of the design flood, and also a silt-free environment near the intakes for trouble-free operation, by transporting sediments together with flood discharges through the sluice spillway. Consequently, the chosen spillway configuration is at the highest possible level consistent with a sound and economical design and satisfactory construction and operation of the works.[13]

In support, the Indian side cited Paragraph 8 (d) of Annexure D-Part 3:

> There shall be no outlets below the Dead Storage Level, *unless necessary for sediment control or any other technical purpose; any such outlet shall be of the minimum size, and located at the highest level, consistent with sound and economical design and with satisfactory operation of the works.*[14]

In his final decision, which flatly endorsed the Indian position on gated spillways, the neutral expert Lafitte maintained that the design of the spillways had as its clear objective not control of flood discharge (that worried the Pakistanis) but control of sediments or silting. This he found not to contravene, or at least not to be disallowed by, either Paragraph 8 (d) or (e) of the IWT.

Clearly recognizing that his determination on this point would not suit the Pakistanis, Lafitte explained his reasoning at considerable length. He noted in particular that the IWT had been drafted in the 1950s, decades before the modern technology of sedimentation management had been fully developed. He observed:

> It appears that the Treaty is not particularly well developed with respect to its provisions on sediment transport. This is not a criticism: the Treaty reflects the status of technology on reservoir sedimentation in the 1950s. The consequence is that the provisions of the Treaty, which explicitly mention sediment, acquire a special significance.
>
> Everybody recognizes the necessity to take into consideration the lessons of the past, in particular the last decades, from the design, construction and operation of dams and hydropower plants on rivers with important sediment transport....

Lafitte concluded by asserting his reasons for enabling the Indians to control waters held in Dead Storage. He said:

> The definition of the Dead Storage given in the Treaty states that it cannot be used for operational purposes. The operational purpose of Baglihar is power generation, and so this purpose is not allowed for the Dead Storage. This is precisely the role of the Live Storage, which has the purpose of generating power. But the capacity of the Live Storage should be protected against sedimentation. This is an essential matter of sustainability. To meet this objective, 'maintenance' of the Live Storage and of the Dead Storage should be carried out — and this is not

excluded by the Treaty — in accordance with the various known processes of sedimentation control, and in particular, drawdown sluicing and flushing.[15]

The response of the Pakistani team to this — from their standpoint — mischievously circuitous reasoning was predictably angry. The IWT, they declared, was drawn up as a bilateral instrument for the prevention of conflict — not to prevent silting up of dams. The neutral expert's mandate, as they understood it, was to determine not how to help the Indians build a perfect dam but to ascertain whether the dam in contention, the Baglihar, had been designed in conformity with the IWT. What Lafitte chose to do, according to the Pakistanis, was, in effect, to rewrite the Treaty, to modify its intent from one of *conflict prevention* to one of *dam sustainability*.

From the Indian point of view, the results of the arbitration were largely consistent with its long-term hydropower plans for Jammu & Kashmir. The Baglihar hydropower plant, a run-of-the-river project with a capacity of 450 MW in its first stage and an additional 450 MW in its second stage, is one of fifteen hydroelectric schemes in the Chenab river catchment area or basin. Four are already operating, two (including Baglihar) are under construction, and nine are at some stage of investigation or preparation. Were all to be completed, their total installed power-generating capacity would come to 7,160 MW — a not inconsiderable figure considered in the light of India's overall energy (including hydropower) requirements.[16]

By any measure, these requirements are vast.[17] By 2010, India is expected to take South Korea's place as the world's fourth largest energy consumer, after the United States, China, and Japan.[18] Its energy requirements are growing at a rate of 5.6 to 6.4 per cent per annum, which translates into a four-fold increase in India's energy needs over the next quarter century.[19] Coal, which presently meets about 55 per cent of India's energy requirements, is bound to take centre stage well into the future; but with energy consumption rising astronomically, greater efforts to expand and diversify energy sources are inescapable.[20]

As of the end of April 2007, India's total installed power generating capacity was 132,110.21 MW. Thermal resources (coal, oil, gas) accounted for 85,575.84 MW, hydro for 34,653.77 MW, nuclear for 4,120 MW, and renewable (including wind and solar) for 7,760.60 MW.[21] In 2003, the government of India identified a planned target

(Mission 2012: Power for All) by the end of the Eleventh Plan in 2011–12 of an additional 107,000 MW — a seemingly unrealizable aspiration that would mean a near doubling of the current installed capacity in less than a decade. Hydropower, whose share in total power generation has ironically been progressively declining over time, was being counted upon to supply about 50,000 MW of the targeted additional capacity.[22] If, when and where, a target on this scale would be realistically reachable were major questions.

India's hydropower quest

India ranks fifth in the world in exploitable hydroelectric (hydel) potential. According to a re-estimate made in April 2006 by India's Central Electricity Authority (CEA), identified hydel potential is 148,701 MW.[23] The breakdown of this potential by river basin, region and state is shown sequentially in Tables 5.1, 5.2, and 5.3. Apparent in Table 5.1 is that the Indus basin serving India's northern region, including Jammu & Kashmir, has a hydel potential second only to that of the Brahmaputra. Table 5.2 shows that almost two-thirds of the potential hydel capacity of India's northern region is as

Table 5.1: **Hydel Potential of India's Major River Basins/Systems**

River Basins/Systems	Potential installed capacity (MW)
Indus Basin	33,832
Ganga Basin	20,711
Central India River System	4,152
Western Flowing Rivers of Southern India	9,430
Brahmaputra Basin	66,065
Total	**148,701**

Source: *India Energy Outlook 2006*, KPMG International.

Table 5.2: **Status of Hydroelectric Potential Development in India, 2006**

Region	Identified capacity (MW)	Capacity developed/under development (%)	Capacity undeveloped (%)
Northern	53,395	36.0	64.0
Western	8,928	68.9	31.1
Southern	16,458	59.7	40.3
Eastern	10,949	31.9	68.1
North-Eastern	58,971	6.8	93.2
All India	**148,701**	**28.7**	**71.3**

Source: Central Electricity Authority, Government of India.

Table 5.3: State-wise Status of 50,000 MW Hydel Initiative

State	Number of schemes	Planned installed capacity (MW)
Andhra Pradesh	1	81
Arunachal Pradesh	42	27,293
Chhattisgarh	5	848
Himachal Pradesh	15	3,328
Jammu & Kashmir	13	2,675
Karnataka	5	1,900
Kerala	2	126
Madhya Pradesh	3	205
Maharashtra	9	411
Manipur	3	362
Meghalaya	11	931
Mizoram	3	1,500
Nagaland	3	330
Orissa	4	1,189
Sikkim	10	1,469
Uttaranchal	33	5,282
Total	**162**	**47,930**

Source: Central Electricity Authority, Government of India.

yet undeveloped. Table 5.3 gives state-wise data on 162 new hydel dam schemes, totalling a little less than 50,000 MW, approved by the Indian government in May 2003. In all three tables, the importance of the northern and north-eastern sectors is immediately evident. Considering the 16 states listed in Table 5.3, for instance, only 29 (17.9 per cent) of the new hydel schemes will be located outside of the northern and north-eastern sectors of the country. The importance of the north-eastern state of Arunachal Pradesh, where almost one-fourth of the dams are to be constructed, and the Indus basin states of Himachal Pradesh and Jammu & Kashmir in the country's north, targeted for 28 (over 17 per cent) of the new hydel schemes, stands out in particular. Equally evident is that these sectors are precisely the ones that border on India's regional neighbours, including Pakistan, and with whom the waters to be tapped are shared.

Water scarcity in South Asia

The Indian government's dogged efforts to expand the country's hydroelectric power-generating capacity — in considerable measure by exploiting the hydroelectric potential of the Indus river basin — have to be seen in the context of the increasingly dire circumstances of water scarcity in the South Asian region. The evidence is over-whelming that there is now a marked decline in renewable per capita fresh water availability in the region as a whole, and that the decline is currently more immediately threatening in some countries than in others. Keeping in mind the substantial regional variation in water availability that exists within each country in the region, it is apparent that the region's largest and most populous country, India, is moving steadily closer to a danger zone in terms of water supply. Per capita availability of water in India has declined by roughly 60 per cent over the last half-century or so, and the next half-century may well witness an equally precipitous drop.[24] This seemingly inescapable fact inevitably affects the thinking of India's water planners *and* those entrusted with negotiating river water agreements with India's co-riparian neighbours — the five countries (Bangladesh, Bhutan, China, Nepal, and Pakistan) with whom India shares the waters of major river systems.

However, when it comes to looming water scarcity, there can be little doubt that Pakistan — one of the world's most arid countries, dependent for most of its fresh water supplies on the waters of one major river system — the Indus river system — can claim top honours in the region. Per capita water availability in Pakistan, according to one recent estimate, slipped from 5,000 cubic metres per annum in 1951, a few years after the country's founding, to 1,100 cubic metres per annum in 2006. According to internationally recognized standards, Pakistan is today one of the most water-stressed countries on earth with severe water shortages becoming a fact of life. With the country expected to have a population of 173 million in 2010, it is certain that by that date it will have moved significantly closer to the internationally recognized 'water scarcity' limit of 1,000 cubic metres of fresh water availability per capita per year, an alarming rate of decline that is projected in some estimates to dip even further — to less than 700 cubic metres per capita by 2025, when Pakistan's population may have reached 221 million.[25] The unpleasant fact of the matter, according to a recently published and immensely disturb-ing World Wildlife Foundation (WWF) report on Pakistan's water crisis, is that 'Pakistan is already one of the most water-stressed countries in the world, a situation which is going to degrade into outright water scarcity.'[26]

The cited WWF report paints an extraordinarily grim portrait of Pakistan's water pathologies. Included among them are: serious deterioration in groundwater quantity and quality in almost all urban centres, severe depletion and drying up of water sources in many areas due to uncontrolled extraction of groundwater and extended dry periods, huge daily discharge of raw sewage to surface water bodies, steep decline in the quality of drinking water, a mounting problem of arsenic contamination of groundwater, and an alarming spread of water-borne diseases. The WWF report concludes that 'water use practices in [Pakistan] fall far short of the required minimum for water conservation and water quality. In simple terms, Pakistan's water is drying up, and what little remains is heavily polluted.'[27]

Whatever opinion one holds about the neutral expert's findings in regard to Baglihar, the plain fact is that India's plans for hydropower development in the Indus basin run squarely up against Pakistan's irrefutable water scarcity. For Pakistanis, this is not a time for taking lightly the restrictions on Indian use of the waters of the three western rivers of the Indus system — the Chenab, the Jhelum, and the Indus itself — that were reserved mainly for Pakistan's use in a bilateral treaty that took nearly a decade to negotiate. Pakistanis are not going to be easily persuaded that their reading of Indian intentions in regard to the water resources of the Indus basin is unjustifiably suspicious. Indeed, what the dispute over Baglihar most clearly signifies is that the river resource rivalry between India and Pakistan is fated to a lengthy, and probably contentious, future.

Energy (Oil & Natural Gas) Resource Rivalry

Signs of probable future contention are also evident when one turns to consider the interactions of these two states over hydrocarbon (oil and natural gas) resources. As was apparent in the case of water, the region's hydrocarbon resources themselves suffer from a huge and mounting gap between demand and supply. India's chronic power shortages are now described routinely as having reached a 'crisis' stage. Major financial, industrial, and political centres, like Mumbai, Kolkata, and New Delhi, are being hit with extended power cuts for which no relief is in sight. To conserve power, the citizens of Mumbai, until recently untroubled by such cuts, are facing unprecedented appeals to check the use of ACs and to keep computers on sleep mode when not in use.[28] A steady stream of worried commentaries on India's energy issues — in relation to energy deals the government is attempting to make, for instance, with Myanmar or Iran — pours forth from the country's political and strategic analysts.[29] Annual reports of India's Ministry of Defence highlight the critical nexus between Indian security and energy needs. 'The Indian Ocean Region', the *Year 2006 Annual Report* observed in the opening paragraph of its first chapter, 'has assumed enormous importance considering our energy requirements. The oil flow in this region is estimated at 15.5 million barrels per day through the Persian Gulf, 10.3 million barrels per day through the Malacca Straits and 3.3 million barrels per day through the Babel–Mandab (Gulf of Aden). This traffic raises security as well as environmental concerns.'[30]

Energy rivalry crops up in India–Pakistan relations most visibly in two sectors of the relationship — one in their proposed direct collaboration in the building of a natural gas pipeline from Iran's South Pars field, across Pakistan to India; the other, more indirectly, in the development by Pakistan of a new deep sea port at Gwadar on the Arabian Sea coast of Baluchistan. In both these cases, energy rivalry finds itself entangled in the rivalry of opposed alliance systems — a rivalry that mirrors the region's emergence as an important arena of global strategic conflict.

The Iran–Pakistan–India (IPI) natural gas pipeline

Often hailed as a promising 'peace pipeline', the proposed 2,700 km IPI pipeline project for transporting Iranian gas across Pakistan to India has been under discussion since the mid-1990s.[31] The trilateral project, which gained ground with the re-launching in 2004 of the India–Pakistan peace process, has had to labour against a number of weighty obstacles — an estimated cost of $7 billion not the worst of them. Although the three parties to the deal have shown promising signs in the past year or so of a determined will to bring the project to fruition, the obstacles are formidable and may yet prove insurmountable.

The deep distrust that has characterized India–Pakistan relations for more than a half of a century naturally heads the list of obstacles. For Indians, placing their country's energy security, to any serious extent, in the hands of their traditional enemy inevitably prompts second thoughts. Another serious obstacle has been Pakistan's domestic instability, in particular the threatened resurfacing of a Baluch nationalist insurgency in Pakistan's sprawling south-western province of Baluchistan. The IPI pipeline, irremediably vulnerable to acts of sabotage, would have to pass through this province.[32] Yet another obstacle has been the price to be set for gas delivered at the Indian border, which apart from Iranian desires in this regard, had to take account not only of Pakistani demands for both a hefty transit fee and transportation tariff, but also of the potentially more favourable price of gas delivered from India's own huge Krishna Godavari (KG) natural gas fields in the Bay of Bengal.[33]

These obstacles have been given substantial reinforcement by Washington's stiff opposition to the project. Conveyed repeatedly and over several years to both Pakistan and India, the Bush Administration's distaste for Iranian ambitions in the region, foremost among them, perhaps, its alleged nuclear arms ambitions, is extremely difficult for either country to ignore. Pakistan, anointed by Washington as a 'major non-NATO ally', is the recipient of billions in American aid for its cooperation in the war against terrorism; India, in turn, is extremely reluctant to place at risk the critically-important civilian nuclear agreement, signed by the United States and India in July 2005, that has yet to be finally approved by the currently contumacious US Congress. To ensure against India's backsliding on the matter, Washington dispatched Energy Secretary Samuel W. Bodman to India in March 2007 with the stern message, publicly delivered, that the IPI pipeline, if allowed to go forward, would 'contribute to the development of nuclear weapons'. And that, he made clear, had to be stopped.[34]

Running through the natural gas pipeline issue is the transparent fact that India and Pakistan are not entirely free to pursue what logic suggests is a 'win-win' project for meeting their energy requirements. It is equally clear, moreover, that their lack of freedom in this connection arises to no small extent from their mutual and understandable reluctance not to jeopardize their friendship with the United States, the loss of which could result not only in severe economic and other penalties but also, and at least as important, in a major strategic gain for their neighbour. Just how much pressure Washington would be willing to exert on either country to block the project is not now clear; as far as the IPI pipeline is concerned, the region's huge energy needs may ultimately trump America's security priorities. If the IPI pipeline project does eventually see the light of day, it will mean that India and Pakistan will have taken a significant step away from being unsparing hydrocarbon competitors towards being facilitators of one another's energy security.

Pakistan's deep sea port at Gwadar

On 20 March 2007, President Musharraf inaugurated the Gwadar deep sea port in the presence of the Chinese Minister for Communication Mr Li Shen. President Musharraf paid tribute in his address to the friendship between China and Pakistan that had made the port a reality. He dwelt at some length on the new seaport's potential for opening a major trade corridor to Central Asia, China and Turkmenistan. Included in the address was a blunt warning to 'extremist elements' in Baluchistan who would be 'wiped out of this area' if they failed to surrender their weapons.[35]

Musharraf's inaugural comments at Gwadar, brief and inelegant as they were, commemorated an event of far more than passing interest to the countries in the region. An obscure fishing village with a population of about 5,000 when the project was begun in 2001, Gwadar has already grown into a bustling town of about 125,000 — with prospects, if the current boom in real estate investment is any sign, of far greater expansion. Its location 650 kilometres west of Karachi provides some needed strategic depth for Pakistan's modest-sized naval force, subject in the past to the blockade of its major base at Karachi by the much more powerful Indian navy. However, the obvious military advantages gained by Pakistan from the new port are only one dimension of Gwadar's significance.

Interviewed by the author in March 2007, an official of Pakistan's Ministry of Ports & Shipping asserted with apparent confidence that Gwadar would within a few years rank among the world's biggest, best, and busiest deep sea ports. It had at the time of the inaugural event three functional berths, with space for eventually fourteen or more. It had enormous advantages, he claimed, over its rivals in the region, including Iran's port of Chabahar, located in the province of Baluchistan & Sistan near the Pakistan border on the coast of the Gulf of Oman. Like Chabahar, the official insisted, Gwadar lies on major maritime shipping lanes, close to the region's vast oil and gas resources, and also close to the rapidly growing and dynamic Gulf economies. In contrast to Chabahar, however, Gwadar is an all-year, all-weather, deep channel port that will eventually be able to handle the largest oil tankers, promising ease of access to the docking area and unusually short turn-around times.[36]

Pakistani plans for Gwadar envision it evolving into a major and multidimensional hub of economic activity, to be linked in coming years by a rapidly expanded web of road, rail and pipeline networks to neighbouring states, and potentially including an LNG terminal, a steel mill, an automobile assembly plant, a cement plant, and facilities for oil-refining. Plans also call for a first-rate international airport at Gwadar.

Undoubtedly, it was 'the convergence of Sino-Pakistani strategic interests [that] put the port project onto a fast track to its early completion'[37] and it is the Chinese connection with Gwadar, of course, that has attracted most attention from regional security observers. The principal contributor (of about $200 million) to the project's first phase, China, has transparent interests in both monitoring the supply routes for its rapidly increasing energy shipments from the Gulf as well as in opening an alternative route via Pakistan for import/export trade, serving China's vast, at times restive, and rapidly developing Muslim-majority Autonomous Region of Xinjiang.

From New Delhi's point of view, the strategic implications of the Gwadar project are substantial — and for the most part they are worrisome. In the first place, Gwadar clearly complicates the Indian Navy's strategic planning: It is one of the several naval bases mentioned by President Musharraf in his inaugural comments — two of them on the Baluchistan coast — which Pakistan is building to diversify and deepen its naval defences. It is but one of the several signs that Pakistan aspires to a significantly greater naval presence in the Indian Ocean.

Second, the construction of Gwadar and its associated road, rail, and pipeline networks has been openly justified as a means to materially strengthen Pakistan's reach into and influence with Afghanistan and the Central Asian states. New Delhi has launched its own projects, including construction of a 200-kilometer road in western Afghanistan to connect Chabahar with Afghanistan and Central Asia, aimed at the same objective. New Delhi's plans, which seek access to Central Asia via the so-called North–South Corridor transiting Iran, essentially bypassing Pakistan, were driven to a considerable extent by Pakistan's reticence about opening a land transit corridor for Indian trade with Afghanistan and Central Asia. In this connection, Christine Fair has highlighted for us the enormous importance India currently attaches to its Iran initiatives — an importance in which Pakistan looms large. 'Militarily and strategically', she points out in a recent essay, 'Central Asia is an important theatre for India. While India's objectives in the region reflect interests that reach far beyond Pakistan, the fact remains that India is interested in countering Pakistan in this region.'[38]

All of this would appear to put India and Pakistan on opposite sides in a supremely high stakes contest for access to the energy resources and markets of Central Asia.

Third and most important, Gwadar inevitably gets interpreted in New Delhi as another link in the China-built chain encircling India on its eastern, northern, and western borders. Gwadar — more perhaps than any other development in the history of Sino-Pakistan relations — lays the groundwork for substantially strengthened military and economic ties between Pakistan and China, as well as for Pakistan's full absorption into a China-centric strategic partnership.

Thus, Gwadar, though it serves multiple objectives, seems bound to stand also as a symbol of energy resource-driven rivalry between India and Pakistan; and as Pakistani and Chinese plans for Gwadar gradually evolve, the probability is great that the impact of these plans will add considerable fuel to this rivalry.

▧ Conclusion

Recall if you will the task I set for myself at the beginning of this paper — to weigh the prospects of the current détente in India–Pakistan relations without falling prey to the seductive arguments served up by either the optimistic or pessimistic schools of analysis, but at the same time making a sincere effort to avoid concluding on a note of complete bafflement. It should by now be clear that neither of the alternatives offered in the title to this article — the one (new chapter) obviously optimistic, the other (strategic charade) pessimistic — is wholly satisfactory. A new chapter has certainly opened in India–Pakistan relations, but it would be naïve to think that it spells an assured deepening of friendly relations and resolution of major issues standing between them. Enough has been said in this article to warrant abundant scepticism in that regard. As for strategic charade, there is undeniably much theatre, much posturing, and much appealing to the (global) gallery in the public performances today of both Indian and Pakistani leaders. Both sides invest heavily in the shaping of perceptions or what in Washington is fashionably labelled today 'strategic communications' — attempts to win favour for one side, and disfavour for the other, in the court of world opinion. The argument advanced in this article, however, is that India–Pakistan initiatives regarding Kashmir (and, indeed, regarding other aspects of their relationship as well) are not just propaganda ploys: on the contrary, much progress *has* been made. The Kashmir issue, for all intents and purposes, has reached a de facto settlement; and that is a major achievement.

Recall also if you will, this article's principal thesis — namely, that the positive changes going on in regard to Kashmir provide no guarantee at all that a positive transformation of the relationship as a whole is in the cards. This article maintained instead that the change now in progress in India–Pakistan relations is entirely compatible with a future as turbulent and inclined to conflict as ever in the past. This paradoxical circumstance was explained as a product of the bilateral relationship's other drivers, foremost among them being the rapidly mounting regional rivalry over natural resources, specifically over energy and river water resources. These drivers, I said, were insufficiently counterbalanced by existing cooperative tendencies, neither in regard to energy and water resources themselves, nor in regard to regional integration and economic trade.

What I am arguing is that the understanding of India–Pakistan relations has suffered for many years from a Kashmir-centric vision of regional conflict that blocked recognition of other forces driving the relationship. The discussion here focused on natural resource rivalry; there are other forces — including religious identity, demographic change (including population growth), and developments in the realm of conventional and strategic weaponry — that might have been included. The point is that a broader and more complex analytical framework or strategic canvas is required than can possibly be fashioned from a narrow focus on Kashmir — so frequently and misleadingly hailed as the 'core issue' between India and Pakistan.

Implicit in the foregoing discussion is that the road ahead in India–Pakistan relations is strewn with trends that can lead in any number of directions, including intensified rivalry and violent conflict. Needed in the world's major capitals is better appreciation among strategic analysts and the policy-makers they serve of the multiplicity and complexity of these trends, of the manner in which they impact the bilateral relations of India and Pakistan, of the role extra-regional great powers play in negatively affecting these trends, and, finally, of how these same great powers might positively, innovatively, and effectively address them.

⬚ Notes

1. Joseph E. Schwartzberg, 'A Way Forward in Kashmir', Paper presented at the 19th European Conference on Modern South Asian Studies, 29 June 2006, University of Leiden, The Netherlands.
2. Sumit Ganguly, 'Will Kashmir Stop India's Rise?', *Foreign Affairs*, July–August 2006, 85(4), p. 45.
3. Dennis Kux, *India–Pakistan Negotiations: Is Past Still Prologue?* (Washington, DC: United States Institute of Peace Press, 2006), p. 65.
4. Robert G. Wirsing, *Kashmir in the Shadow of War: Regional Rivalries in a Nuclear Age* (Armonk, NY: M.E. Sharpe, Inc., 2003), p. 8.
5. Sultan Shahin, 'Resolving Kashmir with a Musharraf Model', *Asia Times*, 29 October 2004, http://www.atimes.com/atimes/South_Asia/FJ29Df01.html (accessed 9 August 2008). Musharraf has by no means converted all Pakistanis to his view of Kashmir. See, for instance, Ashraf Mumtaz, 'Musharraf's Plan to Divide Kashmir: Sultan', *Dawn*, 15 April 2007, http://www.dawn.com/2007/04/15/nat14.htm (accessed 9 August 2008).
6. A. G. Noorani, 'The Truth About the Lahore Summit', *Frontline*, 16 February–1 March 2002, 19(4), http://www.hinduonnet.com/fl1904/19040850.htm (accessed 9 August 2008).
7. Devesh Kapur and Kavita Iyengar, 'The Limits of Integration in Improving South Asian Security', in Ashley Tellis and Michael Wills (eds), *Strategic Asia 2006–07: Trade, Interdependence, and Security* (Seattle, WA: The National Bureau of Asian Research, 2006), p. 248.
8. Nisha Taneja, *India–Pakistan Trade*, Working Paper No. 182 (New Delhi: Indian Council for Research on International Economic Relations/ICRIER, June 2006), p. 38. Taneja states that formal two-way trade between India and Pakistan in 2006 came to $613 million; and that informal trade between them was believed to range anywhere from $250 million to $2 billion. By her reckoning, formal trade at the time should have been in the neighbourhood of $6.6 billion.
9. For a recent, regionally focused discussion of water resource rivalry, see Robert Wirsing and Christopher Jasparro, 'River Rivalry: Water Disputes, Resource Insecurity, and Diplomatic Deadlock in South Asia', *Water Policy*, April–May 2007, 9(3), pp. 231–51.
10. Professor Raymond Lafitte, *Executive Summary: Baglihar Hydroelectric Plant–Expert Determination on Points of Difference Referred by the Government of Pakistan under the Provisions of the Indus Waters Treaty*, Lausanne, 12 February 2007 [hereinafter cited as *Expert Determination–Executive Summary*]. The entire arbitration documentation, including Executive Summary, is available online on the Ministry of Water &

Power at the Government of Pakistan website, http://www.pakistan.gov.pk/ministries (accessed 9 August 2008).

11. Three members of Pakistan's official Baglihar team were interviewed by the author in the course of January and March–April 2007 visits to Islamabad and Lahore. Identities have been withheld on request.

12. Cited in *Expert Determination–Executive Summary*, p. 11.

13. Ibid., p. 11.

14. Ibid., p. 11.

15. Ibid., p. 12.

16. See Annex 1: Hydro-electric Projects in the Chenab River Basin, *Expert Determination–Executive Summary*.

17. The following paragraphs draw heavily on my article, 'Hydro-Politics in South Asia: The Domestic Roots of Interstate River Rivalry', *Asian Affairs*, Spring 2007, vol. 34.

18. Pramit Mitra, 'Indian Diplomacy Energized by Search for Oil', *YaleGlobal*, 14 March 2005, http://www.yaleglobal.yale.edu/display.article?id=5419 (accessed 9 August 2008).

19. 'Energy Overview', *India Core: Information on Indian Infrastructure & Core Sectors*, http://www.indiacore.com/overview-energy.html (accessed 9 August 2008).

20. Expanding India's energy sector is going to be expensive. According to the International Energy Agency, India will have to spend upwards of $800 billion on its energy sector by 2030. Vibhuti Hate, 'India's Energy Dilemma', *South Asia Monitor*, no. 98 (Washington, DC: Center for Strategic and International Studies, 7 September 2006).

21. Ministry of Power, Government of India, http://powermin.nic.in/indian_electricity_scenario (accessed 9 August 2008).

22. Central Electricity Authority, http://www.cea.nic.in/hydro/status; and *India Energy Outlook 2006*, KPMG International, http://www.in.kpmg.com/pdf/India_Energy_Outlook_2006.pdf (accessed 9 August 2008).

23. Central Electricity Authority, http://www.cea.nic.in/hydro/status.

24. Toufiq A. Siddiqi and Shirin Tahir-Kheli, project coordinators, *Water Demand–Supply Gaps in South Asia and Approaches to Closing the Gaps*, vol. 1, Project on Water and Security in South Asia (Honolulu, (HI): Global Environment and Energy in the 21st Century, 2003), Table 4, p. 18.

25. Figures given in the *Pakistan Strategic Country Environmental Assessment Report 2006*, cited in *Pakistan's Waters at Risk*, Special Report (Lahore: World Wildlife Foundation, February 2007), p. 1. For a no less alarming account of Pakistan's water predicament, see the World Bank report *Water Economy: Running Dry*, Report No. 34081-PK (Washington, DC: World Bank, 14 November 2005).

26. *Pakistan's Waters at Risk*, p. 1. Pakistanis (all South Asians, in fact) can today draw equally dismal inferences from two reports by blue ribbon

panels released in mid-2007 — one by the prestigious Intergovernmental Panel on Climate Change, *Climate Change 2007: Impacts,
Adaptation and Vulnerability*, Summary for Policymakers, 13 April 2007,
http://www.ipcc.ch/ipccreports/ar4-wg2.htm.; the other by the Military
Advisory Board, a panel of senior retired American admirals and
generals, *National Security and the Threat of Climate Change* (Alexandria,
VA: CNA Corporation, April 2007), especially pp. 24–27, http://www.
SecurityAndClimate.cna.org/report/ (accessed 9 August 2008). Both of
these reports make a number of especially worrisome predictions about
the likely impact of climate change on the South Asian region.

27. *Pakistan's Waters at Risk*, p. 23.
28. Krittivas Mukherjee and Hiral Vora, 'Mumbai Shortages Highlight India
   Power Crunch', *Reuters* news service, 26 April 2007, http://www.in.reuters.
   com/news (accessed 9 August 2008). See also Archana Chaudhary,
   'Mumbai, Lagging Shanghai, Faces First Power Cuts in a Century',
   Bloomberg.com, 22 March 2007, http://betruesimple.wordpress.com/
   2007/03/23/mumbai-lagging-shanghai-faces-first-power-cuts-in-a-
   century-bloomberg-22-mar-2007/ (accessed 9 August 2008).
29. See, for instance, Siddharth Srivastava, 'India Grapples with Energy
   Issues', *Asia Times*, 24 March 2007, http://www.atimes.com/atimes/
   South_Asia/IC24Df01.html (accessed 9 August 2008).
30. Government of India, Ministry of Defence, *Annual Report Year 2005–
   2006*, p. 2, http://www.mod.nic.in/reports.
31. For an optimistic forecast at an early stage of the project's development, see Shamila N. Chaudhary, 'Iran to India Natural Gas Pipeline:
   Implications for Conflict Resolution & Regionalism in India, Iran,
   and Pakistan', *TED Case Studies: An Online Journal*, January 2001,
   11(1), http://www.american.edu/TED/class/iranpipeline.htm (accessed
   9 August 2008).
32. Gal Luft, 'Iran–Pakistan–India Pipeline: The Baloch Wildcard', *Energy
   Security*, Institute for the Analysis of Global Security, 12 January 2005,
   http://www.iags.org/n0115042.htm (accessed 9 August 2008).
33. On the pricing issue, see 'Iran–Pakistan–India Gas Pipeline Viable:
   India', *IranMania Current Affairs*, 18 April 2007, http://www.
   iranmania.com/news; Bill Samii, 'Analysis: Iran–Pakistan–India Gas
   Pipeline Imperiled', *Radio Free Europe/Radio Liberty*, 18 March 2005,
   http://www.parstimes.com/news/archive/2005/rfe/iran_india_pipeline.
   html (accessed 9 August 2008); and 'Cheap Gas to Dent Reliance
   Bottomline', *The Telegraph*, 25 June 2007.
34. 'We Need to Stop Pipeline, Says Bodman', *The Hindu*, 23 March
   2007, http://www.hinduonnet.com. See also, Paranjoy Guha Thakurta,
   'Iran–Pakistan–India Gas Pipeline in Trouble', *Counter Currents* online,
   14 February 2006, http://www.countercurrents.org/india-thakurta

140206.htm (accessed 9 August 2008); and Paranjoy Guha Thakurta, 'US Frown Turns Gas Pipeline into Pipe Dream', Inter Press Service News Agency, 22 March 2007, http://www.ipsnews.net (accessed 9 August 2008).

35. 'President Musharraf''s Address at the Inauguration of Gwadar Deep Seaport', http://www.presidentofpakistan.gov.pk/FilesSpeeches/ Addresses (accessed 9 August 2008).

36. Interviewed in Islamabad in March 2007. Name withheld on request.

37. Tarique Niazi, 'Gwadar: China's Naval Outpost on the Indian Ocean', *Association for Asian Research* online, 28 February 2005, http://www. asianresearch.org/articles/2528.html (accessed 9 August 2008).

38. C. Christine Fair, 'India–Iran Security Ties: Thicker Than Oil', in Henry Sokolski (ed.), *Gauging U.S.–Indian Strategic Cooperation* (Carlisle, PA: Strategic Studies Institute of the US Army War College [SSI], March 2007), p. 267.

✳

6

Pakistan's Relations with Central Asia[1]

C. Christine Fair

▣ Pakistan's Central Asian Predicament

Pakistan has been chastened by successive failed — and dangerous — efforts to develop 'strategic depth' in Afghanistan and the rest of Central Asia. Many critics and analysts alike have come to view Pakistan as a major source of global insecurity, due to, among other things, its past and present support for a number of militant groups operating in the region, the connections between its militant groups and several recent international terrorist conspiracies, and the disturbing revelations about the extent of A.Q. Khan's nuclear arms bazaar.[2] After the terrorist attacks against the United States in September 2001 (henceforth '9/11') and President Pervez Musharraf's historic decision to join the US-led war on terrorism, Pakistan was able to redeem itself within the international community and obtain relief from layers of sanctions related to Musharraf's military coup as well as nuclear and missile proliferation. Tainted by their government's dubious past policies, Pakistani officials are loath to concede that Pakistan has a Central Asia strategy, preferring instead to focus upon Pakistan's contribution to the war on terror and its own efforts to deal with its myriad domestic problems, including expanding Islamist militancy within its own territory.

Pakistan's need to focus inwards is dire. While the country has been victimized by suicide attacks since 2002, 2006 witnessed a serious innovation in targeting. Following unilateral military strikes in Bajaur and a series of inept Pakistani military operations throughout North and South Waziristan, several groups employing suicide terrorism began targeting non-traditional targets such as the judiciary and troop formations in the tribal areas. Never before 2006 had such entities been targeted by suicide attacks. Suicide attacks became sanguinary in 2007 more than ever before with several more attacks on military installations, troop formations and high-value civilian leadership. With President Musharraf's increasingly tenuous grip on power and the political instability following the assassination of former Prime Minister Benazir Bhutto in December 2007, Pakistan is facing one of its most severe crises in governance. Even though democracy has returned to Pakistan since, with a fragile coalition government in power and a polity increasingly hostile to the US-led war on terrorism, it remains unclear whether and if so, how, Pakistan will be able to rein in the militant threat from within. Doubtless, the need to deal with its domestic turmoil diminishes Pakistan's ability to project and secure its regional interests.

However, as is well known, this was not always the case. Throughout the 1990s, Pakistan tried to forge an 'Islamic bloc' to expand its political clout and to promote its commercial interests in Central Asia and beyond. This was seen as an important component of Islamabad's much-sought strategic depth to guard against any conflict with India — its nuclear-armed nemesis. In principle, Pakistan interpreted the demise of the Soviet Union and the emergence of several Muslim Central Asian republics as an opportunity to project its influence onto the region and position itself to restrict India's access to the same, turning the entire region into a new theatre for Indo-Pakistani strategic competition. Islamabad hoped that its Muslim identity and long-standing cultural and historical ties to the Central Asian region would afford it welcome access — especially to the region's hydroelectric and hydrocarbon resources.[3]

This article argues that while Pakistan may deny embracing a Central Asia strategy publicly given the realities of the region and the expanding presence of its rival India, it has no viable option but to remain engaged in the region in efforts to secure its varied objectives.[4] This article argues that Islamabad has retained two main objectives in relation to the region. First, it seeks to discourage its neighbours from providing India a base from which it can put pressure on or even destabilize Pakistan. For example, Pakistan claims that India is exploiting its base in Afghanistan to cause problems in Baluchistan and in Pakistan's restless tribal areas along the Pakistan–Afghanistan border. Similar accusations abound regarding India's expanding presence in Iran, especially its 'listening post' in Zahedan in the Sistan-o-Baluchistan province, abutting Pakistan's own restless Baluch province. Second, Pakistan seeks enhanced commercial access to the region, especially to its hydrocarbon and hydroelectric resources. While these goals are more humble than the objectives it embraced in the 1990s, there are formidable barriers to achieving them. This article will address the prospects for Pakistan as it seeks to achieve its more modest objectives in the region.

The rest of this essay evaluates Pakistan's options in Central Asia following 9/11. For the purpose of this essay, Central Asia will include Iran, Afghanistan, Tajikistan, Uzbekistan, Turkmenistan, Kazakhstan, and Kyrgyzstan. It will conclude with some consideration of the massive constraints that bind Pakistan as it seeks to establish itself in Central Asia.

▣ Squandered Opportunities and Failed Policies

Pakistan — like India — squandered early opportunities to strengthen its ties to the newly emergent Central Asian republics in the 1990s and ultimately, its efforts to form a Muslim security belt that spanned the expanse of Turkey to Pakistan did not succeed. This failure was due at least in part because of the chronic instability in Afghanistan — the land bridge connecting Pakistan to much of Central Asia.[5] In the wake of the Soviet withdrawal from Afghanistan, the country was engulfed by a sanguinary civil war in which the various warlords fought over the remains of post-occupation Afghanistan. To achieve a reasonably stable Afghanistan whose leadership was positively disposed towards Islamabad, Pakistan supported a Pashtun militant faction, Hizb-e-Islami, led by Gulbaddin Hekmatyar.[6] Pakistan hoped that Hekmatyar could deliver a corridor to Central Asia that would begin in Peshawar, continue through Jalalabad and Kabul, stretching onwards to Mazar-e-Sharif, and finally reaching Tashkent. Kabul remained the choke point in this passageway. Islamabad also hoped that Hekmatyar would recognize the Durand Line as the international border.

Later, under Benazir Bhutto and with the guidance of her interior minister General Naseerullah Babar, Pakistan began supporting the newly emergent Taliban when it became obvious that Hekmatyar could not deliver a stable Afghanistan friendly to Islamabad, much less a corridor to Central Asia, and formal recognition of the Durand Line as the de jure border. From 1994 until 2001, Pakistan provided military, diplomatic, and financial assistance to the Pashtun Taliban movement. As one analyst in an official thinktank in Pakistan explained:

> Increasingly disillusioned by the seemingly endless cycle of violence, Pakistan began to view the Taliban as the only force in the country

capable of restoring the tranquillity that it so desperately required after over a decade and a half of war. Besides, a friendly Pashtun-dominated government in Kabul would provide Pakistan the strategic depth that it required to buttress its defence against India, as well as facilitate its moves to extend its influence in the energy-rich Central Asian Republics (CARs).[7]

Yet, the Taliban too disappointed Islamabad. Not only did their government flounder on providing the much-anticipated stability, they pursued embarrassing policies and did not acquiesce to Islamabad as hoped. It harboured sectarian terrorists and criminals despite Pakistan's repeated requests that they be remanded to Pakistani authorities.

The Taliban, over time, proved to be more of a liability than an asset for Pakistan, especially from 1998 onwards when the Al-Qaeda organized the simultaneous attacks on two American embassies in Kenya and Tanzania. In response, the United States showered Afghanistan (and mistakenly, a suspect pharmaceutical factory in Sudan) with cruise missiles, targeting the Al-Qaeda's facilities near Khost. During that strike, the Pakistan militant group, Harkat-ul Mujahideen, said that five of its members, who were training there, were killed. (This group was and is on the US Department of State list of Foreign Terrorist Organizations.)[8]

Despite repeated requests (and indeed payments of cash and vehicles) by Saudi Arabia, and later by Pakistan, the Taliban refused to hand over Osama bin Laden. Indeed, while the Taliban may have been dubious about Osama bin Laden initially, the 1998 US missile strikes against him cemented the alliance between the Taliban and the Al-Qaeda leadership. This relationship persisted and strengthened in subsequent years, putting Pakistan in an even more difficult position. Pakistan came under renewed fire for supporting the Taliban after they destroyed the world heritage site, the Bamiyan Buddhas in 2001.[9] Finally, the terrorist attacks on the United States in September 2001 made Islamabad's position simply untenable, and it was faced with the stark choice of abandoning its support for the Taliban and joining the war on terrorism, or becoming the target of the same. Despite Pakistan's efforts to encourage the Taliban to hand over Bin Laden and preserve its control over Afghanistan, the Taliban refused. Instead, Pakistan was forced to turn on its erstwhile proxies. It is debatable whether this was a permanent decision or temporary.[10]

While Pakistan's alliance with the Taliban drew the ire of virtually every near and far neighbour, so did Pakistan's support for a collective of Sunni *tanzeems* (militant organizations). Uzbekistan, Tajikistan, Turkmenistan, China (in the Xinjiang province), Russia (in Chechnya and Dagestan), India and even some Arab states all began experiencing bloody violence perpetrated by Islamist militants in the 1990s.[11] These states tended to hold Pakistan directly responsible for the situation: Uzbekistan's President Karimov, for example, directly accused Pakistan of training Uzbek Islamist militants.[12]

Chechens, Uyghurs, Tajiks, Uzbeks, Arabs — among other foreign fighters — sought and received refuge and training in Pakistani militant camps in the 1980s, with support and encouragement from the United States and other western and Arab states to resist the Soviet invasion of Afghanistan. After the end of the Soviet invasion, foreign militants from all over the region took refuge in Pakistan, some of whom married and built families in Pakistan's tribal areas. Subsequently, a variety of these militants obtained support from Pakistani *tanzeems* and from the Pakistan-sponsored Taliban, found ready access to Pakistan's madrasas and enjoyed the patronage of Pakistan's Islamist parties such as Jamaat-e-Islami (JI) and Jamiat Ulema-e-Islam (JUI).[13]

Rather than pursuing security ties with Pakistan, many of the Central Asian states chose to re-establish security relations with Russia, which has been historically an ally of India and wary of Pakistan's Islamist adventurism. Iran too was chary of Islamabad, holding Pakistan responsible for the murder of eleven of its purported diplomats in Mazar-e-Sharif in northern Afghanistan in 1998.[14] Ironically and perversely, while Pakistan supported this collective of Sunni militant extremists to bolster some of its foreign policy objectives in India and Afghanistan, this same policy undermined other important strategic goals such as improved relations with its proximate and distant neighbours. Indeed, most of its neighbours chose India as their most likely South Asian partner, recognizing that they shared a common problem: Sunni militancy based in and originating from Pakistan.

Since reversing its policy towards the Taliban and joining, although with little choice, the US-led war on terrorism, Pakistani officials work assiduously to communicate Islamabad's declared policy of supporting Afghanistan's President Hamid Karzai and backing international efforts to achieve a stable Afghanistan.[15] Castigated for its decades of interference in Afghanistan and subjected to ongoing claims of continued involvement in Afghanistan's internal affairs,[16] Pakistani officials no longer talk of 'strategic depth' and indeed refute the concept and its architect, the former Chief of Army Staff Mirza Aslam Beg.[17] President Musharraf himself had disowned the concept as irrelevant for today's Pakistan.[18] It remains to be seen whether Pakistan has in fact abandoned this policy of strategic depth or simply found it expedient to say it has. As one Pakistan-based analyst noted 'Pakistan's foreign policy regarding Afghanistan is based on pragmatism rather than on what the country actually desires. In fact, in the given situation, Pakistan has had to replace desirability with acceptability — often against its own choice.'[19]

In spite of the denials, Pakistan does not have the luxury of simply abandoning its strategic planning for Central Asia. The demise of the Taliban has brought about a number of adverse changes in Pakistan's security environment. First and foremost, India now has unprecedented access to Afghanistan. During the Taliban period, India — along with Russia, Iran and Tajikistan among others — aided the Northern Alliance, in opposing the Taliban. In fact, many Northern Alliance personalities and their relatives were either educated in or residents of India for some period of time. As the aforementioned Pakistani scholar opined:

> With the Taliban having now been removed from power, and with a government in Kabul manned heavily by members of the Northern Alliance, India has dramatically increased its involvement in Afghanistan and is seeking to marginalize Pakistan's role in the political and economic reconstruction of the latter's war-ravaged neighbour. At the same time, India has taken a determined stride into Central Asia by establishing a military base in Tajikistan and extending its economic and diplomatic activities throughout the region.[20]

During the Taliban period, the regional powers fought a proxy war that pitted Pakistan, Saudi Arabia and the UAE with their client — the Taliban under the leadership of Mullah Omar, against Iran, Russia and India — the Northern Alliance. The Northern Alliance was a conglomeration of militant commanders (such as Ahmad Shah Massoud, Abdul Rashid Dostum, Karim Khalili, Mohammed Fahim, and Ismail Khan) under the titular political leadership of Burhanuddin Rabbani, the then President of Afghanistan. The influence of the Northern Alliance remained restricted to the north and in September 1996, the Taliban captured Kabul and soon thereafter most of Afghanistan.[21]

The Taliban's presence severely limited India's access to Afghanistan, restricting its zone of influence only to those areas in the north under the control of the famed Northern Alliance commander, Ahmed Shah Massoud. This may have been one of the few successes that the Taliban actually delivered to Islamabad. Afghanistan had always enjoyed better ties with Delhi than with Islamabad and indeed Afghanistan was the only country to object to Pakistan's inclusion in the United Nations, citing dissatisfaction with the disposition of Pakistan's Pashtun population. While shortly thereafter Kabul withdrew its objection, the die had been cast.[22] Justifiably vexing Islamabad, Afghanistan's leadership has never missed an opportunity to make maximalist claims on Pakistan's Pashtun areas in the North West Frontier Province, the tribal areas and even Baluchistan.

With the Taliban's defeat, India now enjoys unrivalled access to President Karzai and his government. President Karzai openly proclaims India to be his country's most important ally while India has made investment in Afghanistan a top priority.[23] Indeed, the Indian ambassador in Kabul is one of the few ambassadors who enjoy unfettered access to President Karzai. India has opened several consulates throughout Afghanistan, including missions in cities near the Pakistan–Afghanistan border in Jalalabad and Kandahar.[24] The Indian presence in Afghanistan discomfits Pakistan, which claims that New Delhi uses these consulates as bases from which to run covert operations to destabilize Pakistan. The alleged operations include printing counterfeit currency, sponsoring terrorism and sabotage in Pakistani territory, including the establishment of several 'terrorist training camps' near Qushila Jadid (north of Kabul), Gereshk (in southern Helmand province), in the Panjshir Valley, and in Kahak and Hassan Killies in Nimruz province.[25]

In a May 2006 interview, Senator Mushahid Hussain Sayed (Pakistan Senate foreign relations committee chairman) alleged that:

> These Indian diplomatic missions serve as launching pads for undertaking covert operations against Pakistan, from Afghan soil. Particularly, the Indian consulates in Kandahar and Jalalabad and their embassy in Kabul are used for clandestine activities inside Pakistan in general and the Federally Administered Tribal Areas (FATA) and Baluchistan in particular.[26]

India's presence in Afghanistan is a part of Delhi's overall strategy for projecting its influence in Central Asia and denying Pakistan the luxury of the 'strategic depth' that it struggled for decades to achieve.[27] India's footing in Afghanistan is also desirable as it affords India the ability to 'punish' Pakistan for its covert operations in Indian-held Kashmir and the rest of the country, *and* to deter Pakistan from undertaking any future misadventures in India, particularly Kashmir.

No doubt, Pakistan's distrust of India's intentions and activities in its various missions in Afghanistan stems from its own lengthy history of using its embassy and consulates in Afghanistan to run covert operations throughout the country. Colonel Sultan Amir (a.k.a 'Colonel Imam') is now famous for his covert portfolio of assisting the Taliban. In a 2006 interview, he explained his 'emotional attachment to the Taliban' which was a force of 'angels' that 'brought peace, eradicated poppies, gave free education, medical treatment and speedy justice. They were the most respected people in Afghanistan.'[28] Pakistan also complains bitterly about the use of India's Border Roads Organization(an arm of the Indian army)to rebuild sensitive roads and the deployment of several hundred soldiers from the Indo-Tibetan Police Force to protect Indian workers building key stretches of the ring road as evidence of India's military presence and capacity for making trouble.[29]

While goodwill for Pakistan is in short supply in Afghanistan, Iran too looks warily towards its eastern neighbour, Pakistan. Whereas once Pakistan could count on Iran for 'strategic depth', Tehran cooled to Pakistan throughout the 1990s due to Pakistan's support of the Taliban and due to its patronage and deployment of Sunni Islamist militants operating throughout the region, including anti-Shia *tanzeems*. Tehran, for its part, is guilty of starting the sanguinary sectarian violence that continues to plague Pakistan to date, resulting in reciprocal suspicion and concern in Pakistan about Iran's influence. With anywhere between 10 to 25 per cent of its population comprised of Shias, Pakistan has reason to be concerned.[30] Iran's involvement in sectarian conflicts in Iraq does not bolster Pakistani confidence that a more influential Iran will be benign. While Tehran and Islamabad have made limited progress in overcoming these antagonisms, Tehran and Delhi have quickly forged a comprehensive 'strategic' bilateral relationship that encompasses economic, political and defence-related areas of cooperation. At the same time, India now has two airbases in

Tajikistan. Even Pakistan's historical ally, China, has pursued closer relations with India. Whereas once Pakistan had hoped to project its natural Islam-based influence in the region, Islamabad now finds itself increasingly encircled and outflanked by India with few options to improve this strategic picture in the near future, particularly on account of its current suite of policies that has not thoroughly repudiated or denunciated the use of Islamist proxies to pursue foreign policy objectives.[31] Moreover, it is becoming increasingly apparent to all, including some of Pakistan's own security managers, that Islamist militancy *within* Pakistan threatens the entire region. It is not yet clear whether Pakistan has the will — much less the capability — to contend with this emerging threat.

▨ Pakistan's Great Hope: Energy and Commerce

Pakistan's interests in Central Asia beyond Afghanistan have traditionally been dominated by economic objectives. Islamabad's primary bilateral structure to achieve these goals was the Economic Cooperation Organization (ECO), which grew out of the Regional Cooperation for Development (RCD). The RCD was founded in July 1964 and included Iran, Pakistan and Turkey — the three strongest US allies in the region at that time. The RCD became the ECO in 1985, and in 1992 expanded to include Afghanistan, five of the newly created Central Asian republics and one Caucasus country (Turkmenistan, Kyrgyzstan, Uzbekistan, Tajikistan, Kazakhstan and Azerbaijan).[32] The ECO was intended to establish a common market for goods and services and foster the development of capital and financial markets among Muslim countries. Pakistan also hoped that the ECO would permit it to develop access to the region's energy resources while exporting textiles, telecommunications equipment and machinery. Pakistan also seems to have understood the ECO's territorial configuration to comprise a 'web of strategic interests around it as a way to contain India's potential influence in the region.'[33] Through the ECO, Pakistan was able to tender several credit offers to the Central Asian states. However, as will be discussed below, Pakistan was unable to bring these agreements to fruition due to regional problems and its own fiscal weaknesses.[34]

Pakistan's strategic situation weakened with the establishment of the Shanghai Five in 1996, which developed into the Shanghai Cooperation Organization (SCO) in 2001.[35] The SCO is comprised of China, Russia, Uzbekistan, Tajikistan, Kyrgyzstan, and Kazakhstan and has maintained the agenda of the Shanghai Five of advancing mutual economic interests, fostering military trust among its members *and* combating Islamist radicalism.[36] (In many senses, Pakistan could be seen as an early target of this anti-Islamist radicalism objective.) In recent years, the SCO has developed an explicitly anti-US position and opposes American military and political presence in Central Asia.[37] While several countries have expressed interest in joining as full-fledged members (India, Pakistan, Iran, Mongolia, Turkmenistan), Chinese and Russian officials explained prior to the May 2007 summit that no additional countries could be admitted until an accession mechanism is created.[38]

The SCO significantly constrained Pakistan's Central Asian as pirations, at least in part, because it permits non-Islamic states such as Russia and China to have greater access to the region and preferentially situates them to access the region's energy resources. For this reason, a number of states including India, Pakistan, Afghanistan, and Iran, among others, have expressed interest in participating in this regional forum in different capacities. While Russia and Kazakhstan support India's entry into the SCO as a full-fledged member, China's support for Pakistan's bid has been joined by Tashkent, reflecting significant rapprochement between Pakistan and Uzbekistan. Islamabad and Tashkent now opine that they share a common enemy in terrorism. Uzbekistan's manoeuvring towards Pakistan, in all probability, reflects its interest in accessing the Arabian Sea through Pakistan's ports in Gwadar and Karachi. Until 2005, considerable friction existed between the two due to, among other concerns, the presence of Islamist militants associated with the Islamic Movement of Uzbekistan (IMU) based in and operating out of Pakistan. Indeed, the 2007 purges of Uzbeks from Pakistan's tribal areas is widely believed to be the result of an agreement reached by Presidents Musharraf and Islam Karimov during the latter's May 2006 visit to Pakistan, during which they inked a counter-terrorism agreement.[39] That visit was notable because it was Karimov's first official visit to Pakistan in over fourteen years.[40]

As a part of Pakistan's overall strategy for increasing its presence in Central Asia and beyond is the deep water port that it is building with Chinese assistance in Gwadar, in Pakistan's violence-prone Baluchistan province. As described elsewhere in this volume, this port is important for Pakistan's Central Asia strategy and economic growth for several reasons. Given the chronic instability in the Gulf region and its proximity to the Straits of Hormuz, the port may provide stable access for the Gulf ports. (This may remain elusive due to the ongoing strife in Baluchistan that has arisen in part due to the modalities of the port's construction.) Second, the port is likely to become an important regional shipping hub, providing the landlocked Central Asian republics, Afghanistan and the Chinese Xinjiang region, with coveted access to the Arabian Sea. Pakistan is building a road link between Gwadar and Saindak, which will run parallel to the Iran–Pakistan border. This will be the shortest route linking Central Asia and the Arabian Sea, facilitating the movement of Central Asian energy resources to world markets, augmenting Pakistan's coffers with significant profits from transit fees.[41]

However, before Pakistan can reap the rewards of Gwadar, including the allure of foreign investment in the area, it will have to find some means of contending with the violence that episodically takes place in Gwadar and elsewhere in Baluchistan. While some of this violence is the handiwork of the Al-Qaeda, local Baluchi militants who are deeply distrustful of the Gwadar project and angry over Islamabad's utilization of Baluchistan's gas resources, frequently attack gas pipelines, disrupting energy flows. These attacks are probably intended to impose significant financial loss to punish the centre for its policies and to coerce Islamabad to be more accommodating towards the Baluchis' interests. Some Baluchis worry that the economic gains of the project will benefit the other provinces, not Baluchistan and the Baluchis.

Islamabad must find some means to accommodate the demands of the local Baluchis who view the port as detrimental to their own economic interests and who harbour numerous grievances about the federal government's chronically low-levels of investment in the region. With the ongoing domestic turmoil in Pakistan over the return to democracy, the residual role of the army in Pakistan's governance and the modalities of this next phase of democracy, resolving the Baluchistan impasse may not be likely in the near term. As such violence and terrorism may continue to plague Baluchistan and mitigate the benefits that Pakistan could otherwise realize from the Gwadar port project and related expanded infrastructure.

▩ Afghanistan

Pakistan's goals for Afghanistan remain largely unchanged over the past sixty years. Since Pakistan's inception, it has sought to counter the demand advanced by nearly every Afghan government that an independent state be established for Pakistan's Pashtun population. Second, Islamabad would like the future Afghan government to drop its juridical vacuous claim that the Durand Line is not the de jure border separating the two states. (In 1893, Sir Henry Mortimer Durand, a diplomat and civil servant of colonial British India and foreign secretary of India from 1884 to 1894, negotiated and demarcated the boundary between Afghanistan and British India with agents of the Amir of Afghanistan, Abdul Rahman Khan. Today, the Durand Line is considered the international border between Afghanistan and Pakistan.) Third, and related to the first two objectives above, Islamabad has sought to establish a regime in Kabul that is 'friendly', if not deferential, to Islamabad. Pakistan has yet to see Afghanistan as a neighbour rather than a proxy and this is, in part, due to Kabul's own noxious rhetoric regarding the border and Pakistan's Pashtun population. Pakistan also seeks to thwart India's influence on its western flank and to deny India access to Afghanistan, from where it could harass Pakistan. All of these goals are interrelated and derive in large measure from Pakistan's fears that India may encourage Afghanistan to stoke ethnic fissures within Pakistan as just desserts for Pakistan's efforts to exploit India's ethnic and religious differences.

Finally, Pakistan has long hoped that Afghanistan could provide it access to Central Asia, especially to its commercial and hydrocarbon markets, as well as to permit Pakistan to project its influence politically and culturally. India and Pakistan — along with China and Russia, among others — are competing for access and influence in the new Great Game.

To achieve these objectives, Pakistan has exploited Afghanistan's ethnic fissures and has prosecuted a variety of (largely failed) policies to support Afghanistan's Pashtuns out of the belief that a Pasthun-dominated Afghanistan would be more pliable and even sympathetic towards Pakistan. As described before, Pakistan supported a number of jihadi organizations in the 1990s, preferring the Pashtun Gulbaddin Hekmatyar over others and switched to the Taliban in the early 1990s when Hekmatyar proved to be a failure. However, as noted, the Taliban too failed to deliver and many within the Pakistani security establishment argued for a revised policy with respect to the Taliban long before 9/11. For them, 9/11 afforded an excuse to dump the Taliban at long last.

Indeed, it is clearly in Pakistan's interests to have a stable Afghanistan. A prosperous Afghanistan would no doubt create numerous opportunities for Pakistani products and services. If Afghanistan was to be pacified and safe roads and other lines of communications could be constructed and used, Pakistan would have access to the Central Asian markets that it craves. Similarly, a stable Afghanistan would make several gas pipelines more feasible (such as the proposed Tajikistan–Afghanistan–Pakistan–India pipeline). Currently, Pakistan's bilateral trade with Afghanistan surpasses $2 billion annually. (Pakistani exports to Afghanistan total $1.2 billion and Afghanistan's exports to Pakistan total $700 million.) Indeed, trade volume has increased since the fall of the Taliban, when bilateral trade was only $25 million. In 2003–04, bilateral trade was only 492 million and for 2004–05, the figure climbed to $1.63 billion, mainly because of exports. Because of its geographic, ethnic and cultural proximity, Pakistan has emerged as a major Afghan trading partner in the reconstruction efforts. Worryingly, Pakistani manufactures may be losing out to Indian and Iranian competition. In 2006–07, exports actually declined by almost $400 million over the previous year.[42]

While there is little doubt that a stable and prosperous Afghanistan is in Pakistan's long-term interests, Pakistan must ultimately maintain a contingency plan. In many ways, Pakistan' strategic picture with respect to Afghanistan has decisively worsened since 11 September. As noted above, India and Kabul have forged extremely prominent ties and Kabul openly antagonizes Pakistan about the disposition of their border, which some Pakistanis believe is tacitly goaded on by India. Pakistan also notes with anxiety the under-representation of Pashtuns in the current government, whose composition favours the Tajiks, Uzbeks and Hazaras — the ethnic minorities that comprised the Northern Alliance and which closely allied with India, Iran, Tajikistan and Russia during the Taliban period.

While a strong international presence — especially an American presence — may dampen India's unfettered access to Afghanistan and its ability to harm Pakistan's interest, Islamabad has few illusions that Washington will remain in Afghanistan for very long. Pakistan's security managers also believe that once Washington withdraws, so will the other international actors, once again leaving Afghanistan open to predation by its near and distant neighbours. Thus, it is in Pakistan's interests to maintain ties with Pashtun militants and to support passively — if not actively — some elements of the Taliban currently at work. In the end, geography dictates Pakistan's compulsions. Unfortunately, Pakistan's preference for instability in order to curb India's influence decreases the likelihood of a stabilized Afghanistan, which would no doubt bring Pakistan greater value in the long run. Moreover, Afghan perceptions that Pakistan is at the core of Afghanistan's problems encourages Kabul to seek closer ties to Delhi and to adopt antagonizing postures on issues such as the Durand Line. Prospects are bleak that this self-defeating cycle of distrust and contingency planning can be broken.

▨ Iran

Prior to the Iranian Revolution, Iran and Pakistan were allied with the United States through the Baghdad Pact, which later became the Central Treaty Organization (CENTO). During the 1965 and 1971 Indo-Pakistan wars, Iran provided Pakistan with modest support during the war but substantial post-war recovery assistance. The Iranian revolution broke the strategic relationship between Tehran and Washington, and by extension with Islamabad. The Iran–Iraq war put Islamabad and Tehran upon divergent paths with Pakistan supporting the Arab Gulf states and Iran employing belligerent rhetoric to chastise the same. During their war, Iran and Iraq turned Pakistan into a proxy battlefield that fostered the enduring sectarian conflict that persists in Pakistan to date.[43]

While Tehran became a chief antagonist to Washington after 1979, Islamabad became ever more tightly allied to the United States, following the Soviet invasion of Afghanistan. While Pakistan became a key player in that conflict, Iran remained a marginal player. Pakistan's territory was the primary training and staging ground for the mujahideen who were also recruited from Pakistan, particularly among Afghan refugees. In contrast, Iran's material support to the resistance was minimal and focused upon the Hazara Shias. The collapse of the Afghan state sharpened the difference between Iran and Pakistan. Saudi Arabia — Iran's strategic rival — supported the Afghan mujahideen and later the Taliban, along with Pakistan and the United States and in fact solidified Riyadh's sphere of influence in both Afghanistan and Pakistan.

Afghanistan has been, and remains, a significant point of contention between Tehran and Islamabad. Iran, like Pakistan, bore a heavy burden with several million Afghan refugees living in

Iran before the fall of the Taliban. Iran was deeply bothered by the presence of Deobandi and Salafist militants in Pakistan and Afghanistan who were tightly allied with its strategic competitor and exporter of Wahhabism, Saudi Arabia. This is, at least in part, because for Iran, security implies the preservation of its state ideology as well as the promotion and protection of its Shia tradition and the protection of Shias beyond Iran. All of these interests were threatened by the Taliban and anti-Shia Sunni groups operating in Pakistan.[44]

As noted above, relations between the two precipitously soured after the fall of Mazar-e-Sharif to the Taliban in 1998. The Taliban assassinated the above-noted Iranian diplomats (believed by many to be spies) and slaughtered thousands of Hazara Shias as well. Iran remains concerned about the fate of Shias in Pakistan as they are the predominant victim in Pakistan's sectarian clashes. This is indeed ironic: Iran was responsible, in large measure, for initiating the sectarian conflicts in Pakistan in the 1970s, both to frustrate Zia-ul-Haq's efforts to Islamize Pakistan as a decisively Sunni state and to promote its revolutionary ideals during the Iran–Iraq war. In response, Zia welcomed the patronage of Arab Gulf states to build Deobandi and Ahl-e-Hadis madaris in Pakistan and supported a number of Sunni militias to counter those supported, trained and armed by Iran. Thus the issue of sectarian violence in Pakistan persists as an irritant for both capitals.

Despite the fall of Taliban and Pakistan's ostensible abandoning of its former clients, they continue to disagree on the preferred political arrangement in Afghanistan with Iran continuing to support those associated with the 'Northern Alliance' and Pakistan's persistent preference for the Pashtuns as once embodied in the Taliban. Indeed, Iran remains dubious of Pakistan and continues to see Pakistan as a 'corrupt, unstable, historically pro-American and basically artificial nation-state' and derides its short history as inferior to its own ancient civilization.[45] While Iran has tried to work with the various Pakistani governments, fundamentally Tehran distrusts Islamabad. Since 2000, Iran has worked to develop important security ties with India, despite the substantive and expansive security relations that Delhi enjoys with both Tel Aviv and Washington.[46]

Since 9/11 and Pakistan's alliance with the United States and concomitant use of Pakistani territory for US and coalition military activities in Afghanistan, Iran remains dubious of Pakistan. Relations between the two have been further strained by the election of Iran's hard-line president Mahmoud Ahmadinejad and the evolving nuclear confrontation between Iran and the West. Pakistan's position towards Iran's nuclear programme is delicate as Iran acquired technology and hardware from Pakistan via A.Q. Khan's nuclear arms market. Moreover, Pakistan fears Iran's alliance with India and believes that India now enjoys a solid military, intelligence and commercial presence in Iran. Indeed, India's relations with Iran are critical to India's own Central Asia strategy and afford India access to Afghanistan, as noted above. Pakistani interlocutors increasingly claim that India has exploited its consulate (read 'listening post') in Zahedan in Iran's Sistan-o-Baluchistan province both to instigate Baluchi separatists in Pakistan and to fuel the instability in this resource-rich region.[47]

Despite geographical proximity, the overall trade volume between the two is low ($394 million in 2004).[48] While Pakistan surely could benefit from better ties with Iran (especially with regard to hydrocarbon resources), there are serious sources of economic and strategic competition between the two. Pakistan is building a deep water port in Gwadar with Chinese assistance. The port is essential to China's efforts to diversify its crude oil supplies and both Beijing and Islamabad anticipate that the port will deliver them important economic and military gains. For this reason, India and Iran construe the port as a potential threat to their economic interests and security and as an important competitor to Iran's Chahbahar port, built with Indian assistance. Notably, Chahbahar is only a few hundred kilometres upon the Makran coast from Gwadar. Indeed, Gwadar has 'raised eyebrows in neighbouring India and Iran over Sino-Pakistan maritime activities and has sparked a tacit competition over whether Pakistan's Gwadar port or Iran's Chabahar port …will serve as Central Asia's conduit to warm waters.'[49]

▨ Central Asian Republics

When the Central Asian states became independent, Pakistan expressed what one Pakistan-based analyst called 'over enthusiasm' for establishing closer ties to those states.[50] Pakistan's initial ventures in the Central Asian republics were economic in nature and relied heavily upon the aforementioned ECO. Pakistan began its courtship of the Central Asian countries with a high-level delegation, led by the then minister of state for economic affairs, Sardar Asif Ahmed Ali. Between 24 November and 15 December 2001, his team visited Russia and the Central Asian republics. Remarking upon the initiative, the then secretary general of foreign affairs Akram Zaki pronounced that 'recognition of the Central Asian states would open new vistas of bilateral cooperation with these states with whom Pakistan has close ties of history, faith and culture'.[51]

From this engagement, Pakistan tendered some $10 million each in credit to Kazakhstan, Kyrgyzstan and Tajikistan in an effort to 'establish joint ventures in cotton, textiles, garments, pharmaceuticals engineering goods, surgical instruments, telecommunications and agro-industry'.[52] Pakistan also made an agreement with Uzbekistan to establish satellite communications, build highways, produce tele-communications equipment jointly and manufacture some of the materials for the Central Asian Railways.[53] Pakistan's cooperation with Uzbekistan in fact became most prominent, with wide-ranging agreements in the areas of joint trade ventures, scientific and cultural cooperation, education, and tourism. Pakistan signed agreements to import hydroelectric power from Tajikistan and Kyrgyzstan in 1992 and forged joint economic commissions with all of the Central Asian states. Pakistan also set up fully funded training facilities for these states, spanning 'English language instruction, banking, accounting, insurance, and postal service to diplomacy.'[54] Despite the turbulence that later emerged, these programmes continued.

However the success of these early ventures was limited because of the yawning gap between Pakistan's intent and its capability. Dianne Smith suggests that these failures were due do regional in-stability (in Tajikistan, Afghanistan), Pakistan's inadequate lines of communication and control, and its limited financial resources.[55] However, Pakistan's decision to support Pashtun elements in Afghanistan's civil war against the Uzbek and Tajik ethnic groups became deeply problematic, particularly when Pakistan shifted its support to the Taliban in 1994. Tajikistan and Uzbekistan, which share borders with Afghanistan, were particularly vexed by Pakistan's policies. Islamists opposing the regimes in both Tajikistan and Uzbekistan had ties with the Al-Qaeda and the Taliban and received training in Afghanistan. Given Pakistan's commitment to a Pashtun-dominated Afghanistan, the gap between Islamabad, on the one hand, and Tashkent and Dushanbe, on the other, widened.[56]

After 2001 and Pakistan's refurbished regional image, Pakistan has reinvigorated its efforts with continued high-level delegations to the region and has again found an opportunity to re-engage its

Central Asian neighbours. However, acrimony that arose during the Taliban period has not entirely diminished. Indeed, since 2005, analysts increasingly believe that Pakistan is passively, if not actively, supporting anti-government elements in Afghanistan, which is not welcome news to its near and distant neighbours.[57]

Another hindrance to Pakistan solidifying its ties with Central Asia (and for that matter with Russia) is the presence of foreign fighters in Pakistan's tribal areas (the Federally Administrated Tribal Areas along the Pakistan–Afghanistan border). Many of these fighters were in Afghanistan supporting the Taliban when US forces came in from the north, forcing those fighters out of Afghanistan and into Pakistan's tribal belt. Since 2002, and especially since 2004, Pakistan has sustained military operations against those militants in South and North Waziristan. (Those operations tend to rely upon the Frontier Corps, a paramilitary organization.) As noted, it is widely believed that purported 'tribal rebellion' in North Waziristan to oust Uzbeks came out of the May 2006 Karimov–Musharraf summit in Islamabad.

The basic objectives that animate the government of Pakistan and those of the Central Asian states remain stable, emphasizing commercial and economic interests and fundamental political goodwill. Pakistan necessarily hopes to situate itself advantageously vis-à-vis India. All parties involved recognize Pakistan's potential as an important trade and energy corridor, as reflected not only in China's investments in Gwadar but also in its commitment of $350 million to upgrade the Karakoram Highway, linking Pakistan to China and onwards to Central Asia. Additionally, Pakistan, China, Kazakhstan and Kyrgyzstan signed a quadrilateral trade and transit agreement that has worked since 2004. In principal, this can also be extended to Uzbekistan and Tajikistan.[58] Many in the region are also hopeful that an Iran–Pakistan–India pipeline may emerge, despite Washington's vociferous and vigorous objections. There is also support for the Turkmenistan–Afghanistan–Pakistan–India pipeline, which Washington prefers.[59]

As noted above, Pakistan is in principle an ideal corridor for Central Asia's international trade. However, Afghanistan's continued instability and Pakistan's lack of adequate lines of control linking Gwadar and Karachi to Torkham (the prominent legal crossing point for goods between Pakistan and Afghanistan) dampen the prospects for this corridor's emergence in the policy-relevant future. Tajikistan and Kyrgyzstan has significant potential for hydroelectric power, which Pakistan would like to access.

▧ Conclusions

Fundamentally, Pakistan's strategic objectives with respect to Iran, Afghanistan and the Central Asian republics remain unchanged since the early 1990s. However, Pakistan's strategic environment *has* changed substantially and largely for the worse since the demise of the Taliban regime in Afghanistan. In the wake of 9/11, Pakistan was able to recuperate its international image by turning on the Taliban and joining the war on terrorism. Pakistan has received wide accolades for its enormous sacrifices in the war on terrorism. This praise is deserved: Pakistan has sacrificed more troops than any other ally in the war.

However, in the intervening years since 2001, there have been consistent accusations that Pakistan has once again begun supporting Pashtun militants in Afghanistan. These allegations along with deepening domestic terrorist problems in Pakistan and the discovery of episodic international terror groups with ties to Pakistan — howsoever tenuous — jeopardize the goodwill that Pakistan's heroic decision garnered in the early years after 9/11. Pakistan's ability to continue improving its relations with its near and distant neighbour may well depend on the veracity — or lack thereof of those claims — and upon Pakistan's own domestic instability.

Many of the impediments to success that plagued these efforts in the 1990s persist and are likely to do so for the foreseeable future. Afghanistan remains unstable and some analysts have even argued that Pakistan may prefer an unstable Afghanistan to one that is stable and solidly aligned with India — even if this imposes economic opportunity costs to Pakistan over the long term.[60] Pakistan's fiscal weaknesses, dearth of extant lines of control, domestic instability in key areas (such as Gwadar, Karachi) are all important internal hindrances that do not auger well for Islamabad's success.

Meanwhile, India with its large and growing economy continues to establish strong relations with Iran, Afghanistan and the Central Asian states based upon a wide swathe of common interests, including economic cooperation, cultural exchanges, as well as counter-terrorism, defence and other intelligence and security-related forms of engagement. Increasingly, Pakistan is finding itself outflanked in its own backyard. Dismantling the substantial barriers precluding Pakistan's success in Central Asia may simply be beyond Islamabad's capabilities at present and for the foreseeable future.

▩ Notes

1. This article first appeared in the *Journal of Strategic Studies*, 31(2), April 2008. The author is grateful to the editors of the *Journal of Strategic Studies*, the editors at Routledge and Dr Jetly for their accommodation. The author is also thankful to the external reviewer as also Dr Jetly for their thoughtful suggestions for revisions to this chapter. While this chapter was written while the author was Senior Research Associate at the United States Institute of Peace, she is currently Senior Political Scientist at RAND. This essay reflects the personal views of the author and not of USIP or RAND. The information cut-off for this chapter is October 2007.

2. Simon Scot Plummer, 'Pakistan, Epicenter of Global Instability', *Telegraph.co.uk*, 27 September 2007 (accessed 7 October 2007).

3. Juli A. MacDonald, 'South Asia', in *Central Asia and the South Caucasus: Reorientations, Internal Transitions, and Strategic Dynamics-C*, Conference Report, National Intelligence Council, October 2000, http: // www. fas.org/irp/nic/central_asia.html (accessed 1 August 2008). For a solid Pakistani assessment of its interests, see Asma Shakir Khawaja, *Pakistan and the 'New Great Game*, IPRI Paper 5 (Islamabad: Islamabad Policy Research Institute, April 2003), http:// www.ipripak.org/papers/ pakandnewgame.shtml (accessed 1 August 2008).

4. For a recent assessment of India's relations with Central Asia, see Scott Moore, 'Peril and Promise: A Survey of India's Strategic Relationship with Central Asia', *Central Asian Survey*, June 2007, 26(2), pp. 279–91.

5. Ross H. Munro, 'Security Implications of the Competition for Influence among Neighboring States: China, India, and Central Asia', in Jed C. Snyder (ed.), *After Empire: The Emerging Geopolitics of Central Asia* (Washington, DC: National Defense University Press, 1999), p.133; Jefferson E. Turner, 'What's Driving India's and Pakistan's Interest in Joining the Shanghai Cooperation Organization?', *Strategic Insights*, August 2005, IV(8), http://www.ccc.nps.navy.mil/si/2005/Aug/ turnerAug05.asp (accessed 2 August 2008).

6. During the Soviet jihad, Pakistan backed seven Pakistan-based militant groups, six of which were Pashtun dominated. Burhanuddin Rabbani's, Tajik-dominated Jamiat-i-Islami was the only non-Pashtun group supported by Pakistan.

7. Aly Zaman, 'India's Increased Involvement in Afghanistan and Central Asia: Implications for Pakistan', *IPRI Journal* (Summer 2003), http: //www. ipripak.org/journal/summer2003/indiaincreased.shtml (accessed 1 August 2008).

8. Chidanand Rajghatta and Kamal Siddiqui, 'Pak cries foul over US revenge strike', *Indian Express*, 22 August 1998, http:// indian-express.com/res/web/pIe/ie/daily/19980822/23450784.html (accessed 1 August 2008).

9. 'Reporters see wrecked Buddhas,' *BBC News*, 26 March 2001, http.//news.bbc.co.uk/1/hi/world/south_asia/1242856.stm (accessed 1 August 2008).

10. See Frederic Grare, *Pakistan–Afghanistan Relations in the Post-9/11 Era*, Carnegie Papers, No. 72 (Washington, DC: Carnegie Endowment for International Peace, October 2006), www.carnegieendowment. org/publications/index.cfm?fa=view&id=18740&prog=zgp&proj=zsa, (accessed 1 August 2008); and Seth G. Jones, 'Pakistan's Dangerous Game', *Survival*, Spring 2007, 49(1), pp. 15–32.

11. Fazl-ur-Rahman, 'Pakistan's Evolving Relations with China, Russia and Central Asia', in Iwashita Akihiro (ed.), *Eager Eyes Fixed on Eurasia: Russia and Its Neighbors in Crisis* (Sapporo, Hokkaido: Slavic Research Center, 2007), p. 226, http://src-h.slav.hokudai.ac.jp/coe21/publish/no16_1_ses/contents.html (accessed 1 August 2008).

12. Shireen T. Hunter, 'Religion, Politics, and Security in Central Asia', *SAIS Review*, Summer–Fall 2001, XXI(2), p. 81.

13. Ahmed Rashid, 'The Taliban: Exporting Terrorism', *Foreign Affairs*, November–December 1999, 78(6), pp. 22–35; Dietrich Reetz, 'Islamic Activism in Central Asia and the Pakistan Factor', *Journal of South Asian and Middle Eastern Studies*, Fall 1999, XXIII(1), pp. 1–37; Hunter, 'Religion, Politics, and Security in Central Asia'.

14. 'Taliban resumes Afghan offensive as Iran gathers forces', *CNN Online*, 12 September 1998, http://edition.cnn.com/WORLD/meast/9809/12/iran.afghanistan/index.html (accessed 1 August 2008).

15. See Frederic Grare, *Pakistan–Afghanistan Relations in the Post-9/11 Era*; Marvin Weinbaum, *Afghanistan and its Neighbors: An Ever Dangerous Neighborhood*, USIP Special Report No. 162 (Washington, DC: United States Institute of Peace, June 2006), www.usip.org/pubs/specialreports/sr162.pdf (accessed 1 August 2008).

16. Jones, 'Pakistan's Dangerous Game'.

17. Pakistani officials interviewed by the author in Kabul in August 2007 have used extremely pejorative language to describe Aslam Beg's once-praised approach to the region. Similarly, a high-ranking Pakistani army official visiting Washington in May 2007 also rubbished the concept.

18. 'Musharraf rejects using Afghanistan as strategic depth in case of aggression: TV', *People's Daily Online*, 20 May 2006, http://english. peopledaily.com.cn/200605/20/eng20060520_267145.html (accessed 1 August 2008).

19. Adnan Sarwar Khan, 'Pakistan's Foreign Policy in the Changing International Scenario', *The Muslim World*, April 2006, vol. 96, p. 241.

20. Aly Zaman, 'India's Increased Involvement in Afghanistan and Central Asia: Implications for Pakistan'.

21. Daniel P. Sullivan, 'Tinder, Spark, Oxygen, and Fuel: The Mysterious Rise of the Taliban', *Journal of Peace Research*, 2007, 44(1), pp. 93–108; Barnett Rubin, 'Afghanistan Under the Taliban', *Current History*, February 1999, 98(625), pp. 79–91.

22. Noor-ul-Haq, Sadia Nasir, *Pak-Afghan Relations, IPRI Factfile*, V(8) (Islamabad: Islamabad Policy Research Institute, August 2003).

23. Government of India, Ministry of External Affairs, 'Rebuilding Afghanistan: India at Work', CD on India's efforts provided to the author by the Embassy of India, Kabul.

24. For a list of Indian consulates in Afghanistan in addition to the embassy, see http.//www.meaindia.nic.in/cgi-bin/db2www/meaxpsite/indmission. d2w/Generals (accessed 7 October 2007).

25. Scott Baldauf, 'India–Pakistan Rivalry Reaches into Afghanistan', *Christian Science Monitor*, 12 September 2003, cited Frederic Grare, *Pakistan–Afghanistan Relations in the Post-9/11 Era*, p. 12.

26. Gaurang Bhatt, 'RAW is Training 600 Baluchis in Afghanistan: Mushahid Hussain', *boloji.com*, 14 May 2006, http.//www.boloji.com/ analysis2/0116.htm (accessed 1 August 2008).

27. Stephen Blank, 'India: The New Central Asian Player. A EurasiaNet Commentary', *Eurasia Insight*, 26 June 2006, http://www.eurasianet. org/departments/insight/articles/eav062606a.shtml (accessed 1 August 2008). Stephen Blank, 'India's Rising Profile in Central Asia', *Comparative Strategy*, April–June 2003, 22(2), pp. 139–57.

28. Declan Walsh, 'As Taliban insurgency gains strength and sophistication, suspicion falls on Pakistan', *The Guardian*, 13 November 2006,http:// www.guardian.co.uk/world/2006/nov/13/afghanistan.declanwalsh (accessed 1 August 2008).

29. A Pakistani official at the Embassy of Pakistan in Kabul claims that there are in fact more than '300 Indian commandos in Afghanistan'. (This is clear from the rest of the note!) Indian interlocutors claim that there are several hundred personnel from the paramilitary outfit, the Indo-Tibetan Police Force (ITPF). They argue that the ITPF is perfectly suited for this task given that it routinely works in challenging security areas at altitude. Based on interviews with high-level Pakistani embassy officials in Kabul in August 2007 and with high-level embassy officials at the Indian Embassy in Kabul in August 2007.

30. Estimates of Pakistan's Shia population vary wildly because areas that are traditionally heavily populated with Shia (e.g. Pakistan's Northern Areas) are not enumerated in its census. Thus estimates range anywhere from 10 to 25 per cent.

31. C. Christine Fair, 'India and Iran: New Delhi's Balancing Act', *The Washington Quarterly*, Summer 2007, 30(3), pp. 145–59.

32. Shah Alam, 'Iran–Pakistan Relations: Political and Strategic Dimensions', *Strategic Analysis*, October–December 2004, 28(4), pp. 526–44.
33. Hamid Gul, ECO, 'Strategic Significance in the Context of Islamic Resurgence and Geopolitical Environment', in Tarik Jan et al. (eds), *Foreign Policy Debate: The Years Ahead* (Islamabad: Institute of Policy Studies, 1993), pp. 188–89.
34. Khan, 'Pakistan's Foreign Policy in the Changing International Scenario'; Tahir Amin, 'Pakistan, Afghanistan and the Central Asian States', in Ali Banuazizi and Myron Weiner (eds), *The New Geopolitics of Central Asia and its Borderlands* (Bloomington, IN: Indiana University Press, 1994), pp. 216–31; Dianne L. Smith, *Central Asia: A New Great Game?* (Washington, DC: Strategic Studies Institute, U.S. Army War College, 1996), http://www.strategicstudiesinstitute.army.mil/pdffiles/PUB117.pdf (accessed 1 August 2008). Turner, 'What's Driving India's and Pakistan's Interest'.
35. Ibid.
36. See Alyson J. K. Bailes, Pal Dunay, Pan Guang and Mikhail Troitskiy, *The Shanghai Cooperation Organisation*, SIPRI Policy Paper No. 71 (Stockholm: SIPRI, May 2007); Rajan Menon, 'The New Great Game in Central Asia', *Survival*, Summer 2003, 45(2), p. 198; Hunter, 'Religion, Politics, and Security in Central Asia', in *The Shanghai Cooperation Organisation*. For more information about the SCO, please see website of the Shainghai Cooperation Organization: www.sectsco.org (accessed 1 August 2008).
37. Joshua Kucera, 'Shanghai Cooperation Organisation Summiteers Take Shot at US Presence in Central Asia', *Eurasia Insight*, 20 August 2007, http://www.eurasianet.org/departments/insight/articles/eav082007a.shtml (accessed 1 August 2008).
38. Ibid.
39. For information about the conflict between the Ahmedzai Wazir militant commander Mullah Nazir who led the charge against Uzbeks under the leadership of IMU commander Qari Tahir Yuldashev, see M. Ilyas Khan, 'Pakistan's tribals–who is killing who?', *BBC Online*, 5 April 2007, http://news.bbc.co.uk/2/hi/south_asia/6529147.stm (accessed 1 August 2008). According to interlocutors in Pakistan interviewed in August 2007, the Ahmedzai Wazir tribesmen were 'assisted' by Pakistani military personnel who were called 'Punjabi tribesmen' casting aspersions upon Pakistan's official line that the uprising was a spontaneous effort of Pakistani tribesmen to route foreign terrorists seeking refuge in the Waziristan. For information on the Karimov visit, see Gulnoza Saidazimova, 'Uzbekistan: President Karimov Courts Pakistan to Boost Security, Trade', *Radio Free Europe/Radio Liberty*, 3 May 2006, http.//www. rferl.org/featuresarticle/2006/05/4b240d75-0485-49e1-83a3-91e29be566cd.html (accessed 10 October 2007).

40. Rahman, 'Pakistan's Evolving Relations with China, Russia and Central Asia'.
41. See Ziad Haider, 'Baluchis, Beijing, and Pakistan's Gwadar Port', *Georgetown Journal of International Affairs*, Winter–Spring 2005, pp. 95–103.
42. Marvin G. Weinbaum and Jonathan B. Harder, 'Pakistan's Afghan Policies and Their Consequences', *Contemporary South Asia*, March 2008, 16(1), pp.25–28; Barnett Rubin and Abubakar Siddique, *Resolving the Pakistan–Afghanistan Stalemate* (Washington, DC: U.S. Institute of Peace, 2006). Ashfaq Yusufzai, 'Trade-Pakistan: Smugglers Profit From Landlocked Afghanistan', *IPSNews.net*, 4 August 2007, http.//www.ipsnews.net/news.asp?idnews=38794 (accessed 7 October 2007).
43. John Calabrese, 'The Struggle for Security: New and Familiar Patterns in Iran–Pakistan Relations', *Journal of South Asian and Middle Eastern Studies*, Fall 1997, XXI(1), pp. 61–80; Hafeez Malik, 'Iran's Relations with Pakistan', *Journal of South Asian and Middle Eastern Studies*, Fall 2002, XXXVI(1), pp. 56–71.
44. Alam, 'Iran–Pakistan Relations: Political and Strategic Dimensions'.
45. Fred Halliday, 'Iran and the Middle East: Foreign Policy and Domestic Change', *Middle East Report*, Autumn 2001, No. 220, p. 44.
46. Fair, 'India and Iran'.
47. Ibid.
48. 'Pakistan–Iran preferential trade accord', The *Daily Times*, 3 March 2004, http://www.dailytimes.com.pk/default.asp?page=story_28-3-2004_pg5_8 (accessed 1 August 2008).
49. See Ziad Haider, 'Baluchis, Beijing, and Pakistan's Gwadar Port', p. 96.
50. Rahman, 'Pakistan's Evolving Relations with China, Russia and Central Asia'.
51. Cited by Fazl-ur-Rahman, 'Pakistan's Evolving Relations with China, Russia and Central Asia', p. 226.
52. Amin, 'Pakistan, Afghanistan and the Central Asian States', p. 221 cited by Turner, 'What's Driving India's and Pakistan's Interest in Joining the Shanghai Cooperation Organisation?'
53. Ibid.
54. Fazl-ur-Rahman, 'Pakistan's Evolving Relations with China, Russia and Central Asia', p. 227.
55. Smith, *Central Asia: A New Great Game?*
56. Fazl-ur-Rahman, 'Pakistan's Evolving Relations with China, Russia and Central Asia'.
57. For a recent example of such suspicion, see Jones, 'Pakistan's Dangerous Game'.
58. Fazl-ur-Rahman, 'Pakistan's Evolving Relations with China, Russia and Central Asia'.

59. Dan Millison (Asian Development Bank, South Asia Energy Division), 'Turkmenistan–Afghanistan–Pakistan–India Natural Pipeline Project', November 2006, http://meaindia.nic.in/srec/internalpages/tapi.pdf (accessed 1 August 2008).

60. See Frederic Grare, *Pakistan–Afghanistan Relations in the Post-9/11 Era*; Weinbaum, *Afghanistan and its Neighbors: An Ever Dangerous Neighborhood.*

✳

7

The Spectre of Islamic Fundamentalism over Pakistan (1947–2007)

Ishtiaq Ahmed

Pakistan emerged as a Muslim-majority state on the Indian subcontinent on 14 August 1947 as a result of the north-western and north-eastern zones — where the Muslims were in a majority in contiguous areas — being separated from the rest of India. The basic argument put forth by the Muslim League, a party of the Western-educated modern Muslim elite that spearheaded the struggle for Pakistan, was that Indian Muslims, by virtue of their religion, constituted a nation separate and distinct from Hindus and other religious communities of India. Therefore, they were entitled to a separate, independent and sovereign state, where they could practise their way of life freely.

The modernist elite that came to power in independent Pakistan tried to accommodate Islamic precepts and norms in the constitutional process with a view to making Pakistan both Islamic and democratic. What such a practice, however, facilitated was incremental movement of the constitutional process towards fundamentalist Islamic ideology at the expense of democracy and equal rights of citizens. In 1977, when power passed into the hands of a man with unequivocal fundamentalist sympathies — General Muhammad Zia-ul-Haq, he unabashedly employed state power to enforce a comprehensive programme of 'Islamization' on Pakistan. Later, in the early 1980s when Pakistan became a front-line state in the jihad, sponsored by the United States and Saudi Arabia, against the Soviet Union's intervention in neighbouring Afghanistan, fundamentalism was cultivated as a violent creed and holy warriors were trained to use force and violence to defeat the enemies of Islam. However, after the terrorist attacks of 11 September 2001, General Pervez Musharraf, a modernist by conviction, was pressured by the United States and other nations to change course: Pakistan joined the 'war on terror'. This greatly angered the fundamentalists, with the result that the Pakistani state came into direct conflict with the fundamentalists.

It is concluded that Islamic fundamentalism is incompatible with a pluralist, democratic, and human rights-friendly social and political order. It is violence-prone and therefore amenable to terrorist activities.

The current estimated population of Pakistan is nearly 165 million. The 1998 population census gives a total population of over 132 million. The Muslim component (Sunnis and Shias) is given as 96.28 per cent; Christians 1.59 per cent; caste Hindus 1.60 per cent; scheduled castes 0.25 per cent; Qadianis or Ahmadis 0.22 per cent; and others 0.07 per cent. The Sunni and Shia proportions of the Muslim population are not given. This has been the consistent standard policy over the years. The CIA's online World Fact book gives the estimated current population of Pakistan as over 165 million, of which the religious and sectarian composition is given as: Muslim 97 per cent (Sunni 77 per cent, Shia 20 per cent), others (including Christians and Hindus) 3 per cent. According to the Demographic Research Institute of Karachi University, the Shias make up 12–15 per cent of the Muslim population.[1]

▨ Fundamentalism

The term 'fundamentalism' originated in the United States in the early twentieth century as a reaction by some Protestant laymen to the challenges posed by modernity, liberalism, evolutionism and the scientific method to their *Weltanschauung,* deriving from dogmatic theology. The inerrancy of revealed truth as preserved in the Bible was the core belief of Christian fundamentalism. Moreover, a literal reading of biblical text was declared imperative and binding. In the 1970s, 'fundamentalism' began to be applied as a generic term to revivalist and puritanical religious movements the world over that felt intellectually threatened by modernity and its concomitant uncertainties as well as politically by liberal notions of human rights and democracy.

In *The Fundamentalism Project* — a multi-year study of fundamentalist movements around the world, the editors, Martin E. Marty and R. Scott Appleby, have brought together an impressive array of scholars on religion and culture, although Islamic fundamentalism in South Asia is conspicuous by its absence in the two central volumes, *Fundamentalisms and Society* and *Fundamentalisms and the State.*[2] The editors point out that fundamentalist trends are to be found in all cultures (religions). They observe that religious fundamentalism has appeared in the present times as a mindset prevalent among religious communities and certain individuals and movements whereby they try to preserve their distinct identity. Perceiving that such identity is threatened, they fortify it by a selective retrieval of doctrines, beliefs and practices from a sacred past.[3]

▩ Islamic Fundamentalism

Islamic fundamentalism can be defined as a totalitarian ideology — anti-liberal, anti-pluralism, anti-democratic and anti-gender equality — derived from a selective and literal interpretation of sacred sources such as the Quran and the Sunnah (sayings and doings of the Prophet Muhammad preserved in several authoritative collections known as books of Hadith), and pristine Islamic history from the time of Muhammad and his immediate successors. This ideology, the fundamentalists hope to realize through the agency of the Islamic state, which is believed to have been established by the Prophet Muhammad in the seventh century.

The ideal of a perfect Islamic state has fascinated Muslims throughout history, and movements have emanated from time to time to re-establish it. The Sunnis consider the period of 29 years after Muhammad's death (AD 632–61) when his four successors, the pious caliphs, were in power as a continuation of the ideal state and hence worth emulating.[4] The Shias restrict the period of the ideal Islamic state after Muhammad only to the time when Ali, the last of the first four successors, was briefly in power (AD 656–661). There are other serious theological differences too between these two major groups. Over the centuries, other sects and sub-sects within the Sunnis and Shias, have also come into being.

Core Ideas of Fundamentalist Ideology

The centrepiece of the Islamic fundamentalist project is the imposition of dogmatic Islamic law, the sharia, in all departments of life — individual, collective, cultural, and political, and so on. The sharia is believed to be based on divine revelation and represents God's will. It was revealed to the Prophet Muhammad over a period of 22 years and is preserved in the form of ethical principles and legal precepts in the Quran and the Sunnah. There are some other sources too for elaboration of the sharia but the Quran and Sunnah are the most authoritative. The Islamic state is expected to maintain a social and political order reflecting the will of God and includes laws that maintain a normative standard according to which violations of sharia can be punished.[5] The sharia was developed and systematized during the pre-modern period: between the seventh and the sixteenth centuries. Consequently, it reflects the norms and values of tribal and agrarian societies that obtained during that period.

Fundamentalist Politics

A political programme derived from Islamic fundamentalism invariably sets in motion a backward-looking political thought process and concomitant activities purporting to revive the ideal Islamic state. Any effort to realize such a project is bound to come into conflict with the social, economic and political conditions that exist objectively in the contemporary period. But however backward-looking and reactionary Sunni and Shia fundamentalist movements may be in relation to perceived worldwide Westernization and secularization trends underway in Muslim societies, they are nevertheless not totally opposed to token accommodation of modern ideas in case the situation in hand demands some adjustments.

Consequently, while in tribal societies such as Saudi Arabia, no concessions have been made to modern ideas of universal adult franchise, in more urbanized and developed milieus such as Iran, elections and the right to vote have been accepted as legitimate additions to the political system, albeit not in consonance with the familiar liberal norms and values that underpin Western constitutionalism.[6] However, as a comprehensive ideology for reforming and restructuring state and society, Islamic fundamentalism is amenable to varied interpretations and applications in practice. In the political realm, Islamic fundamentalist parties and movements can adhere to constitutional means or rely on violence, or combine them both into a multi-faceted strategy to realize the objective of an Islamic state based on the full application of the dogmatic sharia.

The most well-known fundamentalist movement in the Muslim world in the twentieth century was the Muslim Brotherhood, founded by the Egyptian Hassan Al-Banna in 1928. The Muslim Brotherhood gained supporters in all corners of the Arab World, where it came into conflict mainly with radical, secular regimes such as those of Gamal Abdul Nasser in Egypt and the Baathists in Syria and Iraq. Shia fundamentalism began to assert itself from the 1950s to challenge the modernistic but authoritarian regime of the Shah of Iran. The Muslim Brotherhood was supported covertly by the American CIA against Nasser, while the Iranian fundamentalists received the same backing during the nationalist regime of Mohammad Mossadegh.[7] The Muslim Brotherhood maintained links with the spearhead of fundamentalism in Pakistan — Maududi's Jamaat-e-Islami. During the 1960s, the Muslim World League (founded 1962) emerged under the patronage of Saudi Arabia as a major international network of fundamentalist movements in Africa, the Middle East and Pakistan.[8] The three main ideologues of fundamentalism in the Muslim world who exercised great influence after the Second World War on Muslim societies have been the Sunni Syed Abul Ala Maududi of Pakistan and Syed Qutb of Eygpt and the Shia Ayatollah Khomeini of Iran.

Proto-fundamentalism in the Indian Subcontinent

However, revivalist Islamic movements, which can be termed as variants of proto-fundamentalism, predate Western modernity and the colonial intervention. In the Indian subcontinent, proto-fundamentalist movements began to emerge in reaction to the Mughal Emperor Akbar (1556–1605) seeking closer cooperation with the Hindu majority. During the time of the Emperor Akbar, Hindu princes and warrior castes were increasingly recruited into the army and given representation at the court. During his successor, Emperor Jahangir's reign, Shia influence also increased at the court. In these circumstances, Shaikh Ahmed Sirhindi emerged as a strong critic of those unorthodox trends.[9]

Later, in the eighteenth century when the main symbol of Muslim power in India, the Mughal Empire, began to weaken, Shah Waliullah started a revivalist Sunni movement with a view to restoring Islamic supremacy in the subcontinent. This was followed in the early nineteenth century by a militant jihad movement (holy war) led by Syed Ahmed Shaheed Berelvi against the Sikhs in the NWFP. It was inspired by the puritanical doctrines propounded by Shaikh Muhammad bin Abdul Wahab in the Arabian Peninsula in the eighteenth century. The Wahabis believed in armed struggle or jihad: they directed their ire not at the West, which at that time had no significant presence in the Middle East, but at the perceived deviation from unadulterated and true monotheistic Islam by traditional Sunnis and Shias. The belief in the cults of saints and Imams prevalent among them was considered accretions that had to be purged to establish pristine Islam.[10]

In 1867, an orthodox Sunni seat of learning was established at Deoband in northern India. Politically, the Deobandis adopted an anti-British approach and many of them were involved in clandestine anti-colonial movements. The Deobandis concluded that cooperation with the Hindu majority to drive the British out of the subcontinent was consistent with the Islamic idea of *wataniyat* (love for the homeland). Socially, the Deobandis remained conservative adhering to the conventional notion that women should be excluded from the public realm.[11]

However, the expanding British Empire in India relegated fundamentalist forces among not only Muslims, but also the Hindu majority, to the margins. Only for a short period of time after the First World War, between 1919 and 1921, did the Muslim *ulema* (clerics) play an active role in politics when they led a countrywide agitation, known as the Khilafat Movement, to dissuade the British from dismembering the Ottoman Empire.[12]

Most Muslims, however, belonged to the traditionalist Brelawi Sunni school of thought, given to saint worship and Sufi ideas. They maintained a distance from anti-colonial politics until after the Second World War when it became clear that the British would soon be withdrawing from India. They then switched their loyalty to the Muslim League and became the main religious force comprising clerics and incumbents on the Sufi shrines to support its idea of Pakistan.[13]

The Demand for a Muslim State

It was modern-educated Muslims, organized in the All-India Muslim League (founded 1906), who became leaders of the substantial Muslim minority of India. Although the demand for a separate Muslim state for the Muslim nation began to be aired by prominent Muslims from the early twentieth century, conventionally the presidential address delivered by Dr Muhammad Iqbal at the annual session of the Muslim League at Allahabad in 1930 is considered the first major claim to a separate Muslim state in India. However, it was not until the Muslim League passed the 23 March 1940 Lahore Resolution demanding separate Muslim state(s) that the idea of Pakistan began to be recognized as a serious manifestation of Muslim aspirations. Interestingly, thenceforth the focus of Muslim separatism shifted decisively from the Muslim minority provinces to the Muslim majority provinces of north-western and northern-eastern India. In particular, Muslim-majority Punjab became the focal point of separatist politics.[14]

Jinnah skilfully never clearly spelled out his vision of an independent Muslim state. When asked to elaborate on the kind of state that Pakistan would be, Jinnah dismissed the allegations that it would be a theocracy. This theme was consistently emphasized in interviews to foreign newspapers and broadcasting companies. For example, in 1946, he told the Reuters correspondent Doon Campbell: 'The new state would be a modern democratic state with sovereignty resting in the people and the members of the new nation having equal rights of citizenship regardless of their religion, caste or creed'.[15]

However, in order to galvanize support for Pakistan, he needed the help of the *ulema* (Muslim clerics) too as they had access to networks already existing through the mosque, and religious ceremonies and activities. The fundamentalist dimension in the Pakistan movement developed most strongly sometime in 1944, when the *ulema* and *pirs* (spiritual guides and teachers) of the Brelawi sub-sect were mobilized to support the demand for Pakistan.[16] The Brelawis represented a more traditional, Sufi-oriented type of Islam. Some dissident Deobandi *ulema* such as Maulana Ashraf Ali Thanvi and Shabbir Ahmed Usmani and their factions were also attracted to the idea of Pakistan and they rallied around the Muslim League.[17]

On the other hand, the anti-imperialist Deobandi Jamiyat Ulema-e-Hind remained opposed to a separate Muslim state and refused to recognize the Western-educated Muslim League and its leaders as representative of Islamic interests. Also, the future ideologue of Islamic fundamentalism in Pakistan, Syed Abul Ala Maududi, opposed the idea of creating a separate Muslim national state. His standpoint was that only when the purpose of creating a state was to establish a chaste Islamic order in the light of the sharia, could pious Muslims support such a movement.[18]

The strength of the Muslim League in the Muslim-majority provinces was going to be put to the test during the 1945–46 election campaign. Consequently, in the public meetings and mass contact campaigns, the Muslim League openly employed Islamic sentiments, slogans and heroic themes to rouse the masses. This is clearly stated in the fortnightly confidential report of 2 February 1946 sent to Viceroy Wavell by the Punjab Governor Sir Bertrand Glancy:

> The ML (Muslim League) orators are becoming increasingly fanatical in their speeches. Maulvis (clerics) and Pirs (spiritual masters) and students travel all round the Province and preach that those who fail to vote for

the League candidates will cease to be Muslims; their marriages will no longer be valid and they will be entirely excommunicated ... It is not easy to foresee what the results of the elections will be. But there seems little doubt the Muslim League, thanks to the ruthless methods by which they have pursued their campaign of 'Islam in danger' will considerably increase the number of their seats and unionist representatives will correspondingly decline.[19]

Similar practices were prevalent in the campaigns in NWFP. In his doctoral dissertation, *India, Pakistan or Pakhtunistan?*, Erland Jansson writes:

The Pir of Manki Sharif ... founded an organisation of his own, the Anjuman-us-asfia. The organisation promised to support the Muslim League on condition that Shariat would be enforced in Pakistan. To this Jinnah agreed. As a result the Pir of Manki Sharif declared jihad to achieve Pakistan and ordered the members of his *anjuman* to support the League in the 1946 elections.[20]

In this regard, Jinnah's letter to Pir Manki Sharif is quite revealing. He wrote:

It is needless to emphasize that the Constituent Assembly which would be predominantly Muslim in its composition would be able to enact laws for Muslims, not inconsistent with the Shariat laws and the Muslim will no longer be obliged to abide by the Un-Islamic laws.[21]

The idea of an Islamic state coming into being was viewed with great apprehension by non-Muslims in the Muslim-majority provinces as they feared that they would be reduced to an inferior status in such a polity. Moreover, the minority Shia and Ahmadiyya communities were fearful that it would result in Sunni domination. This is obvious from the correspondence between the Shia leader, Syed Ali Zaheer and Jinnah in July 1944.[22] Although the Council of Action of the All-Parties Shia Conference passed a resolution on 25 December 1945 rejecting the idea of Pakistan,[23] most Shias had shifted their loyalty to the Muslim League in the hope that Pakistan will be a non-sectarian Muslim state. Initially the Ahmadiyya community was also wary and reluctant to support the demand for a separate Muslim state.[24] It is only when Sir Zafrulla was won over by Jinnah that the Ahmadis started supporting the demand for Pakistan.

In any event, the demand for Pakistan was conceded by the British, and accepted by the main opponent to the partition of India, the Indian National Congress, only months before the British withdrew from the subcontinent.[25] The actual process of partitioning India resulted in the biggest involuntary migration in history, claiming the lives of some two million Hindus, Muslims and Sikhs.[26]

Westernized Elite's Views on the State, the Constitution and the Law

Although the Muslim League had used Islam as a rallying point and had coopted the *ulema* and *pirs* to its election campaign, once that objective had been achieved, Jinnah tried to base his vision of Pakistan on progressive principles. Just three days before Pakistan came into being on 14 August 1947, he delivered an address in Karachi as President of the Pakistan Constituent Assembly to its elected members in which he painted his vision of Pakistan with a very secular and liberal brush. Among other things, he observed on 11 August 1947:

> You are free; you are free to go to your temples, you are free to go to your mosques or to any other place of worship in this state of Pakistan. You may belong to any religion or caste or creed — that has nothing to do with the business of the state.... We are starting with this fundamental principle that we are all citizens and equal citizens of one atate ... I think we should keep that in front of us as our ideal and you will find that in due course Hindus would cease to be Hindus and Muslims would cease to be Muslims, not in the religious sense, because that is the personal faith of each individual, but in the political sense as citizens of the state.[27]

Jinnah's early death on 11 September 1948 closed the chapter on secular nation-building as his successors decided to ground Pakistan on Islamic identity as it had served as the rallying point for Muslim unity in favour of Pakistan. Thus the Objectives Resolution moved in the Pakistan Constituent Assembly by Prime Minister Liaqat Ali Khan on 7 March 1949 proclaimed the novel idea that sovereignty over the entire universe belonged to God. The first Constitution of Pakistan adopted in 1956 contained a commitment to bring all laws into conformity with Islam.[28] It could not be put into operation because the government was overthrown in a military coup in October 1958.

The second Constitution given in 1962 by General Mohammad Ayub Khan reiterated the commitment to bring all laws in conformity with Islam. The third Constitution adopted by the National Assembly of Pakistan in 1973 reiterated the same commitment and went some steps further towards ascribing an Islamic identity to Pakistan. Thus, unlike the first two Constitutions that required only the president of the republic to be a Muslim, the third required the prime minister to be a Muslim too. It further obliged both of them to take an oath testifying their belief in the finality of Prophet Muhammad's mission. In 1974, the National Assembly declared the Ahmadiyya sect non-Muslims on the grounds that it did not believe in the finality of the prophethood of Muhammad.[29] These incremental steps towards a doctrinally purer Islamic identity were interpreted by the fundamentalists as a commitment to making Pakistan a true Islamic state.

Fundamentalist Initiatives

Meanwhile the fundamentalists had started a campaign claiming that since Pakistan was won in the name of Islam, it was immanently an Islamic state. The first indication that the fundamentalists were seeking to wrest state power from the modern-educated leadership in Pakistan was when in 1951 the leader of the Jamaat-e-Islami, Syed Abul Ala Maududi, compiled a 22-point political programme that sought Islamization of Pakistan. All the leading Sunni and even Shia *ulema* signed that programme.[30] That established Maududi as the chief ideologue of Islamic fundamentalism in Pakistan. His overall writings on Islam, state, society and politics indicated a clear preference for totalitarianism. He succinctly and candidly described his idea of an Islamic state as a totalitarian utopia. He remarked:

> A state of this sort cannot evidently restrict the scope of its activities. Its approach is universal and all-embracing. Its scope of activities is coextensive with the whole of human life. It seeks to mould every aspect of life and activity in consonance with its moral norms and programme of social reform. In such a state, no one can regard any field of his affairs as personal and private. Considered from this aspect the Islamic State bears a kind of resemblance to the Fascist and Communist States.[31]

With regard to the position of women and non-Muslims, Maududi assumed the dogmatic position that women and non-Muslims would enjoy all those rights given in Islamic law, the sharia, to them. They could not claim such rights that contradicted the sharia. Thus for example, he insisted that women must accept the leadership of men as was laid down in the Quran. Equally, non-Muslims were entitled only to limited citizenship. They could not hold key positions in the state.[32]

In his major work, *Al-Jihad Fi al-Islam,* Maududi wholeheartedly endorsed the classical Islamic ideas of Dar-ul-Islam (abode of peace where Islamic law applies) and Dar-ul-Harb (enemy territory).[33] It meant that the Islamic state and its neighbours through treaty could establish peace, but in the ultimate sense no real peace could be consolidated between the world of Islam and non-Muslims and Dar-ul-Islam was bound to prevail universally at some point in the future. Moreover, Maududi argued that jihad could be declared only by an authentic Islamic state. The sole purpose of jihad should be to spread the Islamic faith in the world. Wars for territory, or in other words wars in the name of nationalism, were not to be treated as jihad.

Anti-Ahmadiyya Riots

The first challenge to the liberal-Muslim political dispensation in Pakistan occurred when the mainly Sunni clerics started a campaign in 1953 to have the Ahmadiyya sect declared non-Muslim. The Ahmadiyya sect owes it origins to the preachings of Mirza Ghulam Ahmad (1835–1908). Mirza was born at Qadian in the Punjab in a Sunni landowning family. He began his religious career as a keen debater who combated both Christian missionaries and Hindu reformers with clever doctrinal arguments, which won him acclaim from other Muslims. However, soon Mirza staked the claim to being a prophet and made heterodox statements on doctrine. Moreover, he took political positions that were openly pro-British and thus acquired the reputation of an impostor and a British stooge among the orthodox *ulema*.[34]

The Ahmadiyya mission was formally declared in 1901 and upon the request of Mirza himself was shown as a separate sect in the census records.[35] During the colonial period, the Ahmadis received government protection and were recruited in the civil administration and army. The conversions to the Ahmadiyya faith occurred mostly in Punjab. According to Wali Khan, it was Sir Zafrulla Khan, a leading loyalist Ahmadi, who on the instructions of the viceroy,

Lord Linlithgow, prepared the memorandum on the concept of two dominion states — India and Pakistan — in the second week of March 1940 and communicated it to the Muslim League.[36] It based its 23 March 1940 Lahore Resolution on lines suggested in the memorandum.

In any case, Sir Zafrulla was made Pakistan's first foreign minister by Jinnah. The head of the community, Mirza Bashir-ud-din, and some other senior Ahmadis made statements to the effect that Ahmadi influence on the state would be employed to spread their faith in Pakistan, particularly in Baluchistan.[37] Such utterances provoked a reaction among the *ulema* of Punjab among whom the anti-Ahmadiyya sentiment was strongly entrenched. Riots broke out, and killing and looting of Ahmadis took place in many parts of the Punjab. The military, which was called in to restore law and order, acted firmly and the agitation was crushed.

The government appointed a Court of Inquiry, comprising Justice Muhammad Munir and Justice Rustam Kayani, to examine the causes behind the disturbances. They found that not only Sunni and Shia clerics, but also some key figures of the Muslim League provincial government in Punjab, were involved in the riots. They interrogated the various representatives of the Sunni and Shia sects on the nature of the Islamic state, definition of a Muslim, rights of non-Muslims and so on. They were told that non-Muslims could not hold key positions in an Islamic state and Ahmadis who had not inherited their heretical faith from their parents but had voluntarily converted to it could be put to death for apostasy. When asked to define a Muslim, it was found that not only Sunnis and Shias held conflicting views, but also that within the Sunni sub-sects, there was no agreement. The presiding judges made this classic remark:

> Keeping in view the several definitions given by the *ulema*, need we make any comment except that no two learned divines are agreed on this fundamental. If we attempt our own definition as each learned divine has done, that definition differs from that given by all others, we unanimously go out of the fold of Islam. And if we adopt the definition given by any one of the *ulema*, we remain Muslims according to the view of that alim but kafirs according to the definition of every one else.[38]

▣ Towards Islamic Nation- and State-Building

The growth and ascent of a fundamentalist political jargon in Pakistani politics can also be traced to the polarization that took place in the mid-1960s. Ideas of Islamic socialism gained momentum when Zulfikar Ali Bhutto founded the Pakistan People's Party in 1967. It created a scare among the propertied classes of Pakistan. At that juncture, Maududi's version of an Islamic state appeared as a formidable counterweight that could be wielded against the emerging radical threats. Some of his ideas were incorporated into official proclamations. Thus an ordinance issued by the military government of General Yahya Khan in 1969 declared Islam as the exclusive Ideology of Pakistan.[39]

This trend gained the upper hand only in 1977 when Zulfikar Ali Bhutto was toppled by General Muhammad Zia-ul-Haq (1977–88). Unlike other Pakistani rulers who saw 'Islam only as an instrument of policy, Zia-ul-Haq had the fire of a true believer'.[40] He was profoundly influenced by Maududi and the puritanical Deobandi school of Islam. Zia declared succinctly his political mission: 'I consider the establishment of an Islamic order a *prerequisite* for the country'.[41] He wanted to establish a social order in which all sectors of life, including administration, judiciary, banking, trade, education, agriculture, industry and foreign affairs were regulated in accordance with Islamic principles.

In 1979, he announced the imposition of the Hudood Ordinance, that is, punishments laid down in the Quran and the Sunnah for the offences of adultery (death by stoning), fornication (100 lashes), false accusation of adultery (80 lashes), drinking alcohol (80 lashes), theft (cutting off of the right hand), and highway robbery (when the offence is only robbery, cutting off of hands and feet. For robbery with murder, the punishment is death either by the sword or crucifixion). It is interesting to note that apostasy, which traditionally had been part of Hudood law, was not included in the Hudood Ordinance.[42]

Women

In 1984, a new Law of Evidence was adopted, which reduced the evidence of a female witness to half in worth with that of a male witness, in a court of law.[43] The establishment of sharia courts in 1986, as a complement to the Hudood Ordinance, included the Zina (adultery and rape) Ordinance, and instituted processes and procedures that greatly weakened the legal position of women. Rape as sexual intercourse forced upon a woman is not recognized in the Quran, but it was acknowledged by Muslim jurists as *zina bil jabr* or sexual intercourse under duress. Under the previous laws based on Anglo-Muhammadan codes from the colonial period, the evidence of the victim in rape cases was accepted. Under the Zina Ordinance, the evidence of the victim was not admitted, nor was that of any other woman. To prove that adultery and rape have been committed, the traditional requirement of four male witnesses was instituted. Moreover PPC Section 375, as the earlier law on rape was called, had protected girls under fourteen by providing that even with their consent, sexual intercourse with them would constitute rape: this immunity was not included in the Zina Ordinance.[44]

The well-known women's rights activists, sisters Asma Jahangir and Hina Jilani — both lawyers — noted that the such misogynist legislation resulted in harsh punishments being meted out to many victims simply because they could not produce male witnesses who could give evidence that they saw the actual penetration of their vagina by the male phallus of the accused culprit.[45]

General Zia-ul-Haq undertook several other measures to impose chaste Islamic conduct on women. In 1980, a circular was issued to all government offices prescribing a proper Muslim dress for female employees. Wearing of a *chador* (loose cloth covering the head) was made obligatory. A campaign to eliminate obscenity and pornography was also announced: it, however, took the form of a campaign against the general emancipation and equal rights of women. Leading Muslim theologians, hostile to female emancipation, were brought on national television to justify various restrictions on women.[46] It has also been noted in its annual reports by the Human Rights Commission of Pakistan that the incidence of so-called honour killings by close relatives or through hired killers increased significantly in the wake of the legal and social oppression introduced by General Zia-ul-Haq.[47]

Non-Muslims

With the declaration of the Ahmadis as non-Muslims in 1974, Pakistan had already acquired a definite confessional character as it meant that the state distinguished between those it declared Muslims and those it did not. In other words, membership in the true Pakistani nation was made dependent on holding the correct Islamic faith. In 1983–84, General Zia-ul-Haq imposed further restrictions on the Ahmadis who had been declared non-Muslims by the Pakistan National Assembly in 1974. They were forbidden to use Islamic nomenclature for their worship, places of worship and so on. Further discrimination against non-Muslims was introduced through the system of separate electorates in 1985. It barred non-Muslim voters from voting in the general elections for general seats. Non-Muslims were to vote for non-Muslim candidates only. In 1986, a law on blasphemy was adopted that made disrespect to Islam and the Prophet Muhammad a major crime. In subsequent years the blasphemy law was invoked many times to punish alleged offenders who happened to be mostly Christians. Terrorist attacks on Christians, Hindus and Ahmadis, burning of churches, temples and Ahmadi mosques, and forced conversion of Christian and Hindu girls increased dramatically throughout the 1990s and into 2007. The Human Rights Commission has provided data in its annual reports on such incidents.[48]

▨ Internationalization and Sectarian Terrorism of the 1990s

The oil crisis of the 1970s resulted in a massive increase in the wealth of oil-producing states of the Gulf region because those states greatly increased their share of the revenue from the sale of that strategic primary commodity. As these societies went about building modern infrastructure and acquiring modern comforts, a vast field for employment opened up for foreigners. Both Z.A. Bhutto (1972–77) and General Zia-ul-Haq cultivated good relations with the Arab states in the Gulf, and secured employment opportunities for Pakistanis. More than a million-strong Pakistani work force found work in the Gulf states. However, such linkages also meant an increasing role of external actors in Pakistani politics.

The age-old rivalry between Shia Iran and her Sunni Arab neighbours assumed worldwide ramifications after Ayatollah Khomeini captured power in Iran in 1979. As two major oil producers, and leaders of Shia and Sunni fundamentalism respectively, Iran and Saudi Arabia became involved in a frantic competition to extend their influence in Pakistan. This had an adverse bearing on the sectarian problem in Pakistan. Both began covertly to arm sectarian militias. As a result, large sums of money, leaflets, books, and audio as well as video tapes began to circulate in Pakistan. During the 1990s, Pakistan witnessed ugly sectarian killings in which hundreds, mostly innocent people, died.[49] During 1990–2002, 593 Shias and

388 Sunnis had been killed, including leaders and cadres of the two groups. Also killed in such incidents, were 44 persons, belonging to the police and other law-enforcing agencies.[50]

Radicalization of the Pakistan Army

The erstwhile military top brass were trained in the liberal Sandhurst tradition during the British colonial system. Later, when Pakistan joined the Western military alliances of SEATO and CENTO, Pakistani officers began to be trained in American institutions and military schools.[51] However, the military establishment began increasingly to emphasize the Islamic identity of Pakistan's armed forces after General Zia-ul-Haq came to power. The syllabus at Command and Staff College, Quetta came increasingly to rely on the Islamic theory of war and related subjects as officers were groomed to become genuine Muslim warriors. Moreover, from the 1970s onwards, Pakistan military personnel, were stationed in significant numbers in Saudi Arabia and some Gulf states. Such exposure played an important role in the growth of the extremist Wahabi ideology on which the Saudi state is premised.

The Afghan Jihad and Fundamentalism

The 1979 intervention of the Soviet Union in Afghanistan, in support of the Communists who had captured power a year earlier, resulted in millions of Afghans fleeing to Pakistan. The United States had for a long time been involved in building an anti-Soviet front in the region and Pakistan was a close ally in that policy of containment of Communism.[52] With generous military aid from the United States and financial assistance from Saudi Arabia and certain other Arab states, a jihad (holy war) against the Soviet occupation began to be propagated worldwide. Muslim zealots from different parts of the world began to arrive in the Pakistani city of Peshawar where the CIA and retired British officials (with first-hand experience of the North West Frontier Province of Pakistan from the colonial period) were available for training the Pakistani military in modern fighting techniques and in the use of weapons and explosives. The CIA gave US$ 51 million to the University of Nebraska to produce illustrated textbooks to be taught in madrasas in Afghanistan in which the killing of Russians was made sufficiently entertaining and morally justified.[53] The fundamentalist parties in Pakistan — the Jamaat-e-Islami and the Deobandi, Jamiat Ulema-e-Islam became involved in recruiting and indoctrinating young men for the Afghan jihad. Even Sufi-oriented Sunnis, doctrinally the same as the Brelawis, took part in that religious war.[54]

After the Soviets withdrew in 1989 from Afghanistan, a power struggle between different ethnic and sectarian factions broke out in Afghanistan. Pakistan initially supported the Pashtun leader Gulbadan Hekmetyar in his opposition to the government of the Tajik Burhanuddin Rabbani and his Uzbek ally Shah Ahmed Masud. Later, a more Pakistan-loyal group known as the Talibans (pupils) was promoted.[55] The Talibans comprised mainly Afghan and Pakistani students who were indoctrinated in the madrasas set up in the North West Frontier Province and in the Baluchistan province, both bordering Afghanistan.[56] It is interesting to note that in 1956 there were only 244 madrasas in Pakistan, producing prayer leaders and other scholars of Islam. Their number rose up to 15,000 during the Afghan jihad. It was estimated that between 1.5 and 1.7 million pupils attended these madrasas at one point in time. The areas on the Pakistan–Afghanistan border became the strongholds of extremism and terrorism and remain so at present.

More significant was that fact that many of the mujahideen from the Afghan theatre shifted their activity to the Indian-administered Kashmir after the withdrawal of the Soviet Union from Afghanistan.[57] After the congregational Friday prayers, funds began to be collected openly in Pakistan for waging jihad against India. Militant fundamentalist organizations such as the Laskhar-e-Taiba and Jaish-e-Muhammad began to recruit and train volunteers for the Kashmir jihad.[58]

Brief Restoration of Democracy

General Zia-ul-Haq died in a plane crash in 1988. In the elections that followed, Zulfikar Ali Bhutto's daughter, Benazir Bhutto, won the largest number of seats but fell short of a majority. She formed a coalition government, but was thrown out of office by President Ghulam Ishaq Khan on charges of corruption in 1990 and fresh elections were held. Nawaz Sharif, a protege of Zia-ul-Haq, formed the next government but was also dismissed on charges of corruption. In the next round, Ms Bhutto again returned to power only to be dismissed again on corruption charges. Sharif returned to power in 1997 on a landslide victory. He introduced the Fifteenth Amendment; had it been passed by Parliament, the dogmatic sharia would have become the supreme law of the land. Thus, the fact that an elected government was now in power after a long period of fundamentalist rule by a military strongman did not alter the fact that the hegemony of Islamic fundamentalism continued. Nawaz was overthrown by General Pervez Musharraf on 12 October 1999 on charges of conspiring to refuse permission to the Pakistan International Airline's flight from Colombo, Sri Lanka, which carried General Musharraf and hundreds of other passengers from landing in Pakistan and thus endangering many lives.

▦ The 9/11 Terrorist Attacks

Although, since the time of General Zia-ul-Haq, a prominent fundamentalist lobby has been strongly entrenched at all levels of the military apparatus as well as in the civil bureaucracy, more professional-minded officers with quite Westernized lifestyles were also always present. In fact a majority might not have had an active fundamentalist commitment; however, they made their careers during his regime. General Pervez Musharraf belongs to the said category of officers. Soon after capturing power, he spoke highly of the Turkish leader Mustafa Kemal Ataturk's reforms, which resulted in loud protests and condemnation from the clerics and militants.[59] Thereafter, Musharraf chose not to antagonize them. He had initially declared, for example, that murders of females in the name of so-called 'honour killlings' will be severely punished: after the fundamentalists objected, he quickly withdrew from that commitment.

Events outside, however, were to compel Musharraf to make a commitment to changing course. On 11 September 2001, a group of terrorists believed to be members of the Al-Qaeda movement led by a veteran of the Afghan jihad, the Saudi, Osama bin Laden, hijacked civilian aircrafts in various US cities and flew them into the World Trade Center and the Pentagon, killing several thousand people. The United States quickly mustered its armed forces and established an anti-terrorist coalition, securing a UN Security Council resolution to launch military action on Afghanistan. It demanded that the Taliban leader Mullah Omar should surrender Osama bin Laden and his associates. This was refused and on 7 October 2001, the United States launched a major military offensive on Afghanistan.

Pakistan was served notice to choose sides. Musharraf quickly and decisively moved to unlink his administration from the Pakistani militants and join the 'war on terror'.[60] While doing this, he continued to maintain that the militancy in the Indian-administered Kashmir was not to be linked to the Al-Qaeda terrorism and that those who took part in it were freedom fighters.

Terrorist Attacks in Srinagar and Delhi

On 1 October and 13 December 2001, Muslim militants carried out terrorist attacks on the Kashmir Assembly in the capital of the India-administered Kashmir, Srinagar and the Indian Parliament at Delhi, respectively. India responded by ordering its troops to mass up along the 2900 kilometres India–Pakistan border and the Line of Control in Kashmir. Pakistan followed suit. Earlier, in May 1998, both India and Pakistan had demonstrated their ability to explode nuclear devices. In May 1999, both had been engaged in fighting in Kargil inside the Indian side of Line of Control in Kashmir. It was widely feared that nuclear weapons might be used by them in case that conflict escalated.

Thus after 13 December, the two armies faced each other; ready to start a war if ordered. International concern and pressure increased enormously on the two states to withdraw from their standoff. India, however, refused to do that as long as Pakistan supported what it described as cross-border terrorism. The United States, Britain and other Western powers backed the Indian demand for Pakistan to forgo its support to militant groups.

In an address to the Pakistani nation on 12 January 2002, General Pervez Musharraf finally made a complete break with fundamentalist tendencies and movements. He described Pakistan as a modern Islamic state based on a moderate, tolerant interpretation of Islam.[61] Later in an address to the clerics, he spoke about a middle path, a tolerant non-divisive approach to Islam.[62] Most significantly, he abolished the system of separate electorates whereby non-Muslims were required to vote separately from the Muslims. In subsequent clarifications, he dispelled speculations that Pakistan might become a secular state. He reiterated that Pakistan will remain an Islamic Republic. He categorically stated that the Hudood and Blasphemy laws were an intrinsic part of the Pakistani Constitution and will remain in force, but measures will be taken to see to it that they were not used in an arbitrary manner.[63]

October 2002 Elections and Fundamentalist Gains

The electoral process in Pakistan has functioned irregularly because of recurring military takeovers, but whenever elections have been held, some of the fundamentalist parties in Pakistan have taken part in elections. Among them the Jamaat-e-Islami has been the most prominent in terms of ideological leadership and activism in student and national politics. The Jamiat Ulema-e-Islam representing Deobandis and the Jamiat Ulema-e-Pakistan of the Brelawis have also taken part in elections. The Shia minority too has fielded the Tehrik Nifaas-e-Fiqh Jafaria (movement for the imposition of Jafari law) to represent their interests but none has ever made any noteworthy impression in the elections. Their combined votes before the 2002 elections did not exceed 10 per cent of the total votes cast.[64] Most Pakistanis voted for pragmatic, relatively secular parties in the middle or even left-oriented parties committed to social justice.

However, in 2002, the government of President Pervez Musharraf manipulated the electoral system and rigged it to enable the rightwing alliance of the *ulema*, the Muttahida Majlis-e-Amal (MMA), to increase its strength at the expense of the PPP and PML-N. The MMA gained 11.3 per cent of the popular vote. That gave it 58 seats of the 342 seats in the National Assembly.[65] The MMA increase in votes was also a result of the anti-American sentiment that prevailed among the fundamentalists in Pakistan after the United States attacked the Talibans in Afghanistan in October 2001. The MMA was able to form the government in the NWFP and in alliance with some Baluch factions also in Baluchistan. While in power, the MMA tried to introduce harsh Islamic laws and generally followed a patently misogynist social policy.

Later, the MMA split as some groups were opposed to Musharraf's close alliance with the United States and his modernistic approach on Islam, while others continued to work with him. Among the former, a strong support for the Talibans and the Al-Qaeda existed and in their strongholds in the tribal belt, safe haven and sanctuary was provided to the extremists.[66]

▣ Proliferation of Fundamentalist Terrorism

In the aftermath of the 9/11 terrorist attacks, the relations between the ruling elite in Pakistan, headed by General Musharraf and the Talibans and pro Al-Qaeda forces deteriorated quickly as Pakistan joined the war on terror. Notwithstanding total backing of the United States in terms of military and economic aid, the Musharraf government was not able to crush the Talibans and Al-Qaeda operatives in enclaves in NWFP and Baluchistan. On the contrary, the armed encounters between the Talibans and their hosts in the tribal belt on the one hand, and the Pakistan security forces on the other, proliferated during 2002–07. Also, Shia–Sunni terrorism and attacks on non-Muslims continued.

Attacks on Christians, Ahmadis, Shias and Foreigners

On 22 February 2002 the world was shocked to learn that an American journalist, Daniel Pearl, was kidnapped by Islamists and brutally murdered. A video recording showing his execution was mysteriously circulated on the Internet.[67] A terrorist attack on 8 May near the Sheraton Hotel caused the death of 11 Frenchmen and three Pakistanis.[68] Some weeks later, a powerful car bomb explosion took place near the US Consulate in Karachi on 14 June. 12 people were killed and more than 50 injured.[69] Karachi witnessed another atrocity when on 25 September 2002 gunmen entered the offices of the Idara-e-Amn-o-Insaf (Institute for Peace and Justice), a Pakistani Christian charity located in the country's biggest city, Karachi. Victims were tied up in chairs with their hands behind their backs, their mouths taped, before being shot point-blank in the head.[70]

During 2003, Shia mosques were targeted causing several deaths and in 2004, there was a sharp increase in such activity. Suicide bombers began to be employed increasingly in the sectarian killings. Retaliations by Shias also took place, resulting in several deaths but clearly the Shias were on the receiving end most of the time. Sectarian bloodletting proliferated, especially in 2005. Among them the attack on a Sufi shrine, of Bari Imam (revered both by Shias and Sunnis) on 27 May in Rawalpindi, was indicative of the extent to which the Taliban-inspired extremists were willing to go to strike awe among those that did not conform to their strict version of Islam. Twenty people were killed and 82 were wounded.[71] These outrages were followed by an assault on 7 October on an Ahmadi mosque: eight Ahmadis were killed in Mandi Bahauddin, Punjab, while praying.[72] A car bomb explosion outside a Kentucky Fried Chicken shop in Karachi killed at least three people and injured eight.[73] Terrorism continued to ravage lives in Pakistan during 2006. On 11 April fanaticism reached its height when over 50 people, including many leaders of the Brelawi Sunni sub-sect, were killed when they were attending a meeting to celebrate the birthday of Prophet Muhammad in Nishtar Park, Karachi.[74] It was widely believed that the group behind the attack were Deobandis who perceived the Brelawis to be 'soft' on Shias and followed doctrines that were not consistent with pure monotheism. On 14 July, a Shia religious scholar, Allama Hassan Turabi, and his 12-year-old nephew were killed in a suicide attack near his residence in Karachi.[75]

Direct Clash with the State in 2007

Violent attacks directed against state functionaries and installations escalated dramatically in 2007 but several assassination attempts on General Musharraf and other military top brass had already taken place earlier. Thus on 14 December 2003 a powerful bomb went off minutes after Musharraf's convoy crossed a bridge in Rawalpindi. He survived it and another one on 25 December. It was found out that some junior personnel were involved in the conspiracy to assassinate him.[76] The Musharraf regime intensified its military operations against the Taliban and Al-Qaeda enclaves in the tribal areas and during 2004–06 there were recurrent clashes between the Pakistani troops and the Taliban and Al-Qaeda forces. A truce was reached in September 2006 but did not last long. Missile attacks from the air by the Pakistan Air Force at Chenagai on a madrasa on 30 October 2006 left 80 people dead. Some reports suggested that the Americans directly hit those targets. In retaliation on 8 November 2006 a suicide bomber killed 42 soldiers and injured another 20 in Dargai.[77] It was the beginning of a more focused campaign against military personnel that in 2007 reached hugely alarming proportions.

On 26 January, two persons — the suicide bomber and the security guard — were killed in the blast at the prestigious Marriott Hotel in Islamabad. A meeting to celebrate the Indian Republic Day was scheduled in the hotel and Indian diplomats were going to attend it. The bombing was undoubtedly planned for that reception but went off earlier.[78] The garrison-type security arrangements in the Islamabad–Rawalpindi area were further challenged when an insurgency headed by hardcore fundamentalists began to surface in the Pakistani capital in March 2007.

On 28 March, *niqab*-wearing armed women of the Jamia Hafsa at Lal Masjid in Islamabad, the Lal Brigade as they were called, raided the premises of a 'madam' who allegedly ran a brothel, arresting her and her family and forced a confession from her that she was guilty of running a prostitution den. On 6 April, they set up a sharia court inside the mosque. The most senior cleric, Maulana

Abdul Aziz, vowed to launch thousands of suicide attacks if the government interfered in the activities of the court. On 9 April, the sharia court issued a fatwah (edict) against the Punjab Tourism Minister Nilofer Bakhtiar, accusing her of committing a sin when she was shown in newspaper photographs embracing a parachuting instructor following a charity jump in France.[79]

On 28 April, an assassination attempt on the then Interior Minister Aftab Ahmad Khan Sherpao took place in Charsadda, NWFP. He survived but 28 people were killed.[80] In Islamabad, once again the situation reached explosive proportions when on 23 June the Lal Brigade cadres raided a Chinese massage parlour and abducted seven Chinese and two Pakistanis from its premises. They released the Chinese couple who owned the parlour and five Chinese girls who worked there.

The Chinese Minister for Public Security Zhou Yongang Zhou, in a rare display of concern, publicly told the visiting Pakistani Interior Minister Sherpao, 'We hope Pakistan will look into the terrorist attacks aiming at Chinese people and organizations as soon as possible and severely punish the criminals'.[81] On 8 July, gunmen opened fire and killed three Chinese workers and wounded another near Peshawar.[82] The same day in Islamabad, a senior military officer Lt. Colonel Haroon Islam stationed outside the Lal Masjid was gunned down by the militants inside.[83]

At this juncture, Musharraf felt compelled to act ruthlessly. Security forces were ordered to carry out Operation Sunrise (initially named Operation Silence) in full blast.[84] While many inside the mosque panicked and surrendered or tried to escape, several hundred die-hards decided to go down fighting. On 10 July, the army launched the attack in full blast. The total number of people reported killed was 150, of which 10 were army personnel, including an officer.

While the United States supported the assault on the Lal Masjid, the Al-Qaeda's second in command, Ayman al-Zawahiri, issued a video recording calling for Pakistanis to join the jihad against Musharraf to avenge the deaths of the Islamists.[85] Retaliation followed soon after in the form of several attacks on army camps and security personnel. Almost every day, there were media reports of violent conflict in the tribal areas or attempts by suicide bombers seeking government targets in other parts of Pakistan. On 4 September, for example, at least 25 people were killed and 66 injured in two suicide bomb attacks in Rawalpindi cantonment. Among the dead were uniformed officials as well as civilians in a bus travelling to their workplace.[86] Again on 13 September, at least 20 off-duty commandos were killed and 11 injured in an apparent suicide blast at an army officers' mess, near the Tarbela Dam, NWFP. Among the targeted men were commandos from the Special Services Group (SSG) Karar Company, apparently because they were believed to have taken part in the assault on the Lal Masjid.[87]

On 18 October, Benazir Bhutto returned to Pakistan. Hundreds of thousands of people had come to receive her at the airport and a long convoy was formed to escort her to the city. Five minutes past midnight on 19 October, two bomb blasts took place. 189 people died and more than 500 were injured.[88] It was the single most deadly act of terrorism in Pakistani history.

There was still no let-up on terrorism. On 30 October, a suicide bomber struck a police checkpoint in a high security zone of Rawalpindi, less than a kilometre from General Musharraf's camp office.[89] The present author was in Islamabad on that day, attending a conference only a couple of kilometres away. On Thursday, 1 November, another suicide bomber blew himself up and seven officers of the Pakistan Air Force and three civilians at Sargodha, where the Pakistan Air Force has its headquarters.[90] More attacks, mostly by suicide bombers continued in December. On 21 December, a suicide bomb blast again targeted Aftab Ahmad Khan Sherpao, killing at least 57 and injuring over 100 at Jamia Masjid Sherpao, in Charsadda district. Sherpao survived the blast, but his younger son Mustafa Khan Sherpao, was injured.[91]

The Assassination of Benazir Bhutto

2007 culminated with the assassination of Benazir Bhutto on 27 December. She had addressed a mammoth public meeting in Rawalpindi to solicit votes for the general elections announced for 8 January 2008.[92] About 20 other people, among them five PPP volunteers, were also killed in the bomb blast that took place. The government claimed to have intercepted a telephone conversation between the Al-Qaeda leader, Baitullah Mahsud, and a cleric in which they congratulated each other over her death and praised the men who took part in it. An Al-Qaeda statement described her death as the end of 'America's most precious asset in Pakistan'. However, a spokesperson for Mahsud denied that the Al-Qaeda leader had anything to do with the murder.[93]

▣ Links of International and Regional Terrorism to Pakistan

While terrorism within Pakistan raged throughout 2002–07, on 7 July 2005, terrorists struck in London. The first bomb blast took place in the morning rush hours in an underground train and the second followed on a bus an hour later. The authorities reported that more than 50 people had died and 700 injured. The bomb blasts were linked to madrasas in Pakistan, which, according to the British police, three of the four suicide bombers had visited recently. (Their families confirmed that the visits did take place.) One of the suicide bombers, Muhammad Siddiq Khan, left behind a 14-month old daughter and a young wife. There is little doubt that Siddiq and his three younger comrades were idealists who had been brainwashed to believe that their faith and the *ummah* (whole Muslim world) needed their supreme sacrifice. Whereas their mentors have yet not been traced and the network uncovered, the fact remains that the jihadi madrasas churning out a nihilistic worldview are still in business in Pakistan.

Apart from the London bombing, terrorist assaults by Pakistan-based Islamist organizations, primarily the Lashkar-e-Taiba and the Jaish-e-Muhammad, continued not only in the Indian-administered Kashmir but also in other parts of India. The scale and frequency have gone down noticeably, however, after Pakistan officially dissociated itself with extremist ideas and the Kashmir jihad following President Musharraf's speech on this theme on 12 January 2002. Some of the terrorist acts allegedly undertaken by these organizations include the 25 August 2003 bomb blasts in the centre of the Indian megalopolis of Mumbai in which 52 died and hundreds were wounded. On 29 October 2005, three bombs exploded in the shopping markets of Delhi killing more than 65 people. It was on the eve of the major Hindu festival of Diwali. The worst was the bomb blasts on 11 May 2006 on a Mumbai local train that killed 179 people and injured nearly 800. The Indian Prime Minister Manmohan Singh directly accused Pakistan of supporting the groups that carried out that outrage.[94] Similar incidents took place in 2007 and 2008. Pakistan has consistently denied a hand in these outrages and condemned all such acts.

▦ Conclusion

Pakistan emerged as a Muslim-majority state on the Indian subcontinent on 14 August 1947 as a result of the north-western and north-eastern zones where the Muslims were in a majority in contiguous areas, being separated from the rest of India. The basic argument put forth by the Muslim League, a party of the Western-educated modern Muslim elite was that Indian Muslims, by virtue of their religion, constituted a nation separate and distinct from Hindus and other religious communities of India.

A whole body of scholarly literature, Western as well Pakistani, is premised on the assumption that the *ulema* as a whole opposed Pakistan whereas the Westernized elite that led the struggle for Pakistan were secular and modernistic. The subsequent rise of Islamic fundamentalism known by different names — radical Islam, Islamism, extremist Islam and so on — has therefore puzzled them. This study argues that although the movement for Pakistan was led by the Westernized elite, it gained popular momentum only when a substantial section of the *ulema*, the Brelawi Sunnis, were mobilized to present Pakistan to the masses as a panacea in which Islam will be allowed to flourish.

Soon after the death of the founder of Pakistan, Mohammad Ali Jinnah, on 11 September 1948, the modernist ruling elite began to make nominal concessions to Islamic ideas by trying to frame a Constitution that would be both democratic and Islamic. In doing so, they included some constitutional provisions that required that all laws should be brought in conformity with Islam. On the other hand, the fundamentalists from the very beginning had begun to campaign for an Islamic state in Pakistan.

When General Muhammad Zia-ul-Haq, came to power in July 1977, the fundamentalists had a man in power who shared their goal of making Pakistan a 'true Islamic state'. Thereafter began what the Zia-ul-Haq regime described as 'Islamization' of state and society in Pakistan. The Islamization process, coupled with the Afghan jihad of the 1980s, resulted in the constitutional and legal weakening of the position of women, non-Muslims as well as minority sects. Violence and terrorism proliferated as social protests and political agitation broke out among disgruntled sections of society and external actors began to interfere in Pakistani politics.

However, after the terrorist attacks of 11 September 2001, General Pervez Musharraf, a modernist by conviction, was pressured by the United States and other nations to change course: Pakistan was forced to join the 'war on terror'. This brought his regime unavoidably into conflict with the fundamentalists. During 2002–07, terrorism proliferated in Pakistan to alarming proportions.

There can be no doubt that most of the attacks during 2002–07 were carried out by extremists belonging to Sunni fundamentalist organizations connected to the Afghan jihad and having links with rogue elements in the military and security services. Shia–Sunni terrorism and attacks on sub-sects of Sunnis by other sub-sects were indicative of the deep malaise and cleavages present among the various denominations.

One need not labour the point that Islamic fundamentalism is incompatible with a pluralist, democratic, and human rights-friendly social and political order; further, that it is violence-prone and can be used as an incentive to carry out terrorist activities. Unless Pakistan can bring it under control, there will be no return to normality, stability and peace within Pakistan and indeed around it.

▦ Notes

1. Ishtiaq Ahmed, *State, Nation and Ethnicity in Contemporary South Asia* (London and New York: Pinter Publishers, 1998), p. 170.
2. Martin E. Marty and Appelby. R. Scott, *Fundamentalisms and Society* (Illinois and London: University of Chicago Press, 1993). Martin E. Marty and Appelby. R. Scott, *Fundamentalisms and the State* (Illinois and London: University of Chicago Press, 1993).
3. Martin E. Marty and Appelby. R. Scott, *Fundamentalisms and Society* (Illinois and London: University of Chicago Press, 1993), p. 3.
4. Ishtiaq Ahmed, *The Concept of an Islamic State: An Analysis of the Ideological Controversy in Pakistan* (London: Frances Pinter; New York: St. Martin's Press, 1987), pp. 54–55.
5. Kemal Faruki, *The Evolution of Islamic Constitutional Theory and Practice* (Karachi: National Publishing House, 1971); Anwar Ahmad Qadri, *Islamic Jurisprudence in the Modern World* (Lahore: Sh. Muhammad Ashraf, 1981).
6. Ishtiaq Ahmed, *The Concept of an Islamic State: An Analysis of the Ideological Controversy in Pakistan* (London: Frances Pinter; New York: St. Martin's Press, 1987), pp. 93–116.
7. Robert Dreyfuss, *Devil's Game: How the United States Helped Unleash Fundamentalist Islam* (New York: Metropolitan Books, 2005), pp. 94–119.

8. Ibid., pp. 131–50.
9. Ishtiaq Ahmed, 'South Asia', in David Westerlund and Ingvar Svanberg (eds), *Islam Outside the Arab World* (Richmond, Surrey: Curzon, 1999), p. 216.
10. Ibid., 216–19.
11. Zia-ul-Haq Faruqui, *The Deoband School and the Demand for Pakistan* (Lahore: Progressive Books, 1980).
12. Gail Minault, *The Khilafat Movement: Religious Symbolism and Political Mobilization in India* (New Delhi: Oxford University Press, 1999).
13. David Gilmartin, *Empire and Islam: Punjab and the Making of Pakistan* (Delhi: Oxford University Press, 1989).
14. Ishtiaq Ahmed, 'The Fundamentalist Dimension in the Pakistan Movement', *Friday Times*, Lahore, 22–28 November 2002.
15. Quoted in Muhammad Munir, *From Jinnah to Zia* (Lahore: Vanguard, 1978), p. 29.
16. David Gilmartin, *Empire and Islam: Punjab and the Making of Pakistan* (Delhi: Oxford University Press, 1989); Ian Talbot, *Khizr Tiwana, the Punjab Unionist Party and the Partition of India* (Richmond, Surrey: Curzon Press, 1996).
17. Ishtiaq Ahmed, 'South Asia', in David Westerlund and Ingvar Svanberg (eds), *Islam Outside the Arab World* (Richmond, Surrey: Curzon, 1999), p. 224.
18. Syed Abul Al Maududi, *Therik-i-Azadi-i-Hind Aur Musalman*, vols 1 and 2 (Lahore: Islamic Publications Ltd, 1981).
19. Lionel Carter, *Punjab Politics, 1 January 1944–3 March 1947: Last Years of the Ministries, Governors' Fortnightly Reports and other Key Documents* (New Delhi: Manohar, 2006), p. 171.
20. Erland Jansson, *India, Pakistan or Pakhtunistan?* (Uppsala, Sweden: Acta Universitatis Upsaliensis, 1981), p. 166.
21. *The Constituent Assembly of Pakistan Debates*, vol. 5 (Karachi: Government of Pakistan Press, 1949), p. 46.
22. G. Allana, *Pakistan Movement: Historic Documents* (Lahore: Islamic Book Service, 1977), pp. 375–79.
23. S. R. Bakshi, 'Resolution adopted by Council of Action of the All-Parties Shia Conference' (Poona, 25 December 1945), in *The Making of India and Pakistan: Ideology of the Hindu Mahasabha and other Political Parties*, vol. 3 (New Delhi: Deep & Deep Publications, 1997), pp. 848–49.
24. *The Report of the Court of Inquiry constituted under Punjab Act II of 1954 to enquire into the Punjab Disturbances of 1953* (also known as Munir Report) (Lahore: Government Printing Press, 1954), p. 196.
25. N. Mansergh and P. Moon (eds), *The Transfer of Power 1942–47, vol. 11, May 31 to July 7, 1947* (London: Her Majesty's Stationery Office, 1982), pp. 86–87.
26. Ishtiaq Ahmed, 'The 1947 Partition of India: A Paradigm for Pathological Politics in India and Pakistan', *Asian Ethnicity*, March 2002, 3(1).

27. *Speeches and Writings of Mr. Jinnah*, vol. II (Lahore: Sh. Muhammad Ashraf, 1976), pp. 403–04.

28. Leonard Binder, *Religion and Politics in Pakistan* (California: University of California Press, 1961).

29. Ishtiaq Ahmed, 'South Asia', in David Westerlund and Ingvar Svanberg (eds), *Islam Outside the Arab World* (Richmond, Surrey: Curzon Press, 1999), pp. 227–28.

30. Syed Abul Ala Maududi, *The Islamic Law and Constitution* (Lahore: Islamic Publications Ltd, 1980), pp. 332–36.

31. Ibid., 146.

32. Ishtiaq Ahmed, *The Concept of an Islamic State: An Analysis of the Ideological Controversy in Pakistan* (London: Frances Pinter; New York: St. Martin's Press, 1987), pp. 101–10

33. Syed Abul Ala Maududi, *Al-Jihad Fi al-Islam* (Lahore: Idara Tarjuman-ul-Quran, 1981).

34. Ishtiaq Ahmed, 'South Asia', in David Westerlund and Ingvar Svanberg (eds), *Islam Outside the Arab World* (Richmond; Surrey: Curzon, 1999), pp. 233–35.

35. *The Report of the Court of Inquiry constituted under Punjab Act II of 1954 to enquire into the Punjab Disturbances of 1953* (Lahore: Government Printing Press, 1954), p. 10.

36. Wali Khan, *Facts Are Facts: The Untold Story of India's Partition* (New Delhi: Vikas Publishing House, 1987), pp. 29–30.

37. *The Report of the Court of Inquiry constituted under Punjab Act II of 1954 to enquire into the Punjab Disturbances of 1953* (Lahore: Government Printing Press, 1954), pp. 199–200.

38. Ibid., p. 218.

39. Ishtiaq Ahmed, 'South Asia', in David Westerlund and Ingvar Svanberg (eds), *Islam Outside the Arab World* (Richmond, Surrey: Curzon, 1999), p. 230.

40. Husain Haqqani, *Pakistan: Between Mosque and Military* (Washington, DC: Carnegie Endowment for International Peace, 2005), p. 132.

41. Omar Noman, *The Political Economy of Pakistan* (London and New York: KPI, 1988), p. 118.

42. Ishtiaq Ahmed, 'South Asia', in David Westerlund and Ingvar Svanberg (eds), *Islam Outside the Arab World* (Richmond, Surrey: Curzon Press, 1999), p. 231.

43. Ibid., pp. 231–32.

44. Rubya Mehdi, *The Islamization of the Law in Pakistan* (Richmond, Surrey: Curzon Press, 1994), p. 123.

45. Asma Jahangir and Huma Jilani, *The Hudood Ordinances: A Divine Sanction?* (Lahore: Sang-e-Meel Publications, 2003).

46. Khawar Mumtaz and Farida Shaheed, *Women of Pakistan: Two Steps Forward, One Step Back?* (Lahore: Vanguard, 1987), pp. 77–96.

47. *State of Human Rights in Pakistan* (Lahore: Human Rights Commission of Pakistan, 1990–2006).
48. Ibid.
49. Ishtiaq Ahmed, *State, Nation and Ethnicity in Contemporary South Asia* (London and New York: Pinter Publishers, 1998), pp. 177–78.
50. Muhammad Amir Rana, *A to Z of Jehadi Organizations in Pakistan* (Lahore: Mashal Books, 2004), p. 586.
51. Stephen Cohen, *The Idea of Pakistan* (New Delhi: Oxford University Press, 2005), pp. 99–106.
52. Dennis Kux, *The United States and Pakistan 1947–2000: Disenchanted Allies* (Oxford: Oxford University Press, 2001).
53. Ishtiaq Ahmed, 'The Madrassa Industry', *Daily Times*, Lahore, 26 July 2005.
54. Kamal Matinuddin, *The Taliban Phenomenon: Afghanistan 1994–1997* (Oxford: Oxford University Press, 1999).
55. Ahmed Rashid, *Taliban: Militant Islam, Oil and Fundamentalism in Central Asia* (New Haven, CT: Yale University Press, 2000).
56. Kamal Matinuddin, *The Taliban Phenomenon: Afghanistan 1994–1997* (Oxford: Oxford University Press, 1999).
57. Zahid Hussain, 'In the Shadow of Terrorism', *Newsline*, Karachi, February 2000.
58. Anthony Davis, 'Inside Jihad International', *Asiaweek*, November 1999.
59. Stephen Cohen, *The Idea of Pakistan* (New Delhi: Oxford University Press, 2005), pp. 274–75.
60. Pervez Musharraf, *In the Line of Fire* (London: Simon and Schuster, 2006), pp. 199–207.
61. Pervez Musharraf, 'Address to the Nation', 12 January 2002, http://www.presidentofpakistan.gov.pk/FilesSpeeches/Addresses/1020200475758 AMword%20file.pdf (accessed 14 March 2008).
62. *Dawn*, 19 January 2002.
63. Mohammad Kamran, 'Blasphemy Law, Hudood Order to Stay', *Daily Times*, Lahore, 25 May 2002.
64. Iftikhar Ahmad Lodhi, *Forthcoming Pakistani Elections: A Profile on the Islamic Parties*, ISAS Brief No. 39 (Singapore: Institute of South Asian Studies), 26 December 2007.
65. Ibid.
66. Iftikhar Ahmad Lodhi, *The Grand Jirga Imperative: Is this the Solution to the Taliban Insurgency?* ISAS Brief No. 23 (Singapore: Institute of South Asian Studies), 20 September 2007.
67. Pervez Musharraf, *In the Line of Fire* (London: Simon and Schuster, 2006), p. 225.
68. *Daily Times*, 9 May 2002.
69. Ibid., 15 June 2002.
70. Ibid., 26 September 2002.

71. Ibid., 28 May 2005.
72. Ibid., 29 May 2005.
73. Ibid., 16 November 2005.
74. Ibid., 12 April 2006.
75. Ibid., 15 July 2006.
76. Pervez Musharraf, *In the Line of Fire* (London: Simon and Schuster, 2006), p. 252.
77. B. Raman, *Dargai and Chenagai, Waiting to Hear Zawahiri's Version.* International Terrorism Monitor, Paper No. 152 (also designated as Paper 2022), South Asia Analysis Group, 13 November 2006. http//www.southasiaanalysis.org/%5Cpapers21%5Cpaper2022.html (accessed 2 April 2008).
78. *The News*, 27 January 2007.
79. Ishtiaq Ahmed, 'Biased Moralities', *The News International*, 16 July 2007.
80. *The News*, 29 April 2007.
81. *Shanghai Daily*, 27 June 2007.
82. *The News*, 9 July 2007.
83. Ibid.
84. *Dawn*, 12 July 2007.
85. *The News*, 12 July 2007.
86. Ibid., 5 September 2007.
87. Ibid., 14 September 2007.
88. Benazir Bhutto, *Reconciliation, Islam, Democracy and the West* (London: Simon and Schuster, 2008), p. 12.
89. *The News*, 31 October 2007.
90. Ibid., 2 November 2007.
91. Ibid., 22 December 2007.
92. Ibid., 28 December 2007.
93. Ishtiaq Ahmed, 'The Assassination of Ms Bhutto', *The News*, Karachi–Islamabad–Lahore, 31 December 2007.
94. Ibid., 15 July 2006.

✳

8

Civil–Military Relations in Pakistan

Mohammad Waseem

◈ Introduction

Civil–military relations in Pakistan in the year 2008 were underscored by transition from a military-led government to a civilian government in a post-electoral framework. This can be seen as the second phase of democratization in that country, after the first phase (2002–07) had left the process of transition incomplete inasmuch as President Musharraf continued to control the business of the state. While the 'civilian' government from 2002 to 2007 had a public profile of being subservient to the general on top, the 'civilian' government sworn in after the February 2008 elections had a clear anti-Musharraf mandate. Pakistan faced the challenge of cohabitation between the army represented by President Musharraf, now a retired general, and Prime Minister Yusaf Raza Gilani at the head of a Pakistan People's Party (PPP)–Pakistan Muslim League (PML-N)–Awami National Party (ANP) coalition government.

The tug of war between the two sides was characteristic of the combative nature of civil–military relations in the country. The PPP's coalition partners, lawyers, retired judges, the media and the civil society in general, incessantly called for the exit of Musharraf from office. On his part, Musharraf insisted that he was the duly elected president for five years in October 2007. Being well-equipped with constitutional powers, enshrined in the 2003 17th Amendment, to dissolve the National Assembly and appoint judges of higher courts and chiefs of armed services, Musharraf posed a grave threat to the newly elected government. It was generally maintained that there were two parallel governments operating in the country from April 2008 onwards, one led by Prime Minister Gilani representing the Parliament and the other led by President Musharraf representing the extra-parliamentary forces.[1] The former gained strength only after Musharraf resigned on 18 August 2008.

The chequered history of civil–military relations in Pakistan is dotted by military coups, constitutional breakdowns, dissolution of elected

assemblies and periodical reform efforts in the direction of restructuring the state. Pakistan shared the praetorian phenomenon
with various other Third World countries from Latin America, Asia
and Africa, including Argentina, Brazil, Chile, Burma, Indonesia,
Thailand, Ghana, Nigeria and Uganda. A generation of scholars, from
Finer, Janowitz and Huntington onwards, drew upon various case
studies to build theoretical formulations to explain the problematic
nature of civil–military relations in these countries.[2] Subsequently,
scholarly research moved into the domain of transition from military
to civilian rule. Combined with two other streams of transition, one
from communist to representative rule such as in Eastern Europe as
well as in Vietnam and Kampuchea and the other from dynastic to
parliamentary rule such as in Nepal, the process of democratization
has produced a huge amount of research in the framework of comparative politics. The two processes of militarization and civilianization of the state system, especially when these represent recurrent
patterns of rule such as in Pakistan, together shape the political
context, which is the subject of the present enquiry.

The civil–military 'gap' is not a phenomenon confined to countries
such as Pakistan. Somewhat reverberating the 'gap' project in the
United States,[3] public opinion surveys in Britain point to a divergence of opinion about public life between the society and the
armed forces. These opinions relate to matters ranging from the
former's preference for individualism over group cohesion to its
support for liberalism as the moral and philosophical foundation
of democracy.[4] Liberal democracies live with this division in their
midst.[5] In a comparable situation in France, the military has been
traditionally considered to be an embodiment of the 'nation in arms',
which according to Vennesson is a powerful myth with its roots in
conscription, cushioned by nationalism.[6] While studies based on
opinion surveys in Western societies have looked at the problems
relating to the 'gap', no empirical data of that kind has been generally
available, relating to countries such as Pakistan. However, a recent
survey of democracy in South Asia brought out some interesting
observations about Pakistan. On the one hand, people wanted the
army to set things right in the political system. On the other hand,
they overwhelmingly favoured the rule of public representatives.[7] It is
obvious that there are no straight dichotomies of political behaviour
or public policy that crystallize and epitomize civil–military relations
in Pakistan.

While it is interesting to search for the roots of militarism, it is equally significant to look at the pattern of military disengagement from an overt political role. The way the military seeks to establish a link with the civilian institutions in a post-withdrawal scenario brings out its potential to secure its interests as a stakeholder in the power structure of the state such as in Pakistan after the 2002 and later the 2008 elections. In a long-term perspective, this transition shapes the politico-constitutional vision of the ruling setup from a position of strength. Egypt presents a classic case of a successful military disengagement from politics in recent decades. This process instantly transformed the military into an interest group, imbued with a relatively constrained access to society. However, like other militaries engaged in a similar process, the Egyptian military was not without 'politicism' even after disengagement.[8] It has been argued that military disengagement is conceptually separate from transition to democracy. It can be limited only to formal civilian control over the armed forces such as in Syria and Iraq under the Baath Party and in Egypt under Sadat and Hosni Mubarak.[9] The process of withdrawal most typically leaves 'authoritarian enclaves', 'reserved domains' and other manifestations of incomplete disengagement, along with conditions for re-engagement in certain cases such as in Nigeria, Sudan, El Salvador and Pakistan.[10] Indeed, in Pakistan, control over the nuclear command and control system, the policy framework covering conflicts across the border with Afghanistan and India and later the army's Strategic Plans Division (SPD), among others, remained the military's 'reserved domains' from Benazir Bhutto's assumption of office in 1988 to Gilani's induction as prime minister in 2008.[11] Civil–military relations in post-military 'democratic' states assume a high level of significance insofar as these provide a measure of the potential of the armed forces to establish a working relationship with civilian institutions in general.

The Latin American case studies of democratization present two broad perspectives on transition.[12] First, the military effectively maintains the ability to exercise control over public policy and safeguard its institutional interests after the transfer of power: Brazil and Chile comprehensively represent this model. Here, the mode-of-transition perspective characterizes the democratization process with continuity rather than change in terms of the military's pre-eminent role in decision-making on top. The second perspective focuses on the electoral dynamics and its impact on public attitudes towards participatory politics, institutional accountability and patron-client relations. It has been argued that the transformative nature of the whole process of civilianization through elections, formation of a representative ruling set-up and the ongoing discursive practices in and outside the Parliament should not be underestimated. This process involves decline in the military's power in terms of control over policy as well as public discourse. In other words, there is more to democratization than a mere farcical transfer of power. In certain other cases, such as in El Salvador, it was the US pressure that led to reforms in police, judiciary, the electoral system, and the improved human rights situation in the early 1990s, after the military regime had resisted outside efforts to curb oppression and allow internal criticism and contestation for a decade.[13]

The case of electoral politics in Pakistan clearly points to the dynamics of public mobilization playing a crucial role in taking the initiative away from the military-led government. For example, Musharraf laid out the turf for victory for the so-called 'king's party' Pakistan Muslim League–Quaid-i-Azam (PML-Q) in the 2008 elections. However, the election campaign was influenced by unforeseen circumstances, which foiled the plans of the government. The pattern of public mobilization was underscored, among other things, by: the year-long lawyers' movement for restoration of the judiciary; return of the two former prime ministers Nawaz Sharif and Benazir Bhutto from exile; imposition of emergency rule on 3 November 2007 along with dismissal of scores of judges of higher courts; the lifting of emergency on 15 December; assassination of Benazir Bhutto on 27 December; and postponement of elections from 8 January to 18 February 2008. Musharraf lost the game as the campaign brought in a new set of issues and policies, newly mobilized identities, and vastly reinvigorated leadership profiles.

In an attempt to conceptualize civil–military relations in Africa in the period of transition, Jendayi Frazer finds it ironical that democratization focuses on electoral and constitutional reforms rather than new institutional arrangements to control the military.[14] In his view, an institutional strategy would involve putting in place structural counterweights in terms of re-chartering the relationship between the executive, the legislature and the security apparatus. The transition process shapes policy choices. However, these choices are path-dependent, pulled by 'forks in history' such as mega events in the past or 'policy martingales' reflecting chance fluctuations of history.[15] In the context of the present enquiry, we can observe that the institutional imbalance in the realm of civil–military relations has typically underscored the two processes of military takeover and civilianization in Pakistan. In both cases, the military's security orientation operates as dependent and independent variables in international and domestic politics respectively. The military is oriented more to the world outside the national boundaries than inside them because its defence mechanism is operative quintessentially against the external enemy. This puts it in a category different from other institutions of the state. The fact that a typical Third World state undergoes tremendous institutional pressures in the process of state-making at home, as well as the fact that it does not control the international environment in which it operates, finally creates an acute security predicament.[16] This situation can lead to even further securitization of the national vision if global powers subordinate the regional security dynamics to their own strategic framework such as through proxy wars or troop deployment in the region.[17] In Pakistan, consciousness and projection of national security as the leading determinant of the army's world view assumed an ideological dimension under General Zia in the 1980s in pursuit of a vehement Islamization programme. Two decades later, Prime Minister Gilani was still 'harking back to Zia's days' by claiming that the army was the guardian of the country's ideological frontiers.[18] It is instructive to compare this phenomenon with the way the 'national security syndrome' operated in Turkey, which has been afflicted with a similar problem in civil–military relations. The Turkish military assumed control as well as oversight of public policy, merged issues of security with politics, played the role of agency for defining security and constrained the civilian authority.[19] Again, somewhat along the lines of securitization of the national vision in Pakistan in the perspective of asymmetry with India, the perceived regional imbalances underscored the national security orientation at the cost of democratic deficit in Turkey.[20]

How far can structural factors, in this case the institutional apparatus of the military overriding a weak political community, operate without a substantive input from human agency? Can political leaders emerging in the transition period adopt strategies that can lead to civilian supremacy over armed forces? In a comparative study of South Korea and Indonesia, Kim, Liddle and Said argue in favour of initiatives of the political leadership as determinants of the fate of the democratic project.[21] In their view, political leaders can be constrained or enabled by structural factors into taking autonomous and consequential decisions in the direction of establishing civilian supremacy. Thus, President Chun Hwan (1980–88) of South Korea played the opposition leaders Sam and Jung against each other, pulled the emergent middle class out of its conservative mould, depoliticized the officer corps, stopped appointment of military personnel as civil servants and put up the defence spending for parliamentary scrutiny. As opposed to this, under successive Indonesian Presidents, Habibie, Abdurrehman Wahid and Megawati, officer corps barred the way to civilian control over the defence budget as well as to prosecution of those accused of war crimes in East Timor.[22] In Pakistan, Z.A. Bhutto was able to save 195 declared war criminals from being prosecuted by the post-Independence Bangladesh government for perpetrating atrocities on Bengalis during the 1971 civil war.

The civil–military gap in Pakistan operates in terms of the generals' preference for concentration of power in the hands of the head of the state, the Central government and the executive at the expense of the prime minister, the provincial governments and the legislature respectively. While army coups were followed by civilianization of military regimes after a few years, the 'reserved domains' of its power and privilege remained and even expanded under the formal civilian set-ups led by military presidents. Under the civilianization process, the electoral dynamics reinvigorated political parties and patterns of leadership through issue-formation and mobilization of the voting public in general. The transition from military to civilian rule involved the army's quest for putting in place such security mechanisms that would keep the ultimate policy choices in strategic areas in its own hands. Thus, both direct military rule and effective military presence behind a civilian government kept the political initiative with the army and securitized the national vision in the long run. After Z.A. Bhutto, who was able to operate with relative autonomy from the overwhelming influence of the army in its hour of defeat in East Pakistan, no leader was able to override the latter's structural presence at the heart of the state with a view to establishing civilian supremacy.

▣ Setting the Analytical Context

Pakistan is a classic example of a praetorian state. Here, the army has emerged as a guardian of the state, initiator of national agenda and chief arbiter of conflict between social and political forces.

The longevity and recurrence of the army's role in the business of the state has a temporal dimension related to the period and duration of direct military rule, indirect military rule, informal but effective military input in governance and military's subordination to civilian supremacy. Any project of analysis into the nature and character of the army's involvement in politics would need to define and categorize its role through various phases of Pakistan's history. Table 8.1 seeks to give a broad profile of the army's role in Pakistan.

Table 8.1: Patterns of Civilian and Military Rule in Pakistan, 1947–2009

	Type	*Duration*	*Period*
1	Direct military rule	17 years	1958–62, 1969–71, 1977–85, 1999–2002
2	Elected government under a military president (retired or serving general)	16 years	1962–69, 1985–88, 2002–08
3	Elected government under a civilian president: 'Rule of Troika'	12 years	1988–99, 2008–09
4	Supremacy of non-parliamentary forces under the formal parliamentary rule	11 years	1947–58
5	Civilian supremacy	6 years	1971–77

The army's direct rule covers 17 out of the 62 years of the post-Independence period. Another span of 16 years was characterized by the rule of the elected governments under successive military presidents — Ayub in mufti, Zia in uniform and Musharraf in uniform and later in mufti. The ruling generals insisted that they presided over 'real' democracy, free of all the ills of a 'sham' democracy under politicians.[23] Twelve years were taken by 'rule of troika' comprising a civilian president, a prime minister and a Chief of Army Staff (COAS), and eleven years by rule of non-parliamentary forces led by the civil bureaucracy in the early post-Independence period. The period of credible civilian supremacy under Z. A. Bhutto was as short as 6 years.

The discussion in the following sections focuses on three major aspects of civil–military relations in Pakistan: (i) state formation, (ii) genesis of military politics and, (iii) project of constitutional engineering. First, we argue in favour of going beyond the army's corporate interests and institutional ethos to analyzing the shape and character of the postcolonial state in Pakistan, which led to the ascendancy of extra-parliamentary forces. We propose to look into the 'forks in history', which pulled the administrative, financial, and intellectual resources of the state in the direction of a resilient and overarching 'policy martingale' in the post-Independence period, bearing a heavy stamp of military thinking. As Hamza Alavi argues, the ruling elite in the new state emergent from British India drew upon the two institutions of the army and the bureaucracy.[24] In his view, the role of agency in bringing up the new structure of power through the pursuit of a vehement agenda of state formation through the partition of India was played by the Muslim *salariat*, which was socially embedded in the middle class.[25] Partition gave birth to a relatively new ethnic hierarchy led by the Urdu-speaking and Punjabi-speaking migrant elite. These two factors of class and ethnicity determined the shape of the emerging power structure in the country. We shall focus on the way the state elite, supported by its constituency in the educated, professional and commercial middle classes, dealt with the political leadership typically drawn from the tribal and landed elite in the context of share-out of the state's resources. The clue to the army's ascendancy to power lies in the dominance of extra-parliamentary forces over the state system operating along the lines of non-representative rule, which gradually opened up space for generals on top of the ruling hierarchy.

The second aspect of our present enquiry relates to the historical-structural analysis of the economic and political power of the army. The strategic role of the top brass in the policy-making process draws heavily on its historical progression of power and privilege. We shall follow a model of path dependence in the context of the evolving position of the army in the constellation of powers ruling Pakistan. The function of preservation of the social and political order in the country devolved squarely on the officer corps in the tortuous process of state-building. The more the army entered into the business of the state, the more adversely it affected the growth of political institutions. It is almost a structural requirement of a post-coup ruling set-up to adopt the agenda of de-institutionalizing politics. We propose to look at the way the army pursued its nation-building project and lent its worldview to other institutions and groups. The direct army rule, encompassing less than two decades, somewhat dispensed with the need to negotiate terms of reference with rival elite groups. At other times, the army was obliged to co-opt or coerce members of the executive, the legislature and the judiciary. In addition, the army leadership felt the need to establish the legitimacy of its rule for acceptance in the wider public. This led to adoption of ideologies ranging from developmentalism under Ayub and Musharraf to Islamization under Zia.

Finally, we plan to focus on the patterns of civil–military relations as part of the process of democratization. This entails a discussion of the army's preferences and priorities in terms of putting in place constitutional formulas for government-formation. The Pakistan army continues to be shy of committing its institutional resources to the day-to-day administration of the country.[26] Instead, it typically relies on the existing state institutions to deliver on that score. It is true that the number of retired and serving officers appointed in various sectors of the state apparatus always jumped manifold under military rule. However, it did not bring about a qualitative change in the nature and character of the administrative structure, which continued to be in the hands of the civil bureaucracy. All the four military coups were followed by the process of civilianization through elections. One can argue that politics in Pakistan is in a perennial process of democratization, which is dotted with periods of military and non-military rule. This has brought about a more or less stable pattern of civil–military relations whereby all civilian ruling set-ups remain acutely sensitive to the army's preferred set of policies. The previous phase of post-military democratic dispensation (1988–99) was characterized by the 'rule of troika', with the COAS as the key person popularly perceived to be at the helm of affairs from behind the scene. The two stints of Benazir Bhutto and the first stint of Nawaz Sharif in office were cut short by the President ostensibly at the behest of the army, while the latter's second term in office was put to an end through the 1999 coup. In this context, the discretionary space available to civilian governments shrank considerably. In 2003 and again in 2008, elections were held in order to provide the political class formal representation in the process of decision-making on top. While the Musharraf government manipulated the former elections successfully, the latter produced unexpected results. This in turn led to the challenge of cohabitation, beyond the older options of co-option and coercion of politicians by military governments.

▧ State Formation

We shall argue that the army in Pakistan has a larger-than-life role beyond its corporate interests and security orientation. This role is enmeshed with state-craft proper, underscored by the requisite constitutional framework. Generals in Pakistan swear by the Constitution. This puts them in a category different from the Latin American officer corps, essentially because the institutional-constitutional framework of the state in Pakistan has a presumably higher potential for defining and sanctioning the exercise of legal authority than its counterpart in the latter. At the core of this issue lies the fact that British imperialism was maturer than the French and the Dutch and, with a larger margin, the Spanish and the Portuguese maritime empires in terms of establishment of the rule of law, internally differentiated administrative structure and non-arbitrary sources of legitimacy. Transplantation of British laws and institutions in colonial India 'objectified' the patterns of authority and lent a potentially autonomous role to the bureaucracy, the judiciary and later the emergent legislative bodies.[27] The principle of constitutional legitimacy to be operationalized in the form of rule of public representatives provides the legal foundation of the state of Pakistan.

The army is constrained to operate accordingly by temporarily suspending the rules of the game relating to the elective principle and division of powers between the various organs of the state. It then rewrites these rules and incorporates them in the corpus of laws. It is the 'constitutional' approach of the Pakistan army to the business of the state that distinguishes it from its counterparts in Latin America. This lends special significance to the institutional-constitutional framework put together repeatedly by the army. In Pakistan, the law has typically operated at the centre of the power struggle between the army and the political elite. Politics in Pakistan is characterized by a regime of basic human rights protected through the writ jurisdiction of higher courts, electoral expression of the public will and commitment to search for a legal cover of the perceived non-democratic measures taken by the government. Constitutional wrangling over issues of policy and exercise of power by various institutions of the state characterizes the period of transition when the outgoing military dispensation seeks to preserve as much of the legal and institutional space under the future 'civilian' set-up as possible.[28] The army has abrogated or suspended, amended and restored the Constitution in that order. This shows its commitment to what it considers the need for preservation of the social and political order as reflected through the recurrent mode of judicial-thinking remembered as the doctrine of state necessity.[29]

It is argued that the process of state-building in Pakistan has led to ascendancy of the non-parliamentary forces — first the migrant-led civil bureaucracy and later the army. The sources of this phenomenon can be located in the way Partition and later migration from India to Pakistan took place. The partition of India created a grossly anomalous situation. The Pakistan movement was led by the Muslim elite from northern and western India comprising the Muslim minority provinces. The elite dominated the umbrella national party Muslim League that established Pakistan in Muslim majority areas in the northwest and the northeast of India. The government of Pakistan was dominated by the elite which had migrated to the new country after Partition. Both the first governor general Muhammad Ali Jinnah and the first Prime Minister Liaqat Ali Khan were migrants from India. Similarly, the higher bureaucracy and the judiciary as well as the business elite were dominated by migrants.[30] By 1951, 7.2 million Muslims had migrated, constituting 20 per cent of the population in (West) Pakistan, as opposed to India where migrants accounted for 1 per cent.[31] Migrants shaped the new state in important ways. Politics in Pakistan suffered from structural discontinuity in terms of establishing a state apparatus from scratch. Migrants shaped the psyche of the new nation along feelings of insecurity at the hands of India, commitment to Islamic ideology and the need to unite against all odds. The political imagination of the migrant community was characterized by an all-Pakistan approach to public life and relative intolerance of sub-national identities.

The new state was characterized by institutional imbalance. While the executive wing of the state was dominated by migrants, the Constituent Assembly formally represented 'local' elements. It had been elected before Partition by provincial assemblies from the Muslim majority areas now constituting Pakistan. The federal government sought to bypass the Parliament whenever possible and rule through the higher bureaucracy, which was itself migrant-dominated. This pattern of asymmetrical distribution of power between the executive and the legislature was reflected through the loss of parliamentary sovereignty. For six decades, politics in Pakistan has been typically characterized by a low power-potential of the Parliament. The country experienced a situation of parliamentary sovereignty, at least in a legal sense, only from 1972 to 1979 and 1997 to 1999. The migrant elite, and later unrepresentative elites of one persuasion or the other, dreaded the prospects of their exit from power in the event of elections, which would have shifted the locus of power and legitimacy to the Parliament. The perceived dys-functionality of elections for the ruling elite has been a permanent feature of politics in the country. Aversion to electoral politics and parliamentarism in general was combined with commitment to unitarian models of government with a provision for a strong Centre. Feelings of insecurity vis-à-vis India revolving around the Kashmir conflict led to a cult of unity in Pakistan at the obvious cost of provincial autonomy. Bureaucracy, which was re-organized on an all-Pakistan basis, controlled the financial and institutional resources in the provinces much to the chagrin of local leaderships. Four out of five provinces — East Bengal, Sindh, NWFP and Baluchistan — demanded autonomy in the face of the perceived hegemony of the Centre, especially in its bureaucratic incarnation.[32]

Katharine Adeney and Andrew Wyatt look at the interplay of structure-agency dynamics in South Asia, respectively identified with the legal-constitutional framework and the power-wielding elite on top.[33] In ethnic terms, the role of the agency was played by the migrant leadership and the Punjab elite. In the 1950s, a process of Punjabization of the state set in.[34] In terms of class dynamics, the establishment continued to draw on the middle class from Punjabi and Muhajir communities, remotely followed by Pashtuns. This class displayed a 'statist' perspective characterized by centralization of power in the hands of the federal government at the cost of provin-cial autonomy, Islamic ideology as a supra-legal source of legitimacy and a relative lack of tolerance for ethnic identities. Both the struc-ture and agency gravitated towards the state elite represented by the Punjabi-Muhajir middle class. Elections were constantly post-poned ever since the promulgation of the Constitution in 1956. The prospects of transfer of the political initiative, along with its implications for policy and privilege, to the elected representatives of the people, increasingly engaged the army in the business of the state.

The political and constitutional perspectives of the migrant-led bureaucracy defined the national agenda, which was shared and upheld by the army. One can argue that the state in Pakistan in its formative years was almost predisposed to giving the army a predominant place in the power structure. By 1958, the decade-long process of state formation had led to the emergence of an establishment that managed to wrest initiative from the hands of politicians. The first 'civilian' coup had already taken place in 1954, when Governor-General Ghulam Mohammad dissolved the Constituent Assembly. The judiciary, which extended its blessings to the dissolution of the Parliament in 1954, subsequently legitimized the 1958 coup.

▨ Genesis of Military Politics

Research about the ascendancy of the army in Pakistan typically focuses on the vacuum in the political system due to disintegration of the Muslim League after Partition and the decay of political institutions in general.[35] Some scholars point to the ambitions of generals to forestall the shift of power to public representatives, such as in 1958, while others focus on the army's serious reservations about rapprochement with India, which it resisted at various times in history.[36] In this context, estrangement between civil and military wings of the state can be located to various developments ranging from the 1948 UN-sponsored ceasefire in Kashmir, which led to an aborted coup known as the Rawalpindi Conspiracy Case, to the 1999 visit of Indian prime minister Vajpayee to Lahore, which was followed by the Kargil conflict. Still others argue that the American connection strengthened the Pakistan army and authoritarian rule in general, especially during the three phases of strategic relationship between the two countries in the 1950s–60s, the 1980s and the in new millennium.[37] It has been argued that Pakistan's pursuit of parity with India in defence potential put the army in a commanding position in the corridors of power.[38] This phenomenon, known as the 'India syndrome', continued to operate for half a century after Partition.[39] It was pointed out that threat perceptions vis-à-vis India produced two major schools of thought among the elite: one conservative, which looked at India as a potentially hegemonic power in the region; the other ultraconservative, which saw India seeking to destroy Pakistan at the first opportunity.[40]

Ayesha Siddiqa has drawn a six-fold typology of civil–military relations, which includes three clusters of roles and functions: civilian supremacy in democratic and authoritarian systems; domination of ruler, arbitrator or parent-guardian military; and, finally, warlordism.[41] She characterizes the role of the military in Pakistan as arbitrator prior to 1977 and, as parent-guardian in the post-1977 period. In the former role, the army played a backseat driver, balancer of power, stabilizer and watchdog vis-à-vis the civilian authority. In the latter role, civilian partners of the army played a crucial role while the army sought an institutional presence in the political system as guardian of its expanding political and economic interests.[42] For the purposes of our present enquiry, we need to outline the power base of the army in the society and the state, spread over decades or even generations. We plan to focus on a path-dependent approach to political ascendancy of the army inasmuch as it was able to identify its institutional interests with the national interest, both symbolically and ideologically.

The major strength of the army drew on Punjab, which has been the power base of the country. The GHQ (General Headquarters) of the Indian army for north-western provinces was located in Rawalpindi. By the First World War, Punjab alone accounted for two-thirds of the cavalry — almost 90 per cent of the artillery and slightly less than half of the infantry of the Indian army.[43] The tribes from northern Punjab, including Awans, Janjuas, Gakhars and Rajputs in general were characterized as martial races. At the turn of the twentieth century, when lands from newly irrigated canal colonies were allocated, half a million acres went to soldiers and ex-soldiers.[44] This tradition has continued to operate for a hundred years now. On the eve of the First World War, the recruitment drive of the army brought the rural-based Unionist Party on board and turned Punjab into a 'quasi-military state'.[45] During the period between the two world wars, the welfare of peasant soldiers from the recruitment areas was a top priority of the government. This was reflected through the pattern of expansion of franchise for elections for the Punjab Assembly, whereby special provisions were made to give the right to vote to soldiers. In due course, almost one-third of the provincial electorate comprised soldiery. This figure jumped to more than two-thirds of the electorate in the case of military recruitment areas.[46] All this transformed the army into a formidable social and political presence in Punjab on the eve of Independence.

As Partition degenerated into communal riots in West Punjab, certain military units were put together as Pakistan Military Evacuation Organization (PMEO) to safely escort Muslim refugees from East Punjab. In this process, army officers and soldiers were politicized.[47] Anti-Indianism took deep roots in Punjab where refugee families suffered casualties while crossing the border. The army's sense of insecurity at the hands of India accelerated during and after each armed conflict or confrontationist posture. This happened after the Kashmir war of 1947–48; Indo-Pakistan wars of 1965 and 1971; the Indian occupation of the Siachen Glacier in 1984; Indian military exercises Brass Tacks, 1987; the nuclear stand-off between India and Pakistan, 1990; the Kargil conflict, 1999; and the troop deployment on borders, 2002. Each episode increased the sense of national insecurity in the army and the ruling elite. As the army got politicized, politics became militarized, in the sense that national policies and priorities were increasingly set by the army.

Over time, the army built the myth of simple, honest, innocent and hard-working masses who were exploited by politicians. This was in continuation of the tradition of paternalistic rule of 'guardians', which had been carefully cultivated under the colonial government.[48] According to this view, political leaders mobilized the people of Pakistan in pursuit of their personal, factional, tribal and ethnic agendas at the cost of national interest. This process of state-formation was destined to bring up the military as a leading factor. Politics in Pakistan displayed major features of military politics even before the military takeover. Generals had made their preferences known in terms of foreign and defence policies and domestically in the direction of controlling leftist and ethnic parties through various means. In the broader context of international diplomacy, Commander-in-Chief General Ayub conducted strategic negotiations directly with his counterparts in Washington, DC, bypassing his political bosses at home. The army enjoyed a level of autonomy that was denied to all other institutions. The army largely upheld and reinvigorated the new state's institutional, constitutional and attitudinal perspectives.

The army's superordinate role in the elite structure was clearly established under Ayub (1958–69), even as civil bureaucracy continued to be in charge of administration in major fields of public life. The Ayub system was dynamic in terms of economic activity. However, that led to unbridled urbanization, income inequalities across classes, regions and sectors and job insecurity in general. At the same time, that system was extremely predisposed towards status quo. It represented a rigid institutional model of rule under the 1962 Constitution, which rendered the Parliament and the political parties powerless. There was no way to enter the system for politically active or ambitious individuals, groups or communities.

The failure of the Ayub system in 1969, subsequently followed by a vehement year-long campaign for elections held on 7 December 1970, put the army on the defensive. It has been argued that the image of the army moved downwards from a saviour of the nation to less charitable roles through various stages before and after Ayub's fall.[49] Ayub's successor General Yahya was acutely conscious of the need to preserve the high profile of the army as custodian of the nation's faith and trust. He soon moved to install a civilian cabinet, even as important decisions continued to be taken by the martial law secretariat or directly by the GHQ in Rawalpindi. Sensitivity about its public image influenced the army in terms of deciding the level and scope of its involvement in the day-to-day administrative and oversight functions. In the initial phase of the coup, the army typically exercised control over administrative activity through supervisory teams and military courts. Soon after, the army was withdrawn to the barracks, and civil bureaucracy continued to be in charge as before.

Stephen Cohen has mentioned three generations of army leadership — British, American and Pakistani, corresponding to Ayub, Yahya and Zia.[50] Ayub represented a generation of Sandhurst-trained generals, imbued with an ethos of guardianship and orientation towards status quo in terms of maintenance of the social and political order. Yahya and his colleagues belonged to the 'American generation' trained under the Military Assistance Programme (MAP). They were less paternalistic and more liberal towards the reformist agenda. Zia, on the other hand, was 'local' in vision and style, and thus represented the 'Pakistani' generation. It can be surmised that the army generals after Zia belonged to the third category, along with variations of style and approach according to the nature of their exposure to foreign training. In style, the army leadership moved from the elitism and modernism of Ayub and the conservatism and populism of Zia onwards to the liberalism and reformism of Musharraf. However, all along, army rule represented exclusivism, pragmatism and authoritarianism, punctuated by political repression. Pakistan underwent a change in the recruitment pattern of the army in class and regional terms in the 1960s and the1970s.[51] This brought in hawkish elements who would typically like to set things right in all spheres of public activity, nab corrupt politicians and uphold a right-wing reformist agenda as well as embrace Islamic ideology as the ultimate ideational sanction of the state.

The Z.A. Bhutto government (1971–77) represented a major set-back to the ongoing ascendant position of the army in its overt or covert political role, at least for a short time. Under Z.A. Bhutto, a number of military officers were retired, including the chiefs of army and air force. He condemned Bonapartist tendencies in the army and restructured its leadership by replacing the commander-in-chief with the Chief of Army Staff (COAS) and bringing in the Chairman of the Joint Chiefs of Staff Committee on top of the three services.[52] One can see a parallel situation of civilian assertion of suprem-acy over armed forces in South Korea under Chun as mentioned earlier and even more significantly, in Argentina after the defeat in the Falklands War in 1982.[53] The Supreme Court verdict in Asma Jillani Case in April 1972 declared Yahya's coup as an act of usurp-ation, illegal and unconstitutional in nature. It maintained that the coup maker should be 'tried for high treason and suitably punished. This alone will serve as deterrent to would-be adventurers'.[54] The Bhutto government remains the only example of a civilian ruling setup in Pakistan's history that enjoyed formal as well as effective supremacy over the armed forces.

The central point of our argument about the army's role in Pakistan is that it enjoyed support from various elite sections of the population within the dominant Punjabi and Muhajir commu-nities. This fact transcended the conceptual formulation of 'gap' between the military and the society. The clue lies in the specific elite composition of Pakistan, which served as the ultimate and stable constituency for praetorianism. From the 1968–69 anti-Ayub movement through the 1970 elections and the 1977 anti-Bhutto movement to Zia's martial law (1977–85), populist forces including industrial labour, students, lawyers, intelligentsia, party workers from the leftist and ethnic parties and the general masses found themselves on the opposite side of the army, the bureaucracy, the *ulema*, the capitalist class and the landed elite. Z.A. Bhutto symbolized these forces as a charismatic leader riding the wave of popularity in West Pakistan through the 1970 elections and later as president (1971–73) and prime minister (1973–77).

The elite groups of various persuasions joined hands during the 1977 anti-Bhutto movement and subsequently gravitated to-wards Zia's martial law government (1977–85). The mainstream politics, with its epicentre in Punjab, was divided into pro-Bhutto and anti-Bhutto camps for the following quarter of a century, the latter comprehensively identified with the army in general and Zia in particular. This explains the way Islamists joined hands with the army under several military and non-military governments for three decades after 1970. The actual or potential alliance between the mosque and the army continued to be a formidable challenge to the mainstream political parties, ethnic parties and, in its post-9/11 reincarnation, to the liberal project of the Musharraf government.[55] From the 1980s onwards, the ISI (Inter Services Intelligence) operated and sponsored links with various Islamic groups. These groups ranged from the Afghan mujahideen and Taliban in the 1980s and 1990s respectively to Islamic parties in Pakistan led by Jamiat Ulema-e-Islam (JUI) and Jamaat-e-Islami (JI) during these decades.[56] In the post-9/11 situation, American scholars, politicians and media commentators often accused the Musharraf government for continuing to operate these relations with impunity.[57] In the context of a war against terrorism, Musharraf was considered a 'marginal satisfier' who had become 'adept over time at manoeuvring with the religious political establishment'.[58] Pakistan was advised not to develop its national identity on the basis of 'radical Islam nor in reflexive opposition to India'.[59]

As noted earlier, the army has enjoyed a vehement support base in the state bureaucracy as well as in the big business outside the state structure. Civil bureaucracy has been conceived as a potential ally of the army in its opposition to politicians. Alavi's conceptual formulation about the state in Pakistan focuses on the military-bureaucratic establishment. Relations between the two state apparatuses have not moved along unilinear lines. Civil bureaucracy lost its power and prestige proportionate to the comprehensive inroads into decision-making channels of the state made first by the Pakistan People's Party (PPP) in the 1970s and later by the army in the 1980s. However, the bureaucracy continued to be the main institutional vehicle through which military rule was operationalized.[60] The Musharraf government's devolution plan took away both power and lustre from various bureaucratic positions, especially at the district level. However, the higher bureaucracy was able to thwart major reform efforts in the direction of decentralization, accountability and performance-related career patterns.[61] At the other end, the business community comprised the Muhajir commercial elite from Bombay followed by Calcutta and Delhi in the early years after Partition. It was augmented by the emergent bourgeoisie of Punjab led by migrants from East Punjab in India in the last quarter of the twentieth century. The business community has been a stable constituency of successive military regimes from Ayub to Musharraf. Showing its acute dependence on the development planning channels of the government from the early post-Independence years to the late 2000s, the bourgeoisie in Pakistan fully availed official patronage in pursuit of the latter's project of industrialization. Z.A. Bhutto's policy of nationalization in the 1970s had acutely damaged the leading industrial houses. The latter lent full financial backing to the anti-Bhutto movement in 1977 and made a common cause with Islamic opposition during the movement. The business community has been against the PPP for nearly four decades. It shuns all politics, especially of the populist variety identified with the PPP, and finds army rule a stabilizing factor.

In recent decades, the army made substantive inroads into big businesses in various sectors of economic activity. In her study of the military economy, Ayesha Siddiqa applied the concept of 'milbus' (military business) to the expanding network of financial and commercial activities of the defence establishment. She outlined the military's economic empire at three distinct levels of operations: (i) organizational level, which included the profit-making activities of the National Logistic Cell (NLC), the Frontier Works Organization (FWO) and Special Communications Organization (SCO) as well as various cooperatives; (ii) the four subsidiaries, two belonging to the army (that is, Fauji Foundation and Army Welfare Trust), and one each to the Air Force, (that is, Shaheen Foundation) and to the Navy, (that is, Bahria Foundation); iii) allotment of real estate and provision for employment and business opportunities for military personnel, both serving and retired.[62] It can be argued that the military's economic power correlates very closely with its political power. The three armed forces have sought to go beyond the defence budget into large-scale market activities, in addition to allocation of landed property and creation of jobs for officers and soldiers. The military's subsidiary organizations accumulated immense power. Sometimes, they gave clear signals that they did not accept civilian supremacy. The head of the Fauji Foundation Lt. Gen. (retd.) Amjad was accused of selling a sugar mill for Rs 300 million against a higher bid of Rs 387 million: In the face of a furore in the Senate on the information about the deal, which was officially provided to the house, the Fauji Foundation published large advertisements in the press rejecting the information altogether. It practically de-acknowledged the jurisdiction of the Parliament over military affairs.[63]

▩ Constitutional Engineering

Current approaches to the phenomenon of praetorianism dwell on a dichotomy between constitutional politics and military politics.[64] Formally, a military coup displaces a constitutional government through extra-constitutional means. Thus Generals Ayub, Yahya, Zia and Pervez Musharraf intervened in politics in 1958, 1969, 1977 and 1999 respectively by dissolving the Parliament and dismissing the lawful government. However, the story does not end there. Constitutionalism provides the strongest undercurrent for political and administrative activity in Pakistan. Constitutionalism bounced back after each coup. Military governments in various countries have been obliged to hold elections and sometimes quit office, such as in Nigeria, Turkey, Bangladesh and Ghana. The constitutional tradition continues to haunt military leaders in government till they transfer power to civilians, except in such atypical cases as Myanmar.

In Pakistan, all the four military governments sought to keep the prevalent constitutional set-up intact with the exception of those articles and clauses that related to the elective principle, one way or another. When President Iskandar Mirza launched his coup on 7 October 1958, he declared that the country would be governed as nearly as possible 'in accordance with the late Constitution'.[65] Courts were to continue their functions as before. The military government resolved to build a new democratic system and tighten up existing laws.[66] When the spectre of elections loomed large on the horizon in 1957–58 and threatened to disrupt the prevalent privilege structures, the army moved in. It thwarted the process of installation of an elected government in office and thus prevented the balance of power from tipping in favour of the political leaders who would have enjoyed a new source of legitimacy in the form of an electoral mandate. Weber points to the modern state as a bearer of sovereign prerogatives and creator of legal norms whereby elections provide legitimacy to rulers without necessarily opening up the state system to general masses.[67] The competing forces tend to find their respective stable positions in the state through parliamentary elections.[68] However, in a typical Third World society, the institutional potential of political actors is somewhat limited in terms of directing the election campaign along the pre-planned means and ends. Not surprisingly, an election tends to assume a movement character.[69]

In 1958, the Pakistan military acted before the impending elections and saved the situation for the ruling elite. In 1970, circumstances forced Yahya's military government to go ahead with elections because social and political groups had been far too mobilized during the anti-Ayub movement to be kept out of the system any more. The 1970 elections produced results that were dreaded by the army for 23 years. These results radicalized politics along ethnic, linguistic, class and sectarian lines. In 1977, Zia's coup was launched in a spirit of reactive militarism,[70] inasmuch as the interests of various groups — military, bureaucracy, *ulema* and the business community — were threatened by an all-out lawlessness. The 1977 coup, as indeed the 1999 coup, did not abrogate the 1973 Constitution. Typically, only certain articles relating to elections and elected assemblies were rendered inoperative.

The first speech of all the four coup-makers after takeover is symptomatic of the vision and strategy of the army. Most typically, they 'suggest that the country is on the verge of destruction, condemn the politicians and the toppled government, pat the people on the back, lionize the army, describing the takeover as something "unpleasant", emphasize publicly the "reluctance" with which they had to take the action, suggest that the action is taken in the greater national interest, claim that the country has been saved by this action and promise greener pastures for the masses'.[71] Charles Kennedy has given an interesting checklist of measures, which the coup-makers in Pakistan felt obliged to take after taking over power. They would typically 'avoid legal chaos', 'make things legal in the short term', 'reinvent local government', 'intimidate the civil bureaucracy and the superior judiciary' and 'rewrite the Constitution'.[72] Each time a new Bonaparte launched a coup, he faced the issue of 'constitutionalizing' his action in various steps. This involved, beyond mere stretching of the interpretation of law, the assumption of powers to change the law itself. That in turn required the higher courts to provide legitimacy to the military government. This came through in several cases starting with the Tamizuddin Case in 1954, followed by the Dosso Case in 1958 to the Zafar Ali Shah Case in 2000, with the exception of the Asma Jillani Case in 1972.

In the 1978 Begum Nusrat Bhutto Case and the 2000 Zafar Ali Shah Case, the Supreme Court also allowed the military government to amend the Constitution. The judiciary was subjected to taking a fresh oath after the 1977 and 1999 coups, in the backdrop of continuation in force of the 1973 Constitution sans its provisions relating to electoral entities. Both Zia and Musharraf, under their respective Provisional Constitution Orders (PCOs) of 1980 and 2000 forced the judges of the higher courts to show allegiance to the new 'constitutional' reality instead of the Constitution itself. In November 2007, Musharraf again subjected the higher judiciary to take oath on the new PCO promulgated under the Emergency. Appointment of senior judges under Musharraf, much as under Zia, was carried out with extreme partiality. Lower down, appointment of district and sessions judges was similarly scrutinized with a view to eventually rigging the elections, in which they would serve as returning officers.[73]

In the context of elections and elected governments, the army's political vision focused on the leadership factor and not on the participation factor. It believed that an executive president was ideally equipped with the authority and vision to lead the nation to the promised land. For half a century, the army has favoured the presidential system for Pakistan. In the view of the army, 'parliamentarism' meant dispersion and dilution of state authority, because the leader of the house would be typically committed to keeping his majority on the floor. In this process, he would be obliged to accommodate members of minority communities, smaller parties and many others who were suspect in the eyes of the state for one reason or the other. Ayub's military government (1958–62) served the function of transition from the parliamentary to the presidential system. Later, when Yahya's government was bogged down in military operation in East Pakistan in 1971, he allegedly prepared a draft Constitution that was reportedly presidential. This despite the fact that the presidential system was comprehensively rejected by the nation during the 1968–69 anti-Ayub movement. Similarly, Zia's military government (1977–85) again served the function of bringing about transition from a parliamentary to semi-presidential system by changing the 1973 Constitution from within under the 1985 8th Amendment. Successive presidents dissolved assemblies and dismissed governments in 1988, 1990, 1993 and 1996 under Article 58(2) (b) of the 8th Amendment, allegedly at the behest of army. The Nawaz Sharif government took away presidential powers to dissolve the National Assembly by passing the 13th Amendment in April 1997. However, the political situation changed after the 1999 military coup: In the aftermath of the 2002 elections, the Musharraf government restored Article 58(2)(b), first through LFO (Legal Framework Order) and then by getting the 17th Amendment passed by the newly elected Parliament.

While the Constitution explicitly provides for civilian supremacy over armed forces, the latter have generally sought a role for themselves in the business of the state.[74] General Zia announced the establishment of the National Security Council (NSC) as a supra-cabinet advisory body with a strong military presence, as part of his Revival of the Constitution Order (RCO) in 1985. However, in the face of opposition from the newly elected parliamentarians prior to lifting of martial law in December 1985, Zia agreed to drop it from the draft of the 8th Amendment. As opposed to this, Musharraf established NSC as part of his LFO in 2003, which was subsequently formalized through an act of Parliament, as part of a deal with the religious opposition Muttahida Majlis-e-Amal (MMA). The idea was that if the army did not rule directly, it should remain an active player on the political stage in an informal capacity. Even without the NSC, the army chief's presence behind the scene was popularly acknowledged throughout the 1990s. Not surprisingly, the government under the two prime ministers Benazir Bhutto (1988–90 and 1993–96) and Nawaz Sharif (1990–93 and 1997–99), with civilian presidents in place, Ishaq (1988–93), Leghari (1993–97) and Rafiq Tarar (1997–2001), was often described as the 'rule of troika' comprising the President, the Prime Minister and COAS. The army hoped that the NSC would leave a strong imprint of the army's thinking not only on the specific context of formulation of defence and foreign policies but also on the way the state exercised its authority in general.

Generals in Pakistan developed an innovative approach to bringing the masses into a participatory mould without giving them any role in the business of the state. This strategy focused on votes rather than seats in the local bodies' elections, whereby the public input was channelled through the ballot at the district and sub-district levels, but no transfer of power was envisioned at these levels. The idea of local self-government has taken deep roots in the army's mind. One can find a rationale for this in the quest for keeping the social and political order safe from politicians operating at higher levels. Following a powerful streak of paternalism, somewhat along the pattern of internal differentiation in the army, between the officer cadre and soldiers, local self-government has attracted the imagination of successive military rulers. Ayub introduced a comprehensive system of Basic Democracies (BD) that became a part of the 1962 Constitution. People elected members of local bodies who acted as an electoral college for the election of the President as well as the National and provincial assemblies. Ayub's BD system was conceived essentially as a subordinate structure vis-à-vis the district administration. The system was meant to depoliticize the society, thereby seeking to revive the classical British colonial model of a top-down flow of patronage outside the domain of the emergent nationwide political activity. The idea was to disenfranchise the masses in terms of a direct political input into the business of the state. Under Ayub, politics was effectively boxed into districts and thus localized to the detriment of political parties.[75] At the same time, the BD system served the function of providing a source of legitimacy at the grassroots level where people craved for an exercise in ballot in one form or another.[76] This model was rendered unpopular through a nationwide movement against Ayub Khan in 1968–69. However, later Zia found the Ayub model useful inasmuch it could take care of linking the grassroots leadership with the state's patronage system via the district administration, bypassing the political parties. The non-party dynamics of local bodies was arbitrarily extended to elections for the National and provincial assemblies in 1985.

Over time, local bodies emerged as the support base of military governments. Not surprisingly, the political leadership and parties all along looked at military initiatives in the direction of devolution of power with great suspicion. In the face of public demand for general elections, the Musharraf government chose to go for local bodies elections instead in 2001. He formulated a devolution plan to establish 'grassroots' democracy by forming a third tier of government at the district level, led by an indirectly-elected district officer called *Nazim*. The local bodies' office holders emerged as the nationwide support base for Musharraf for his presidential referendum in 2002. He again mobilized *nazims* (similar to mayor, coordinator of cities and towns in Pakistan) for organizing a public rally for him in Islamabad on 12 May 2007, as a response to the lawyers' movement in opposition to his reference against Chief Justice of Pakistan filed in March 2007. It was widely believed that *nazims* were politically active on behalf of Musharraf, during the campaign for the 2008 elections.

A military-led government found several advantages in reactivating local bodies. Most notably, these provided a semblance of legitimacy in the form of exercise in mass voting. Local bodies localized politics, thereby minimizing the role of such extra-local entities as political parties. Public activity surrounding local bodies elections was tied down to local issues while larger issues concerning sectoral allocation of resources and distribution of power remained outside the purview of these elections. As electoral contestants did not represent political parties, they could not promise a change in policy. By default, policy remained firmly in the hands of the state elite. The military governments clearly undermined the influence of political workers at the constituency level in the face of local patterns of leadership elected into Union Councils and District Councils.

Military presidents in mufti or uniform generally suffered, to borrow a term from the United States, from a '6-year itch'. Ayub in 1964–65, Zia in 1983 and Musharraf in 2007 faced street agitation after their initial aura was dissipated. In each case, the image of the military as a 'parallel state' spread far and wide.[77] The dismissal of Chief Justice Iftikhar Chaudhry on 9 March 2007 led to a lawyers' movement, which created a landmark inasmuch as there was no turning back to the halcyon days of uninterrupted rule for Musharraf. The chief justice issue simply exploded and set in motion a series of events, which challenged the status quo.[78] The lawyers' movement, supported most prominently by the media and the civil society, brought to bear moral pressure on Musharraf to move forward to the lifting of emergency, shedding of uniform and holding of elections. The new COAS General Ashfaq Kayani felt that the profile of the army had suffered in the face of public protests of one kind or another. He announced withdrawal of 300 serving military officers, including a 3-star general and several major generals from civilian positions. Quite a few of them were on jobs in Earthquake Reconstruction and Rehabilitation Authority (ERRA), National Accountability Bureau (NAB), Survey of Pakistan, Airport Security Force (ASF), Anti-Narcotic Force (ANF) and other public corporations or bureaus.[79] In early January 2008, controversy about the military's role in politics spread to such unlikely quarters as retired military officers who openly criticized Musharraf for selling out to America, political repression at home and destabilization of the country. They asked him to resign from his office. In a rare show of collective embarrassment, they publicly regretted mistakes of the past, especially regarding military intervention in politics.[80] The President dismissed them as a bunch of job-seekers whom he had not obliged. In the post-election framework of politics, Musharraf refused to resign after the nation had voted against his party PML-Q. A new deadlock emerged, characterized by what Rajni Kothari described in a different context as a situation of state against democracy.

◙ Conclusion

Our observations point to the fact that civil–military relations in Pakistan drew on the lack of domestic institutional potential of the state to deliver on the promise of democracy, as enshrined in the 1935 India Act as amended by the 1947 India Independence Act. The insecurity syndrome relating to state-building at home in the context of regional security complex kept the military establishment from letting the political initiative go out of its hands, even when it was not in government. The constellation of powers ruling Pakistan has a stable policy agenda and ideological orientation. The army has increasingly moved into the centre stage of this constellation. We have observed that the function of safeguarding socioeconomic and political order in Pakistan was assumed by the army in the background of structural discontinuity that occurred at the time of Partition. The migrant-led state put in place an institutional apparatus and a tradition of constitutional thinking and practice which, at least by default, prepared the ground for military takeover. We have noticed that the army's role was path-dependent in terms of its historical roots in British India and its presence in the decision-making channels on top after Independence. Finally, we showed how the army developed a set of constitutional preferences and priorities relating to the form of government, distribution of power between various institutions of the state, both horizontally and vertically as well as parliamentary sovereignty. We have argued that the ruling elite's worldview has been subsumed under the army's commitment to a set of policies, ideological formulations and institutional mechanisms.

Musharraf faced difficulties on all these counts in the year 2007–08. Both the bar and the bench rebelled against his act of rendering the Chief Justice non-functional in March 2007. Political parties struggled to take the initiative in their own hands. Musharraf's erstwhile Islamist allies turned against him in the backdrop of military operation against the madrasa Jamia Hafsa in Islamabad in July 2007, followed by a spate of suicide attacks on government installations. Subsequently, the military operations in Swat further cost Musharraf support from Islamic parties. Former Prime Minister Nawaz Sharif organized an All Parties Conference in London in July 2007 that vowed to launch a movement against Musharraf to restore democracy. While Washington's support had been relevant for keeping Musharraf in power, an all-out mobilization of political forces soon created serious problems for the Musharraf government and ended up in the defeat of the 'king's party' in the 2008 elections. However, none of the setbacks faced by the top brass before and after the elections meant that the power of army would diminish significantly.[81] Indeed, the deteriorating security situation in January 2009, after the Mumbai attacks, again tilted the balance in favour of the army. The dualism, which characterized the prevalent constitutional arrangement for sharing power between the parliamentary and extra-parliamentary forces, was expected to continue to define the role of the army in Pakistan in one form or the other.

▨ Notes

1. Mohammad Waseem, 'Two Governments or One?', *Dawn,* Lahore, 1 April 2008.
2. S. E. Finer, *The Man on Horseback* (London: Oxford University Press, 1969); Morris Janowitz, *The Professional Soldier: A Social and Political Portrait* (New York: The Free Press, 1965); Samuel Huntington, 'Patterns of Violence in World Politics', in S. Huntington (ed.), *Changing Patterns of Military Politics* (New York: The Free Press, 1962).
3. See Ole R. Holsti, 'A Widening Gap between the U. S. Military and Civilian Society?', *International Security,* Winter 1998–99, 23(3).
4. Hew Stratchan, 'The Civil–Military "Gap" in Britain', *The Journal of Strategic Studies,* June 2003, 26(2), pp. 43–45.
5. Ibid., p. 44.
6. Pascal Vennesson, 'Civil–Military Relations in France: Is there a Gap?', *The Journal of Strategic Studies,* June 2003, 26(2), pp. 31–39.
7. Harsh Sethi (ed.), *State of Democracy in South Asia* (New Delhi: Oxford University Press, 2006).

8. Imad Harb, 'The Egyptian Military in Politics: Disengagement or Accommodation', *Middle East Journal*, Spring 2003, 57(2), pp. 271–72.

9. Ibid., pp. 272–74.

10. Ibid., pp. 272–76.

11. Cyril Almeida, 'Retaking Bomb Project', Lahore, *Dawn*, 23 April 2008.

12. Wendy Hunter, 'Continuity or Change? Civil–Military Relations in Democratic Argentina, Chile and Peru', *Political Science Quarterly*, Autumn 1997, 112(3), pp. 453–54.

13. William Deane Stanley, 'El Salvador: State-Building before and after Democratization: 1980–95', *Third World Quarterly*, 27(1), p. 102.

14. Jendayi Frazer, 'Conceptualizing Civil–Military Relations During Democratic Transition', *Africa Today*, 1995, 42 (1–2), pp. 1–3, http://elin.lub.lu.se/link2elin?genre=article&issn=00019887&year=1995&volume=42&issue=1-2&collection=ebsco&pages=39-49&resid=204415 063fe08a5887f240b99238ff30&lang=en (accessed 11 August 2008).

15. Ibid., p. 3.

16. Mohammad Ayoob, 'The Security Predicament of the Third World State: Reflections on State Making in a Comparative Perspective', in Brian L. Job (ed.), *The Insecurity Dilemma: National Security of Third World States* (Boulder, CO and London: Lynne Rienner Publishers, 1992), p. 65.

17. Barry Buzan, 'Third World Regional Security in Structural and Historical Perspective', in ibid., p. 174.

18. 'Harking back to Zia days', *Dawn*, Lahore, 26 April 2008.

19. Umit Cizre, 'Demythologizing the National Security Concept: The Case of Turkey', *Middle East Journal*, Spring 2003, 57(2), pp. 214–17.

20. Ibid., p. 217.

21. Yong Cheol Kim, R. William Liddle and Salim Said, 'Political Leadership and Civilian Supremacy in Third Wave Democracies: Comparing South Korea and Indonesia', *Pacific Affairs*, Summer 2006, 79(2), pp. 247–54.

22. Ibid., pp. 258–67.

23. Pervez Musharraf, *In the Line of Fire* (London: Simon and Schuster, 2006), pp. 154–63.

24. See Hamza Alavi, 'The Army and the Bureaucracy in Pakistan Politics', in A. Abdel Malek (ed.), *Armée et Nations dans les Trios Continents* (Alger, 1975). Originally in English, mimeograph.

25. Hamza Alavi, 'Authoritarianism and Legitimation of State Power in Pakistan', in Subrata K. Mitra (ed.), *The Postcolonial State in South Asia* (London and New York: Harvestor-Wheatsheaf, 1990), pp. 32–33.

26. Stephen Cohen, *The Idea of Pakistan* (Lahore: Vanguard Books, 2005), p. 129.

27. Mohammad Waseem, *Politics and the State in Pakistan* (Islamabad: National Institute of Historical and Cultural Research, 1994), pp. 42–59.
28. Ibid., pp. 400–01.
29. Hamid Khan, *Constitutional and Political History of Pakistan* (Karachi: Oxford University Press, 2001), pp. 1–153.
30. Mohammad Waseem, 'Mohajirs in Pakistan: A Case of Nativization of Migrants', in Crispin Bates (ed.), *Community, Empire and Migration* (New York: Palgrave, 2001), pp. 248–49.
31. Calculated from Government of Pakistan, *Census of Pakistan 1951*, Report and Tables, Karachi, n.d., vol. 1, pp. 19–23 and vol. 6, p. 65.
32. See Ayesha Jalal, *The State of Martial Rule* (Cambridge and New York: Cambridge University Press, 1990), pp. 110–11.
33. Katharine Adeney and Andrew Wyatt, 'Democracy in South Asia: Getting beyond the Structure-Agency Dichotomy', *Political Studies*, 2004, 52(1), pp. 1–4.
34. Yunas Samad, *A Nation in Turmoil: Nationalism and Ethnicity in Pakistan 1937–1958* (New Delhi: Sage Publications, 1995), pp. 124–30.
35. See Ian Talbot, *Pakistan: A Modern History* (London: Hurst and Company, 1998), pp. 125–34.
36. See for discussion, Hasan-Askari Rizvi, 'The Pakistan Military: A Bibliographical Study', in Charles Kennedy, Kathleen Mcneil, Carl Ernst and David Gilmartin (eds), *Pakistan at the Millennium* (Karachi: Oxford University Press, 2003), pp. 106–09.
37. Mushahid Hussain and Akmal Hussain, *Pakistan: Problems of Governance* (Lahore: Vanguard, 1993), pp. 29–47.
38. Veena Kukreja, 'Pakistan's Political Economy, Misplaced Priorities and Economic Uncertainties', in Veena Kukreja and M.P. Singh (eds), *Pakistan: Democracy, Development and Security Issues* (New Delhi: Sage Publications, 2005), p. 13.
39. Jean-Luc Racine, 'Pakistan and the India Syndrome: Between Kashmir and Nuclear Predicament', in Christopher Jefferson (ed.), *Pakistan: Nationalism Without a Nation* (New Delhi: Manohar, 2002), p. 197.
40. Ayesha Siddiqa, 'Pakistan's Political Economy of National Security', in Veena Kukreja and M.P. Singh (eds), *Pakistan: Democracy, Development and Security Issues* (New Delhi: Sage Publications, 2005), p. 124.
41. Ayesha Siddiqa, *Military Inc.: Inside Pakistan's Military Economy* (Karachi: Oxford University Press, 2007), pp. 33–35.
42. Ibid., pp. 37, 47–54.
43. Tan Tai Yong, 'Punjab and the Making of Pakistan', *South Asia*, 1995, xviii, p. 178.
44. Ibid., p.180.
45. Ibid., p.182.
46. Ibid., p.187.

47. The Government of Pakistan, *The Journey to Pakistan: A Documentation on Refugees of 1947* (Islamabad: National Documentation Centre, 1993), p. 16.
48. For a historical study of British paternalism, see Philip Woodruff, *The Men who Ruled India: The Guardians* (London: Cape Publishers, 1954), p. 76.
49. Brig. (retd.) A. R. Siddiqi, *The Military in Pakistan: Image and Reality* (Lahore: Vanguard, 1996), Chapters 3, 7 and 8.
50. Stephen P. Cohen, *The Pakistan Army* (Berkeley and Los Angeles, CA: University of California Press, 1984), pp. 55–74.
51. Vali Nasr, *Jamat Islami: Vanguard of Islamic Revolution* (London: I.B. Tauris, 1994), p. 171.
52. Hasan-Askari Rizvi, *The Military and Politics in Pakistan 1947–86* (Lahore: Progressive Publishers, 1986), pp. 195–201.
53. Edward Viola and Scot Mainwaring, 'Transitions to Democracy: Brazil and Argentina in the 1980s', *Journal of International Affairs*, 1985, 38(2), pp. 193–97.
54. *Asma Jilani vs Government of Punjab*, Criminal Appeal no. 19 of 1972, PLD *(Pakistan Legal Decisions)* 1972 Supreme Court 139, Lahore, n.d., xxiv, p. 243.
55. Hussain Haqqani, *Pakistan: Between Mosque and Military* (Lahore: Vanguard, 2005), pp. 311–19.
56. Mushahid Hussain and Akmal Hussain, *Pakistan: Problems of Governance* (Lahore: Vanguard, 1993), pp. 73–74.
57. See Robert Wirsing, 'Pakistan's Transformation: The Limits of "Extreme Makeover" in US Counter Terrorism Strategy', Paper for Conference on 'Ethics, Values and Society: Social Transformation', LUMS, 31 March–3 April 2005, p. 3.
58. Marvin Weinbaum, 'Musharraf as Catalyst: Balancing Counterterrorism and Reforms', Testimony before the Senate Foreign Relations Committee, 14 July 2004, quoted in ibid., p. 5.
59. Ashley Tellis, 'US Strategy: Assisting Pakistan's Transformation', *The Washington Quarterly*, Winter 2004, 28(1), p. 101.
60. See Maya Chadda, *Building Democracy in South Asia* (London: Lynne Rienner, 2000), p. 68.
61. Charles H. Kennedy, 'Analysis of Pakistan's Devolution Plan', Mimeograph, Islamabad, 2001, pp. 7–10.
62. Ayesha Siddiqa, *Military Inc.: Inside Pakistan's Military Economy* (Karachi: Oxford University Press, 2007), pp. 112–18.
63. M.T. Butt, 'Generals Defy, Degrade Parliament to Protect a Corrupt Colleague', *South Asia Tribute*, Washington, DC, 8 June 2005.
64. Examples of this dichotomy abound in the literature on civil–military relations. In Pakistan's context, see Prologue, Hasan-Askari Rizvi, *Military, State and Society in Pakistan* (New York: St. Martin's Press, 2000), pp. xiv–xix.

65. *The Pakistan Times*, 11 October 1958.

66. *The Pakistan Times*, 9 October 1958.

67. Max Weber, 'Bureaucracy', in H.H. Gerth and C. Wright Mills (eds), *From Max Weber: Study in Sociology* (New York: Oxford University Press, 1958), p. 239.

68. Robert A. Dahl, *A Preface to Democratic Theory* (Chicago: University of Chicago Press, 1961), pp. 137–38.

69. Samuel P. Huntington, *Political Order in Changing Societies* (New Haven, CT: Yale University Press, 1968), pp. 459–60.

70. Shirin Tahirkheli, 'The Military in Contemporary Pakistan', *Armed Forces and Society*, Summer 1980, p. 647.

71. Shahid Siddiqui, 'Military–Political Discourse', *Dawn*, Lahore, 13 February 2008.

72. Charles Kennedy, 'A User's Guide to Guided Democracy: Musharraf and the Pakistani Military Governance Paradigm', in Charles Kennedy and Cynthia Botteron (eds), *Pakistan 2005* (Karachi: Oxford University Press, 2006), pp.122–38.

73. Hamid Khan, 'Military and Judiciary in Pakistan October 1999 Onwards', *Journal of South Asian and Middle Eastern Studies*, Summer 2003, 26(4), pp. 42–47.

74. See for discussion, Pakistan Institute of Legislative Development and Transparency (PILDAT), *National Security Council: A Comparative Study of Pakistan and Other Selected Countries*, Background Paper, August 2005, pp. 12–16.

75. See Mohammad Waseem, *Democratization in Pakistan: A Study of the 2002 Elections* (Karachi: Oxford University Press, 2006), pp. 67–68.

76. Ibid., pp. 69–74.

77. See Mazhar Aziz, *Military Control in Pakistan: The Parallel State* (London and New York: Routledge, 2007).

78. 'Weinbaum: On the Eve of Re-election Musharraf has Bought Some Time', Interview for Council on Foreign Relations, US Congress, by Bernard Gwertzman, 3 October 2007.

79. http://www.paktribune.com/news/print.php?id=197130 (accessed 4 October 2008).

80. *The Daily Jang*, Lahore, 31 January 2008.

81. Katharine Adeney, 'What Comes After Musharraf?', *Brown Journal of World Affairs*, Fall/Winter 2007, 14(1), p. 49.

※

9

Resurgence of the Baluch Movement in Pakistan: Emerging Perspectives and Challenges

Rajshree Jetly

Most states in South Asia have been confronted with the problem of forging a cohesive national identity by accommodating the diverse and heterogeneous populations within their boundaries. Though not unique to South Asia, the assertion of separate identities has been the biggest challenge to the stability and integrity of the states in the region, which are mainly multi-ethnic pluralist societies. Each country relied upon its own forms of nation-building, some more successfully than the others, but the essential contradiction between the nature of the state and the multi-ethnic social system has persisted, in varying degrees, in most of the countries. Overall, the task has not been easy for any country; it has been often made even more difficult by the ruling elite's general reluctance or failure to decentralize political and economic authority and encourage cultural plurality. This remains particularly true of certain movements in South Asia, which if handled in a more accommodating manner, might not have become as militant and intractable as they are today.

Pakistan is no exception to this: in fact, ethnic conflict has presented the most formidable challenge to Pakistan since its inception and has already led to two civil wars and to the secession of the country's most populous province, East Pakistan, in 1971. Pakistan has sought to use Islam as a unifying force to bring different ethnic groups together, with few, if any, efforts on the part of the central elites to incorporate the history, language or cultural experiences of these ethnic groups into a modern sense of national identity. It was mistakenly assumed that different ethnic groups such as the Sindhis, the Baluch and the Pashtuns would willingly surrender their rich historical and cultural tradition in return for a narrowly defined Pakistani identity; this has not happened. Failure of the state to articulate a viable national identity only on the basis of Islam, and the simultaneous politicization of ethnic identities, has only complicated matters for Pakistan.

Added to this, the successive federal governments' preferential treatment of certain ethnic groups over others has worked to the disadvantage of the other groups and led to a fundamental imbalance in the Pakistani polity. Highly centralizing policies of a predominantly Punjabi military and bureaucratic structure have only widened the cleavages between the provinces and the centre. This has engendered feelings of alienation among most other groups such as the Sindhis, the Muhajirs and the Baluch in terms of access to socio-economic development and adequate share of financial resources. Rectification of these grievances has become the basis of demands for greater autonomy in various provinces of Pakistan at different points of time.

▣ Re-emergence of the Baluch Crisis

Baluchistan is the traditional homeland of the Baluch who account for a mere 3.5 per cent of the entire population of Pakistan. They are, however, spread across a vast area covering 222,000 square kilometres and occupy almost 43 per cent of Pakistan's total land area. Notwithstanding the many divisions within the closed tribal structures of the Baluch — in terms of class contradictions, religious differences, linguistic variations, population dispersion and levels of socio-economic development — the Baluch have remained very proud of their distinct identity, value systems and tribal affiliations. The Sardari system is deeply rooted in the political and social psyche of the Baluch. Despite the decline in their power following the formal abolition of the Sardari system in 1976, the Sardars have continued to be respected to this day within their tribes and exercise de facto control over their respective areas. It is this fierce sense of tribal identity and loyalty which has more than anything else sustained their desire for national self-determination.

The Baluch have had strained relations with the Pakistani state since its inception. Over the years, the Baluch have been involved in many armed rebellions against the federal government, whether democratic or authoritarian. As Ataullah Mengal, a noted Baluch leader pointed out, the Baluch have always been discriminated against by the Punjabi-dominated federal government: 'We stand nowhere. Under the military regime, we are ruled with an iron heel. And during democracy, it is more of the same, but sugar-coated. There is no substantive difference.'[1]

Baluchistan witnessed a fresh wave of insurgency in the last few years breaking a lull of more than two decades. The last major insurgency was in the 1970s, which had been largely fuelled by the Baluch's perception of disenfranchisement by the federal government in terms of their economic, social and political expectations. Fundamentally, the same issues that dominated the 1970s civil war are still looming large on the Baluch scene: underdevelopment of the province, lack of economic and political participation at the national and provincial levels, exploitation of the province and lack of trust between the Baluch and the federal government are just as potentially explosive today as they were in the 1970s.

Insurgency in the province began to grow noticeably during the years 2003–04 following the Musharraf government's plans to establish additional army cantonments in sensitive areas such as Gwadar, Dera Bugti and Kohlu in Baluchistan in order to help the United States curtail terrorist activities in pursuance of its global war on terror. Not surprisingly, these establishments had a provocative effect on the Baluch nationalists, who were already resentful of the federal governments' construction of the Gwadar port. Increased military presence in the region was seen by the Baluch as a deliberate move by the federal army to consolidate its presence in Baluchistan. By 2003, the Baluch insurgents had started targeting the developmental projects related to the construction of highways and cantonments around Gwadar. They were fighting mainly under the banner of the Baluch Liberation Army (BLA), a shadowy underground organization, with reportedly more than 5000 fighters, the majority of whom had been trained in Afghanistan.[2] Continued attacks on military and government installations all through 2004 and the retaliatory military action by President Musharraf led to a steep escalation of tensions in the province. In May 2004, three Chinese engineers were killed and eleven others, including nine Chinese and two Pakistanis, were injured in a daring bomb blast in Gwadar, creating a major embarrassment for Islamabad.

Yet another unfortunate incident that added fuel to the fire was the violent rape of a female doctor in January 2005 by Pakistani soldiers in a Sui hospital complex. The government's tardiness in responding to the situation sparked off widespread protests among the Baluch.[3] The late Akbar Bugti's support, in whose areas the Sui gas fields were located, gave a new momentum to the movement. The BLA launched a massive attack on the government forces, resulting in a pitched battle with the security forces that lasted for many days. Railway lines, gas supply lines and gas installations were attacked by the rebels, affecting gas supply to the rest of the country, including major industrial units in Punjab and Sindh. The capital city of Quetta and other areas were plunged into total darkness by the massive power failure. The Pakistani military responded with full force, killing many of the insurgents and innocent civilians in the ensuing warfare.

It was just a matter of time before the Baluch retaliated in a daring rocket attack on a paramilitary camp in Kohlu that President Musharraf was scheduled to visit in December 2005. This was, in some ways, a turning point, which brought matters almost to a breaking point. The security forces launched a full-fledged attack on Marri camps in Kohlu district, which later extended to the Dera Bugti area. The intensity and magnitude of the Army operation — evoking memories of East Pakistan in some quarters — led to a widespread criticism of the Musharraf government's heavy-handedness in dealing with the Baluch. The opposition parties in Parliament seized the opportunity to criticize the federal government for carrying out genocide against the innocent citizens. The Human Rights Commission of Pakistan (HRCP) came out in open denunciation of the federal government's gross violations of human rights.[4]

The government, on its part, maintained that regular armed forces were not used on the Baluch rebels and described the HRCP accusations as exaggerated accounts. The US intelligence sources however, reported otherwise. According to one report, six Pakistani army brigades, and paramilitary forces totalling 25,000 men were involved in fighting the BLA guerrillas in Baluchistan.[5] The independent Pakistan Human Rights Commission also reported 'indiscriminate bombing and strafing' by 20 US-supplied Cobra helicopter gunships and four squadrons of fighter planes, including US-supplied F16 fighter jets, leaving hundreds of civilians dead and many more injured.[6] According to another report, the Pakistan government had used the American helicopters, supplied to it to fight the Al-Qaeda, against the Baluch rebels.[7]

In August 2006, Baluch nationalist leader Nawab Akbar Bugti, labelled by the government as the kingpin of Baluch insurgency, was killed in a massive operation by the Pakistani army. The government maintained that the killing had happened by accident when army officers had gone in to negotiate with the leader. The Baluch, however, had good reasons to call it a deliberate act of personal vendetta, particularly in view of the fact that Musharraf had publicly vowed to take on Bugti and said, 'I do not consider him Nawab (baron) any more, he and two other tribal chieftains are indulging in anti-state activities with the help of foreign money and weapons. We will soon sort them out.'[8]

Bugti's killing and the humiliating manner[9] in which he was buried noticeably widened the gulf between the Baluch and the Pakistani federal authorities. It also helped to bring the Sardars together in a show of defiance against the government. For instance, the historic grand Jirga (an assembly or council of the headmen of Baluch tribes) was revived after nearly 130 years in September 2006 to review the 1948 pact under which the former state of Kalat (now part of Baluchistan) had acceded to Pakistan, putting the government on the defensive.[10]

A tense situation has continued to prevail in Baluchistan since. According to US Intelligence sources, during Musharraf's rule, as many as six Pakistan army brigades or a quarter million regular troops plus paramilitary forces were deployed in Baluchistan against the BLA which had been fighting the Pakistan army, mainly in the Kohlu Mountains and the surrounding areas. At the same time a great deal of resentment was building up against the government for unleashing a wave of unlawful arrests, detention, and extrajudicial killings in Baluchistan. The number of people who had disappeared in Baluchistan also rose to an all-time high creating a climate of fear and terror.[11] The Baluch seemed to be, however, more determined than ever before to challenge the writ of the government. This hardly augurs well for the return of normalcy to the province in the near future.

Socio-Economic Underdevelopment

It may be useful at this point to recount some of the factors that have led to a sense of deep resentment among the Baluch and put them on a collision course with the federal government. Baluchistan has remained the poorest and the most underdeveloped province of Pakistan. Socio-economic growth indicators such as literacy, health facilities, civic amenities, industrial infrastructure and per capita income underline its extremely backward status. Forty-five per cent of the population has been reported to be still living below the poverty line. More important, there has been a huge gap in terms of socio-economic indicators between Baluchistan and the other provinces. In 2006–07, Baluchistan's literacy rate was the lowest (42 per cent) as compared with the other provinces (Punjab 58 per cent, Sindh 55 per cent, North West Frontier Province [NWFP] 47 per cent) and the national average at 55 per cent.[12] The Human Development Index for Baluchistan in 2003 was the lowest at (0.499) as compared with the other provinces; in descending order Punjab (0.557); Sindh (0.540); NWFP (0.510).[13] Its health facilities have remained minimal; the number of hospitals, dispensaries, maternity and child welfare centres being far less than other provinces. Only 20 per cent of the people in Baluchistan have access to drinking water as opposed to 86 per cent at the national level.

Exploitation of Natural Resources

Paradoxically, Baluchistan, the most backward region of Pakistan, is a land abounding in natural resources with large reserves of gas, minerals, fisheries, and coal. The Baluch have harboured deep resentment against the federal government for pursuing discriminatory and exploitative policies that have brought Baluchistan to the present state of affairs. As the Baluch nationalist leader Sardar Ataullah Mengal observed in 2007 'Balochistan has been turned into a colony, all its resources have been usurped and the Baloch are being treated as slaves in their own land.'[14]

The Baluch have blamed successive governments in Islamabad for cornering the lion's share of profits from the state's resources without diverting any of the benefits to the province itself. Baluchistan presently accounts for 36 per cent of Pakistan's total gas production but less than half of that is consumed by the province itself with the remaining being piped off to other provinces. It was equally difficult for the Baluch to accept that even though gas was being supplied to cities in Punjab by 1964, their own capital, Quetta, remained bereft of it until 1986.[15] Even now only four out of 28 districts in Baluchistan have access to piped gas; only 5–6 per cent of the population have a gas connection, and there is a total absence of CNG stations in the province.[16]

Baluchistan has also not had a fair deal in terms of the royalties from the gas it produces and has received only 12 per cent of the royalties due. The natural gas reserves from the province generated revenue of $1.4 billion annually, but the Baluch received only $116 million as royalty.[17] Their long-standing demand for a revision of royalties on Sui gas had also fallen on deaf ears; to make matters worse, the federal government has under-priced Baluch gas, as compared with other provinces.[18]

Issues of Development

It is not then surprising that the level of Baluch distrust against the federal government has remained so high that even efforts made by the federal government to create a modern infrastructure, improve the means of communication and develop the province have not had the desired effect. While the government's objectives may have been well-meaning, the residual hostility and mistrust among the people totally undermined their effectiveness. Most Baluch were quick to trace the lack of any visible progress in Baluchistan to the fact that instead of promoting development, the Pakistani federal authorities had been more interested in pursuing their own socio-economic agenda and strengthening their own political base.

They claimed that the federal government has either stalled or delayed many development projects because these did not serve its purpose. For instance, the copper project in Saindak had remained in a limbo for almost ten years (1996–2005). It was revived only in 2005 when it was leased to the Metallurgical Construction Corporation (MCC) of China, with China investing US$ 1.4 billion in the project. More important, out of the 50 per cent of the plant's total profits, 48 per cent was to be retained by the federal government and barely 2 per cent was allocated for the Baluch.[19]

Under the circumstances, the construction of roads and highways came to be largely viewed by the Baluch as a ploy for extension of the federal machinery to exercise control over them, penetrate their strongholds and open their province to outsiders for purposes of trade, settlement and exploitation of their resources. Lamenting on the depressing state of affairs, the Baluch leader Khair Bux Marri, had pointed out that most of the roads built in Baluchistan were 'not for our benefit but to make it easier for the military to control us and for the Punjabis to rob us. The issue is not whether to develop, but whether to develop with or without autonomy. Exploitation has now adopted the name of development.'[20]

▨ Marginalization of the Baluch

Over the years, the Baluch have also felt increasingly marginalized in their own land. Historically, Pashtun, Sindhi, and Punjabi merchants have maintained control over the commercial life in Quetta, the only urbanized part of Baluchistan. Steady influx of Sindhis, Punjabis and, in particular, the Pashtuns, whose numbers rose considerably after the Afghan crisis, not only disturbed the balance of the local population but also generated fears in the Baluch of being turned into a minority in their own homeland. According to one source, the Baluch comprised only 45 per cent of the population of Baluchistan. The rest was made up of the Pashtuns (38 per cent), followed by others who comprised the remaining 17 per cent.[21]

The Baluch have also been aggrieved about being steadily dispossessed of their land. The federal government, dominated by the Punjabis, over the years allowed many Punjabi civilian and military personnel posted to Baluchistan to buy prime land in the province. In recent years, the government acquired land around the Gwadar port at below the market value and distributed much of it to navy and coastguard personnel who were largely non-Baluch. This created a speculative market, with the cost of land soaring in Gwadar and being grabbed by outsiders.[22] According to one estimate, once the Gwadar port is completed, the population of Gwadar and its surrounding districts is expected to rise from 70,000 to a staggering 2 million. This is bound to bring about a drastic change in the ethnic composition of the region to the disadvantage of the Baluch.[23]

The small population size of the Baluch in their own province remained a major constraint for the Baluch for securing their rightful share of jobs and resources in their homeland. Regular entry of people from other provinces seeking employment had worked to their disadvantage in terms of employment opportunities in the development projects. The Gwadar project has been cited by the Baluch as a prime example of this: of the 600 people employed in the first phase of the Gwadar project, only 100 of them were Baluch, largely in the lower-end jobs. Nawab Akbar Bugti, the late veteran leader of the Baluch movement, bemoaned the fact that even though 'the government had promised that all jobs that the locals could do would be given to them ... people are being brought in, even for unskilled labour.'[24]

The Ormara Naval base, the second largest naval installation, had also failed to provide adequate employment opportunities to the Baluch. The Ormara town itself witnessed little or no progress in its development, continuing to have poor infrastructure with lack of educational institutions and the absence of regular power supply.[25]

Baluch Representation at the Political Level

Fear of progressive marginalization of the Baluch at the provincial level has been compounded by their perceived deprivation vis-à-vis other ethnic groups in Pakistan — in particular the Punjabi ruling elites at the centre. The share of Baluch in the structures of power sharing and decision-making has remained dismal in both the political and economic spheres. Their woeful lack of representation in the civil–military complex in Pakistan has resulted in their progressive alienation from the national mainstream.

The quota system that was introduced by Zulfikar Ali Bhutto to give proportionate representation to all provinces has operated to the disadvantage of the Baluch due to the fact that the population of Baluchistan constituted a very small percentage of the national population. Further, the Pashtuns and the Punjabis domiciled in Baluchistan were able to count themselves under the Baluchistan provincial quota, diluting ethnic Baluch representation.[26] According to Ataullah Mengal, 'all positions in Balochistan — from officers to *sepoys* — in the Secretariat, the police and the Frontier Corps, are filled up by outsiders. The local Baloch people are nowhere to be seen.'[27] As recently as 2002, only four out of fourteen provincial government secretaries in Quetta were Baluch; even key positions of the Chief Secretary and the Inspector General of Police in the province were filled by non-Baluch.[28]

Besides the provincial level, the Baluch have also felt discriminated at the federal level, aggrieved as they have been by the domination of the Punjabis who constitute more than half of Pakistan's population and occupy most of the top echelons of power in the state bureaucracy. The Baluch have attributed their poor representation in the federal services to a deliberate policy on the part of the government to keep them out of key administrative positions. According to one study, from 1947 to 1977, of the 179 persons who were named to central cabinets in Pakistan, only four (2.2 per cent) were Baluch tribesmen from Baluchistan and only one of them was named prior to the 1980s.[29] Similarly, in the seniority list of federal secretaries issued by the Establishment division, 29 federal secretaries were from Punjab, 10 from NWFP, five from Sindh (rural), four from Sindh (urban) and one from AJK (Azad Jammu and Kashmir — the Pakistani-controlled territory of the former princely state of Jammu and Kashmir). There was no representation from Baluchistan.[30]

In the defence forces, the Baluch have been as poorly represented as in the bureaucracy. The ethnic group composition of the Pakistan military corps in the 1970s was approximately: 70 per cent Punjabi, 15 per cent Pashtun, 10 per cent Muhajir and 5 per cent Baluch and Sindhi.[31] By the early 1990s, the official quota for soldiers from Baluchistan and Sindh was raised to 15 per cent, but this quota was never filled and these communities have continued to remain under-represented in the military till date. More important, since the quota has been determined on a provincial basis, most of the recruits from Baluchistan comprise Pashtuns and other settlers.[32]

The Government Perspective

On its part, the government of Pakistan has maintained that lack of development in Baluchistan only tended to reflect the unwillingness of the Baluch themselves to break away from their tribal ways and integrate into the national mainstream. Islamabad has projected the Baluch as an insular community, which has remained backward not because of lack of government initiatives to promote development, but because of its resistance to change its economic and social structures. President Musharraf openly accused the tribal chiefs of politicizing development issues in order to maintain the status quo and thus preserve their power. According to government sources, the discontented groups themselves had a vested interest in the continuation of the conflict in order to ensure that their leadership positions as well as access to funds and support remained secure.

The late Akbar Bugti came in for open criticism from Musharraf's government for espousing the Baluchistan cause and at the same time receiving payments from the Ministry of Finance in lieu of Sui gas revenue.[33] In his address to the nation on 20 July 2006, President Musharraf described the Marri, Bugti and Mengal tribal chiefs as being 'anti-democracy, anti-development, anti-government and anti-Pakistan', putting their people 'under subjugation of the worst kind'.[34]

As for lack of development in Baluchistan, the federal government has been quick to point out that extensive economic concessions have been given to the Baluch to spur development and improve their socio-economic profile. Vast amounts of money, totally dispro-portionate to the population of Baluchistan, which stands at a mere 4.9 per cent, have been pumped into the province in the past few decades. During Zulfikar Ali Bhutto's period, for example, there was a visible increase in federal funds for Baluchistan, which rose from Rs 120 million in 1972–73 to Rs 210 million in 1974.[35] Vast amounts of money were invested in building roads; opening schools, colleges and technical institutions; extending credit and banking facilities; electrification; harnessing groundwater resources; and installing tube wells for irrigation and improving the health sector. Bhutto's successor, General Zia, followed suit. From 1977 to 1984/85, a record Rs 4,000 million was injected into Baluchistan. Among the major projects completed in this time were the extension of Sui gas to Quetta; completion of the RCD highway; the New Quetta airport, airstrips at Pasni and Turbat, a TV complex in Quetta, radio stations at Khuzdar and Turbat, and the completion of the Bolan Medical College.[36]

Like the previous regimes, the Musharraf government also ploughed money into Baluchistan in the hope of winning over the Baluch. Whilst unveiling the 'Vision for Development of Baluchistan' former Prime Minister Shaukat Aziz announced a special package of Rs 19.5 billion in 2006 to expedite development in the province. He also announced the creation of 32,124 jobs for the province for that financial year.[37] Interestingly, the vision package was the first major incentive announced by the government to pacify the Baluch after Bugti's killing in August 2006 and also comprised financial packages for Dera Bugti and Kohlu districts, which were adversely affected during the battles between the Baluch and the federal government.

On the uplift of Baluchistan, Musharraf announced grants of Rs 1 billion for the development of Quetta and Rs 100 million each for each of the 28 districts of the province in December 2006. An additional grant of Rs 2.5 billion was announced for parliamentarians to launch development schemes in their respective constituencies. Other economic incentives included seven new cadet colleges, two more campuses of the Baluchistan University at Gwadar and Turbat and 1,000 scholarships for Baluch students.[38] In addition, Musharraf as-sured the people of Baluchistan that the government would press ahead with a network of new roads linking Loralai with DG Khan and Zhob with DI Khan to ensure that development benefits reach all parts of the province.

Citing this record, the government discounted the Baluch allegations and maintained that the lack of any visible improvement was not due to want of effort on their part but due to rampant corruption and massive misappropriation of funds at the provincial level.[39]

It is clear from the foregoing discussion that while there may have been some basis for the government's assertion that the Baluch had not been able to break away from their tribal ways and integrate into the national mainstream, this was not the entire truth. There is little doubt that it had been the government's apathy to the Baluch demands for greater participation in the speedy development of the province that had led to their increasing disillusionment. Also, the governments' strategies for socio-economic development had not been followed by adequate power-sharing arrangements, which could have redressed the long-standing Baluch grievances. These factors put the two on a virtual collision course over the last few decades.

The Baluch sense of strong injustice and relative deprivation have been the most significant factors in mobilizing their demands ranging all the way from provincial autonomy to an independent Baluchistan. The recent crisis has been no exception.

▨ Differences with the 1970s Insurgency

The last time that the government was involved in a civil war with the Baluch nationalists was in the 1970s when it had been able to quell the insurgency with a mix of coercion and conciliation. The picture today is more complex and complicated for the Pakistani government. This is because there are some critical differences with the earlier situation, which makes the government's task much harder now. Presented below is a quick overview of the decline of Baluch insurgency in the 1970s. The main reasons for this decline were the weak nature of the movement; the efficacy of the strategies pursued by the central leadership, particularly Zia-ul-Haq; and, more importantly, the lack of any meaningful outside support.[40] With low literacy rates, and the absence of an educated middle class, the Baluch movement could not develop a mass character and remained confined to a few tribes only. Moreover, differences among the Baluch leadership on the means and ends of their struggle, the fragmented character of the Baluch tribes, and competing rivalries between the Baluch and the Pashtuns in the province, militated against political assertion of the Baluch community. These weaknesses were cleverly exploited by General Zia to outmanoeuvre the Baluch who were by then directionless.[41] It was just a matter of time before the leaders were bought or mollified by the government, rendering the Baluch cause a non-issue by the early 1980s.

Today, the situation is very different.[42] The Baluch are no longer as fragmented and guerrilla fighting is being carried out under the aegis of the Baluch Liberation Army (BLA), which comprises the influential Marri, Bugti and Mengal tribes. Although the BLA was officially outlawed in 2006, it continues to draw support from many Baluch. Sanaullah Baluch, a Senator belonging to the Baluch National Party, admitted that the BLA is very popular among the Baluch as 'they have internationalized the Balochistan cause, which we (the politicians) have failed to do'.[43]

Unlike the 1970s, when there was some friction and rivalry between these tribes, there is relatively speaking, greater cooperation among them today. Indeed, when Akbar Bugti's tribal territory came under attack by Pakistani troops, the Marris offered him sanctuary in their tribal area.[44] According to some analysts, a new leadership is emerging, which is moving away from the traditional feudalistic system of patronage and loyalty and for the first time, Baluch society is witnessing a process of 'horizontalization', cutting across regions and classes, which could have long-term implications for the traditionally closed tribal system.[45]

The BLA has also attracted many educated Baluch from a middle-class background into its fold and the leadership also appears to be more united in pursuing the goal of greater provincial autonomy. The four main Baluch political parties (Baluch National Party [Mengal], the Baluch National Party, the National Party and Nawab Akbar Bugti's party, the Jamhoori Watan Party [JWP]) came together for a common cause under the umbrella of Baluch Ittehad. All this made it more difficult for President Musharraf to exploit the differences between the various tribes, as General Zia was able to do successfully in the 1970s.

Furthermore, the Baluch are now better equipped with heavy weaponry and sophisticated equipment. It is reported that they are getting enough money from the Persian Gulf to buy weapons in the black market.[46] More importantly, today the Pakistani military is stretched to its maximum, as it is engaged on three visible fronts — the US-led global war on terrorism in the North West Frontier Province and the Afghan border, the Line of Control in Kashmir and the revived Baluch insurgency. This could appreciably limit its manoeuvrability and effectiveness in Baluchistan.

Renewed Baluch insurgency is operating in a geo-political environment that is different from the 1970s.[47] The province covers some 562 miles of the Persian Gulf's Makran coast, which includes the Strait of Hormuz through which about 40 per cent of the world's oil tankers pass. Given its strategic location, the area has acquired special significance for South Asia, Central Asia and the Persian Gulf in the era of global terrorism. Thus all major powers including the United States, China, Afghanistan, Iran and to a lesser degree, India, have a stake in the way the Baluch crisis unfolds in the days to come.

In recent years, the importance of energy has triggered a race amongst the big powers for acquisition of gas and oil pipelines, hydro-power projects in and around the region. The Gwadar port, which is at the cusp of South Asia, West Asia and Central Asia, is particularly significant in this context. China, for example, wants the Gwadar port facilities to import oil and gas and is negotiating with Pakistan for five oil and gas pipelines from Central Asia. In addition, China is eyeing a trans-Himalayan pipeline to carry the Middle Eastern crude oil to Western China through the Gwadar port, so as to present a shorter alternative to the Malacca straits route through which is shipped 80 per cent of its present oil supply.[48] There is considerable Chinese investment in terms of both capital and labour; the first phase of the Gwadar port has been completed with the Chinese investment of US$ 200 billion. The gas pipeline will pass from there connecting Central Asia with South Asia. Many road links are also being built to make Gwadar accessible to China through overland links that will stretch to and from Karakoram highway in Pakistan's northern areas that border the Chinese province of Xingjian. The port is being built with a view to having a modern air defence unit, a garrison, and an international airport.[49]

The United States also has long-term stakes in the developments in the region. First, it remains wary of China's growing power and would like to keep a close watch on its activities in the region. Second, the region has acquired even greater significance in view of the US objective of stamping out international terrorism. Amidst growing reports of the presence of the Al-Qaeda in Baluchistan, the United States would also like to keep its options open on collaborating with Pakistan to enter Baluchistan — both to fight the Al-Qaeda, and perhaps even to prepare for a potential strike against Iran, should its long-term security interests warrant it.

Iran, an important regional power, which had offered support to the Pakistani state during the 1970s, is not likely to extend such support now, in view of the fact that the Baluch current struggle seems to be more for greater provincial autonomy rather than an

Independent or Greater Baluchistan. The latter would have serious ramifications for Iran, which has its own Baluch minority.[50] More important, given the US-Pak strategic entente, and Iran's differences with the United States, it may be in Iran's interest to ensure that Baluchistan does not come under the full control of the Pakistani military.

India is yet another power that has long-term strategic interest in the future course of events in Pakistan. India has long been anxious about growing Sino-Pak collaboration and would be keeping a watch on the likely extension of China's influence in the Indian Ocean region through its involvement in the Gwadar port. India is interested in the shipping routes and energy trading related to Central Asia, as underlined by its collaboration with Iran on the Chabahar port, which is seen by some as a direct competition to the Gwadar port. It is also keen on establishing its presence in Central Asia as made evident by its assistance in building a 200km-long road that will connect Chabahar port with Afghanistan and an airbase in Tajikistan.[51]

Pakistan has repeatedly alluded to India's complicity in Baluch insurgency. Dr Sher Afgan Niazi, the Pakistan Minister for Parliamentary Affairs during Musharraf's regime openly remarked in the Pakistani senate that India was supplying arms and resources to tribal insurgents to carry out acts of sabotage in Baluchistan.[52] Without naming India specifically, President Musharraf also talked about a conspiracy in which some of Pakistan's neighbouring countries were involved in supplying money and weapons to the Baluch.[53] India has denied any such involvement. While India would not like to destabilize Pakistan, it might not be averse to seeing the cauldron boiling in Baluchistan, which would compel Pakistan to increase its military engagement in the area, diverting some of its military resources away from its conflict with India, over Kashmir.

With the United States, India, and China engaged in the great game, stability and peace in Baluchistan has acquired even greater significance for Pakistan than ever before. Pakistan is keen to leverage on Baluchistan's strategic significance as it knows that the competition and control of its energy resources will be the most important factor in determining the economic and political configurations of this region. Pakistan is therefore eager to seize the opportunities available to it through the Gwadar sea port for accessing the oil-rich Central Asia and the emerging new markets in Asia Pacific. By one estimate, the Baluch are sitting on 24 trillion cubic feet of natural gas, and 6 billion barrels of oil, besides vast reserves of copper, zinc, antimony, and chromites in the Chaghai district at Saindak.[54] It is clear from the foregoing discussion that prolonged destabilization in Baluchistan would have unacceptably high costs for Pakistan.

▣ Prolonged Insurgency in Baluchistan: Some Implications

Although it is too early to draw any conclusions on how the Baluch movement would evolve in the days to come, one can draw some possible scenarios:

The first scenario could be that the army is able to stamp out insurgency in the province. Pakistan's economic survival depends in a large measure on a steady supply of gas for industrial and domestic use in both the urban and rural areas. Islamabad is in no mood to tolerate any further disruption of vital supply lines, which could have a have disastrous fallout on Pakistan's economic and social development.[55] Therefore any escalation in militancy in areas that are home to the vital gas field and installations would be put down with a heavy hand. The federal government is set on quelling the growing tide of violence in the province, and would not hesitate to use a higher level of force to do so. According to one estimate, a total of 60,000–80,000 Pakistani troops remain engaged in the battles in Waziristan and Baluchistan,[56] and the number could go up in the days to come. Since the BLA, by most accounts, is still not in a position to challenge the might of the Pakistani state, the army may be able to effectively control the situation in due course of time. However, this may not be easy to achieve for a number of reasons. First, as has been proved over and over again, it is very difficult to put an end to guerrilla movements that have proved notoriously elusive and kept the state on its toes for protracted periods of time. Second, coercion may be a short-term palliative but even in cases where it succeeds, the solutions are seldom lasting. Tensions tend to recur if basic grievances are not taken care of, leading to spiralling instability.

The second scenario could be that the federal government proactively embarks on a policy of active economic and political engagement with the Baluch leaders. This would involve the initiation of a new dialogue with the Baluch leaders to establish more inclusive and transparent economic and political structures in the province. Several efforts have been made by the federal government to win over the Baluch by offering sops and concessions; some economic packages have been in the pipeline to assuage Baluch sentiments in areas that were adversely affected during the hostilities, including the grant of 1 billion for the development of Quetta itself and a number of other schemes for the uplift of the province. There have also been some efforts to deal with Baluch sensitivities on the tardy supply of gas to the province.[57] Such conciliatory gestures would, however, need to be followed by speedy action on the ground to effectively make a dent in Baluch resistance and stop a further downslide in the Baluch situation. The past track record of federal governments and their general disinclination to initiate a simultaneous political dialogue in a restructured Centre-state framework, however, makes this scenario rather difficult to foresee in the near future.

The third scenario is that Baluchistan remains set for a long-lasting confrontation, which could keep the pot boiling for a while. This is because there are several indications that, notwithstanding the economic blandishments, the movement may intensify in the days to come. Issues of uneven distribution of resources and exploitation of the central government remain explosive issues for the Baluch, who are reportedly in no mood to succumb to Islamabad's concessions without a substantive transfer of authority to them. The government, on its part, seems to be in no hurry to work out a conciliatory framework for greater dialogue with Baluch leaders. In the event, insurgency would linger on with no signs of early resolution. This seems to be the scenario that will hold in the days to come.

In such an event, prolonged instability in Baluchistan could have a number of implications for Pakistan. First, economic and political viability would suffer in the long run. Pakistan is already spending a huge proportion of its finances on domestic and cross-border conflicts and can hardly afford an intractable confrontation with the Baluch without serious consequences to its development. More important, continued unrest could spill over to neighbouring Sindh, which has been tense in the past, and trigger ethnic disturbances. These could have an adverse impact on the already fragile political climate of the country. Second, an unresolved crisis in Baluchistan could provide the Al-Qaeda with a strategic opportunity to exploit differences between the Baluch and the federal government. The Baluch are essentially secular in outlook and have in the past not shown an inclination to join hands with Islamic fundamentalist elements. However, with the Taliban now using Baluchistan as a base for its operations,[58] there is a risk that the Baluch will cooperate with the Al-Qaeda/Taliban forces for strategic reasons. This would enhance the internal security threat in Pakistan even as the new coalition government in Islamabad struggles to balance the various competing interests of Pakistan's domestic politics and the United States' strategic interests in its war on terrorism.

Apart from the heavy cost to both the Baluch and the Pakistani state, prolonged Baluch conflict can have broader implications on the region as a whole. Any long-term instability in Pakistan will have a ripple effect on South Asian regional peace and security. Ethnicity in this region is heavily interlinked and a flare-up in Baluchistan could quite easily spread across borders. As mentioned earlier, the Taliban could use the Baluch resistance to join hands with the Baluch against Islamabad. Pakistan's border with Afghanistan makes Baluchistan a key player in terror and war-against-terror politics. If, as indicated above, the Al-Qaeda–Baluch nexus develops, it could well be the tinderbox of fundamentalist terrorism that will engulf the region. Given the interconnectedness of oil and gas pipelines, ports and trade routes, the entire South and Central Asian regions could well end up being hostage to a continued Baluch crisis.

It is clear from the foregoing discussion that the Baluch movement may wax and wane depending on the prevalent situation, but is not going to fade away by itself. The future of the Baluch insurgency would hinge to a large extent on the organizational structure and leadership of the movement. The Baluch reluctance to shed their tribal affiliations, their extremely small numbers — which limit their political, social and economic participation in the federal structure — and failure to organize a coherent and well-structured political leadership, would impede their efforts to achieve their objectives. More important, the strategies of the Pakistani state will be crucial in determining the course of the Baluch movement. The role that Islamabad would play in exacerbating or reducing tensions, and the nature and timeliness of its state's response would decide whether the movement is contained or assumes a more confrontational form. The interplay of all these factors has decided the fate of the Baluch movement in the past and it is suggested that similar dynamics will help to shape the course of the movement in the future. At the end of the day, perceptions are very important and unless both sides are able to arrive at a mutual understanding and demonstrate a genuine willingness to improve relations with each other, Pakistan may be saddled with the Baluch problem for some time to come.

▣ Notes

1. 'Ending the Rule of Punjab, by Punjab and for Punjab': Interview with Ataullah Khan Mengal, *Himal South Asia*, 2007, 20(5), http://www.himalmag.com/2007/may/coverfeature_interview_sardar_ataullah_khan_mengal.htm (accessed 29 August 2007).
2. The BLA has been in existence in one form or the other since the 1980s when the former USSR had extended moral and material support. BLA members mainly comprise both Bugti and Marri tribes though there have been some recruits from the Mengal tribes of late. There are also some reports of another armed group called the Baluch Liberation Front (BLF) that has also been active in the ongoing Baluch insurgency.
3. Even two years down the line, the government has not made public the details of the investigation and revealed the name/s of the guilty.
4. 'Baluchis of Pakistan: On the Margins of History', *The Foreign Policy Centre Report*, London, November 2006, p. 44, http://fpc.org.uk/fsblob/817.pdf (accessed 31 July 2008).
5. Cited in Selig S. Harrison, 'Pakistan's Costly "Other War"', *The Washington Post*, 15 February 2006, http://www.washingtonpost.com/wp-dyn/content/article/2006/02/14/AR2006021401767.html (accessed 31 July 2008).
6. Ibid.
7. Also, three Cessna aircrafts fitted with sophisticated surveillance equipment given to Pakistan to apprehend drug smugglers were being used against the Baluch rebels. See Tim Mcgirk, 'Pakistan's Other War', *Time Magazine*, South Pacific Edition, 26 July 2006, 167(25), p. 26.
8. *The Hindustan Times*, 28 August 2006.
9. Bugti's coffin, according to some reports, was padlocked and sealed and no one but the 'Khateeb' (prayer leader) was permitted to see his face, creating a lot of suspicion among his family members who demanded DNA tests to verify Bugti's body.
10. Relations between the Baluch and the Pakistani state have been strained since 1947. In 1948, resistance by the Khan of Kalat to incorporation in Pakistan was met with military takeover by Pakistan's forces. The grand Jirga of 2006 was hosted by the present Khan of Kalat, Mir Suleiman Dawood (the event was last held in 1838 under Mir Khudaidad Khan, the then Khan of Kalat). It was attended by 1,500 people, including 85 Sardars and 300 tribal elders. See Rahimullah Yusufzai, 'The Baluch Jirga', *The News International*, 16 October 2006.

11. Since the army operation began in Baluchistan, a large number of Baluch people have disappeared after being detained on charges of 'spying for an enemy country', or for alleged connections with the BLA. See Massoud Ansari, 'Between Tribe and Country, The Crisis of Baluchistan', *Himal South Asia*, 2007, 20(5), http://www.himalmag.com/2007/may/ coverfeature_balochistan.htm (accessed 23 May 2007). For details on the disappearances, see Abdul Wahab, 'Missing in Custody', December 2006, http://www.newsline.com.pk/NewsDec2006/newsbeatdec2006. htm (accessed 31 July 2008).

12. Government of Pakistan, Ministry of Finance, *Economic Survey of Pakistan (2007–08)*. See Chapter 10 on Education, pp. 169–70, http:// www.finance.gov.pk/admin/images/survey/chapters/10-Education08. pdf (accessed 3 August 2008).

13. *Pakistan National Human Development Report 2003*, UNDP, Pakistan. Estimation by Wasay Majid and Akmal Hussain, http://www.un.org. pk/nhdr/htm_pages/cp_1.htm (accessed 3 August 2008).

14. *Dawn*, 27 March 2007.

15. See Frederic Grare, 'Pakistan: The Resurgence of Baluch Nationalism', *Carnegie Papers* No. 65, January 2006, p. 5.

16. 'Baluchis of Pakistan: On the Margins of History', *The Foreign Policy Centre Report*, London, November 2006, p. 49.

17. Cited in John C.K. Daly, 'The Baluch Insurgency and its Threat to Pakistan's Energy Sector', *Global Terrorism Analysis*, The James Town Foundation, Terrorism Focus, 21 March 2006, 3(11), http://www. jamestown.org/terrorism/news/article.php?articleid=2369935 (accessed 3 August 2008).

18. A comparison with the prices in other provinces reveals that when the unit price in Baluchistan was Rs 27, the prices in Sindh and Punjab were respectively Rs 170 and 190. See Frederic Grare, 'Pakistan: The Resurgence of Baluch Nationalism', footnote 9, p. 14.

19. The remaining 50 per cent was going to be picked up by China. See Massoud Ansari, 'Between Tribe and Country, The Crisis of Baluchistan', *Himal South Asia*, 2007, 20(5), http://www.himalmag. com/2007/may/coverfeature_balochistan.htm (accessed 23 May 2007).

20. Selig S. Harrison, *In Afghanistan's Shadow, Soviet Temptations and Baluch Nationalism* (New York: Carnegie Endowment for International Peace, 1981), p. 47.

21. Ray Fulcher, 'Baluchistan: Pakistan's Internal War', *Green Left Weekly*, 8 December 2006, http://www.worldpress.org/Asia/2594.cfm (accessed 31 July 2008).

22. According to one report, a 500-square-yard plot that used to cost US$ 130 has shot up to US$ 7,000. Cited in Ziad Haider, 'Baluchis, Beijing, and Pakistan's Gwadar Port', *Politics and Diplomacy*, Winter/Spring 2005, p. 100.

23. Ray Fulcher, 'Baluchistan: Pakistan's Internal War'.

24. Haroon Rashid, 'At the moment, war is being imposed on us', interview with Akbar Khan Bugti, *Newsline* (Karachi), February 2005, http://www.newsline.com.pk/NewsFeb2005/cover3feb2005.htm (accessed 31 July 2008)

25. Zahid Hussain, 'Gathering Storm', *Newsline*, February 2005, http://www.newsline.com.pk/NewsFeb2005/cover1feb2005.htm (accessed 31 July 2008). Also see Zahid Hussain, 'Musharraf's Other War', *Newsline*, January 2006, http://www.newsline.com.pk/NewsJan2006/cover1jan2006.htm (accessed 31 July 2008).

26. The quota system has operated to the disadvantage of the Baluch due to the fact that the Baluchistan population only constituted a very small percentage of the national population. Further, the Pashtuns and Punjabis domiciled in Baluchistan were able to count themselves under the Baluchistan provincial quota, further diluting ethnic Baluch representation. In the regional distribution of quotas from 1973 to 1983, for Grades 16 to 22 of Pakistan's bureaucracy, the quota earmarked for Baluchistan was only 3.5 per cent while the actual strength was down to a lower figure of 3.1 per cent. The Baluch had being arguing that since their population has grown since 1972, their quota should be increased from 3.5 per cent to 5.25 per cent. According to one report, it is only in recent years that the Baluch quota in federal jobs has since been increased from 3.5 to 5 per cent. See *The News International*, 14 January 2007.

27. 'Ending the rule of Punjab, by Punjab and for Punjab', Interview with Ataullah Khan Mengal.

28. *The News International*, 7 September 2006.

29. Shaheen Mozaffar, 'The Politics of Cabinet Formation in Pakistan: A Study of Recruitment to the Central Cabinets, 1947–1977', PhD dissertation, Miami University, Ohio, 1980. Cited in Robert G. Wirsing, *The Baluchis and Pathans*, Minority Rights Group Report no. 48 (London), Minority Rights Group, 1987, p. 9.

30. *The News International*, 7 September 2006.

31. Asaf Hussain, *Elite Politics in an Ideological State* (Kent: Dawson and Sons, 1979), Table 14, p. 129.

32. 'Baluchis of Pakistan: On the Margins of History', *The Foreign Policy Centre Report*, London, November 2006, p. 51.

33. According to one source, a deal was brokered between the Pakistani federal government and Akbar Bugti, in which the latter received 120 million rupees annually as rent for land used by Pakistani Petroleum Ltd. (PPL) for extraction of natural gas in Sui territory; and an additional monthly payment of PKR 2 million for ensuring the safety of their operations. See Amir Siddiqui, 'Unholy Alliance', *Newsline*, February 2005, http://www.newsline.com.pk/NewsFeb2005/cover2feb2005.htm (accessed 3 August 2008).

34. Nirupama Subramanian, 'The Baluchistan Cause Gets a Martyr', *The Hindu*, 29 August 2006.
35. For details see, Government of Pakistan, 'White Paper on Baluchistan' (Rawalpindi: Government of Pakistan, 1974), p. 33; Rajshree Jetly, 'Baluch Ethnicity and Nationalism (1971–1981): An Assessment', *Asian Ethnicity*, February 2004, 5(1), pp. 17–18.
36. *Pakistan Opinion Trends and Analyses POT* (Pakistan series), vol. 7, part 232, 7 December 1984, pp. 3752–53.
37. *The News International*, 14 October 2006.
38. Muhammad Ejaz Khan, 'Musharraf Vows to Rectify Baluchistan's Prolonged Neglect', *The News International*, 8 December 2006.
39. This was reiterated by Mubashir Hassan, Minister of Finance, Planning and Development in the Bhutto government from 1971 to 1974, in an interview with the author in New Delhi, 4 September 1996.
40. For a detailed analysis of the reasons for the decline of the Baluch movement in the 1970s, see Jetly, 'Baluch Ethnicity and Nationalism (1971–1981): An Assessment', *Asian Ethnicity*, February 2004, 5(1), pp. 1–26.
41. The movement got further dissipated with some tribal chiefs maintaining an ambivalent attitude towards the Zia regime: overtly, they opposed his rule, but in practice, they availed themselves of the opportunities offered by the co-optive policies of the regime. Zia's multi-pronged policy of coercion, co-option and conciliation turned the tide in Baluchistan in favour of the federal government.
42. Differences between the recent insurgency and the insurgency in the 1970s are also discussed in Rajshree Jetly, 'The Re-emergence of the Baluch Movement in Pakistan', *ISAS Insights* no. 15, October 2006, pp. 5–6.
43. Naveed Ahmad, 'Accept us as Equal Federating Units or We will Try to Get Rid of You', *Newsline*, January 2006, http://www.newsline.com.pk/NewsJan2006/cover2jan2006.htm (accessed 3 August 2008).
44. Shahzada Zulfiqar, 'Edging Towards Anarchy?', *Newsline*, September 2004, http://www.newsline.com.pk/NewsSep2004/newsbeat1sep.htm (accessed 31 July 2008).
45. 'Baluchis of Pakistan: On the Margins of History', *The Foreign Policy Centre Report*, London, November 2006, pp. 31–32.
46. Selig S. Harrison, 'Pakistan's Costly "Other War"', *The Washington Post*, 15 February 2006, p. 3.
47. In the 1970s, the external environment was not conducive to advance the Baluch cause. Although there were several powers involved in the Baluch crisis, none was willing to extend their wholehearted support for the secession of Baluchistan from Pakistan. Their assistance was largely confined to verbal sympathy and moral empathy. Major powers including the United States, the Soviet Union and China (which had

important concerns in South Asia) remained wary of any trend towards 'Balkanization' in the region, which would have affected their long-term security interests.

48. Syed Fazl-e-Haider, 'Gwadar and Oil Politics', *Dawn* Internet edition, 15 January 2007, http://www.dawn.com/2007/01/15/ebr13.htm (accessed 3 August 2008).

49. Nafisa Shah, 'Baluchistan Geopolitics', *The News International*, 27 September 2006.

50. Some Baluch leaders, such as Ataullah Mengal have, however, taken a more radical position and espoused Independence rather than greater autonomy for the Baluch.

51. Nafisa Shah, 'Baluchistan Geopolitics', *The News International*, 27 September 2006; Ziad Haider, 'Baluchis, Beijing, and Pakistan's Gwadar Port', *Politics and Diplomacy*, Winter/Spring 2005, p. 99.

52. BBC: Monitoring South Asia–Political, 14 September 2006 (Source: *Daily Times* website, Lahore)

53. Massoud Ansari, 'Between Tribe and Country, The Crisis of Baluchistan', *Himal South Asia*, 2007, 20(5), pp. 5–6.

54. Nafisa Shah, 'Balochistan Geopolitics and Akbar Bugi', Part 1, *The News International*, 26 September 2006.

55. Ikram Sehgal, 'Life after Bugti', *The News International*, 7 September 2006.

56. Ayesha Siddiqa, 'The Mystery that is Pakistan', *Newsline*, February 2007, http://www.newsline.com.pk/NewsFeb2007/cover2feb2007.htm (accessed 31 July 2008).

57. The following remark by Musharraf is significant in this context. 'It is unfortunate that the areas which are a source of natural gas remained bereft in the past. Don't blame me for past neglects ... I am here to provide you all facilities', *The News International*, 14 October 2006.

58. For Taliban movement in Baluchistan, see Zahid Hussain, 'The Taliban Strike Back', *Newsline*, June 2006, http://www.newsline.com.pk/NewsJune2006/cover1jun2006.htm (accessed 31 July 2008).

＊

10

Pakistan: Political Economy and Post-2000 Developments

Imran Ali

After a downturn during the 1990s, Pakistan's economy experienced a dramatic revival in the post-9/11 period. In 2007, this economic surge was still in evidence, with an average growth rate in excess of 6 per cent over the period. The country's economy had experienced cyclical patterns in earlier decades, and therefore by 2007, the question remained as to what extent and for how long this upturn could be maintained. Tied to these questions was the issue of how much longer the military dictatorship of 'president' Pervez Musharraf would last. Beginning with the coup that ousted the civilian government of prime minister Nawaz Sharif in October 1999, and initially unable to reverse the economic malaise it had inherited, the Musharraf regime had overseen the return to economic buoyancy since 2002. These developments can be better understood in the context of the broader impacts on the political economy that have shaped Pakistan's economic structures and processes before and after decolonization in 1947. A brief survey of these emerging patterns in the political economy will provide a useful perspective to an analysis of the economic scenario since 2000.

To a large extent, Pakistan's political economy was shaped by developments in the colonial period of British rule. The nature and extent of economic change in the Indus basin had decisive ramifications for the post-colonial period. These developments hinged principally on the emergence of an extensive network of perennial canals, taking off from the Indus and its western tributaries, in the provinces of Punjab and Sindh. Constructed from the mid-1880s, these canals transformed hitherto arid and barren land into an agricultural zone that is of critical value to, and indeed underwrites, the contemporary Pakistani economy. The low population density of essentially semi-nomadic pastoral tribes, and settled communities along riverine tracts, was transformed through colonization and land settlement by allotting land to grantees from more populous areas.

The basis for the selection of grantees, and the patterns of utilization of canal irrigated lands, established the mainsprings of the Indus basin's political economy in the twentieth century.[1]

Land distribution was a process controlled by the state since colonization occurred predominantly on land categorized as 'State Waste', though the extension of canal irrigation to proprietary land also consolidated the position of incumbent landlords. Since the bulk of colonization occurred under imperialist rule, the British were able to gain major political leverage from the transfer of a valuable economic resource to selected segments of native society. Most land was allotted in smallholdings of up to 50 acres, and grantees were chosen not from the landless rural poor, or the lowly 'service castes' in indigenous hierarchy, but from the upper peasant segment of hereditary landholding castes. In their old villages, the proprietary rights of this important class had already been acknowledged by the British in return for land revenue payments, which were the chief source of state revenue. These were the same elements that were also being heavily recruited into the British Indian military after 1857 — a consequence of the support they provided to the British in the crisis of 1857–58. By the twentieth century, the Punjab alone accounted for over half the total army.[2] Sizeable areas were also allocated in the new canal irrigated zones for larger landholdings, thereby shoring up the landlord stratum, which served as an essential intermediary for imperialist rule.

In institutional terms, the authority of both the military and the state bureaucracy were significantly strengthened in the emergent hydraulic society. Significant landed resources were reserved for grants to army pensioners and then veterans of the two world wars, as well as for the extensive breeding of cavalry horses through conditional land grants. The native bureaucracy also gained stature from control over irrigation water, land allotments, and land transfers and mutations; and was heavily embroiled in rent seeking.[3] The post-1947 dominance of the military and bureaucracy, and the continued authority of the landlord element leveraging on upper peasant support, were underlined by their consolidation during colonial rule. By contrast, business groups had also emerged with the major increase in trade, processing and distribution of agricultural commodities; but their access to canal irrigated land was limited to auction purchases. Since they were predominantly non-Muslim in composition, their exit to India in 1947 further emasculated the prospects of the business segment posing any major politico-economic challenge to the traditional order. The exclusion of the rural poor before 1947, from both electoral enfranchisement and occupancy access to landed resources, also reflected their continued neglect in the structure of state expenditures after decolonization.[4]

The Pakistani state then continued for the next half-century to abide by the political economy modes established under imperialist tutelage. Arguably, as later developments were to show, within the framework of supposed sovereignty, imperialist control remained pivotal in the exercise of authority, although with a shift away from Britain to a new hegemon. For one, a vital consequence of the British success at manoeuvring agricultural colonization to their own political advantage had been an extremely weak nationalist stimulus in the region that later became Pakistan. Only in the Frontier province did a political grouping, led by Ghaffar Khan and allied to the Indian National Congress, display nationalist sentiments and achieve electoral success. Significantly, in Pakistan, Ghaffar Khan was humiliated, imprisoned and exiled. In Punjab and Sindh, the British-aligned landlord nominees of the upper peasantry continued to dominate the provincial legislatures right up till decolonization, leading thereby to a continuity of dependent authoritarianism into Pakistan.[5] By contrast, the Congress had severed this nexus with the 1936 elections in the area that became India, and it since then assumed rule for the next half-century in a democratic Indian state that could espouse neutrality. The notion of 'retarded nationalism' should therefore be noted, as it has continued to play an integral role in Pakistan's political economy.

Thus, the weakness of nationalist organization allowed those forces aligned against democracy to remain dominant in the new country. This position could not, however, have been secured without continued acquiescence to neo-imperialist power, a relationship that was to articulate sequentially in the coming decades.[6] The denial of democracy to the people was evidenced through the failure to hold elections in the first decade, characterized by de-institutionalized and factionalized landlord politics. This 'instability' was followed by a decade of military rule, during which the nexus between internal authoritarianism and the dependence of the civilian and military elites on the Anglo-American axis was further reinforced. This dependence was formalized through inclusion in the Southeast Asia Treaty Organization (SEATO) and Central Treaty Organization (CENTO) military nexus. While social-sector spending in Pakistan remained minimal and the real incomes of the vast majority stagnated, both power and resources continued to remain highly concentrated among the agrarian and business elite.[7] Untrammelled by popular sanction, the bureaucracy could also indulge in decision-making with little accountability but increasingly blatant rent-seeking. The military for its part continued to absorb a high proportion of public expenditures.

The reason given for maintaining an army of over half-a-million was the threat from India, and a controlled media plied the people with anti-Indian themes. It could be argued that Indian depredations on the Kashmiri people, and its denial of their right to self-determination, provided the moral basis for this rationalization. Yet, despite the huge and continued resource diversion, the military cannot sustain a conventional war for more than a few days. Such armies in the Third World have also been a pushover when attacked; people's militias are a more effective defence against foreign aggressors, as witnessed in West Asia. In whose interests then was this large military apparatus maintained? Was it perhaps that the Pakistani people, inordinately poor and deprived, paid entirely for a resource-draining military capacity against a possible Soviet–Russian expansionism? The commonly-evoked theme of US military 'assistance' to Pakistan has certainly run dry since the resource drain has been heavily in the other direction; it is high time that this is reversed. Moreover, to maintain this relationship, continued de-institutionalization and the satiation of rent-hungry intermediaries has led over time to a breakdown in orderliness, public management delivery, and state legitimacy. Pakistan wallows at the nether end of societal and institutional indicators worldwide.[8] Hence, the notion of 'retarded nationalism' needs to be associated with that of ongoing 'vassalage', as significant determinants of the nation's political economy.

In the economic sphere, public policy in the first two decades focused on overcoming the almost complete non-existence of an industrial sector.[9] While the Indus region was a substantial exporter of agricultural commodities and raw materials, there had been virtually no large-scale industrial investment there during colonialism. Beginning with the savings accumulated during the Korean War trade upturn, and heavily induced through state subsidies, incentives and tariff protections, an incipient industrial sector began to emerge in the 1950s, and gained further momentum in the 1960s with increasing wealth concentration.[10] The emergence of a few business groups, dominating the large-scale industrial sector and diversifying into the financial sector, began to appear iniquitous, since political rights and labour unions were suppressed, and real wages of workers remained stagnant.[11] Small- and medium-scale enterprises failed to receive the subsidies and public sector divestments accruing to certain selective business beneficiaries. Regional misgivings also arose, with East Pakistan (later Bangladesh) increasingly resenting apparent resource transfers from jute exports to industrial investment in the western wing. In agriculture too, the Green Revolution benefits accrued mostly to middle- and large-scale farmers, who could afford the new inputs needed for optimal profits, such as agricultural machinery, pesticides, fertilizers and high-yielding seeds. The upper peasantry was further squeezed, with tenant expropriations induced by farm mechanization, and undertaken through authoritarian fiat. Rapid economic growth had heightened, rather than reduced, income inequity and wealth concentration.[12]

The consequence of these growing inequalities and tensions was evident in the 1970 general elections — the first in Pakistan's history. These followed on the overthrow of the Ayub Khan military regime after a popular agitation, and in the context of an assertion of popular will, they can be seen as equally an expression of a nationalist struggle as the events leading to 1947. Not only did half the country break away to form Bangladesh, but in the remaining part a reversal of economic strategy under the People's Party government of Zulfiqar Ali Bhutto saw extensive nationalization of large-scale industry, banks and insurance, and even the education and health sectors.[13] Bhutto's 'progressive' policies, however, were heavily overdetermined, and in the end betrayed, by an underlying hostility to business and market forces, inherent in his alliance with the upper peasantry of Punjab, the large landlords of Sindh, and urban workers and intelligentsia. His anti-capitalist 'counter-revolution', initially directed at large-scale business, was reinforced through follow-up nationalization of the intermediate agro-processing sector, and of trade, distribution and export in the major agricultural commodities. This effort to remove the private sector from the agricultural value chain, and the moves against big business, led to private-sector investment constraints in the medium term.[14]

However, it was Bhutto's resistance to renewed superpower pressure that more probably led to his downfall, and eventual execution. With a new military partner, General Zia-ul-Haq, in place by 1977, the efforts to destabilize Afghan neutrality led to the Soviet military invasion in 1979. The subsequent 'jihad' in Afghanistan through American-sponsored armed resistance, and its related induction of an Islamic 'ideology' for Pakistan through military fiat and newly arisen religious 'fundamentalism', has made it more problematical for an impoverished people to normalize their economic and political environment.[15] The price of a freedom with no bloodletting for Eastern Europe and the ex-Soviet republics was paid with over a million dead in Afghanistan, and with Pakistan awash with drugs, arms and religious militancy, apart from the burden of sustaining over three million refugees. While Pakistan's growth rate of around 6 per cent in the 1980s was the highest in a painfully slow-growing South Asian region, much of this was induced by workers' remittances and foreign loans, rather than enhancements in industrial productivity or any significant diversification away from the focus on cotton textiles.[16]

With the anti-Soviet agenda achieved, the intensity of geo-strategic attention on Pakistan waned. After Zia's timely demise in an air crash in 1988, Pakistan returned for the next decade to civilian governments. None of the four governments in this period — two each of Benazir Bhutto and Nawaz Sharif — were allowed to complete their tenures; finally, military rule was again re-established in 1999. Coincidentally, the return to a military regime, more compliant with Western geo-strategic demands, was followed by another war in Afghanistan two years later. Significantly, from being one of the largest programmes in the 1980s, US foreign assistance was virtually eliminated in the period of civilian democracy in the 1990s. Pakistan even suffered sanctions after it conducted a nuclear test in response to India's in 1998.[17]

This period witnessed an economic downturn, in which the growth rate for once went below that of India, and both fiscal deficits and foreign debt rose to unsustainable levels.[18] Political uncertainty discouraged investment, while rapid population expansion virtually negated real growth rates. Ongoing civil conflict in Afghanistan led to a takeover by the Taliban, presumably a further version of the 'Islamist terrorists' originally generated under American sponsorship. The freedom struggle in Kashmir also incurred Indian outrage, thus commencing an intense process of vilification of Pakistan. Such efforts at 'demonization' began to shape perceptions of Pakistan overseas; and they have found their latest expression in those seeking scapegoats for the continuing failure to quell resistance in Afghanistan, following the invasion and occupation of that country by the Western axis.

In the first few years of his rule, Musharraf was unable to turn around the economy, which continued to suffer from the structural weaknesses that had emerged in the 1990s. Especially crippling was a foreign debt burden exceeding US$ 30 billion, which had risen precipitously since the 1980s through the willingness to lend of multilateral agencies like the World Bank, Asian Development Bank and International Monetary Fund, aided by the resource hunger of native intermediaries into whose coffers these funds appeared to have mostly disappeared. The foreign currency deposits held by Pakistanis in overseas banks were said to be roughly equivalent to the country's foreign debt. Loan repayments became difficult to meet, necessitating rescheduling of debts. The problem was compounded by repayment pressure of debt that had been raised at commercial rates, to meet interest payments on soft loans. This action had apparently been taken by the interim 'caretaker' regimes established after the dismissal of elected governments in the 1990s, when some multilateral agency hirelings, like Moeen Qureshi and Shahid Javed Burki, took over temporary control of the administration and public finance. By mid-2001, the foreign exchange reserves had sunk to a mere $200 million, and inability to maintain repayment schedules was even moving the country towards sovereign default.[19]

These fiscal adversities had significant linkage effects in the economy. In the face of fiscal deficits of 6 per cent or more, which reflected an excess of even current expenditures over revenues, public finances began to suffer a continuing resource gap. With military expenditures continuing at high levels, the development budget had to be severely curtailed. This left little room for any decisive improvements, or even increments, in infrastructure, communications, energy resources, social sector amenities and health and education, and human resource development. The financial stringency, as well as perceptions of heightened country risk, kept interest rates above 20 per cent with financial institutions, and at even higher levels in the highly pervasive informal money market. These prohibitive rates affected investment levels as well as the overall growth rate, which stagnated at around 4 per cent. A drought also affected agricultural performance at this time, accompanied by emerging scarcities in irrigation resources and the failure to develop any major hydroelectrical projects.[20]

Efforts at widening the income tax base proved unsuccessful, in the face of corruption in the revenue bureaucracy, lack of documentation in the widely diffused informal sector, and resistance by the rural elite to taxation of agricultural incomes. Under pressure from the international money-lending agencies for meeting interest payments on external debt, the government started a process of reducing subsidies and moving towards user charges in utilities. It then resorted to indirect taxation by introducing a high general sales tax, at the rate of 15 per cent, thereby transferring the revenue and fiscal burden on to the poor, since further state income could not be derived from the upper income segments through direct taxes. The higher input costs that both agriculture and industry began to experience made them uncompetitive with economies like China and India, where producers continued to enjoy substantially subsidized energy rates. Also, other low income countries, like Bangladesh and Vietnam, threatened to erode Pakistan's competitiveness in the staple industry — cotton textiles, especially in the value-added segments of apparels and made-ups. Margins there tended to be higher than in the commoditized yarn and grey cloth segment, where the bulk of Pakistan's investment in textiles remained concentrated.

Despite these deep-seated problems, Pakistan's economy experienced a considerable turnaround after the September 2001 attacks in New York. With the American invasion of Afghanistan and the ensuing campaign against the 'Al-Qaeda', Pakistan again became a front-line state in geopolitical conflict, and an essential ally for meeting Western military objectives. Once again, the economic benefits that it obtained were a pittance compared to the strategic contributions that it was called upon to make. Pakistan has never been the destination of any sizeable investment flows from the West, in comparison with the substantial amounts directed towards first East Asia, then Southeast Asia, and more recently India.[21] From 2002, a certain level of foreign assistance was resumed, and the more onerous sanctions were lifted; but the real dynamics behind the turnaround were the inflows of money from expatriate Pakistanis, in the face of greater accountability and vigilance over money laundering and the funding of 'terrorism' networks. Another source of inflows was the bounty money paid to the Pakistani military for handing over 'terrorist' suspects to be sent to concentration camps and torture facilities, run by or for the United States. Investment funds have also reached Pakistan from Arab oil economies, largely to purchase industrial and infrastructure assets and financial institutions under the privatization programme.[22]

Under the changed circumstances, Pakistan's macroeconomic outlook also improved. There was a rise in export earnings, though these are still inadequate for a country of 160 million people. By 2007, they had exceeded US$ 15 billion, from a level around US$ 10 billion in 2000. Pakistan's exports were still higher than India on a per capita basis, but it had nowhere near the latter's performance in the information technology business. Pakistan's foreign exchange reserves rose from the desperate level of US$ 200 million in 2000 to a purported US$ 13 billion by 2006. The government also claimed that the country had paid off the more harmful high interest component of the foreign debt, which still nevertheless stood above US$ 35 billion. The external debt to GDP ratio also improved, leading to greater fiscal space that allowed for more resource allocation to the development sector. The more 'positive' attitude towards Pakistan among foreign donors had arguably the deleterious effect of renewed multilateral and bilateral loan flows into the country, a process induced with the avid support of a bureaucracy that should actually have been questioning the relevance and efficacy of adding on further debt.[23]

The rapid rise in liquidity had a visible impact on Pakistan's economy. Interest rates came down sharply, and at one point hovered around historic lows of 5–6 per cent. This led to a consumption upturn, and also spurred investment to meet the increasing demand for goods and services. A speculative boom in property also ensued, with major price rises taking property values to unprecedented levels. These peaks were followed by downward swings; overall they represented a diversion from more productive employment of resources, in areas that would have had a more positive impact on prospects of longer term economic growth, such as infrastructural development and industrial deepening and efficiency. The property value escalations indeed allegedly diverted industrialists towards raising bank credit for quick returns on property speculation, to the neglect of their core businesses. The involvement of senior military personnel in land scams also began to erode the Musharraf regime's reputation. The cancellation of the allotment of 240,000 acres to 'institutions' in the area around the new sea port development of Gwadar was one of the grievances the regime had against the Chief Justice of Pakistan's Supreme Court, whose dismissal by Musharraf in March 2007 raised a popular political outburst. In the complex interactions between economic, strategic and political factors, two other stimuli for the dismissal of the Chief Justice were also evident. One was his pursuance of the issue of missing persons, which did not suit the activities of the United States in removing hundreds of young men to torture cells. The other was apprehensions that the Chief Justice could not be relied upon to acquiesce in Musharraf's presumed designs for rigging the forthcoming elections in favour of his political supporters.

The stock market, which had languished around the 1,200 index level in 2000, rose by 2006 to over 12,000. Pakistan had the best-performing stock market in the world for a greater number of years since 2000 than any other country. Again, the index was highly skewed towards pockets of robustly performing firms in the energy, communications and financial sectors, and among consumer product MNCs. By contrast, the predominant number of scrips in the textile sector, representing Pakistan's largest industry, remained well below par value, and in many cases 70–80 per cent below. This anomaly reflected the failure of Pakistani industrial entrepreneurs to meet their obligations to the capital markets. They were able to make a one-time resource gain, through the appropriation of bank loans and public share subscriptions, but failed to reciprocate with dividend payments or bonus or rights issues. They could, of course, repeat the process through new share floats, if the diminishing returns on reputations allowed. Hence business 'groups' ended up with several independent companies, rather than as corporatized entities. Also, uncontrolled insider trading, apparently with the connivance of politically well-placed elements, was allegedly responsible for the wild fluctuations in the share index that periodically convulsed the stock market. During this period and overseen by Musharraf's 'prime minister', Shaukat Aziz, himself an erstwhile banker, some of the major brokers in the Karachi Stock Exchange established their own investment banks, and indeed emerged as the new super rich of the country.

The economic turnaround, however, might not be entirely a function of financial inflows induced by overseas insecurities over money accountability. As I have discussed elsewhere:

Conversely, it could be argued that the money flows into Pakistan had a more positive dimension. They could only partly be explained through insecurities in overseas quarters over money accountability. They also reflected the undervalued levels of the Pakistani share and real estate markets, and were a response to a conducive investment environment. Moreover, the liberalization since the 1990s of financial and currency markets, and the major concessions given to foreign investors, such as 100 per cent equity and full remittance of profits, were bound to produce results. The more business-friendly public policy approach was also designed to stimulate both domestic and foreign investment, through a series of conducive measures, such as export rebates, concessionary import duties on capital goods and industrial raw materials, removal of wealth and capital gains taxes, and control over progressive rates of corporate and individual income taxes. The investment spurt only awaited a more politically stable environment, and this was not forthcoming in the 1990s, owing to internal political factors and Pakistan's external image. After 2001, the greater acceptance of the Musharraf regime by the international community and, to some extent, relief from the prevarications and greed of opportunistic civilian politicians, created a salubrious environment for investment. This would be the more positive interpretation of capital flows into Pakistan, except that these flows came largely in individual remittances, rather than as substantive doses of corporate or business investment.[24]

According to government statistics, the growth rate of the Pakistani economy reached above 5 per cent in 2003, and stayed above 6 per cent in the mid-2000s.[25] The agricultural growth rate, which is important enough to affect overall GDP, also remained positive, with no major reverses since the end of the drought that had affected the economy for a few years prior to 2002. Increasing domestic demand for food crops, from wheat to vegetables and fruits, as well as smuggling of food items to Afghanistan, India and Iran, helped maintain the buoyancy of the agricultural sector. At times seasonal shortages of certain commodities, such as onions, tomatoes and even potatoes, sent their prices spiralling, in some cases necessitating imports from India. These price hikes affected inflation rates and cut into the already meagre disposable incomes of the great majority, thereby even threatening the political stability of the country. Nevertheless with a cultivated area of over 20 million hectares and other impressive indicators, such as a livestock herd roughly equivalent in size to that of the United States and European Union, Pakistan's agribusiness potential remained one of its key resources.

A constraining feature on the maintenance of higher growth rates could be impending shortages in energy and irrigation water. Under the Musharraf regime, there have been no major increments in energy production, since contracts were reached with independent power producers in the 1990s for higher-cost thermal power generation, based on gas and furnace oil. The inability to construct further hydroelectric projects, and especially the ongoing postponement of the Kalabagh Dam on the Indus, has threatened to lead to future energy shortfalls. Robust economic growth has increased the energy demand levels, without commensurate supply enhancements, and with the government caught without an energy strategy. With local gas reserves due to run out in the next decade, Pakistan has yet to take decisive measures to develop its renewable or alternative energy sources. Pakistan has the world's sixth largest coal reserves, but it is of high phosphoric content, and its mining will have environmental repercussions. Nuclear power has yet to supply more than 1 per cent of Pakistan's energy needs. The energy shortfall will not only incur popular wrath — and riot-like situations have already occurred in some cities — but it will also constrain industrial growth and agricultural operations in the future.

Irrigation resources are also considerably stretched, and Pakistan is now seen as a water-scarce zone.[26] Some global warming projections have even estimated a decrease in the water availability in the Indus river system to a staggering 40 per cent by mid-century, which, if it were to happen, would threaten the very survival of a population already swollen beyond sustainability. Pakistan has the largest contiguous irrigation system in the world, which provides the backbone of its economy. Efforts made to decentralize the irrigation management to a more participatory mode, through the creation in 1997 of statutory irrigation development authorities in the provinces of Punjab and Sindh, experienced a failure of implementation under Musharraf. Specifically, there was an inability, or unwillingness in the face of vested interests, to push through the creation of farmers' organizations of local irrigators, and apex area water boards at canal command levels, aimed to take over the operational management from the endemically corrupt and inefficient irrigation departments surviving from the colonial period. More recently, with the World Bank and Asian Development Bank again providing credit for water sector projects, pressure has returned for progress on these reforms.[27] New technologies also enable more accurate measurement of water flows, and identification of water diversions and misappropriations. However, follow-up legal action is resisted by the miscreant alliance of corrupt officials on the one hand and on the other the larger water users that permeate the power structure.

The discrepancy between stated policy goals and actual performance pervades other aspects of public administration. Such significant shortfalls in policy implementation are not confined to Pakistan alone among the developing countries, yet they seriously challenge the equity of high relative resource absorption by ineffective public functionaries and their private sector associates. One glaring example lies in the continuing failure in population planning and control, which is a vital variable in Pakistan's economic sustainability. From a base of 35 million in 1947, the country's population now exceeds 160 million; and current projections take it to well over 250 million by 2025. The administration's response has been to simply descend to untruths over the population growth rate. This was reduced in official claims from 3.1 per cent in the mid-1990s, first to 2.6 per cent by 2000, to another neat downward adjustment of 0.5 per cent, to 2.1 per cent by 2004, and to a more comforting but clearly delusionary level below 2 per cent at 1.9 per cent currently! There is no real explanation of how, in a mere decade, a 30 per cent reversal in demographic behaviour has come about. Meanwhile, with the census process in disarray, the government remains clueless of how many people there really are in the country. One equation is clear, and officially acknowledged: over half the population is under 20 years of age. The demographic implications of such huge numbers reaching school age and employment age, and then entering the reproductive cycle with attitude, as well as their demands on physical and institutional resources, defies the capacity of the state to even conceptualize these problems, let alone devise strategies for their amelioration.

To some extent, the descent to Malthusian mayhem is a product of extreme economic inequalities, combined with major inequities in political economy. Again, these are symptoms shared with other developing countries, but they remain part of the crisis of social economy that is facing Pakistan. The historic low level of expenditures on human development and the social sector, combined with political exclusion and the absence of redistributive mechanisms as well as old age and unemployment benefits, has induced the poor to seek security in numbers. With declines in the death rate and generally improved food security, combined with the weak controls over child labour creating decided generational resource transfers from child to parent, there is a certain logic in the poor wanting to have large families. The state has proclaimed on paper a prioritization for 'poverty alleviation' strategies, but these appear more for the facilitation of funding by the international donor community — the bulk of resources get absorbed by political intermediaries and the middle-class salariat rather than reaching the poor.[28] Patterns experienced in the past, especially in the 1960s, of high growth actually increasing income inequalities, appear to have re-emerged. The shift to indirect taxes, and relief from wealth tax, has helped upper income groups. Inflationary trends in basic commodities have also hit the poor. The relative numbers under the 'poverty level' remains contentious, with the administration claiming a reduction towards 25 per cent, and analysts putting this figure closer to 35 per cent. But such a level is itself arbitrary: clearly the great majority of Pakistan's population suffers from serious to severe economic deprivation.[29]

Perhaps the most major reform under the Musharraf regime has been the setting up of a local government system. This is clearly the most ambitious and innovative in South Asia; and to a large extent its success is challenged by the scale of the transition that is entailed. A three-tier system has been introduced, at the level of the district, sub-district *tahsil* and municipal authority, and local union councils. Elections to non-executive positions are on a non-party basis, while the elections of the district mayor, or *nazim*, are indirect. This has led to allegations that the system was devised to reduce the hold of political organizations on local politics, and to counter the influence of politicians elected to the provincial and national legislatures. Another critique has been that the power of the bureaucracy has been hobbled, by removing the judicial powers of the pivotal Deputy Commissioner position and placing it under the control of the district government. A number of other roles and functions have been devolved to the local level, though in practice the bureaucracy in the provincial governments continues to exercise significant authority, if only because local governments lack the expertise and capacity to handle administrative complexities. In the 2002 local government elections, the military intelligence apparatus did apparently intervene to ensure that supportive groups assumed office; while the fact that the district *nazim* is not directly elected also leaves room for manipulation. Nevertheless, if this new structure continues to articulate, then local development, social sector delivery, and the application of economic resources at the ground level will have experienced a major transition.

A major reform that the Musharraf regime could have attempted, but failed even to consider seriously, owing to the risks attached, was the restructuring of provincial entities. Pakistan has the same four provinces it inherited in 1947, even though the population has more than quadrupled, socio-economic realities are far more complex, and administrative and governance challenges have increased manifold. India has almost doubled the number of states in sixty years, reflecting greater responsiveness to changing conditions and ethnic or linguistic distinctions. In Pakistan, having four large provinces, each carrying major weight, has created seemingly insurmountable problems over such decisions as the construction of the Kalabagh Dam, till recently the sharing of waters of the Indus river system, and even the annual national finance award for the provincial sharing of fiscal resources. The Punjab alone has over 80 million people, larger than any country in Europe outside united Germany. Karachi, with around 15 million people, could easily be a separate province.[30] Around twelve provinces could be created, hopefully with thin administrations, to better serve the needs of a growing population, and to avoid the escalation of controversial issues to federation-threatening levels, as well as the politicization that vested interests are apt to create.

The level of cooperation and integration in the regional economy can make a significant contribution to a country's economic well-being in the contemporary world. Pakistan is uniquely placed in that it lies geographically where all three circles of Central, South and West Asia intersect. Its position has given it an intensity of economic and geo-strategic importance, over millennia, matched by few other regions (it's 'civilization' is now, for better or worse, in its seventh millennium). However, South Asia is the region where its natural alignment lies: and efforts at regional cooperation there have been perhaps the most retarded internationally. Not only is the total external trade of the SAARC (South Asian Association for Regional Cooperation) countries a mere fraction of the total world trade, but only a miniscule fraction of this trade is within the

SAARC region.[31] Moreover, the two largest economies, India and Pakistan, are also the least focused on intra-regional trade. While India has granted Pakistan a Most Favoured Nation (MFN) status, which is now quite common under the General Agreement on Tariffs and Trade (GATT) protocols, Pakistan has not reciprocated; this has been a bone of contention between the two countries. While Pakistan has linked this with a resolution of the core Kashmir issue, India has retaliated by trying to keep Pakistan out of other regional and international networks, such as the Indian Ocean consultative process. In lieu of granting MFN status to India, Pakistan has maintained a 'positive list' of items on which it would allow trade with India: by 2006, this list extended to over 750 items.

Meanwhile, there has been occurring within SAARC a process of moving towards a free trade area. The signing in 1996 of a South Asia Preferential Trade Agreement (SAPTA) was followed by further negotiations on trade liberalization. These culminated in the signing of the South Asian Free Trade Agreement (SAFTA), which came into effect on 1 July 2006 .[32] Under this, all items would be open to free trade, except for a restricted 'negative list' that members could retain. In July 2006, Pakistan announced that in the case of India, it would retain its 'positive list', coupling the move to free trade with a resolution of the Kashmir dispute. India has reacted negatively to this proviso, and the matter remains unresolved. In the meantime, trade with India has increased to over US$ 1 billion dollars, whereas actual trade either through smuggling or via the Gulf states is already considerably higher. In the next few years, India–Pakistan trade flows should gain further momentum. Pakistan has also moved in line with World Trade Organization (WTO) thresholds towards import liberalization; and indeed the subsequent hike in imports has created a worrying trade imbalance since 2006. Fears that a recurring trade gap would result in a return to current account deficits could only be forestalled by either reducing imports or raising exports, both of which appeared problematic. Without these rectification measures, the Pakistani rupee could begin to come under pressure, as it had done with almost 10 per cent devaluation per year in the 1990s.

One of the problems Pakistan continued to face was the lack of diversification in exports. These remained heavily concentrated in a few commodities: three quarters were in the light manufactured goods, comprising cotton, synthetic textiles, leather goods, garments, knitwear and rice. The export destinations were: about 40 per cent to USA, around 25 per cent to the European community, and 25 per cent to Asia, of which 8 per cent was to China (including Hong Kong) but only 1 per cent to India.[33] With concentration in commodities and with weak bargaining power, Pakistan's export resilience was by no means assured. Indeed, the negative effects of the trade imbalance would be much greater, without remittances of approximately 4 billion dollars annually in the mid-2000s. As opposed to exports, fully a quarter of total imports were in petroleum products, one of the highest ratios in Asia. Edible oils also feature high on the import list, reflecting expanding domestic demand and the inability to generate country supply in this commodity. Pakistan is also the world's third or fourth largest importer of tea, with consumption escalating through media advertising on television, and major market share in the branded segment by one multinational, Unilever.

In the wider context, the state of business development in Pakistan also remained sub-optimal. While the post-1990 emphasis on market forces had given more stimulus to the private sector, the post-nationalization disincentives coming through from the 1970s took time to overcome. The 'big business' groups of the 1960s never really re-emerged, and those that had survived through a focus on cotton textiles no longer relished diversification into more sophisticated and value-adding industries.[34] The post-1985 return of private sector investment remained concentrated in lower-value addition segments of cotton spinning and weaving, and increasingly turned to the even more commoditized investment in sugar production. A heavy incursion of rent capitalism in the 1990s, leveraging off civilian politics, left much of the credit portfolios of financial institutions in non-performing loans. Since then, the privatization of the extensive network of state-owned enterprises, and especially the privatization of nationalized banks, has restored confidence in the private sector, and raised levels of foreign direct investment. The latter is claimed to be nearing US$ 5 billion in 2006–07, from levels only one-tenth of this a few years earlier. However, sales in the infrastructure sector, especially the telecommunications parastatal, are responsible for this hike, rather than any decent investment rises in export creation and internationally competitive industrial production. The development of the latter capabilities is the greatest challenge to both Pakistani state and entrepreneur, and in this the assessment must remain one of unfulfilled potential.

Also, the neglect of Pakistan as a zone of foreign investment flows compared unfavourably with those of the recipient economies of the Southeast Asian 'miracle'. This lack of attention also contrasted vividly with Pakistan's own prominence in internationally critical geo-strategic conflicts; and this must rank as one of the great blind spots in the structure of international investment. Perhaps in the 'world system', Pakistan 'was indeed called, and then chosen, by global-ization, but for the latter's strategic and geopolitical imperatives, rather than for its economic and wealth generating virtues'.[35]

The economic momentum that seemed to have built up, and the relative political 'stability' that most countries under military dictator-ships ostensibly experience, began to decompose rapidly from early 2007 in Pakistan. Apprehensions had periodically been voiced that the post-2001 growth spurt had not been based on strong funda-mentals. The structure of growth had been strongly skewed in favour of the financial sector, based on remittance inflows, which in turn led to a large and irresponsible reduction in interest rates by the economic management team headed by Shaukat Aziz. This had led to an unsustainable spurt in demand, fuelled by a newly created 'credit' economy, and this in turn worsened both inflationary pressures and the trade imbalance, as consumers reached out for imported goods, including luxury cars, under a WTO-induced trade liberalization regime. Periodic shortages in some food commodities hit the lower-end income groups, sending worrying signals that agricultural production was not keeping up with demand, and also exposing the continuing inefficiencies of supply chains in the food system. The most serious shortfall appeared in 2007–08 in flour shortages: the crisis stemming from emerging flour scarcity, which drove up the prices of Pakistan's staple food to unprecedented levels, was produced more by hoarding and speculative activity than by shortfalls in the wheat crop. The wheat market, newly opened to the private sector as the main player in the wheat trade, fell victim to unscrupulous elements that purportedly included provincial and federal politicians. These developments were not without pol-itical consequences, as shown by the results of the February 2008 elections.

As interest rates climbed back up, not only did the speculative boom in real estate and the stock market run aground, but the pro-duction sector was also hurt through rising costs. Many industrial entrepreneurs had shifted focus from their manufacturing units, by collateralizing these assets to raise funds from banks for quick profits in property and portfolio investments. They now felt the squeeze of rising financial charges and falling values. Pakistan also began to lose its labour cost advantage in textiles to other low-income economies, like Bangladesh and Vietnam, leading first to a crisis in the knitwear segment, and then increasing strains in spinning and weaving, which were Pakistan's premium export earners. Exacerbating these trends was an emerging energy shortage, which assumed uncontrollable proportions by mid-2008. The Musharraf regime had neglected adding any further capacity in electricity generation during its extended tenure; and the extensive power cuts to which it resorted adversely affected industrial production, and threatened the livelihoods of workers in the micro-enterprise and informal sectors, who could not afford private generators that were expensive to purchase and operate. The power crisis and the squeeze on the manufacturing as well as agricultural production, with endemic power outages in the rural sector, threatened to undo whatever economic gains the Musharraf regime could claim to have achieved.

Coinciding with the return of economic stringency was a developing political crisis that centred around growing public revulsion for the Musharraf dictatorship. This political crisis was brought on by Musharraf's summary decision on 9 March 2007 to dismiss the Chief Justice of the Supreme Court, the country's apex judicial body. The political climate continued to deteriorate with the ensuing lawyers' and civil society movement for the restoration of the Chief Justice, the 're-election' of Musharraf as 'president' for a further term of five years and his relinquishment of the position of army chief, the National Reconciliation Order or NRO, which implicitly lifted corruption charges against Benazir Bhutto and enabled her to return to Pakistan in time for elections, and the contentious Provisional Constitutional Order or PRO on 3 November 2007, which displaced Supreme and provincial High Court judges who were not in favour of the Musharraf incumbency. The assassination of Ms Bhutto on 27 December 2007 and several bomb attacks against security targets plunged the country into further crisis. Bhutto, in the final days of her life, had begun to alter her approach to the 'war on terror'; and her questioning of a mainly military solution as advocated by the US–NATO axis was probably tantamount to her death sentence. Nevertheless, the popular vote in the elections of 18 February 2008 displayed a dramatic rejection of Musharraf's policies, and of both his political manipulations and economic failures. By also rejecting the religious politicians, the Pakistani people showed that their political wisdom was not to be denigrated. The return to a democratic order and of economic equity, not possible without a rollback of the imperialist interventions and native authoritarian forces so ubiquitous in Pakistan's history, now remained the challenge for Pakistan's political economy.

Appendix 10.1

Economic Indicators, 2000–2006

Indicators	2000–01	2001–02	2002–03	2003–04	2004–05	2005–06	July–Sep. 2005	July–Sep. 2006	+ (−) %
Exports (US$ bn.)	9.20	9.13	11.16	12.31	14.39	16.47	4.15	4.27	3
Imports (US$ bn.)	10.72	10.334	12.22	15.59	20.60	28.58	6.55	7.43	13
Trade Balance (US$ bn.)	(1.52)	(1.20)	(1.06)	(3.28)	(6.21)	(12.11)	(2.40)	(3.16)	32
Net Revenue (PKR bn.)	393.9	404.1	460.6	518.8	590.39	712.61	149.2	NA	
FDI (US$ mn.)	322.40	484.70	798.00	949.40	1524	3521	328.7	1029	213
Workers' Remittances (US$ bn.)	1.09	2.39	4.24	3.872	4.17	4.60	1.00	1.23	23
Forex Reserves (US$ bn.)	3.22	6.43	10.72	12.33	12.61	13.14	12.0	12.53	4
Exchange Rate (PKR/US$)	58.4	61.0	57.7	57.92	59.66	60.16	59.5	60.5	2
Stock Exchange Index	1300	1520	3402	5279	7450	9989	8226	10512	28
GDP Growth	2.6%	3.6%	5.1%	6.4%	8.4%	6.6%			
Inflation	4.4%	3.4%	3.3%	3.9%	9.3%	8%			

Source: State Bank of Pakistan (SBP), Federal Bureau of Statistics (FBS), Central Board of Revenue (CBR), Business Recorder.

Appendix 10.2

Key Investment Indicators

Fiscal year (July–June)	1997–98	1998–99	1999–00	2000–01	2001–02	2002–03	2003–04	2004–05	2005–06
Growth of Gross Total Investment	9.00%	–3.60%	10.20%	8.60%	3.20%	10.70%	14.40%	27.50%	29.50%
Growth of Gross Fixed Investment	1.50%	1.60%	10.50%	8.50%	3.20%	8.20%	14.70%	28.60%	30.70%
Growth of Gross Private Fixed Investment	13.30%	–11.40%	14.30%	7.20%	17.30%	9.80%	13.10%	29.10%	31.60%
Total Foreign Investment (US$ mn.)	822.6	403.3	543.4	182	474.6	820.1	921.7	1,676.60	3,872.50
Of which: Portfolio Investment	221.3	27.3	73.5	–140.4	–10.1	22.1	–27.7	152.6	351.5
Foreign Direct Investment	601.3	376	469.9	322.4	484.7	798	949.4	1,524	3,521
FDI Shares by Sector:									
Power	39.80%	27.80%	14.30%	12.50%	7.50%	4.10%	–1.49%	4.80%	9.11%
Chemical, Pharm. & Fertilizer	12.00%	11.50%	25.50%	8.20%	3.70%	11.60%	3.00%	6.10%	–0.29%
Construction	3.60%	2.90%	4.50%	3.90%	2.60%	2.20%	3.37%	2.80%	2.54%
Mining & Quarrying and Oil Exp.	16.50%	23.90%	17.00%	26.30%	56.70%	23.60%	21.43%	12.80%	9.08%
Food, Beverages & Tobacco	3.20%	1.60%	10.60%	14.00%	–1.10%	0.90%	0.47%	1.50%	1.70%
Textile	4.50%	0.40%	0.90%	1.40%	3.80%	3.30%	3.73%	2.60%	1.33%

Transport, Storage & Comm.	55.56%	34.90%	24.29%	14.30%	7.30%	25.30%	6.60%	7.10%	1.70%
Machinery (other than electrical)	0.03%	0.20%	0.07%	0.10%	0.00%	0.10%	0.70%	0.20%	0.00%
Electronics	0.51%	0.70%	0.79%	0.80%	3.30%	0.90%	0.50%	0.30%	0.40%
Electrical Machinery	0.05%	0.20%	0.92%	1.30%	2.20%	0.70%	0.30%	0.40%	1.40%
Financial Business	9.35%	17.70%	25.50%	26.00%	0.70%	-10.80%	6.30%	5.20%	3.40%
Trade	3.35%	3.40%	3.75%	4.90%	7.10%	4.10%	1.60%	1.20%	2.10%
Petrochemicals & Refining	1.16%	1.60%	7.62%	0.40%	1.00%	2.70%	2.60%	8.20%	0.30%
Tourism/Paper & Pulp	0.10%	0.00%	0.19%	0.20%	0.20%	0.40%	0.10%	0.00%	0.90%
Cement/Sugar	1.25%	1.10%	0.24%	0.20%	0.10%	4.70%	1.30%	0.40%	0.50%
Other	5.15%	9.70%	6.09%	6.20%	4.90%	5.80%	7.20%	9.10%	9.60%
FDI Shares by Country:									
USA	14.70%	21.40%	25.11%	26.50%	67.30%	28.80%	35.50%	45.40%	42.70%
United Kingdom	6.90%	11.90%	6.84%	27.50%	6.30%	28.10%	36.00%	18.90%	22.50%
UAE	40.50%	24.10%	14.18%	15.00%	4.40%	1.60%	1.20%	1.50%	3.20%
Germany	0.80%	0.90%	0.74%	0.50%	2.30%	4.80%	2.20%	4.20%	4.00%
France	0.10%	-0.20%	-0.59%	0.30%	-1.40%	0.20%	0.30%	2.10%	0.80%
Hong Kong	0.70%	2.10%	0.66%	0.70%	0.60%	1%	0.20%	0.60%	0.30%
Italy	0.00%	0.00%	0.20%	0.00%	0.00%	0.40%	0.10%	0.00%	0.10%
Japan	1.60%	3.00%	1.59%	1.80%	1.30%	3%	3.80%	12.50%	3.00%
Saudi Arabia	7.90%	1.20%	0.76%	5.50%	0.30%	17.60%	6.10%	4.80%	0.20%
Canada	0.10%	0.10%	0.05%	0.10%	0.70%	0.00%	0.00%	0.10%	0.10%
Netherlands	3.40%	2.40%	1.48%	0.40%	-1.10%	1.50%	2.30%	1.20%	4.50%
Korea	0.05%	0.10%	0.10%	0.00%	0.10%	1.10%	2.00%	1.00%	1.00%
Others	23.20%	33.00%	48.88%	21.80%	19.10%	12.00%	10.30%	7.60%	17.60%

(Appendix 10.2 continued)

(Appendix 10.2 continued)

Fiscal year (July–June)	1997–98	1998–99	1999–00	2000–01	2001–02	2002–03	2003–04	2004–05	2005–06
Selected Industrial Output:									
Fertilizer ('000 tonnes)	3,894	4,242	5,059	5,129	5,187	5,269	5,673	5,989	6,236
Sugar ('000 tonnes)	3,555	3,541	2,429	3,015	3,249	3,676	4,021	3,115	2,960
Cement ('000 tonnes)	9,364	9,634	9,314	9,674	9,935	11,020	12,862	16,088	18,483
Pig Iron ('000 tonnes)	1,016	989	1,107	1,071	1,043	1,140	1,176	1,137	788
Tractors (Units)	40,144	26,644	34,559	31,635	23,801	26,240	35,770	43,746	49,439
Cars (Units)	33,684	38,619	32,461	39,819	41,233	63,095	98,461	126,817	160,642
Paper & Paper Board ('000 tonnes)	345	356	435.4	531.1	547.8	374.4	406.5	400.1	454
Stock Market Indicators:									
KSE-100 Index (Nov. 1991=100)	879.62	1,054.67	1,520.73	1,366.43	1,770.11	3,402.47	5,279	7,450	9,989
SBP General Index (2000–01=100)	98.72	106.38	128.8	118.72	106.7	204.9	312.7	359.99	427.01
Market Capitalization (PKR bn.)	259.3	289.2	391.86	339.3	407.6	746	1357.48	2013.20	2766.41
Turnover of Shares (PKR bn.)	15	25.5	48.1	29.2	29.1	52.7	96.96	88.3	79.45

Source: Board of Investment, Government of Pakistan, Key Investment Indicators, http://www.pakboi.gov.pk.

◙ Notes

1. Imran Ali, *The Punjab under Imperialism, 1885–1947* (Princeton, NJ: Princeton University Press, 1988).
2. Tan Tai Yong, *The Garrison State: The Military, Government and Society in Colonial Punjab, 1849–1947* (Delhi: Oxford University Press, 2005).
3. Imran Ali, 'Malign Growth? Agricultural Colonization and the Roots of Backwardness in the Punjab', *Past and Present*, February 1987, 114(1), pp. 110–32.
4. Imran Ali, 'Past and Present: The Making of the State in Pakistan', in Imran Ali, S. Mumtaz and J.L. Racine (eds) *Pakistan: The Contours of State and Society* (Karachi: Oxford University Press, 2002), pp. 24–39.
5. Imran Ali, 'The Punjab and the Retardation of Nationalism', in D.A. Low (ed.), *The Political Inheritance of Pakistan* (London: Macmillan, 1991), pp. 29–52.
6. Imran Ali and S. Mumtaz, 'Understanding Pakistan — The Impact of Global, Regional, National and Local Interactions', in I. Ali, S. Mumtaz and J. L. Racine (eds), *Pakistan: The Contours of State and Society* (Karachi: Oxford University Press, 2002), pp. ix–xxxvi.
7. Imran Ali, 'Asian Experiences of Development: The Case of Pakistan, 1945–1975', Paper presented at the conference on 'Asian Experiences of Development: Southeast Asia, South Asia and East Asia, 1945–1975', National University of Singapore, June 2006.
8. Imran Ali, 'Historical Impacts on Political Economy in Pakistan', *Asian Journal of Management Cases*, 2004, 1(2), pp. 129–46.
9. Imran Ali, 'Business and Power in Pakistan', in Anita M. Weiss and S. Zulfiqar Gilani (eds), *Power and Civil Society in Pakistan* (Karachi: Oxford University Press, 2001), pp. 93–122.
10. Gustav F. Papanek, *Pakistan's Development: Social Goals and Private Incentives* (Cambridge, MA: Harvard University Press, 1967).
11. Stephen R. Lewis, Jr, *Economic Policy and Industrial Growth in Pakistan* (Cambridge, MA: MIT Press, 1969).
12. Imran Ali, 'Income and Wealth Redistribution Policies in Muslim Countries: The Case of Pakistan', Paper presented at the International Workshop on 'Economic and Social Policies for Income and Wealth Redistribution in Muslim Countries', Trinity College, University of Cambridge, August 2005.
13. Shahid J. Burki, *Pakistan under Bhutto, 1971–1977* (London: Macmillan, 1980).
14. Imran Ali, 'Pakistan Agribusiness Industry Note', Paper presented at the conference 'USA–Pakistan Dialogues in Agribusiness and Agroindustry', Lahore University of Management Sciences, Lahore, June 2006.

15. Craig Baxter (ed.), *Zia's Pakistan: Politics and Stability in a Frontline State* (Boulder, CO: Westview Press, 1985).

16. Ishrat Hussain, *Pakistan: The Economy of an Elitist State* (Karachi: Oxford University Press, 1999).

17. Dennis Kux, *The United States and Pakistan, 1947–2000: Disenchanted Allies* (Karachi: Oxford University Press, 2001).

18. Parvez Hasan, *Pakistan's Economy at the Crossroads: Past Policies and Present Imperatives* (Karachi: Oxford University Press, 1998).

19. Ishrat Hussain, *Economic Management in Pakistan 1999–2002* (Karachi: Oxford University Press, 2004).

20. Imran Ali, 'Pakistan Agribusiness Industry Note', Paper presented at the conference 'USA–Pakistan Dialogues in Agribusiness and Agroindustry', Lahore University of Management Sciences, Lahore, June 2006.

21. Imran Ali, 'Business, Stakeholders and Strategic Responses in Pakistan', Armidale, University of New England Asia Centre, Paper no. 8, 2005.

22. UBS Investment Research, *Asian Economic Perspectives, Pakistan Arrives* (Hong Kong: UBS, 2006).

23. Asian Development Bank, 'Country Strategy and Program Update, 2006–2008', August 2005.

24. Imran Ali, 'Pakistan', in *Regionalism and Trade: South Asian Perspectives 2006* (Singapore: Institute of South Asian Studies, National University of Singapore, 2007), pp. 141–59.

25. *Pakistan Statistical Yearbook, 2006* (Islamabad: Federal Bureau of Statistics, 2006).

26. Imran Ali, 'The Political Economy of Water in Pakistan', Paper presented at the conference on 'The Future of Water: State, Agribusiness and Society', Lahore University of Management Sciences, Lahore, April 2006.

27. World Bank, *Pakistan's Water Economy: Running Dry* (Islamabad: World Bank, 2005).

28. Ministry of Finance, Government of Pakistan, 'Accelerating Economic Growth and Reducing Poverty: The Road Ahead', Poverty Reduction Strategy Paper, Islamabad, 2003.

29. Akmal Hussain et al., *National Human Development Report for Pakistan* (Islamabad: UNDP, 2003).

30. Imran Ali, 'Re-imagining Punjab: Shackled Potential', *Seminar* (New Delhi), November 2006, 567, pp. 21–25.

31. Imran Ali, 'Pakistan', in *Regionalism and Trade: South Asian Perspectives 2006* (Singapore: Institute of South Asian Studies, National University of Singapore, 2007), pp. 141–59.

32. Ibid.

33. *Pakistan Statistical Yearbook, 2006* (Islamabad: Federal Bureau of Statistics, 2006).

34. Imran Ali, 'Business and Power in Pakistan', in Anita M. Weiss and S. Zulfiqar Gilani (eds), *Power and Civil Society in Pakistan* (Karachi: Oxford University Press, 2001), pp. 93–122.
35. Imran Ali, 'Business, Stakeholders and Strategic Responses in Pakistan', Armidale, University of New England Asia Centre, Paper no. 8, 2005.

❋

11

Analyzing Pakistan's Economic Prospects in an Increasingly Integrated World: External Constraints on Sustainable Growth

Arslan Razmi

Like many other developing countries, Pakistan has attempted to pursue the path of internal and external (that is, current account but not so much capital account) liberalization and export-led growth in recent decades. The switch from an emphasis on import substitution to export-promotion, and from somewhat tepid support for the private sector to outright privatization of publicly-owned assets in Pakistan began in earnest with the structural adjustment program (SAP) signed with the International Monetary Fund (IMF) in 1988. However, the evolution of Pakistan's economy has been markedly different from that of other successful exporters of manufactures in Asia, and even from the other industrializing countries in its neighbourhood. The differences can be attributed partly to the trajectory of domestic institutional development, and partly to the political economy of Pakistan's external circumstances. This chapter investigates some of the recent economic developments in the Pakistani economy, explores the sources and sustainability of its recent growth patterns, and aims to shed some light on prospects over the short- to medium-term. Throughout the article, the emphasis is on developments in Pakistan's international trade, current account, and finance regimes.

The last few years have brought an impressive improvement in some macro-economic indicators. However, as we will seek to show in the following sections, this improvement may mostly reflect temporarily benign external conditions, rather than an improvement in the underlying fundamentals of the economy. Moreover, the improved macro-economic indicators in some areas may hide serious (and worsening) deficiencies in others; deficiencies which if not addressed could result in the benefits of growth being limited to increasingly narrow segments of a polarized population.

The next section provides a brief glimpse into the evolution of Pakistan's economy. This is followed by a look at the development of Pakistan's external trade regime. The two sections following that discuss two major recent developments that are likely to impact Pakistan's economy in the coming years: (i) the demise of the Multi-fibre Arrangement (MFA) and its successor Agreement on Textiles and Clothing (ATC) that significantly regulated trade in these sectors before 2005, and (ii) the possible realization of a South Asian Free Trade Area (SAFTA). The following section investigates the prospects for and constraints on the pursuit of export-led growth by Pakistan under the present global circumstances. This is followed by a discussion of the effects of various external sources of financing on Pakistan's economic growth and a brief analysis of the sustainability of Pakistan's present macroeconomic trajectory, along with its medium-run prospects. Some preliminary econometric estimates are presented to ground the analysis. The final section concludes.

◈ Macroeconomic Evolution of Pakistan's Economy

Table 11.1 presents the contributions of various sources of demand to Pakistan's gross domestic product (GDP) as these have evolved. A few interesting details are immediately evident. First, as is the case for most developing countries (but even more so for Pakistan),[1] household consumption has consistently constituted the largest component of aggregate expenditures. Second, the share of government expenditure as a proportion of GDP, which has traditionally been low by global and other developing country standards, had declined by 2003 to its value at the height of the Bhutto regime's relatively state-centred years. Moreover, this contrasts with an *increase* in the share of government expenditures as a source of demand, both at the global and developing country levels. Third, gross capital formation (or gross investment) has traditionally been much lower in Pakistan than in the other developing countries, especially the rapidly growing East and Southeast Asian nations. Fourth, trade (in goods and services) as a proportion of GDP rose from 22 per cent to a little over 33 per cent between 1975 and 2003, although this proportion is still low by global and developing country standards.

Table 11.1: Sources of Aggregate Demand (%), 1975–2003

Economic indicator	1975 World	1975 Developing economies	1975 Pakistan	1990 World	1990 Developing economies	1990 Pakistan	2003 World	2003 Developing economies	2003 Pakistan
Government expenditure	15.5	12.3	9.6	17.2	13.9	12.2	17.4	14.0	9.1
Household expenditure	61.0	61.1	76.4	59.4	59.8	68.9	61.6	57.3	73.6
Gross capital formation	23.0	26.8	22.1	23.7	25.4	20.7	20.9	25.5	16.7
Exports	15.6	19.8	8.0	19.5	25.2	12.7	24.9	36.7	16.9
Imports	16.1	20.2	14.0	19.8	24.0	14.2	24.7	33.0	16.3
Total	**100**	**100**	**100**	**100**	**100**	**100**	**100**	**100**	**100**

Source: United Nations Conference on Trade and Development (UNCTAD), *Handbook of Trade and Development Statistics* (online database), United Nations, Geneva.

Figure 11.1 highlights the evolution of Pakistan's economy in terms of the relative contribution of different sectors to the total value-added. The figure underscores the fact that while the contribution of manufacturing remained more or less stable at around a quarter of the total value-added, the services sector expanded at the expense of the agricultural sector, which shrank from about 40 per cent in 1965 to less than 23 per cent in 2004. This highlights another feature that distinguishes Pakistan from the rapidly industrializing East- and Southeast- Asian economies in that the latter experienced an expansion of the *manufacturing* sector rather than the services sector, at least during their transition from low-income to middle- or upper-middle income status. Moreover, it is worth noting that while the agricultural sector has shrunk over the last few decades in terms of its contribution to total value-added, agriculture and agriculture-related activities continue to employ a much larger proportion of the Pakistani workforce than its proportional contribution to value-added. The latter observation partly reflects the widespread presence of underemployment in this rural, low-productivity sector.

Figure 11.1: Contribution of Various Sectors to Value-Added (% of Total Value Added)

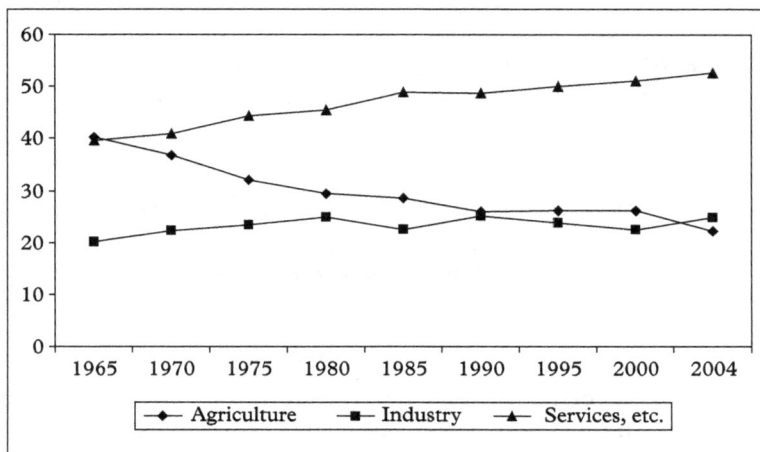

Source: World Bank, *World Development Indicators* (online database), Washington, DC.

With rare exceptions, the Pakistani government ran budget deficits ranging from 4–10 per cent of GDP for most of its history (see Figure 11.2). Interestingly enough, these deficits continued to run high in the post-SAP period, beginning in 1988. However, this was mainly a result of high interest rates and associated debt servicing costs rather than due to any inherent proclivity towards fiscal 'irresponsibility' on the part of the elected governments. Indeed, the primary balance (revenues minus expenditures excluding interest payments) picture remained relatively satisfactory over the period with the parliamentary governments running either surpluses or small deficits during most of the 1990s.[2] Government revenues as a share of GDP fluctuated in the 10–20 per cent range, rising to the upper half of the range in the 1980s and 1990s, before returning to the lower half in recent years (see Figure 11. 2).

Figure 11.2: Evolution of the Fiscal Balance and Government Revenue as a Proportion of GDP, 1953–2005

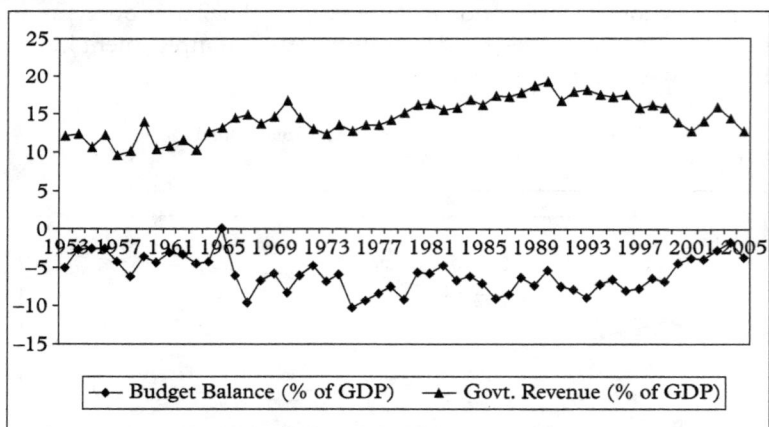

Source: International Monetary Fund, *International Financial Statistics* (online database), Washington, DC.

▣ External Trade Regime

Pakistan is part of the relatively small but growing group of developing countries whose exports overwhelmingly consist of manufactured products. However, Pakistan's exports remain highly concentrated, with a large proportion of value-added in the export sector coming from textiles and clothing. In addition, Pakistan is also a major grower and exporter of cotton.

As part of its efforts to integrate more closely into the global trading system, Pakistan acceded to the World Trade Organization (WTO) in January 1995. In 1996–97, Pakistan significantly accelerated the liberalization of its trade regime. Import tariffs have declined sharply as a result, as have tax revenues from international trade (see Table 11.2 and Figure 11.3, respectively).

Table 11.2: Pakistan's Tariffs on Non-Agricultural and Non-Fuel Imports

Year	Effectively applied rate (simple average)		Effectively applied rate (weighted average)		Effectively applied rate (maximum)	
	1995	*2004*	*1995*	*2004*	*1995*	*2004*
Origin						
World	51.6	16.2	49.2	15.7	265.0	200.0
Developed economies	50.9	15.7	50.3	16.2	265.0	200.0
Southeast Europe and CIS	50.4	15.4	28.6	10.1	70.0	60.0
Developing economies	52.3	16.7	49.0	15.3	265.0	200.0
Least developed countries	53.2	16.2	32.0	10.5	265.0	150.0

Source: United Nations Conference on Trade and Development (UNCTAD), *Handbook of Trade and Development Statistics* (online database), Geneva.

External Accounts

Like most of its South Asian neighbours,[3] Pakistan has been relatively closed to trade, as measured in terms of GDP, compared to many other developing countries of similar size. Figure 11.3 shows Pakistan's trade to GDP ratio, which in spite of the dramatic liberalization in recent years, merely increased from 27 per cent in 1967 to 33 per cent in 2003. However, Pakistan's share of world exports dropped from 0.79 per cent in 1950 to 0.15 per cent in 2004.

As seen in Figure 11.4, Pakistan has run current account deficits (mainly due to negative balances of trade in goods and services) offset by financial account surpluses and official reserve transactions for most of its history since the mid-1970s. However, this picture reversed for a few years in the immediate aftermath of the 2001 terrorist attacks in New York. The reversal owes much to three factors: (a) the write-off or rescheduling of bilateral debts by the United States and other major creditors, resulting in reduced current account outflows in the form of interest and principal payments, (b) increased inflows of new grants and credits from the United States, Japan, and Europe, and (c) the repatriation of huge sums of

Figure 11.3: Evolution of Pakistan's Trade as a Proportion of GDP (left-hand scale) and Taxes on International Trade as Percentage of Total Revenues (right-hand scale)

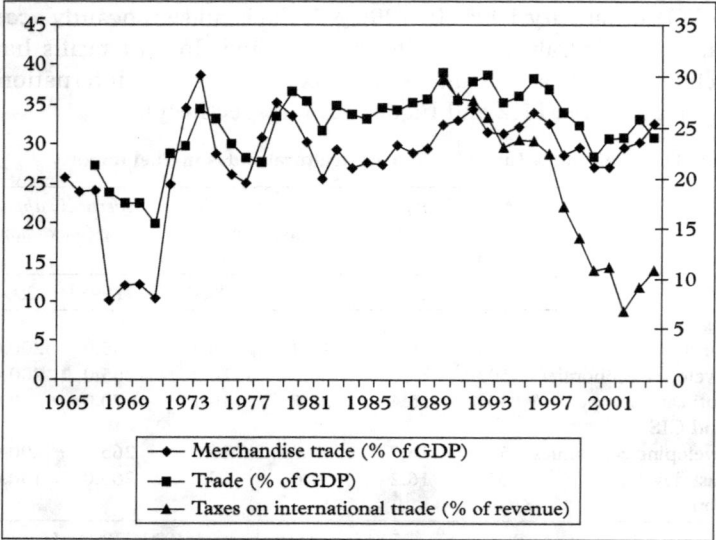

Source: World Bank, *World Development Indicators* (online database), Washington, DC.

Figure 11.4: Current Account, Financial Account and Official Reserves (US$ bn.), 1976–2004

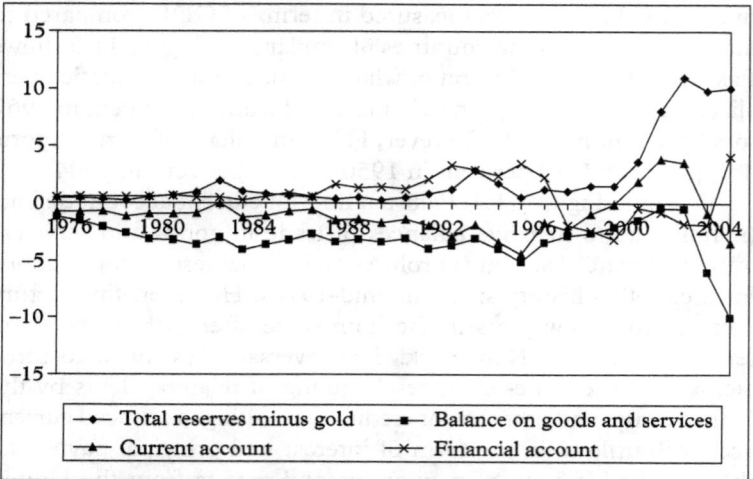

Source: International Monetary Fund, *International Financial Statistics* (online database), Washington, DC.

earnings and savings by overseas Pakistanis. The latter factor, which has had consequences for resource allocation between the tradable and non-tradable sectors of the economy, has in turn resulted from two factors: fear on the part of overseas Pakistanis for the safety of their savings in overseas bank accounts, and the switch to more formal channels of repatriation once the informal 'hundi' system came under stricter international scrutiny.[4]

Table 11.3 illustrates some of these factors. International sanctions following the nuclear tests in May 1998 left the Pakistani economy in a rather vulnerable position on the external front. However, the 9/11 attacks brought significant changes, as Pakistan became an ally in the 'war on terror'. The current account switched from a deficit of $85 million to a surplus of $1.9 billion between 2000 and 2001, just as workers' remittances increased sharply from $1.1 billion in 2000 to $4.3 billion in 2005 (thus growing at an annual rate of over 31 per cent) while net current transfers jumped from $4.1 billion to $9.1 billion over the same period. Foreign direct investment also picked up in 2002, surpassing the billion dollar mark two years later. However, like its trade–GDP ratio, Pakistan's FDI (foreign direct investment)–GDP ratio also remains relatively low compared to other countries at similar income levels.[5] As Pakistan's external position stabilized, international investor confidence and relatively easy international liquidity conditions were reflected in its successful floating of Eurobonds worth $500 million in 2004 after a five-year absence from international bond markets.

The net impact of increased current transfers and worker remittances has been to significantly relax the foreign exchange reserves position.[6] Pakistan's foreign exchange reserves were sufficient for almost 6 months of imports in 2005, up from barely 8 weeks in 2000.

Figure 11.5 highlights Pakistan's persistent current account deficits from another perspective. One can derive the following simple macroeconomic identity from the national income and expenditures identities:

trade balance ≡ net national savings ≡ net domestic private savings + budget balance

Logically, current account deficits (or more simply, trade balances) reflect an excess of national investment over savings, which

Table 11.3: Pakistan's External Acounts (US$ mn.), 1976–2005

	1996	1997	1998	1999	2000	2001	2002	2003	2004	2005
Goods exports (F.O.B.)	8507.3	8350.7	7850.0	7673.0	8739.0	9131.0	9832.0	11869.0	13297.0	15382.0
Goods imports (C.I.F.)	-12163.7	-10750.2	-9834.0	-9520.0	-9896.0	-9741.0	-10428.0	-11978.0	-16693.0	-21560.2
Balance on merchandise trade	**-3656.4**	**-2399.5**	**-1984.0**	**-1847.0**	**-1157.0**	**-610.0**	**-596.0**	**-109.0**	**-3396.0**	**-6178.2**
Services exports	2016.2	1625.2	1404.0	1373.0	1380.0	1459.0	2429.0	2968.0	2749.0	3677.0
Services imports	-3458.8	-2658.3	-2261.0	-2146.0	-2252.0	-2330.0	-2241.0	-3294.0	-5333.0	-7482.0
Balance on goods and services	**-5099.0**	**-3432.6**	**-2841.0**	**-2620.0**	**-2029.0**	**-1481.0**	**-408.0**	**-435.0**	**-5980.0**	**-9983.2**
Income credits	175.4	146.6	83.0	119.0	118.0	113.0	128.0	180.0	221.0	657.0
Income debits	-2197.8	-2366.4	-2263.0	-1959.0	-2336.0	-2189.0	-2414.0	-2404.0	-2584.1	-3173.0
Balance on goods, services and income	**-7121.3**	**-5652.3**	**-5021.0**	**-4460.0**	**-4247.0**	**-3557.0**	**-2694.0**	**-2659.0**	**-8343.0**	**-12499.2**
Current transfers (credit)	2739.5	3980.6	2801.0	3582.0	4200.0	5496.0	6593.0	6300.0	7666.0	9126.0
Current transfers (debit)	-54.1	-39.9	-28.0	-42.0	-38.0	-61.0	-45.0	-68.0	-140.0	-90.0

Current account balance	−4436.0	−1711.7	−2248.0	−920.0	−85.0	1878.0	3854.0	3573.0	−817.0	−3463.2
Capital account (credit)	0.0	0.0	0.0	0.0	0.0	0.0	40.0	1140.0	596.0	214.0
Capital account (debit)	0.0	0.0	0.0	0.0	0.0	0.0	0.0	−2.0	−5.0	−12.0
Capital account balance	**0.0**	**0.0**	**0.0**	**0.0**	**0.0**	**0.0**	**40.0**	**1138.0**	**591.0**	**202.0**
Direct investment outflows	−6.8	24.3	−50.0	−21.0	−11.0	−31.0	−28.0	−19.0	−56.0	−44.0
Direct investment inflows	922.0	716.3	506.0	532.0	308.0	383.0	823.0	534.0	1118.0	2183.0
Portfolio investment in-flows	0.0	0.0	0.0	0.0	0.0	0.0	0.0	−2.0	9.0	18.0
Portfolio investment out-flows	260.9	279.0	−57.0	46.0	−451.0	−192.0	−567.0	−119.0	392.0	906.0
Other investment assets	−163.8	−21.4	44.0	−523.0	−437.0	53.0	−64.0	−542.0	−1339.0	146.0
Other investment liabilities	2483.9	1322.9	−2316.0	−2398.0	−2508.0	−602.0	−948.0	−1603.0	−1934.0	907.3
Financial account balance	**3496.2**	**2321.1**	**−1873.0**	**−2364.0**	**−3099.0**	**−389.0**	**−784.0**	**−1751.0**	**−1810.0**	**4116.3**
Net errors and omissions	159.6	−71.8	1011.2	768.1	556.9	707.6	974.0	−52.4	685.2	−380.5
Overall balance of payments	**−780.2**	**537.6**	**−3109.8**	**−2515.9**	**−2627.1**	**2196.6**	**4084.0**	**2907.6**	**−1350.8**	**474.6**

Source: International Monetary Fund, *International Financial Statistics* (online database), Washington, DC.

Figure 11.5: The Persistent Savings–Investment Gap, 1976–2004

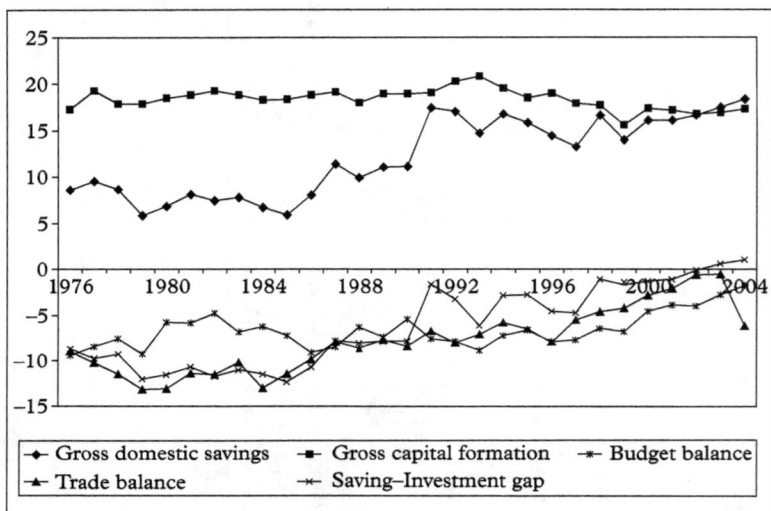

Source: World Bank, *World Development Indicators* (online database), Washington, DC.

have to be financed by net borrowing from abroad (either by the private sector or by the government). Figure 11.5 illustrates these aspects of the identities and shows how Pakistani trade imbalances have been reflected in both excess of investment over savings and budget deficits. Although it is impossible to infer causality without careful econometric tests, it is safe to assume that Pakistan's low domestic saving rates and persistent budget deficits bear at least partial responsibility for difficulties on the external account side.

Composition of Exports and Imports

A look at Table 11.4 reveals that Pakistan continues to export a majority of its products to developed countries although the proportion has declined somewhat over the decades. Europe and the United States have traditionally been the largest destinations for Pakistani exports. Pakistani imports, on the other hand, are geographically less centred on industrialized countries, mainly due to the high proportion of oil imports.

Tables 11.5–11.8 detail the composition of Pakistani imports and exports, as classified under the Standard International Trade Classification (SITC) and Broad Economic Categories (BEC) systems.[7] Pakistan is a part of the group of developing countries

Table 11.4: **Composition of Pakistani Imports and Exports by Origin and Destination (%)**

Partner	1955	1965	1975	1985	1995	2004
Imports World	100.0	100.0	100.0	100.0	100.0	100.0
Developed economies	72.7	89.6	61.4	55.8	50.4	40.3
Europe	45.0	41.5	25.9	23.8	27.7	20.2
US and Canada	12.2	37.4	16.3	15.3	10.4	11.2
Japan	14.6	9.9	13.1	12.6	10.7	6.7
Developing economies	9.2	7.9	33.8	42.3	46.6	57.1
OPEC	3.6	0.7	19.4	25.3	18.7	28.0
Other Asia	4.9	6.8	14.6	13.7	22.1	26.9
Exports World	100.0	100.0	100.0	100.0	100.0	100.0
Developed economies	64.8	51.7	38.6	52.0	56.7	53.0
Europe	43.6	34.4	26.1	28.6	31.7	28.6
US and Canada	8.0	10.0	5.0	11.0	16.8	22.1
Japan	11.8	4.5	6.8	11.3	6.8	1.1
Developing economies	32.6	44.6	54.7	41.5	39.1	45.9
OPEC	1.4	7.0	21.8	16.1	11.0	18.6
Other Asia	24.9	26.2	24.0	16.6	20.5	18.8

Source: United Nations Conference on Trade and Development (UNCTAD), *Handbook of Trade and Development Statistics* (online database), Geneva.

that mainly export manufactured products.[8] Pakistan's exports are heavily concentrated under SITC categories 6 (manufactured goods classified chiefly by material) and 8 (miscellaneous manufactured articles), consisting mainly of textile yarn and fabric (SITC 65) and apparel and clothing accessories (SITC 84). Together, these two SITC categories (that is, 6 and 8) constituted almost 77 per cent of Pakistani exports in 2005. In terms of BEC categories, this translates into almost four-fifths of Pakistan's exports being concentrated under categories 2 (industrial supplies) and 6 (consumer goods). Unlike many other developing countries (including its SAARC neighbour Bangladesh), however, Pakistan is specialized to a greater extent in the relatively capital-intensive textile sector, rather than in the more labour-intensive clothing and apparel sector. We discuss some implications of this pattern of specialization in a later section.

As is generally the case for other countries, Pakistan's imports are much more diverse than its exports. In other words, Pakistan is much 'larger' on the export side than on the import side. Almost half of Pakistan's imports fall under SITC categories 3 (mineral fuels, lubricants and related materials) and 7 (machinery and transport equipment). The former reflects Pakistan's heavy dependence on imported oil and petroleum products. In terms of BEC categories, this translates into almost four-fifths of Pakistan's imports being

Table 11.5: SITC2-Wise Classification of Pakistan's Exports (US$ mn. and %)

Year	SITC2-0	SITC2-1	SITC2-2	SITC2-3	SITC2-4	SITC2-5	SITC2-6	SITC2-7	SITC2-8	SITC2-9	Total
1985	4.56E+08	8.83E+06	5.02E+08	3.90E+07	3.33E+03	9.24E+07	1.19E+09	5.45E+07	3.74E+08	2.48E+07	2.74E+09
	(16.66)	(0.32)	(18.34)	(1.42)	(0.00)	(3.37)	(43.31)	(1.99)	(13.67)	(0.91)	(100.00)
1990	4.86E+08	6.45E+06	6.03E+08	7.09E+07	1.55E+04	2.47E+07	3.02E+09	5.58E+07	1.29E+09	1.24E+07	5.57E+09
	(8.73)	(0.12)	(10.82)	(1.27)	(0.00)	(0.44)	(54.28)	(1.00)	(23.11)	(0.22)	(100.00)
1995	9.31E+08	4.84E+06	3.48E+08	7.98E+07	3.39E+04	5.48E+07	4.58E+09	4.38E+07	2.09E+09	2.13E+07	8.16E+09
	(11.41)	(0.06)	(4.27)	(0.98)	(0.00)	(0.67)	(56.19)	(0.54)	(25.63)	(0.26)	(100.00)
2000	9.24E+08	6.22E+06	2.98E+08	1.31E+08	2.28E+07	1.46E+08	4.82E+09	9.61E+07	2.74E+09	1.66E+07	9.20E+09
	(10.05)	(0.07)	(3.24)	(1.43)	(0.25)	(1.59)	(52.40)	(1.05)	(29.75)	(0.18)	(100.00)
2005	1.79E+09	2.70E+07	3.12E+08	6.75E+08	9.71E+07	4.86E+08	7.82E+09	2.92E+08	4.54E+09	1.22E+07	1.61E+10
	(11.17)	(0.17)	(1.94)	(4.20)	(0.61)	(3.03)	(48.70)	(1.82)	(28.30)	(0.08)	(100.00)

Source: Author's calculations from United Nation's Commodity Trade Statistics (COMTRADE) database. See the appendix for definitions of the SITC categories.

Note: Figures in parentheses are percentages.

Table 11.6: SITC2-Wise Classification of Pakistan's Imports (US$ mn. and %)

Year	SITC2-0	SITC2-1	SITC2-2	SITC2-3	SITC2-4	SITC2-5	SITC2-6	SITC2-7	SITC2-8	SITC2-9	Total
1985	5.89E+08 (9.99)	1.71E+06 (0.03)	3.12E+08 (5.30)	1.43E+09 (24.34)	5.06E+08 (8.60)	6.78E+08 (11.52)	6.32E+08 (10.73)	1.58E+09 (26.89)	1.47E+08 (2.50)	6.36E+06 (0.11)	5.89E+09 (100.00)
1990	7.87E+08 (10.70)	2.67E+06 (0.04)	4.63E+08 (6.29)	1.54E+09 (20.91)	4.71E+08 (6.41)	1.20E+09 (16.27)	8.08E+08 (10.98)	1.88E+09 (25.56)	2.00E+08 (2.72)	9.81E+06 (0.13)	7.36E+09 (100.00)
1995	8.99E+08 (7.68)	8.93E+06 (0.08)	8.18E+08 (6.99)	1.90E+09 (16.25)	1.10E+09 (9.42)	1.97E+09 (16.80)	1.17E+09 (9.97)	3.38E+09 (28.89)	2.70E+08 (2.31)	1.89E+08 (1.62)	1.17E+10 (100.00)
2000	9.18E+08 (8.30)	3.96E+06 (0.04)	6.16E+08 (5.57)	3.61E+09 (32.64)	4.75E+08 (4.29)	1.98E+09 (17.91)	8.59E+08 (7.76)	2.05E+09 (18.49)	2.87E+08 (2.59)	2.68E+08 (2.42)	1.11E+10 (100.00)
2005	1.39E+09 (5.54)	1.08E+07 (0.04)	1.89E+09 (7.51)	5.32E+09 (21.21)	8.89E+08 (3.54)	4.04E+09 (16.11)	2.97E+09 (11.83)	7.40E+09 (29.50)	6.77E+08 (2.70)	5.06E+08 (2.02)	2.51E+10 (100.00)

Source: Author's calculations from United Nation's COMTRADE database. See the appendix for definitions of the SITC categories.
Note: Figures in parentheses are percentages.

Table 11.7: Broad Economic Categories (BEC) Classification of Pakistan's Exports (US$ mn. and %)

Year	BEC-1	BEC-2	BEC-3	BEC-4	BEC-5	BEC-6	BEC-7	Total
2000	9.57E+08	3.53E+09	1.30E+08	2.09E+08	2.05E+07	4.33E+09	1.94E+07	9.20E+09
	(10.40)	(38.40)	(1.42)	(2.27)	(0.22)	(47.09)	(0.21)	(100.00)
2005	1.92E+09	5.16E+09	6.60E+08	4.24E+08	6.71E+07	7.81E+09	1.18E+07	1.61E+10
	(11.93)	(32.16)	(4.11)	(2.64)	(0.42)	(48.66)	(0.07)	(100.00)

Source: Author's calculations from United Nation's COMTRADE database. See the appendix for definitions of the BEC categories.
Note: Figures in parentheses are percentages.

Table 11.8: Broad Economic Categories (BEC) Classification of Pakistan's Imports (US$ mn. and %)

Year	BEC-1	BEC-2	BEC-3	BEC-4	BEC-5	BEC-6	BEC-7	Total
2000	1.43E+09	3.48E+09	3.60E+09	1.54E+09	5.84E+08	3.88E+08	4.78E+07	1.11E+10
	(12.88)	(31.47)	(32.55)	(13.88)	(5.27)	(3.51)	(0.43)	(100.00)
2005	2.43E+09	8.78E+09	5.29E+09	5.78E+09	1.88E+09	8.84E+08	5.70E+07	2.51E+10
	(9.69)	(34.97)	(21.08)	(23.03)	(7.49)	(3.52)	(0.23)	(100.00)

Source: Author's calculations from United Nation's COMTRADE database. See the appendix for definitions of the BEC categories.

Note: Figures in parentheses are percentages.

concentrated under categories 2 (industrial supplies), 3 (fuels and lubricants) and 4 (capital goods).

Table 11.9 shows the technological profile of Pakistan's exports relative to some other developing countries. The percentage of high-tech products in Pakistan's total exports remains abysmally low, especially compared to its competitor exporters of manufactures in East and Southeast Asia.

Table 11.9: Percentage of High-Technology Products in Each Developing Country's Total Exports

Country	1990	1995	2000	Country	1990	1995	2000
Bangladesh	0.13	0.03	N/A	Mexico	8.29	15.08	22.40
China	N/A	10.05	18.58	**Pakistan**	**0.06**	**0.04**	**0.39**
India	2.40	4.30	5.01	Philippines	N/A	34.94	72.58
Jamaica	N/A	0.03	0.06	Singapore	39.87	53.92	62.56
Korea	17.84	25.87	34.82	Sri Lanka	0.53	N/A	N/A
Malaysia	38.18	46.10	59.53	Thailand	20.72	24.42	33.28
Mauritius	0.54	0.94	1.03	Turkey	1.19	1.25	4.86

Source: World Bank, *World Development Indicators* (online database), Washington, DC.

Notes: High-technology exports are products with high R&D intensity, such as in aerospace, computers, pharmaceuticals, scientiûc instruments, and electrical machinery. 'N/A'denotes missing data.

Figures 11.6 and 11.7 yield more insight into the comparative structure of Pakistan's exports as it has evolved over the last couple of decades.[9] Before we discuss these figures, however, a few terminological clarifications are in order. Manufactures are generally classified as products falling under SITC categories 5–8.[10] For purposes of analysis of the sophistication of exports, exports are also sometimes usefully classified into 'resource-based', 'low-tech', 'medium-tech', and 'high-tech' in increasing order of technological sophistication. Resource-based (or RB) exports fall mostly under SITC categories 0–4.[11] Low-tech (LT) exports generally fall under SITC categories 6 and 8.[12] Medium-tech (MT) exports mostly span SITC categories 5, 7, and 8.[13] Finally, high-tech (HT) exports mostly fall under SITC category 7. In the interest of brevity, and as a rough approximation, therefore, we assume that:

- RB exports correspond with SITC categories 0–4,
- LT exports correspond with SITC categories 6 and 8, and
- MT/HT exports correspond with SITC categories 5 and 7.

Figure 11.6: The SITC Category-Wise Composition of Developing Country Exports, 1984–2004

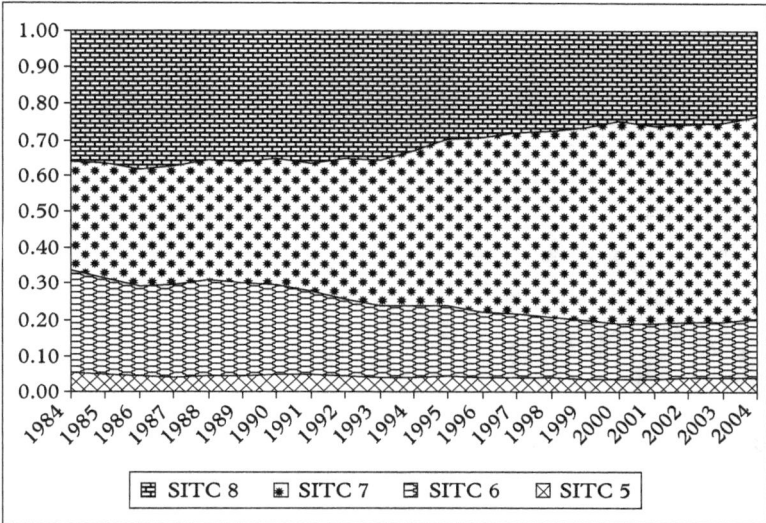

Source: Author's calculations from the United Nations' *COMTRADE* database.

A look at Figure 11.6, which shows the SITC category-wise composition of developing country manufactured exports in 1984–2004, reveals that the share of the relatively sophisticated SITC category 7 expanded dramatically, mainly at the expense of SITC categories 6 and 8. Figure 11.7(a) confirms this pattern in terms of growth rates of manufacturing value-added, revealing that developing countries experienced the highest rate of growth in the MT/HT sectors. Moreover, Figure 11.7(b) indicates that, at the global level, HT products have been the most dynamic in terms of growth in share of world exports in recent decades. Figure 11.7(c), however, presents a starkly different picture for Pakistan, where the most rapid growth in export value took place in the LT sector. Finally, Figure 11.7(d) underscores these concerns by presenting the technological evolution of Pakistan's exports compared to some other developing countries. Unlike some of the other major exporters of manufactures like Thailand, Malaysia, India, and China, HT exports barely make an appearance in Pakistan's export basket, while the share of MT exports too is much lower compared to the other countries. Moreover, these low proportions hardly changed over the period

Figure 11.7: The Technology Composition of Pakistan's Trade Structure in Comparative Terms

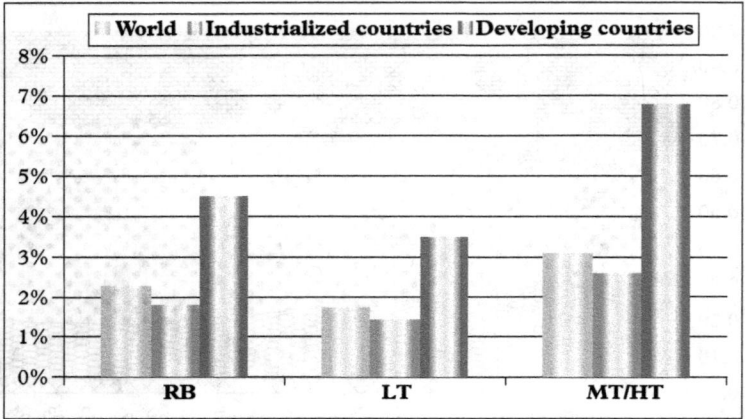

(a) Growth rates of manufacturing value-added, 1980–2000

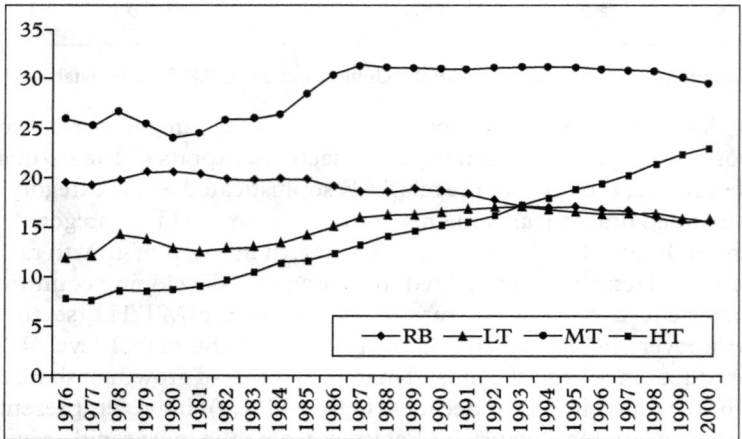

(b) Share of manufactured exports by technology, 1976–2000

(Figure 11.7 continued)

(*Figure 11.7 continued*)

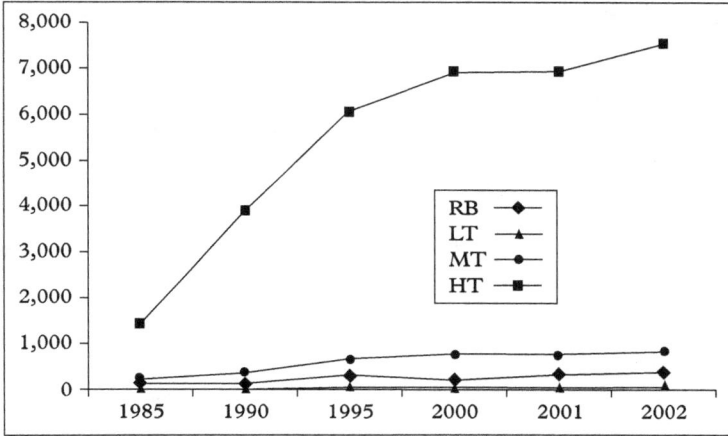

(c) Value of Pakistani exports by technology (US$ mn.)

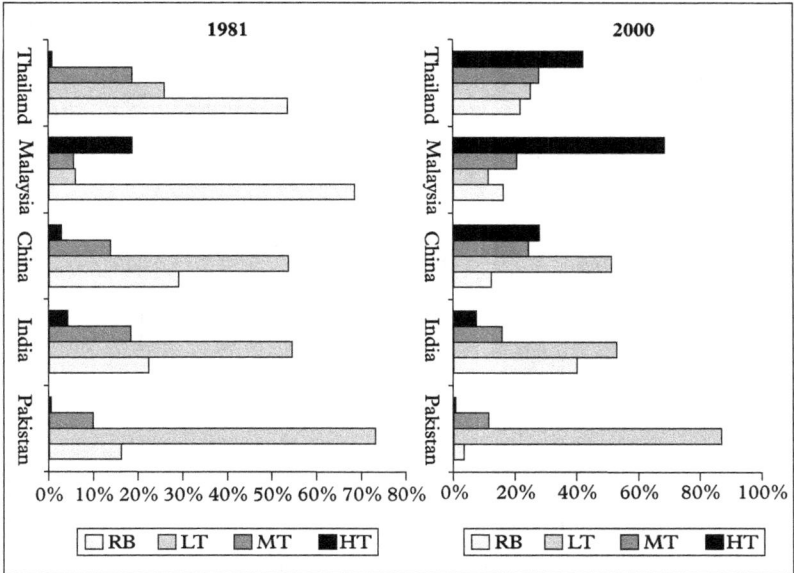

(d) Comparative export structures by technology, 1981–2000

Source: Sanjaya Lall, 'Benchmarking Pakistan's Competitive Performance', Paper presented at the Asian Development Bank Institute Policy Seminar on 'Industrial Competitiveness: The Challenge for Pakistan', 17 November 2003.

1981–2000, although the share of LT exports increased at the expense of RB exports.[14]

Diversification of Exports

Table 11.10 compares the concentration of Pakistan's export basket to other countries and regions using a Herfindahl–Hirschman index developed by the United Nations Conference on Trade and Development (UNCTAD). The table covers the period 1985–2004. Exports remain concentrated relative to other developing countries as a group. Not surprisingly, the table reveals that developed-country exports are much less concentrated than developing-country ones, and the latter are in turn much less so than those for the group of Least Developed Countries (LDCs). Furthermore, the degree of concentration of Pakistan's exports remained more or less stable over the period. Finally, the table also reveals that Pakistan's exports are significantly more concentrated than those from some other major Asian developing-country exporters of manufactures such as India, China, or Malaysia.

The lack of export diversification has implications for policy and welfare. One obvious implication of concentrated specialization is the greater vulnerability to international terms of trade swings for countries that are specialized in exporting primary commodities.

Table 11.10: Concentration of Pakistan's Exports Relative to Other Developing Countries

Category	1985	1995	2004
Developed economies	0.108	0.095	0.112
Developing economies	0.294	0.221	0.184
Developing economies: America	0.257	0.199	0.281
Developing economies: Africa	0.490	0.485	0.325
Developing economies: Asia	0.265	0.199	0.162
Bangladesh	0.280	0.264	0.305
China	0.171	0.063	0.106
India	0.142	0.137	0.120
Malaysia	0.270	0.178	0.194
Pakistan	0.220	0.241	0.217
Least Developed Countries (LDCs)	0.422	0.546	0.483

Source: United Nations Conference on Trade and Development (UNCTAD), *Handbook of Trade and Development Statistics* (online database), Geneva.

Note: The statistic for India is for 2003. The Herfindahl–Hirschman index is a measure of the degree of market concentration. It is based on 239 products at the three-digit level of SITC (revision 2) classification, and ranges from 0 to 1 (in order of increasing concentration).

For example, Figure 11.8 illustrates the volatility of Pakistani cotton prices in international markets. Traditionally, such vulnerability has been seen as a problem only for developing countries that export primary commodities. However, as we argue in a later section, this may be an increasingly important concern for developing countries that are dependent on exports of labour-intensive, low-tech manufactured exports.

Figure 11.8: Free Market Price of Pakistani Cotton (Pakistan Sindh/Punjab, SG Afzal, 1-1/32", CIF North Europe [¢/lb.])

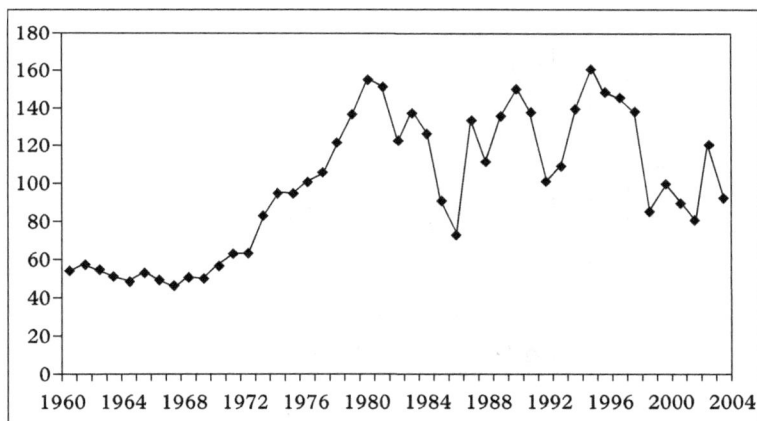

Source: United Nations Conference on Trade and Development (UNCTAD), *Handbook of Trade and Development Statistics* (online database), Geneva.

Trade with other SAARC Countries

In the immediate aftermath of independence from British rule in 1948, intra-regional trade between the newly independent South Asian countries constituted 19 per cent of their total trade.[15] This proportion, however, had declined drastically to 2 per cent by 1967 (following the Indo-Pak war of 1965 and ensuing tensions).

Pakistan was one of the seven founding members of the South Asian Association for Regional Cooperation (SAARC) when it was established in 1985. With almost 1.5 billion people, SAARC is the largest regional agreement in the world in terms of population. However, in terms of intra-regional trade, SAARC is one of the least active associations. Table 11.11 highlights the disappointing performance of SAARC member countries in this regard. Intra-regional trade stood at a mere 3.9 per cent for imports and 5.3 per cent

Table 11.11: A Comparison of Intra-Group Trade within SAARC and Other Regional Trade Groupings (US$ mn. and %)

Group	Trade Partner	Imports				Exports			
		1975	1985	1995	2004	1975	1985	1995	2004
EU 15	Intra-group	200,229.9 (55.3)	416,857.4 (57.5)	1,168,532.3 (61.0)	1,986,487.4 (58.8)	196,617.9 (57.7)	419,134.1 (59.2)	1,259,699.4 (62.4)	2,080,118.3 (61.1)
	Rest of the world	161,985.8 (44.7)	307,751.3 (42.5)	745,639.7 (39.0)	1,390,605.1 (41.2)	143,960.8 (42.3)	289,062.2 (40.8)	758,591.1 (37.6)	1,324,408.3 (38.9)
MERCOSUR	Intra-group	1,017.1 (5.2)	1,965.0 (9.5)	14,495.1 (18.2)	17,909.7 (18.2)	1,035.5 (8.5)	1,952.6 (5.5)	14,198.9 (20.3)	16,720.8 (12.0)
	Rest of the world	18,648.2 (94.8)	18,818.4 (90.5)	65,032.1 (81.8)	80,365.6 (81.8)	11,149.9 (91.5)	33,267.8 (94.5)	55,809.1 (79.7)	122,170.7 (88.0)
NAFTA	Intra-group	55,609.1 (36.9)	159,466.3 (34.4)	396,003.5 (38.4)	729,621.4 (36.2)	49,983.4 (34.6)	143,191.0 (43.9)	394,471.6 (46.2)	723,610.3 (55.2)
	Rest of the world	95,142.7 (63.1)	303,479.3 (65.6)	634,282.6 (61.6)	1,284,664.6 (63.8)	94,654.8 (65.4)	182,840.2 (56.1)	458,700.6 (53.8)	5,861,14.7 (44.8)

ASEAN	Intra-group	2,643.1 (11.1)	11,424.7 (17.2)	65,918.7 (18.3)	114,359.8 (22.5)	3,660.1 (16.7)	13,504.3 (18.6)	79,543.8 (24.6)	125,531.2 (22.0)
	Rest of the world	21,201.0 (88.9)	54,810.8 (82.8)	294,519.7 (81.7)	394,319.5 (77.5)	18,306.7 (83.3)	59,000.3 (81.4)	243,242.7 (75.4)	445,559.2 (78.0)
SAARC	Intra-group	280.0 (2.7)	513.7 (1.9)	2,241.7 (3.9)	5,637.6 (3.9)	293.0 4.7	600.8 (4.5)	2,023.7 (4.4)	5,919.4 (5.3)
	Rest of the world	10,111.6 (97.3)	26,427.1 (98.1)	55,803.6 (96.1)	139,980.6 (96.1)	6,005.7 (95.3)	12,824.4 (95.5)	43,808.0 (95.6)	104,965.3 (94.7)

Source: United Nations Conference on Trade and Development (UNCTAD), *Handbook of Trade and Development Statistics* (online database), Geneva.

Note: EU 15 denotes the European Union. MERCOSUR or Southern Common Market consists of Argentina, Brazil, Paraguay, Uruguay, and Venezuela. NAFTA or the North American Free Trade Agreement includes the US, Canada, and Mexico. ASEAN or the Association of South East Asian Nations consists of Brunei, Cambodia, Indonesia, Laos, Malaysia, Myanmar, the Philippines, Singapore, Thailand, and Vietnam. SAARC or the South Asian Association for Regional Cooperation consists of Bangladesh, Bhutan, India, Maldives, Nepal, Pakistan, and Sri Lanka. Figures in paramtheses are percentages.

for exports in 2004. The corresponding percentages in 2004 were 58.8 per cent and 61.1 per cent for the European Union, 18.2 per cent and 12 per cent for MERCOSUR (or the Southern Common Market), and 22.5 and 22 for the Association of Southeast Asian Nations (ASEAN). It is important to note, however, that a major proportion of trade between SAARC countries occurs through 'informal' channels and does not appear in the records.[16]

▣ The Expiration of the Multifibre Arrangement (MFA)

The textiles and clothing (T&C) sector accounts for approximately 27 per cent of Pakistan's total industrial output, and absorbs about 38 per cent of the industrial labour force.[17] Until recently, trade in textiles and clothing (or T&C) was governed under the Multifibre Arrangement (MFA) and its post-Uruguay Round incarnation — the Agreement on Textiles and Clothing (ATC).[18] The MFA/ATC regimes, under which developing countries were allotted quotas for access to markets in industrialized countries, expired on 31 December 2004. Given the importance of this sector in determining Pakistan's (and those of many other semi-industrialized developing countries) economic performance, and considering that some of the studies carried out in the wake of the Uruguay Round of negotiations attributed as much as two-thirds of the expected global gains from it to the expiry of the MFA,[19] we now turn to a brief discussion of the likely implications of the new post-MFA environment.

Since quotas under the MFA regime were bilateral, and their degree of restrictiveness varied across countries, it was expected that the benefits of quota removal will be distributed unequally across and within countries. Industrial country consumers and competitive exporters from countries that exported mainly to non-industrial countries were expected to gain from lower industrial country prices and higher international prices, respectively, while exporters from countries that faced effectively binding quotas were expected to gain from greater export volumes.[20] Exporters from countries that previously benefited from quota-protected access and developing country consumers, on the other hand, were expected to lose, owing to the same factors.[21] Finally, domestic producers in industrialized countries were also expected to lose due to lower domestic prices. Turning to cotton producers, it was expected that the effects will be mixed. They will gain in the sense that greater trade in textiles and clothing will create greater demand for cotton. On the other hand, however, since the expiration of the MFA was expected to shift production of these goods to the developing countries that favour domestic fibre producers, cotton growers in countries with limited domestic fibre production were expected to suffer losses on this account. Yet another dimension along which countries were expected to lose or gain was created by the emergence of quota-hopping foreign direct investment by multinational firms from binding quota to non-binding quota countries during the MFA years. The expiration of the MFA was expected, for obvious reasons, to result in concentration of T&C supply chains in a smaller number of more competitive countries.

As a low-wage exporting country that produces a significant amount of cotton, Pakistan was initially expected to gain from the expiration of the ATC regime. However, the entry of China into the WTO persuaded some observers to revise these expectations downwards. Indeed, China's exports grew sharply in early 2005, leading the United States and Europe to take 'safeguard' measures in the form of 'voluntary' export restraints and anti-dumping measures against China.[22]

The jury is still out on the impact of the WTO on Pakistan's T&C exports. Pakistan's share of world exports seems to have increased marginally.[23] For example, according to Whalley, Pakistan's share of world clothing exports to the United States increased from 1.76 per cent to 1.83 per cent between 2004 and 2005.[24] However, this increase is insignificant compared to that in the Chinese share of world exports, which in spite of safeguard measures, increased from 13.8 per cent to 22.1 per cent over the same period. Some relatively high-wage suppliers like Turkey, Singapore, and Hong Kong saw their shares decline, in line with ex-ante expectations. On a less rosy note, however, Pakistan's market share of clothing exports to the United States barely increased *in terms of value* from 2.60 to 2.62 per cent over the same period, while China's increased from 14.9 per cent to 26.7 per cent. Moreover, Pakistan's share of the US textile market actually declined, both in terms of value and volume. Finally Pakistan's share of the EU market also declined marginally in 2005 following the demise of the MFA regime in spite of a significant increase in the overall share of Asian countries.[25]

◙ South Asia Free Trade Agreement (SAFTA)

The agreement to establish a South Asian Free Trade Area was signed in January 2004, subsequently coming into force in 2006. Various technical details such as rules of origin and mechanisms for compensation for the least-developed members of the South Asian Association for Regional Cooperation (SAARC) are currently under negotiation. The agreement, which is widely seen as a stepping stone on the way to a Common Market, or even a Monetary Union, envisages sharp liberalization of intra-regional trade by 2016, although the Least Developed Member States are accorded special and differential treatment.[26] More specifically, the member countries have agreed, as part of the broader trade liberalization effort, to gradually harmonize and eventually curtail their tariffs on imports from SAFTA countries to 5 per cent or less. The reduction is scheduled to take place in phases. In the first phase, the LDC members will reduce their maximum rates to 20 per cent by January 2008, while the non-LDC members will reduce their maximum rates to 30 per cent over the same period. In the second phase, beginning 1 January 2008, the LDC members will reduce their import tariffs to 5 per cent or less by January 2013, while the LDC members will reduce their import tariffs to the same maximum level by January 2016. The agreement allows the exclusion of 'sensitive' items through negotiation. The list of sensitive items will be member-specific. Furthermore, there are plans to set up a South Asian Customs Union (SACU) by 2015 and a South Asian Economic Union (SAEU) by 2020.[27] While the idea of an economic union seems far-fetched when one considers the political and economic realities, a customs union may be an achievable target.

Bilateral and regional free trade agreements (BTAs and RTAs) have emerged world-wide as stepping stones to, or even substitutes for multilateral trade liberalization. This development, which has been described by a leading trade economist as the 'spaghetti bowl phenomenon',[28] has gained momentum in the wake of the stalled Doha Round of trade negotiations. The remainder of this section takes a brief look at the potential consequences of SAFTA for Pakistan's economy.

Simple trade theoretic analysis since the early work of Viner has considered two major (and conflicting) static efficiency effects of RTAs.[29] The *net* (static) efficiency effect of RTAs on individual member countries are ambiguous, and can broadly be divided into two categories: (1) trade creation, and (2) trade diversion.[30]

Trade creation is said to have taken place whenever production moves from domestic producers who produce at a higher opportunity cost to lower cost foreign producers. *Trade diversion* is said to have taken place when, as a result of signing an RTA, domestic consumers switch their source of imports from more efficient non-member country producers to member country producers.

While the former effect of a RTA is beneficial in terms of *static* efficiency of resource allocation, the latter is harmful as it implies loss of tariff revenue while purchasing products at a higher than necessary cost. The overall efficiency effects of joining a RTA are, therefore, ambiguous for individual countries. In general:

- the greater the number of countries participating in the RTA, the smaller the (negative) effect of trade diversion is likely to be (in the extreme case, of course, with the whole world becoming a part of the RTA, trade diversion is zero).
- the greater the initial tariff, the smaller the (negative) effect of trade diversion is likely to be (in the extreme case where initial tariffs are so high that there is no trade, subsequent trade diversion would be zero).
- the more closely the price in the member countries approaches the (globally) low-cost price, the smaller the likely trade diversion.

How does South Asia score on these criteria? Partly due to their relatively small economic size, and partly due to their moderate degree of integration into the world trading system, SAARC member countries account for a relatively small proportion of world trade. Moreover, almost all SAARC member countries are significantly dependent on the textile and apparel sectors for their exports, the main destination for these exports being the United States and the EU. Finally, intra-SAARC country trade is relatively small in magnitude. As such, SAARC countries are more appropriately understood as mutual competitors in industrialized country markets who import very little from each other.[31] Put differently, SAARC country traded products are substitutes and compete largely in third (industrialized country) markets only. These factors reduce the scope for trade creation. On the other hand, the fact that SAARC countries are low-cost producers of many labour-intensive products creates wide room for trade creation. Baysan *et al.* argue that it is unlikely that the lowest cost suppliers of the member countries are within the SAARC region; this combined with the restrictiveness of SAFTA's list of sensitive items and rules of origin, leads one to scepticism regarding the economic merits of SAFTA.[32]

A few studies have attempted to evaluate the effects of SAFTA using either computable general equilibrium (CGE) simulations or estimating gravity models of trade for SAARC countries.[33] Pursuing the general equilibrium methodology, Bandara and Yu find that the full elimination of trade barriers between South Asian countries would increase India's welfare, but affect Bangladesh negatively, with the other countries experiencing slight gains.[34] Extending the agreement to ASEAN would result in reduced welfare for all South Asian countries, but an extension to NAFTA or EU would have the opposite effect. Moreover, the simulations suggested that, due to the similarity of their production structures, SAFTA will not have a significant impact on the composition of member country outputs. Srinivasan explores the effects of SAFTA using the gravity approach. The analysis concludes that the smaller countries (Bangladesh and Nepal) would gain the most from the full elimination of tariffs among South Asian members with Pakistan, India and Sri Lanka enjoying only marginal benefits in terms of trade volumes.[35] Rodriguez-Delgado provides another set of gravity model-based estimates.[36] Again, only the smallest countries obtain significant increases in trade volumes, with Pakistan, Bangladesh, Sri Lanka, and India experiencing relatively minor increases.

Baysan *et al.* examine the likely effects of SAFTA in light of the India–Sri Lanka Free Trade Agreement (ISLFTA).[37] The study concludes that the presence of negative lists that exclude a major proportion of the goods that the SAARC countries have a comparative advantage in, and the presence of strict rules of origin requirements increases the probability of trade divergence, and means that trade is likely to take off in new goods that the countries do not presently trade, and which for that reason are not likely to be covered under the negative lists.

In summary, existing studies do not provide much room for optimism regarding the potential gains that SAARC countries in general, and Pakistan in particular, may derive from a South Asian free trade agreement.[38] However, these studies do show more significant gains from multilateral liberalization (or from SAFTA plus NAFTA or SAFTA plus EU).

▩ A Fallacy of Composition?

The last few decades have seen a major shift in the composition of developing country exports, with manufactures having increased as a proportion of total exports from less than 25 per cent in 1980 to more than 70 per cent in 2003 (see Figure 11.9 below). Like many other semi-industrialized developing countries, Pakistan has re-tooled its trade policy in recent decades to pursue manufacturing-focused export-led growth.[39] Compared to many other developing country competitors, Pakistan (along with other South Asian countries such as Bangladesh and India) have an unusual combination of low levels of both skill per worker and land per worker that gives these countries a strong comparative advantage in labour-intensive manufactures. Moreover, as is the case for many other developing countries, developed countries remain Pakistan's major export market. While an export-focused strategy led to rapid success in the form of sustained growth spurts for the East Asian tigers (Hong Kong, South Korea, Singapore, and Taiwan) in the 1970s and 1980s, the viability of such a strategy is more open to question under present international circumstances.

The classical sources of gains from trade between two countries are based on the idea of *reciprocal demand*. As country A exports to

Figure 11.9: Composition of Merchandise Exports from Developing Countries by Major Product Group, 1980–2003

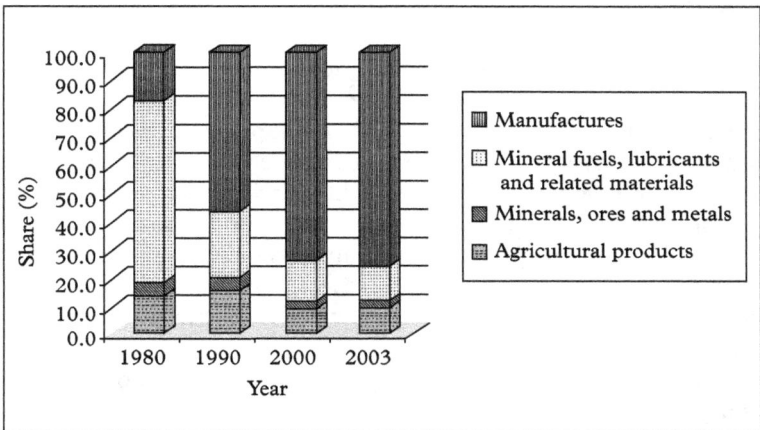

Source: UNCTAD, *Trade and Development Report,* United Nations Commission on Trade and Development 2005, Geneva.

country B, the income generated enables the former to buy more from the latter, creating a virtuous cycle of gains from specialization and exchange. However, in a world where countries A and B are both pursuing third (developed) country markets, reciprocal demand does not come into play, at least to the same extent. Moreover, classical trade models are typically based on the *small* country assumption (a small country is a price taker in international markets). While this may be a good assumption for individual developing countries, it may not be so for a group of developing countries attempting to sell similar products in the same (developed) country markets. Indeed, in the latter scenario, *immiserizing growth*, as first formalized by Bhagwati becomes a distinct possibility as a large country (that is, a group of developing countries) increases its supply of exports to the world market, and as a result, puts downward pressure on its international terms of trade.[40]

To put it somewhat differently, *unless* developed country markets for developing country products expand at a sufficiently rapid pace, developing country exporters of manufactures face significant demand-side constraints on export-led growth in the face of growing competition. If too many developing countries simultaneously pursue export-led growth, a 'fallacy of composition' or 'adding-up constraint' may come into play. The problem assumes added weight in the wake of China's entry into the global trading system, and its (and to a lesser extent, India's) emergence as a global manufacturing powerhouse.

The issue can also be discussed in terms of the 'flying geese' paradigm.[41] A major motivation behind the dramatic shift in developing country exports towards manufactures has been the perception that these products offer better prospects for export expansion without inducing the destabilizing terms of trade changes that have been observed in global primary commodity markets. According to this perspective, less developed countries can move up the development 'ladder' by initially specializing in and exporting low-technology, unskilled-labour-intensive manufactures. As these countries graduate to the rank of middle- or higher-income countries by exporting more technologically sophisticated, skill- and capital-intensive products, they allegedly expand export opportunities for other developing countries further down the development ladder in what is sometimes called the 'flying geese formation'. Advocates of this view of trade and development, not surprisingly, have often encouraged the pursuit of developing countries' comparative advantage in low-skill labour-intensive manufactured products. However, this view generally pays insufficient attention to the problem that if too many developing countries simultaneously pursue similar markets in similar industries, tiers of the flying geese formation may become too clogged to produce desirable forward movement for individual countries.

A few recent studies have empirically tested for the presence of a fallacy of composition in developing country pursuit of export-led growth.[42] Eichengreen found that while China's emergence as a global trading presence benefits the capital goods exporting, upper-middle-income countries of East Asia (such as South Korea and Taiwan), it harms other developing countries that specialize in exporting labour-intensive consumer products.[43] Based on their econometric estimates of export equations, Razmi and Blecker concluded that developing country manufactured exports mainly compete with other developing country manufactured exports rather than with developed country producers, thus creating a potential fallacy of composition.[44] The study also found, however, that the problem of significant price competition from other developing countries mainly exists for countries exporting relatively labour-intensive low-tech products as opposed to developing countries that export more sophisticated high-tech products. In the specific context of Pakistan, the study finds that Pakistani exports face significant price competition from other developing countries, and Pakistan's pursuit of manufacturing-based export-led growth, therefore, faces a potential adding-up problem.

Blecker and Razmi explored the output effects of real exchange rate changes in semi-industrialized developing countries, and found that these countries face a fallacy of composition in the sense that they experience output benefits from real exchange rate depreciations relative to other developing countries but not from such depreciations relative to developed countries.[45] Thus, improved competitiveness relative to other competing developing country exporters may lead to higher growth, at least in the short-run, but the growth comes at the expense of other developing countries.[46] Moreover, since the study also found contractionary effects of real devaluations relative to other developing countries (perhaps due to greater debt burdens or worsened terms of trade), the overall welfare effects of increased competitiveness are likely to be limited (if positive at all) for many countries. Finally, the study found that the terms of trade of major developing country exporters of manufactures have experienced an overall decline relative to industrial countries in recent decades. Figure 11.10 shows Pakistan's real exchange rates relative to developing and industrial countries in the sample used by Blecker and Razmi.[47] Notice that these real exchange rates are the relative prices measured in the same currency (US$).[48] Note also that an upward movement means a depreciation of Pakistan's real exchange rate and vice versa. At least two relevant observations emerge from the figure. First, Pakistan's real exchange rate relative to other developing countries was more stable compared to its real exchange rate relative to other developed countries.[49] Second, the terms of trade almost consistently moved in favour of the developed countries, as indicated by the upward movement of the 'T.O.T' plot, which captures the aggregate producer price index of developed countries relative to an aggregated export price for the major developing country exporters of manufactures. This latter observation suggests that the concerns made famous by Raul Prebisch and Hans Singer may not be limited to primary commodities, and major developing country exporters of manufactures may also have

Figure 11.10: Pakistan's Real Exchange Rate with Respect to Developed and Developing Countries, Respectively, 1984–2004

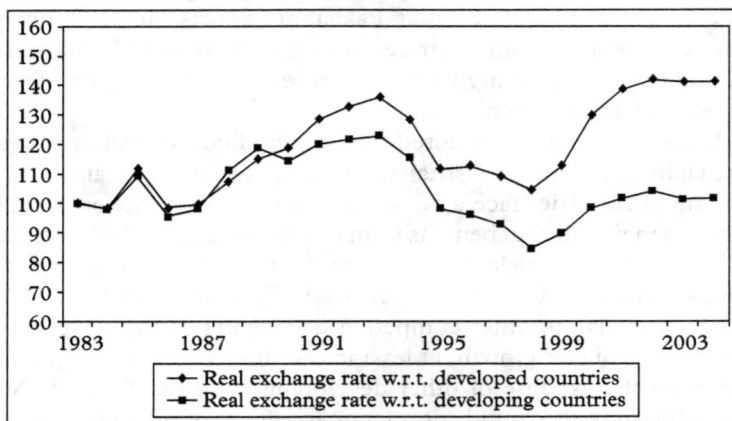

Source: R. Blecker and A. Razmi, 'The Fallacy of Composition and Contractionary Devaluations: Output Effects of Real Exchange Rate Shocks in Semi-Industrialised Countries', *Cambridge Journal of Economics*, 2008, 32(1), pp. 83–109.

experienced the declining terms of trade problem in recent years. A look at Figure 11.11 gives further cause for concern. The figure illustrates the recent evolution of the net barter terms of trade for different groups of countries including: (a) oil exporters, (b) exporters of minerals and mining products, (c) exporters of agricultural products, (d) exporters of manufactures and primary commodities, and (e) exporters of manufactures. Not surprisingly (given the recent surge in oil prices), group (a) has fared the best among developing countries, while group (b) has also benefited from improved terms of trade. Surprisingly, however, group (e) has experienced declining terms of trade, and was the worst off in this dimension.

◉ Remittance and Aid-led Growth?

A significant segment of the Pakistani labour force consists of workers who are temporarily or permanently settled abroad. Since many of these workers retain strong ties to their families back home, their remittances constitute a major source of foreign exchange for Pakistan. This has been particularly true since the 1970s when the

Figure 11.11: Recent Evolution of Net Barter Terms of Trade for Different Groups of Developing Countries

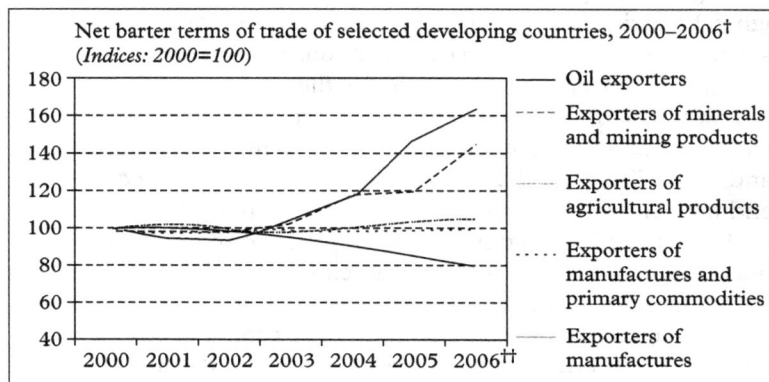

Source: UNCTAD, *World Economic Situation and Prospects*, United Nations Commission on Trade and Development 2007 (Geneva: UNCTAD, 2007), p. 11.

Note: UNCTAD Secretariat calculations, based on UN COMTRADE; United States Department of Labor, Bureau of Labor Statistics, Import/Export Price Indexes Database, Japan Customs, Trade Statistics Database; and UNCTAD. Commodity Prices Bulletin various issues.

[†] Non-weighted average of 51 developing countries.

[††] Preliminary estimates.

sharp upturn in oil prices along with active efforts by the government led to a surge in demand for Pakistani labour in the Persian Gulf and Middle East. In addition, Pakistani-origin workers also have a significant presence in North America and Europe.[50]

Traditionally, a significant proportion of workers' remittances used to enter Pakistan through the informal 'hundi' or 'hawala' system. This system was preferred due to its relatively low transaction costs and its invisibility for tax purposes. However, following the events of 11 September 2001, these informal channels for international financial transactions came under the close scrutiny of global financial regulators. This fortuitous development (from the perspective of the Pakistani balance of payments) then resulted in a dramatic increase in workers' remittances arriving through formal channels. Furthermore, heightened concerns about the security of their assets seem to have encouraged many Pakistanis to send back a greater share of their savings abroad.

Concurrent with the sharp increase in remittances, Pakistan also experienced a rise in official development assistance in the aftermath of the 9/11 terrorist attacks and the ensuing US invasion of Afghanistan. Furthermore, the military regime was able to use its leverage as an ally in the 'war on terror' to get some of Pakistan's foreign debts written off or rolled over. These developments have considerably relaxed the foreign exchange constraints that Pakistan faces, and have been partly responsible for the increase in the coverage of Pakistan's foreign exchange reserves from less than two months' worth of imports in 2001 to over 5 months in 2005. Figures 11.12 and 11.13 illustrate the concurrent change in remittances, ODA, and the debt-servicing burden in the aftermath of 9/11.[51]

An increase in remittances and other forms of foreign exchange injections for a foreign exchange starved economy like Pakistan's can have a significant impact through several channels. On the positive side, it can relax constraints on importing capital goods and intermediate inputs crucial for industrial production. Remittances affect interest rates, and can also help improve the credit-worthiness of a country. Moreover, by increasing household income, and thus boosting consumption and spending, remittances can also have a multiplier effect on significant sectors of the economy.[52] Official development assistance on favourable terms and lower debt-servicing costs can provide breathing space for social spending, especially for heavily-indebted countries.

Figure 11.12: Worker Remittances as a Percentage of GDP, Official Development Assistance (ODA) as a Percentage of GDP, and Pakistan's Share of Total ODA Destined for Developing Countries

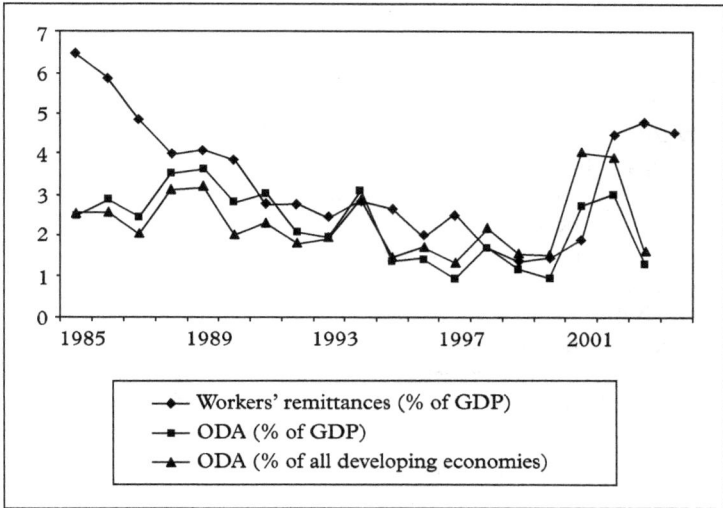

Source: United Nations Conference on Trade and Development (UNCTAD), *Handbook of Trade and Development Statistics* (online database), Geneva.

Figure 11.13: Remittances, Official Development Assistance (ODA), and Debt-Servicing Obligations (US$ mn.)

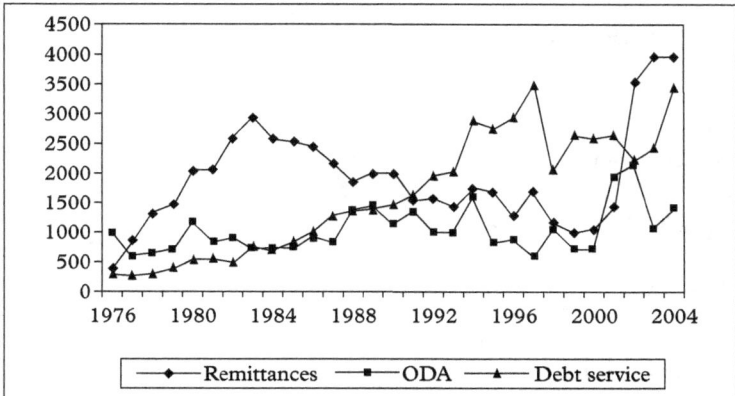

Source: World Bank, *World Development Indicators* (online database), Washington, DC.

On the negative side, remittances and ODA can also lead to the so-called 'Dutch disease' whereby the inflow of foreign exchange resources appreciates the currency (both in nominal and real terms), and results in making the domestic tradable goods sector internationally less competitive. The Dutch disease factor assumes increased importance given the nature of Pakistani exports, which are heavily concentrated in the apparel and textiles sectors, and face highly competitive conditions (low margins) in international markets. Moreover, in Pakistan's case, several studies have concluded that the majority of remitted funds have traditionally been directed towards either domestic consumption or investment in the non-traded goods sector (mainly land and real estate),[53] which, unlike investment in the traded goods sector, does not create a channel for export growth.[54] Finally, it has also been argued that remittances can reduce labour force participation rates.[55]

Figure 11.14 plots Pakistan's GDP growth rates and worker remittances as a proportion of GDP. The two series seem to move together with a lag, except for the late 1990s when the relationship seems to have considerably weakened. We now turn to a closer investigation of the effects of various sources of foreign exchange inflows on Pakistan's growth. Our objective is to take another look at the sustainability of recent growth patterns.[56] In line with our focus on the external regime, we econometrically explore the effects of the following five external account (quantity or volume) variables on output growth in Pakistan:

- Worker remittances
- Exports[57]
- Official development assistance or ODA
- Net FDI inflows
- Debt service-related outflows

Regressions involving time series require a careful look at the time series properties of the variables. While we provide a brief summary of the results here, the interested reader is referred to the unpublished appendix for the technical details.[58] One approach to dealing with some potential econometric problems is to use a cointegration technique to investigate the presence of a long-run relationship between the level instances of the variables. However, our small sample size (we could only estimate equations for the period 1976–2004 due to data availability problems) limits the

Figure 11.14: Time Plots of Worker Remittances as a Percentage of GDP (left-hand scale) and Real GDP Growth Rate (right-hand scale)

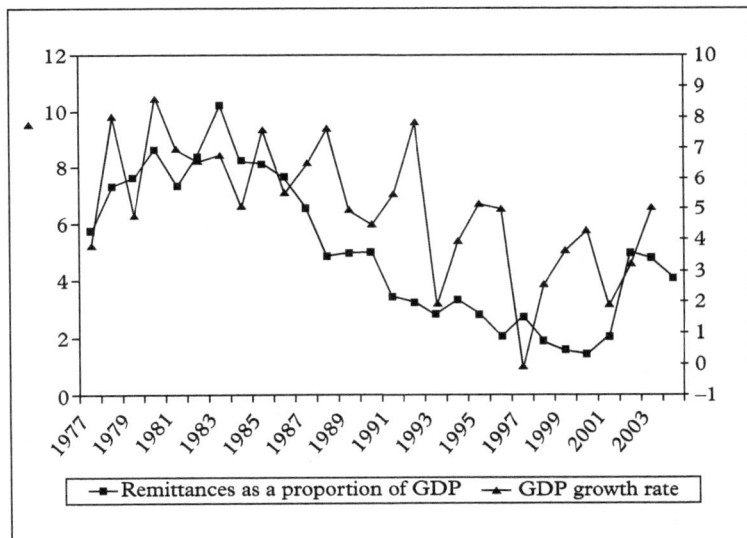

Source: World Bank, World Development Indicators (online database), Washington, DC.

feasibility of this approach. An alternative is to specify the variables in first-differenced form. The drawback of this latter approach is that it focuses on short-run information, leaving out the long-run signal. We, therefore, ran the regressions with the regressors specified in log levels. As a robustness check, we then re-ran the regressions with the variables in first-differenced form. Moreover, in order to control for price or scale changes, we estimated two alternative subsets of specifications, one after deflating the variables by the industrialized country price level index, and the other after expressing the regressors as proportions of GDP. In the case of debt servicing, we specified it alternately both as a proportion of exports and of gross national income. In order to take into account time lags, we specified all the regressors in first-lagged form. Finally, to explore inertial effects, we estimated equations with and without lagged instances of the dependent variable.

Our level estimates indicate that only remittances have a statistically significant (and positive) impact on Pakistan's GDP growth rate.[59] Exports, ODA, and debt service generally have the expected (positive, positive, and negative) signs but are statistically insignificant. Moreover, the FDI coefficient too is statistically insignificant.[60] The estimated coefficients derived using the deflated variables yield values ranging from 0.005 to 0.026, indicating that a 1 per cent increase in remittances raises the annual GDP growth rate by 0.5 to 2.6 per cent.

We should add that these are only preliminary estimates, and more robust conclusions would require much more detailed econometric work that controls for a host of other external factors (such as international interest rates, global growth, domestic quotas, etc.). Our estimates do, however, raise some interesting questions about the recent growth of the Pakistani economy. For example, if the growth has largely originated from remittance-led consumption and investment in the non-traded sector, how consistent are these developments with the government's emphasis on export-led growth? Does Pakistan run the risk of becoming increasingly less competitive in the post-MFA era, especially considering that it mostly exports relatively low value-added products in highly competitive sectors? Would the current surge in foreign exchange inflows lead to the Dutch disease scenario that hindered Pakistan's growth in the aftermath of a similar surge in the 1980s? We briefly revisit some of these questions in our concluding section.

▨ Concluding Remarks

We began this chapter with a brief look at the evolution of Pakistan's macroeconomic performance with a focus on the external accounts. We then looked at the nature and composition of Pakistan's trade, Pakistan's place in the global trade architecture, and Pakistan's prospects in the aftermath of the expiration of guaranteed quotas under the MFA and the agreement to constitute SAFTA. We found that Pakistan's exports remain highly concentrated in the textiles and clothing sectors, and that most studies do not predict major gains accruing to Pakistan in the new international environment for trade in apparel and textiles. Moreover, given the low level of trade between SAARC countries, and the nature of their exports, there are reasons to doubt that SAFTA would lead to dramatic benefits for most countries in the region, including Pakistan.

Next, we turned our attention to exploring aspects of Pakistan's recent efforts to pursue export-led growth. While Pakistan exports have grown relatively rapidly in recent years, this pattern may not be sustainable for several reasons. While the textile and clothing sectors have traditionally provided the stepping stone to industrialization for a number of countries (including most of the successful industrializers over the last two centuries), the likelihood of similar developmental results in present international circumstances may be constrained by demand-side constraints working at a global level. In other words, the simultaneous pursuit by many countries of export-led growth in low-tech, labour-intensive sectors with low barriers to entry may lead to a fallacy of composition if the supply-side of global markets becomes too crowded.

One approach to countering the fallacy of composition problem may be to quickly graduate into more sophisticated sectors where international competition is less severe. However, Pakistan so far shows few signs of moving in that direction. Given Pakistan's low level of human and social development, this is certainly not surprising. Moreover, pursuing remedies to this situation through sharp increases in social sector investment may not be in the self-interest of the narrow base of elites who have traditionally dominated Pakistan's politics, and have under-invested in the human capital of the majority.[61] Finally, to the extent that lower labour costs help maintain competitiveness in the face of international competition in sectors with limited scope for productivity growth, the incentives for wage suppression in an export-led growth regime further constrict the room for the kind of generalized rise in incomes that could lead to significant segments of the populations investing in the human capital of their progeny.[62]

An alternative source of recent growth, lent plausibility in the light of previous studies of growth in Pakistan and our own preliminary econometric estimates, may have been the surge in remittances following the September 2001 attacks. However, this may be a temporary (exogenous) shock over which policy makers have limited control. Moreover, to the extent that foreign exchange inflows in the form of remittances are likely to lead to (real and nominal) exchange rate appreciations, these remittances may undermine Pakistan's hopes of pursuing export-led growth and render the economy vulnerable to Dutch disease effects, unless the funds are used for investment in productivity-enhancing activities rather than consumption. Given past record, it is hard to be optimistic on this account. Indeed, there is plausible evidence that remittances have recently led to real estate booms in the big cities, with land prices skyrocketing after a period of relative stagnation in the 1990s.

Moreover, rising prices of non-tradable assets may also have helped fuel the credit-led consumption boom that contributed to higher growth in recent years.

Finally, another likely source underlying Pakistan's recent impressive growth performance may be the surge of official assistance and debt write-offs. While this is good news in the short-run, the long-run consequences will depend on the use that the state makes of this breathing space. Much of the recent assistance has taken the form of military hardware and infrastructure, which tends to enlarge Pakistan's already bloated military expenditures, while having a limited impact in terms of long-run growth.[63] Moreover, such assistance, if not utilized in productivity-enhancing ways, may also undermine Pakistan's prospects for export-led growth for reasons similar to those referred to while discussing remittances.

In sum, Pakistan's impressive recent performance in terms of output growth may rest on shaky foundations. Moreover, recent shifts in relative prices may result in re-allocation from the tradable to non-tradable sectors over the medium-term, undermining Pakistan's pursuit of export-led and/or domestic investment-led growth. Making room for growth based on more solid foundations in the long-run will require careful planning and targeted investment in the segments of the economy that create human capital and are likely to be under-provided by the private sector because of their public goods nature.

▦ Appendix 11.1

Broad Economic Categories (BEC) Rev.3

BEC 1 – Food and beverages
    11 – Primary
    12 – Processed
BEC 2 – Industrial supplies not elsewhere specified
    21 – Primary
    22 – Processed
BEC 3 – Fuels and lubricants
    31 – Primary
    32 – Processed
BEC 4 – Capital goods (except transport equipment), and parts and accessories thereof
    41 – Capital goods (except transport equipment)
    42 – Parts and accessories
BEC 5 – Transport equipment and parts and accessories thereof
    51 – Passenger motor cars

52 – Other
53 – Parts and accessories
BEC 6 – Consumer goods not elsewhere specified
    61 – Durable
    62 – Semi-durable
    63 – Non-durable
BEC 7 – Goods not elsewhere specified

Standard International Trade Classification (SITC) Rev.2

SITC 0 – Food and live animals
    00 – Live animals other than animals of division 03
    01 – Meat and meat preparations
    02 – Dairy products and birds' eggs
    03 – Fish (not marine mammals), crustaceans, molluscs and aquatic invertebrates, and preparations thereof
    04 – Cereals and cereal preparations
    05 – Vegetables and fruit
    06 – Sugars, sugar preparations and honey
    07 – Coffee, tea, cocoa, spices, and manufactures thereof
    08 – Feeding stuff for animals (not including unmilled cereals)
    09 – Miscellaneous edible products and preparations
SITC 1 – Beverages and tobacco
    11 – Beverages
    12 – Tobacco and tobacco manufactures
SITC 2 – Crude materials, inedible, except fuels
    21 – Hides, skins and furskins, raw
    22 – Oil-seeds and oleaginous fruits
    23 – Crude rubber (including synthetic and reclaimed)
    24 – Cork and wood
    25 – Pulp and waste paper
    26 – Textile fibres (other than wool tops and other combed wool) and their wastes (not manufactured into yarn or fabric)
    27 – Crude fertilizers, other than those of division 56, and crude minerals (excluding coal, petroleum and precious stones)
    28 – Metalliferous ores and metal scrap
    29 – Crude animal and vegetable materials, n.e.s.
SITC 3 – Mineral fuels, lubricants and related materials
    32 – Coal, coke and briquettes
    33 – Petroleum, petroleum products and related materials
    34 – Gas, natural and manufactured
    35 – Electric current
SITC 4 – Animal and vegetable oils, fats and waxes
    41 – Animal oils and fats
    42 – Fixed vegetable fats and oils, crude, refined or fractionated

43 – Animal or vegetable fats and oils, processed; waxes of animal or vegetable origin; inedible mixtures or preparations of animal or vegetable fats or oils, n.e.s.

SITC 5 – Chemicals and related products, n.e.s.

51 – Organic chemicals

52 – Inorganic chemicals

53 – Dyeing, tanning and colouring materials

54 – Medicinal and pharmaceutical products

55 – Essential oils and resinoids and perfume materials; toilet, polishing and cleansing preparations

56 – Fertilizers (other than those of group 272)

57 – Plastics in primary forms

58 – Plastics in non-primary forms

59 – Chemical materials and products, n.e.s.

SITC 6 – Manufactured goods classified chiefly by material

61 – Leather, leather manufactures, n.e.s., and dressed furskins

62 – Rubber manufactures, n.e.s.

63 – Cork and wood manufactures (excluding furniture)

64 – Paper, paperboard and articles of paper pulp, of paper or of paperboard

65 – Textile yarn, fabrics, made-up articles, n.e.s., and related products

66 – Non-metallic mineral manufactures, n.e.s.

67 – Iron and steel

68 – Non-ferrous metals

69 – Manufactures of metals, n.e.s.

SITC 7 – Machinery and transport equipment

71 – Power-generating machinery and equipment

72 – Machinery specialized for particular industries

73 – Metalworking machinery

74 – General industrial machinery and equipment, n.e.s., and machine parts, n.e.s.

75 – Office machines and automatic data-processing machines

76 – Telecommunications and sound-recording and reproducing apparatus and equipment

77 – Electrical machinery, apparatus and appliances, n.e.s., and electrical parts thereof (including non-electrical counterparts, n.e.s., of electrical household-type equipment)

78 – Road vehicles (including air-cushion vehicles)

79 – Other transport equipment

SITC 8 – Miscellaneous manufactured articles

81 – Prefabricated buildings; sanitary, plumbing, heating and lighting fixtures and fittings, n.e.s.

82 – Furniture, and parts thereof; bedding, mattresses, mattress supports, cushions and similar stuffed furnishings

83 – Travel goods, handbags and similar containers

84 – Articles of apparel and clothing accessories

85 – Footwear

87 – Professional, scientific and controlling instruments and apparatus, n.e.s.

88 – Photographic apparatus, equipment and supplies and optical goods, n.e.s.; watches and clocks

89 – Miscellaneous manufactured articles, n.e.s.

SITC 9 – Commodities and transactions not classified elsewhere in the SITC

91 – Postal packages not classified according to kind

93 – Special transactions and commodities not classified according to kind

96 – Coin (other than gold coin), not being legal tender

97 – Gold, non-monetary (excluding gold ores and concentrates)

▦ Notes

1. China being a noticeable contemporary exception.
2. Ministry of Finance, *Economic Survey, 2005–2006* (Ministry of Finance, Government of Pakistan, Islamabad, 2006).
3. With the possible exception of Sri Lanka, which began liberalizing its trade regime in the 1970s.
4. A later section discusses these issues in more detail.
5. The ratio, which was 0.18 per cent in 1972, had merely increased to 1.16 per cent in 2004.
6. Although some of the increased holdings of foreign exchange reserves are almost certainly a reflection of the efforts to maintain a competitive nominal exchange rate through official reserve transactions. In this sense, the State Bank probably pursues a de facto exchange rate target in spite of the de jure float. More below on the pursuit of external competitiveness.
7. See the Appendix for a more detailed presentation of how various industries and sectors are categorized under these systems.
8. In Pakistan's case, the share of manufactures in total exports increased from almost 68 per cent in 1984 to 86 per cent in 2003.
9. Figure 11.7 has been borrowed with slight modifications from Sanjaya Lall, 'Benchmarking Pakistan's Competitive Performance', Paper presented at the Asian Development Bank Institute Policy Seminar on 'Industrial Competitiveness: The Challenge for Pakistan', 17 November 2003.
10. SITC category 68, which consists of the processing of non-ferrous metals, is often excluded, however. This does not affect our discussion in any significant manner.

11. Food and live animals, beverages and tobacco, crude materials, inedible (except fuels), mineral fuels, lubricants and related materials, and animal and vegetable oils, fats and waxes, respectively.

12. Manufactured goods classified chiefly by material and miscellaneous manufactured articles, respectively.

13. Chemicals and related products, machinery and transport equipment, and miscellaneous manufactured articles, respectively.

14. Although not shown in the figure, these shares have remained largely unchanged in the post-2000 years.

15. World Bank, 'Trade Policies in South Asia: An Overview', *World Bank Report* 29949, Washington, DC, 2004.

16. See, for example, J. S. Bandara and Wusheng Yu, 'How Desirable is the South Asian Free Trade Area? A Quantitative Economic Assessment', *The World Economy*, 2003, 26(9), pp. 1293–1323, and T. Baysan, A. Panagariya and N. Pitigala, 'Preferential Trading in South Asia', World Bank Policy Research Working Paper 3813, January 2006.

17. Afia Malik, 'Demand for Textile and Clothing Exports of Pakistan', Pakistan Institute of Development Economics, Research Report Number 180, 2001.

18. Thus the MFA was a major exception to the GATT principle of non-discrimination.

19. See for a discussion, John Whalley, 'The Post-MFA Performance of Developing Asia', Working Paper Number 12178, National Bureau for Economic Research, Washington, DC, 2006.

20. That is, they could have sold more in the absence of quotas.

21. Governments generally distributed the quotas free of charge to domestic firms based on criteria such as past export performance. See C. B. Hamilton (ed.), *Textiles and Trade and the Developing Countries: Eliminating the Multi-Fibre Arrangement in the 1990s* (Washington, DC: The World Bank, 1990). Also, most of the rents accrued to domestic exporters (G. W. Harrison, T. F. Rutherford and D. G. Tarr, 'Quantifying the Uruguay Round', *Economic Journal*, 1997, 107 (444), pp. 1405–30).

22. Under the terms of China's WTO accession, such safeguard measures can be undertaken against China until 31 December 2008.

23. Although one reason for this low growth post-MFA may be the rapid growth in the immediately preceding years as producers prepared for the post-MFA era.

24. John Whalley, 'The Post-MFA Performance of Developing Asia', Working Paper Number 12178, National Bureau for Economic Research, Washington, DC, 2006.

25. Whalley notes that in Pakistan's case, the positive effects of the post-MFA regime were offset by the imposition by the EU of a 13.4 per cent anti-dumping duty on bed wear and the reintroduction of a 12 per cent tariff on textile exports (ibid.).

26. For example, under an 'early harvest' programme, India, Pakistan and Sri Lanka are scheduled to bring down their customs duties to 0–5 per cent by January 2009 for the products from such Member States.

27. The main difference between a *customs union* and an *economic union* is that while the former involves eliminating tariffs among member countries and forming a common tariff position vis-à-vis the rest of the world while the latter proceeds further in the sense that member countries synchronize their fiscal, monetary and economic policies.

28. See J.N. Bhagwati, 'U.S. Trade Policy: The Infatuation with Free Trade Areas', in Jagdish Bhagwati and Anne O. Krueger (eds), *The Dangerous Drift to Preferential Trade Agreements* (Washington, DC: AEI Press, 1995), pp. 1–18.

29. Jacob Viner, 'The Customs Union Issue', Carnegie Endowment for International Peace Report, New York, 1950.

30. The reader is referred to any standard trade textbook such as Robert C. Feenstra, *Advanced International Trade: Theory and Evidence* (Princeton, NJ: Princeton University Press, 2004) for a more detailed discussion of RTAs and their welfare effects.

31. Although, as stated earlier, one important caveat to this picture is the significant presence of trade through unofficial/informal channels.

32. See T. Baysan, A. Panagariya and N. Pitigala, 'Preferential Trading in South Asia', World Bank Policy Research Working Paper 3813, January 2006.

33. See Baysan et al., for a discussion of the relative merits of these two approaches (ibid.).

34. J.S. Bandara and Wusheng Yu, 'How Desirable is the South Asian Free Trade Area? A Quantitative Economic Assessment', *The World Economy*, 2003, 26(9), pp. 1293–1323.

35. T.N. Srinivasan, 'Regional Trading Arrangements and Beyond: Exploring Some Policy Options for South Asia', World Bank Report No. IDP 42, Washington, DC, 1994.

36. J.D. Rodriguez-Delgado, 'SAFTA: Living in a World of Regional Trade Agreements', Working Paper Number WP/07/23, International Monetary Fund, 2007.

37. See T. Baysan, A. Panagariya and N. Pitigala, 'Preferential Trading in South Asia', World Bank Policy Research Working Paper 3813, January 2006.

38. This should not distract from the possibility that a free trade area may be a good idea for political reasons, i.e., to improve India–Pakistan relations, but as Baysan et al. point out, there are other, possibly more direct ways to achieve that goal (ibid.). One such route may be a bilateral free trade agreement between the two countries.

39. As mentioned earlier, more than four-fifths of Pakistani exports now consist of manufactured products.

40. J.N. Bhagwati, 'Immiserizing Growth: A Geometrical Note', *Review of Economic Studies*, 1958, pp. 201–05.
41. See S. Kasahara, 'The Flying Geese Paradigm: A Critical Study of its Application to East Asian Regional Development', Discussion Paper Number 169, United Nations Commission on Trade and Development, Geneva, 2004; also F. Furuoka, 'Japan and the "Flying Geese" Pattern of East Asian Integration', *Eastasia.at*, October 2005, 4(1), http://www.eastasia.at/vol4_1/article01.htm (accessed 9 August 2008).
42. See for example, R. Blecker and A. Razmi, 'The Fallacy of Composition and Contractionary Devaluations: Output Effects of Real Exchange Rate Shocks in Semi-Industrialised Countries', *Cambridge Journal of Economics*, 2008, 32(1), pp. 83–109; R. Faini, F. Clavijo and A. Senhadji-Semlali, 'The Fallacy of Composition Argument: Is it Relevant for LDCs' Manufactures Exports?', *European Economic Review*, 1992, 36(4), pp. 865–82; V. A. Muscatelli, A. A. Stevenson and C. Montagna, 'Intra-NIE Competition in Exports of Manufactures, *Journal of International Economics*, 1994, 37(1), pp. 29–47; T. Palley, 'Export-led growth: Evidence of developing country crowding-out', in P. Arestis, M. Baddeley, and J. McCombie, (eds), *Globalization, Regionalism, and Economic Activity* (Northampton, MA: Edward Elgar, 2003), pp. 175–97; and B. Eichengreen, Y. Rhee and H. Tong, 'The impact of China on the Exports of Other Asian Countries', Working Paper no. 10768, National Bureau of Economic Research, Cambridge, MA, 2004. See A. Razmi and R. Blecker, 'Developing Country Exports of Manufactures: Moving Up the Ladder to Escape the Fallacy of Composition?', *Journal of Development Studies*, 2008, 44 (1), pp. 21–48, for a more detailed discussion and literature review.
43. B. Eichengreen, Y. Rhee and H. Tong, 'The Impact of China on the Exports of Other Asian Countries', Working Paper no. 10768, National Bureau of Economic Research, Cambridge, MA, 2004.
44. A. Razmi and R. Blecker, 'Developing Country Exports of Manufactures: Moving Up the Ladder to Escape the Fallacy of Composition?', *Journal of Development Studies*, 2008, 44 (1), pp. 21–48.
45. R. Blecker and A. Razmi, 'The Fallacy of Composition and Contractionary Devaluations: Output Effects of Real Exchange Rate Shocks in Semi-Industrialised Countries', *Cambridge Journal of Economics*, 2008, 32(1), pp. 83–109.
46. In other words, the growth benefits are of a 'beggar-thy-neighbour' nature.
47. The sample consisted of 10 high income industrialized OECD countries, and 18 major developing country exporters of manufactured products. See R. Blecker and A. Razmi, 'The Fallacy of Composition and Contractionary Devaluations: Output Effects of Real Exchange Rate Shocks in Semi-Industrialised Countries', *Cambridge Journal of Economics*, 2008, 32(1), pp. 83–109.

48. See R. Blecker and A. Razmi for details of how the real exchange rate indices were constructed (ibid.).
49. The coefficient of variance of the real exchange rate with respect to developed and developing countries were 0.13 and 0.10, respectively.
50. In Europe, the United Kingdom has a relatively high concentration, owing in part to past colonial connections and the language factor.
51. Figures on actual levels of military and civilian aid are hard to access. According to Cohen and Chollet, Pakistan has received more than $10 billion in assistance from the US over the past five years, most of it channelled through the Pakistani military. See C. Cohen and D. Chollet, 'When $10 Billion is Not Enough: Rethinking U.S. Strategy toward Pakistan', *The Washington Quarterly*, Spring 2007, 30(2), pp. 7–19. This figure includes waived sanctions and debt forgiveness worth $2 billion. Moreover, the US has encouraged other creditors to follow suit. According to the paper, however, less than 10 per cent of this assistance goes toward humanitarian or development funding. For example, education-related assistance amounted to only $64 million per year, or $1.16 per child per year.
52. See, for example, P. Isard, *Globalization and the International Financial System: What's Wrong and What Can Be Done* (Cambridge, UK: Cambridge University Press, 2005); A.P. Thirlwall and M.N. Hussain, 'The Balance of Payments Constraint, Capital Flows and Growth Rate Differences between Developing Countries', *Oxford Economic Papers*, November 1982, 34, pp. 498–509; and J.S.L. McCombie and A.P. Thirlwall (eds), *Essays on Balance of Payments Constrained Growth: Theory and Evidence* (London: Routledge, 2004).
53. See, for example, R. Amjad, 'Impact of Workers' Remittances from the Middle East on Pakistan's Economy: Some Selected Issues', *The Pakistan Development Review*, 1986, 25(4), pp. 757–82; and H. Alderman, 'Saving and Economic Shocks in Rural Pakistan', *Journal of Development Economics*, 1996, 51, pp. 343–65.
54. Indeed, if anything, by reducing the availability of tradables for export, higher consumption could harm export growth.
55. Chami et al., who used panel data from a dataset containing 113 countries, found a negative correlation between remittances and economic growth, concluding that remittances may serve as counter-cyclical, compensatory mechanisms rather than as a source of capital for economic development. See R. Chami, C. Fullenkamp and S. Jahjah, 'Are Immigrant Remittance Flows a Source of Capital for Development', *IMF Staff Papers*, Washington, DC, April 2005, 52(1), pp. 55–81.
56. Note that our objective is not to study the contribution of workers' remittances to growth in Pakistan but rather to study (more narrowly) the effect of remittances relative to other sources of foreign exchange.

See Z. Iqbal and A. Sattar, 'The Contribution of Workers' Remittances to Economic Growth in Pakistan', Pakistan Institute of Development Economics Research Report Number 187, 2005, for an investigation of the former question.

57. Alternatively, we could have used the trade balance, i.e., net exports of goods and services. However, considering that a significant proportion of remittances, ODA, and FDI inflows is likely to be spent on imports that would create potential simultaneity/endogeneity problems.

58. The unpublished appendix is available from the author on request.

59. Since the specifications with variables in first-differenced forms did not yield any statistically significant estimates, we limit our discussion to the level estimates.

60. This is consistent with several recent empirical studies that have concluded that FDI inflows have a positive effect on growth only in relatively high-income countries that have the 'absorptive capacity' to channel the FDI into productive uses. See, for example, E. Borensztein, J. De Gregorio and J. Lee, 'How does Foreign Direct Investment Affect Economic Growth?', *Journal of International Economics*, 1998, 45 (1), pp. 115–35.

61. See William Easterly, 'The Political Economy of Growth without Development: A Case Study of Pakistan', Paper for the Analytical Narratives of Growth Project, Harvard University, June 2001, who terms Pakistan's economic record as that of 'growth without development'.

62. See Talat Anwar, 'Changes in Inequality of Consumption and Opportunities in Pakistan during 2001–02 and 2004–05', Research Report Number 3, Centre for Research on Poverty Reduction and Income Distribution, December 2006; and Ministry of Finance, *Economic Survey, 2005–2006* (Ministry of Finance, Government of Pakistan, Islamabad, 2006), for evidence of the increase in consumption inequality in Pakistan over the period 2001–02 to 2004–05. See also UNCTAD, *Trade and Development Report,* United Nations Commission on Trade and Development 2003 (Geneva: UNCTAD, 2003), for evidence of wage suppression in some developing countries pursuing export-led growth.

63. Pakistan's military expenditures constitute about 30 per cent of central government revenue, according the World Bank's *World Development Indicators,* but given that this statistic does not include several major defence expenditure items, the actual number is likely to be significantly higher.

✳

12

The Puzzle of Pakistan's Social Sector Development: Finally on Track?

S. Akbar Zaidi

Pakistan's economic growth record, of well over 5 per cent for many decades, with noticeable and not infrequent peaks and troughs, by all accounts, has been quite impressive, especially when compared to other countries at similar levels of economic development. However, the country's record of economic growth has given rise to a dual paradox. First, the high economic growth trajectory has been reached with very low human development fundamentals, where indicators related to education, literacy, health, and access to water and sanitation, have been lower than what one would expect to be required for a country to achieve Pakistan's growth levels. This deficiency in the fundamentals that support growth questions some of the core assumptions of New Growth Theory, in which human development is considered almost a prerequisite for economic growth: Pakistan may have bucked the pattern by achieving high growth with low fundamentals. The second paradox that emerges from an examination of Pakistan's economic performance is that this relatively high and consistent economic growth has not resulted in an equal improvement in human development indicators to the extent that one would expect. This article is an attempt to try to understand this dual paradox, and suggests, that perhaps while Pakistan may have contradicted the general trend in the past, it may now be moving closer to that general pattern, where the relationship between high growth and better human development indicators is seen to be moving together.

While this attempt to examine the relationship between growth and human development is the main aspect of this article, we also examine some historical trends of human development indicators and the relationship between growth and development, and provide some explanations for why they behaved the way they did in Pakistan. We first begin with a brief historical account of the social sectors and of human development in Pakistan after which our focus changes to recent years, where we focus on key issues related to both growth and development.

◙ Economic Growth and Social Development in Six Decades

The sixty years since 1947 can be distinguished by six specific epochs or eras representing different economic policies, and planning and management choices; most of all, they represent different sets of political arrangements. The first eleven years, between 1947–58 are the years when the country and economy were trying to settle down. This period was followed by what many still call the golden era of economic development (or at least economic growth) in the Decade of Development under General Ayub Khan. The economy and the political scene had indeed stabilized and settled down with a consequence that growth rates were unprecedented, and Pakistan was considered to be one of the few countries at that time that would achieve developed-country status. *The New York Times* of 18 January 1965 stated: 'Pakistan may be on its way towards an economic milestone reached by only one other populous country, the United States'. *The Times,* London echoed this sentiment on 26 February 1966 saying that 'the survival and development of Pakistan is one of the most remarkable examples of state- and nation-building in the post-war period'. However, with the war of liberation in East Pakistan, the majority wing left Pakistan to form Bangladesh and two, not one, new countries were born.[1]

Post-1971 Pakistan was a new country in every respect, compared to the one that had existed before. The third brief yet highly significant era in Pakistan's history was the five-and-a-half years of Zulfiqar Ali Bhutto. His populism or Islamic Socialism, or just plain rhetoric, made him the most popular, and at that time, the only elected leader to emerge in what was left of Pakistan. His rule ended by the imposition of Pakistan's second martial law under General Zia-ul-Haq in 1977. There were some similarities between the first and the second martial laws, but the world was now very much changed and a different place compared to the one of the 1960s. The opening up of the Middle East, the Afghan war with its consequences of a drug and arms culture in Pakistan, attempts at the Islamization of the economy and society, and a praetorian sort of democracy between 1985–88, were amongst the salient features of the Zia era.

The death of General Zia, in many ways, brought about the end of the old Pakistan and 1988 — with the rebirth of democracy — signals the third birth of the nation following the two earlier ones of 1947 and 1971. While political and social changes were fast to emerge, the post-1988 economic changes and programmes also represented a departure from the past with very significant impacts on society, many of which were highly deleterious. However, in 1999 once again, Pakistan was set off on yet another different trajectory, in many ways trying to undo the Zia legacy further.

Laying the Foundations: 1947–58

In 1947, Pakistan was indeed, a predominantly agrarian, undeveloped, newly independent nation, with little industry, few services and no infrastructure. In the first few years, Pakistan's main concern was one of survival: adverse international conditions and a precarious domestic situation with millions of refugees made the provision of very basic necessities the primary task of the government. Attempts to restructure the economy and ensure that it was on a strong footing could only have been undertaken after the initial political and economic shocks were dealt with.

The first decade of economic policy and planning reflected the attempts made by the bureaucracy to keep Pakistan on its feet. The herculean task of building an economic base was left to the state sector as the private sector was still in its embryo and did not have the capital to lead an industrial revolution in the country. It was the windfall gain made by the mercantile class during and after the Korean War in 1952 that paved the way for the foundations of industry — an industry which the state sector helped develop and then handed over to the private sector.

The Decade of Development: 1958–68

If we examine Pakistan's economic growth record, the decade of the 1960s stands out as the best performer. Table 12.1 gives a useful indication of the nature of the differences between the decades of the 1960s, 1970s, 1980s and 1990s. While the rates of growth for the 1960s and the 1980s do seem to be quite close in most categories, there are important conceptual and ideological differences in the modes of development under the two military regimes.

Dozens of economists and social scientists have written on Ayub Khan's era and they generally agree that considerable economic growth and development did indeed take place during that period.[2] They argue that significant leaps were made in industrial and agricultural production, where growth rates in excess of 20 per cent

Table 12.1: Growth Rates (%)

	GDP	Agriculture	Manufacturing	Services
1950s	3.1	1.6	–	–
1960s	6.8	5.1	9.9	6.7
1970s	4.8	2.4	5.5	6.3
1980s	6.5	5.4	8.2	6.7
1990s	4.6	4.4	5.8	4.6
1990–91 to 1995–96	5.0	4.2	5.2	5.1
1995–96 to 1999–2000	4.0	4.9	3.2	4.0
1999–2002	3.0	1.3	5.1	4.2
2002-06	6.85	3.95	10.5	7.0

Source: Government of Pakistan, *Pakistan Economic Survey*, various issues, Islamabad.

per annum were witnessed in the large-scale manufacturing sector. In the first five years of the Ayub period, manufacturing grew by as much as 17 per cent, and in the second half of Ayub Khan's reign, agricultural growth increased by 6 per cent, while industry grew by 10 per cent. Table 12.1 shows that the economy in general, and the different individual sectors, grew by phenomenal rates, and Pakistan was considered to be a model capitalist economy in the 1960s.

Observers have pointed out that this aggressive capitalist development caused serious economic, social and political tensions. They argued that there was increased disparity in incomes across different regions, manifest in the concentration of economic prosperity in both the industrial and agricultural sectors in central Punjab, and in industry in Karachi. Critics of Ayub Khan's model of development point out that these two regions were permitted to grow at the expense of the rest of the country and the end result was the feeling on the part of East Pakistan, of utter neglect and betrayal. Apart from the very obvious phenomenon of regional disparities, a number of scholars also took great pains to show that there was a great deal of economic concentration amongst individuals and the numerous business empires that were created, resulting in increasing income inequality.

Of course, all this did happen. There was tremendous growth, but there was also increasing disparity across class and region. The social sectors were also neglected. There was little or no increase in the level of real wages, and social equity was of little concern. Functional inequality was the preferred philosophy of Mahbub-ul-Haq and Ayub Khan's Harvard Advisory Group — their focus was on the rich, who were supposed to generate greater savings, and thus were to be the motors of capitalist growth and development. Ayub Khan's economic policies thus resulted in growth, development, expansion in the forces of production and the birth of a proletariat; compared to the earlier periods, this was indeed, a very progressive era in the evolution of the economic and political process that is Pakistan.

In terms of social development, what is important here is that in the early phases of (low) development and economic growth following Independence, the state played a fundamental role in the provision of services such as schools and health facilities but was unable to cope with the huge demand unleashed on account of structural changes that had taken place over the decade. The existing structures and systems of the provision of health and education services catered to a small urban elite clientele, with the huge majority of the rural populace still cut off from the benefits of high growth. Although many rural health schemes — such as the Barefoot Doctor — were initiated, they reached only a small proportion of the populace. Once economic growth began to affect social formations and structures, the state was not able to deal with the demands of the new social groups that had emerged. The rise of the new middle classes, both in urban and rural areas, where land reforms in particular played a fundamental role, demanding more and better social services, came into conflict with the institutions of the state, which eventually resulted in the ouster of the Ayub government. The state-capitalist model of economic growth was supported by the state provision of social services, but was unable to meet the growing demands of a population that wanted more than just the economic benefits of growth. In other words, not only did the high growth take place with low social development but it also did not translate into higher investment or provision in the social sector.[3]

Bhutto's Populism: 1971–77

Ironically, while most intellectuals condemned Ayub Khan's policies, it was the very same policies that gave rise to populism and defined the brand of policies particular to Zulfiqar Ali Bhutto, who was supported by the same intellectuals. Without Ayub, Bhutto would not have been possible. Bhutto's economic policies were more 'illiberal' than those of his predecessor and his nationalization was said to be the major cause for a huge downward trend in growth. However, Table 12.1 shows that in the 1970s, GDP grew by close to 5 per cent and the propaganda about the failure of the Bhutto regime has been highly exaggerated.

Bhutto's government also laid the foundations for future growth and development by which his successor benefited. Basic industries were set up and a base for a capital goods industry was established, resulting in subsequent growth. The Middle East boom that Bhutto initiated, again another irony in Pakistan's history, helped keep General Zia in power for some years. The interventionist economic policies of Zulfiqar Ali Bhutto were responsible for growth not only in his own tenure, but also in the period after 1977.

Bhutto's intervention in the economic sphere was matched with equally forceful interventions in the social sectors: he undertook land reforms, nationalized industries and banks and enforced price controls, all in an effort to respond to his populist mandate and to truly emerge as the people's elected representative. In addition, he also nationalized educational and health institutions, bringing the social sectors well under state control. Numerous policies were initiated in the social sectors with a 'people's' focus, where the attempt was made to provide free health and education services to all. Interestingly, although Table 12.1 shows that the 1970s, and in particular the Bhutto years, were amongst the worse in terms of economic growth, spending on development was very substantial. In 1974–75, for example, government health expenditure was as high as 1.7 per cent of GDP, the highest it has ever been in Pakistan's sixty-year history. Moreover, development expenditure was a staggering 11 per cent of GDP in 1976–77 when the Bhutto government was removed, again the highest it has ever been.

The Second Military Government: 1977–88

General Zia's regime was more liberal in economic terms — but certainly not in political terms — than any of his predecessors. While the trend to liberalize the economy was escalated consciously in the Zia period, the Soviet invasion of Afghanistan and the excessive involvement in Pakistan by the United States, helped assure steps to increase growth. Remittances from the Middle East and aid from abroad helped launch Pakistan's second economic revolution, where the middle class emerged as a formidable economic and political category. Pakistan's growth rates in the 1980s, as Table 12.1 shows, were quite phenomenal. By becoming the capitalist world's 'front-line' state against all things Soviet, and especially against Soviet expansionism in the region, Pakistan's government gained in terms of financial aid and resources, but the impact of General Zia's martial rule, however, inflicted deep-rooted damage to Pakistani society in terms of ethnic and religious schisms, which still affect Pakistan in major ways. Another major burden from the Zia era that plagued governments after him, was the astronomical debt burden that he bequeathed to the country; the consequences of both domestic and international debt was a major cause for the slowdown in the economy in the 1988–99 period.

With high remittances and unprecedented aid, growth rates soared, as did private enterprise. The pseudo-socialist model of the Bhutto regime was dismantled with the private sector making a huge comeback in the social and economic spheres. A second middle class revolution occurred, but this time as the state began to withdraw under the guise of the global phenomenon of 'liberalization' and the 'withering away of the state', the private sector and the market began to determine all economic and social choices, options and outcomes. Private and market solutions to illiteracy, disease, lack of water and sanitation, etc., began to be found, often aided by the NGO boom that had taken place across the country. Social indicators began to improve and importantly, poverty declined considerably in this period (see Table 12.2) largely on the basis of high economic growth, but also because of the nature and type of that growth, which was predominantly decentralized on account of private transfers from the Gulf states.

Democracy under Structural Adjustment: 1988–99

The decade of the 1990s has been Pakistan's worst in many regards, not least because of the economy performing particularly poorly.

Table 12.2: Trends in Growth, Poverty and Income Distribution

Decade	Growth	Poverty	Income Distribution (Gini)
1950s	Stagnated	Persisted	Unknown
1960s	Rapid increase	Increased	Improved
1970s	Slow, stagnated	Declined	Worsened
1980s	Rapid increase	Declined	Rapid deterioration, followed by rapid improvement
1990s	Substantial decline	Increased considerably	Worsened
1999–2002	Decline continues	Continued to increase	Unknown, but worsening trend probably continued
2003–07	Rapid increase	Declined	Worsened

Explanations for the poor performance in the 1990s range from (i) issues related to poor governance; (ii) the fact that there were eleven governments over the period 1988–99 resulting in frequent changes of government and an environment of instability, something which is not conducive to investment and growth; (iii) the debt burden accumulated over the buoyant Zia period of 1977–88 that finally came home to roost, resulting in annual interest payments having to be paid — equivalent to 60 per cent of the budget each year, with another 25 per cent allocated to defence — which did not allow much left over for development; (iv) sanctions imposed on Pakistan in the early 1990s related to nuclear proliferation; and, (v) the IMF and World Bank-managed structural adjustment programme, which resulted in all Pakistani governments having to make substantial structural interventions in the economy, many of which had a seriously deleterious impact on growth, distribution, social sector investment and on poverty.

Added to all this, was the severely deteriorating law and order situation in Karachi, Pakistan's main economic and financial centre, which made matters far worse. The economic costs and implications of Pakistanis carrying out 'jihad' in different parts of the region and globe, perhaps even supported by state institutions, and the rise of eligious fundamentalist forces, gave Pakistan an image which would not have been very favourable to attract foreign (or even local) investors. Moreover, this jihad factor was a core reason why Pakistan, while not at war with India throughout the 1990s, was certainly not at peace with its neighbour. Interestingly, once we look at the more recent past, since 1999, and certainly since 11 September 2001, many of these constraints on the economy have been removed.

In the period 1988–98, all governments in office in Pakistan were severely constrained by the IMF and the World Bank's structural adjustment programmes enforced throughout that period, and by the huge debt overhang inherited from the profligate Zia decade. Both these factors resulted in a fiscal squeeze being imposed on the economy, and in particular on development expenditure and on the social sectors. Hence, the overall development expenditure, which was on average 7.3 per cent of GDP in the 1980s when there was a lot of liquidity, was slashed to 4.7 per cent of GDP for the 1990s. With severe restrictions on expenditure due to fiscal 'discipline' and due to debt interest payments, as always, the social sectors were the first to have their budgets drastically reduced. Match with this the fact that the economy was constrained and growth rates were low, and the economic and social sector downslide is not surprising. However, while this general pattern continued throughout the 1990s, it was made worse in May 1998 when both India and Pakistan conducted their nuclear tests.

Soon after the nuclear tests, the developed countries, the G-7, imposed a wide range of economic sanctions against Pakistan, a country which was highly dependent on donor funding and on aid. The Japanese, for example, because of having experienced the outcome of nuclear irresponsibility, do not do business with any country that carries out nuclear tests. As a consequence, the Japanese government stopped all funding of projects and aid, both to India and to Pakistan. Other governments also castigated Pakistan (more so than India, who was also in the firing line) for undertaking the tests and cut aid and assistance on which the Pakistani economy and government had become dependent. The IMF also suspended its Enhanced Structural Adjustment Facility (ESAF) and Extended Fund Facility programmes as well as new Official Development Assistance. On all accounts, Pakistan was squeezed by western donors and governments as a consequence of undertaking these nuclear tests.

Hence, the 1990s saw not just a deterioration in economic performance, but also because of fiscal constraints, a squeeze on development funding. Some donor-funded social sector initiatives were initiated, but the economic crisis led to a crisis that was magnified in the social sectors (see Section below).

11 September 2001: The Day the World Changed

There is little disagreement over the fact that the economy benefited immensely — as did General Musharraf's political fortunes and his longevity — as a consequence of 9/11. The single most important attribute of Pakistan's economy through the 1990s was its severe debt burden. With having to repay large amounts of interest each year, little was left for domestic development. Soon after 9/11, a huge part of the country's debt was written off and rescheduled, creating immense fiscal space — a windfall that the government could not have anticipated in its wildest dreams. Remittances and hidden wealth from Pakistanis overseas came back to Pakistan immediately after 9/11, when fearing greater scrutiny of their accounts, many Pakistanis (particularly those in the United States and Dubai) diverted their funds back to Pakistan. (This is evident from the fact that Pakistan's traditional source for remittances — between $2–4 billion — was the Middle East; however, after 9/11 in 2002–03, the United States, uncharacteristically, became Pakistan's single largest source of remittances by Pakistanis abroad, replacing Saudi Arabia). Apart from this, aid flew back into Pakistan, a pattern that we have seen when the two previous military dictators ruled Pakistan in the 1960s and the 1980s. Research has shown that external support to Pakistan, particularly from the United States and from multilateral financial institutions such as the IMF and the World Bank, grows when the military is in power. It has been this windfall gain after 9/11 that has driven this boom, much of it on account of excess liquidity in the banking system.

A high GDP growth rate for the fourth year running (since 2002), resulting in high and increasing per capita incomes, is one of the more positive economic outcomes to emerge over the last few years. There are other positives as well, such as an increase in investment and a rise in exports. Other signs seen as important by the government, as claims of how well the economy is doing, include the exponential growth in the Stock Market Index, all suggesting a 'Pakistan Shining' scenario. However, from the point of view of the citizens of Pakistan, many of these numbers are not transformed into conditions that would result in an improvement in the quality of their lives. Even after three years of high growth and rising per capita incomes, most Pakistanis are still waiting for the benefits of this growth to trickle down. Moreover, a growth strategy focused on the rich and upper middle classes, resulting in growing income disparities, is causing rising resentment levels not seen since the 1960s.

Most of the factors that resulted in the poverty-stricken 1990s decade, delineated earlier, have disappeared. The debt burden has been lifted, creating fiscal space; there were no changes in government and leadership from 1999 to 2008, suggesting perhaps a sense of stability; Karachi is no longer at war with itself; the jihadis have been reigned in on account of which there is talk of serious peace and economic cooperation with India; sanctions have not only been lifted but debt write-offs and large amounts of aid have been made available to the government in its support for the war on terror. One needs to emphasize that, *had the New York attack not taken place, it is quite improbable that Pakistan would have been able to get out of the post-nuclear tests and post-military coup scenario, both of which had been damaging to the economy.*[4]

With the growth rate at 8.6 per cent in 2004–05, the highest in two decades, following a growth rate of 7.5 per cent in the previous year; with the fiscal deficit near its lowest in almost two decades; with remittances at their highest levels ever; and with exports crossing the $17 billion mark for the first time and showing signs of further growth; the government is claiming that the economy has rebounded, that there has been a 'turnaround' and that good times of high growth, human development along with political stability, have returned. Even the stock market has soared to inconceivable levels, setting new records every week. It seems that Pakistan is finally out of the ruinous decade of the 1990s and set on course for growth and development on its way to economic prosperity. However, there is no denying the fact that this change has taken place on account of the developments globally and particularly in the region, on account of 9/11, an issue to which we will return a little later.

⬛ Human Development in the 1990s and Today

International Comparisons 1993–2002[5]

It is probably not very wise to compare countries. There are too many factors — history, culture, governments, institutions — that influence events and consequences in very special and specific ways. The context of each event or development must be recognized and appreciated. Often, standards of a very alien kind are imposed across a general universe, which may result in numbers or results that are not comparable. Even so-called scientific criteria are not insensitive to their social environment, and even simply counting and comparing 'obvious facts' can be hazardous. Hence, there are numerous problems in taking a set of indicators showing the state of the health of the economy and comparing them across countries. Nevertheless, this continues to be done and there is a huge industry churning out Ph.D.s and tomes on indicators comparing diverse nations and countries. We too, despite our criticism and concerns, continue that tradition in order to indicate some salient trends.

In this section, we examine the performance of Pakistan in the social sectors in light of that of other developing countries. While it is difficult to make comparisons across countries, it is possibly more difficult to find some countries across which comparisons can be made. In our choice of countries (see Table 12.3) all the eight belonged to the World Bank's classification of Low Income Countries, that is, those with a per capita GNP of less than US$ 730 based on 1993 data — this year is chosen to see how well or badly, countries have performed since.

While the low income status may be the first criterion for our selection of countries, there are some others as well. India, Bangladesh and Sri Lanka share similar histories and belong to South Asia, and are also grouped together in the South Asian Association of Regional Cooperation (SAARC), and hence, can have some valid grounds for comparison. China is included because it is a key player in the region, had a GNP per capita close to that of Pakistan's, and is cited by many as a country where communist-led growth and development in the past has resulted in an egalitarian social structure with extensive social development. The new China with its liberal and open economic programme — like much of the rest of the region — also makes it worth observing. Ghana and Nigeria, while very different from the Asian countries, are included because they have large populations. (Nigeria), as well as Ghana, had a GNP per capita (in 1993) close to or equal to Pakistan's. Also, like the four South Asian countries, they have both been under British Colonialism, and hence some comparison is probably permissible. The outlier is Vietnam, which is included because it is still a Socialist state (like China), but has not had as many years of capitalism as China; and despite having a per capita GNP of only 40 per cent of Pakistan's (in 1993), has some very interesting and revealing social indicators. Possibly, GNP per capita, as is often assumed, may not be the sole, or even the key, criterion for social development. Political commitment, structure and involvement, may be equally, if not more, important.

Table 12.3 is not easy to interpret; indeed, if there are any interpretations that could be made from it. There are no conclusions or hard overriding truths that emerge from the table; it simply offers certain observations open to conjecture. What Table 12.3 does, then, is allow us to examine the pattern and trend of human development in Pakistan in the 1990s, before we turn to trends in recent years.

The first row gives the GNP per capita in US dollars in 1993 for each of the eight countries, followed by the second row showing the GNP per capita for 2002. These rates indicate the rate at which countries have grown over the 1993–2002 decade. China's example is significant, where in a few years it increased its comparative and absolute position: In 1980, China had a GNP per capita of $206 compared to Pakistan's $285, and was one of the poorest countries in the

Table 12.3: International Comparison of the Social Sectors

	Pakistan	Vietnam	Bangladesh	India	Nigeria	Ghana	China	Sri Lanka
GNP pc 1993 ($)	430	170	220	300	300	430	490	600
GNP pc 2002 ($)	410	430	360	480	290	270	940	840
GNP pc rank 1993*	31	5	12	20	21	30	33	39
GNP pc rank 2002*	30	32	27	38	22	18	53	50
HDI rank 1993**	128	120	146	134	141	129	111	97
HDI rank 2003	144	109	139	127	152	129	104	99
Literacy rate 2001	44.0	92.7	40.6	58.0	65.4	72.7	85.8	91.9
Female literacy 2001	28.8	90.9	30.8	46.4	57.7	64.5	92.5	89.3
GDI rank 2003+	120	89	112	103	124	104	83	80
Poverty Index rank#	65	39	72	53	54	46	26	34

Source: S. Akbar Zaidi, *Issues in Pakistan's Economy* (Karachi: Oxford University Press, 2005).

Notes: * The higher the rank, the better — the poorest country is ranked 1; ** The lower the rank the better — the best country is ranked 1 and the worst 175; + Best ranked 1, worst 175; # Best ranked 1, worst 74.

world; with a phenomenal 8.2 per cent average annual growth rate for over two decades, it improved its position markedly. While China, Sri Lanka, Vietnam, India and even Bangladesh, had all substantially improved their per capita GNP values in the 1990s, significantly, Pakistan with Ghana and Nigeria, had not. Rather than be part of the dynamic growth trends of East Asia, which were being mirrored amongst countries of South Asia, *Pakistan increasingly looked like a poor, underdeveloped, African country.*

The GNP per capita rank lists the positions on the basis of GNP per capita that these countries have in the world; Vietnam was the fifth poorest country in the world with a GNP per capita of only $170 in 1993, and Pakistan, with a GNP per capita of $430 was the 31st poorest country out of the 132 then classified by the World Bank. What is most interesting to read from this comparison of ranks of GDP per capita in 1993 and 2002 is that in line with improvements in absolute levels of GDP per capita, those countries that have done well in 1993–2003 have also done relatively better than other countries. While Vietnam was the fifth poorest in 1993, it is now the 32nd poorest, showing considerable improvement, while Pakistan *joined the African countries whose ranks had worsened in this decade.*

While GNP per capita is a very simplistic and crude (yet indicative) measure of social development, the Human Development Index (HDI) is a larger and broader composite indicator that captures much more than just per capita income. The HDI contains three indicators: life expectancy, representing a long and healthy life; educational attainment, representing knowledge; and real GDP (in purchasing power parity dollars), representing a decent standard of living.

Thus, the HDI in Table 12.3 for our selected countries, unlike the GNP per capita, shows a reverse order: the higher the number, the worse the nature and extent of social development. Using the HDI, Pakistan's rank in 1993 was 128th out of 174 countries showing (a lack of) social development, but had fallen further to the 144th position in 2003, mirroring the worsening trend in per capita income. In our sample, Sri Lanka was in 1993 the best of the eight countries selected (97th) and Bangladesh (146th) the worst; ten years later Sri Lanka still remains the best at 99th position, while Nigeria has become the worst in terms of HDI ranking. Again, India, Bangladesh and Vietnam had improved their ranking, but Pakistan had fallen by as *many as fourteen positions down the HDI ladder* in the 1990s.

Not only did Pakistan's social and human development worsen, but so did its comparative position with regard to other countries. In terms of HDI performance, the worst 27 performers — from rank 149 to 175 — were all African countries. In the lowest HDI category called Low Human Development, of the 34 countries, only four were outside of Africa. Pakistan *at position 144, happened to be one of them.* Pakistan's human and social profile after the decade of Democracy and Structural Adjustment, looked more like that of poor African nations, rather than that of South Asian or Latin American states. Even Nepal, Bangladesh and Bhutan had better human and social statistics than Pakistan.

The next segment in Table 12.3 shows one of the most important statistics cited for social development — that of literacy. Overall adult literacy (and importantly, female literacy) is considered to be a fairly good indicator that reveals the true status of social development in any country. In New Growth Theories, where human capital formation is an essential component and prerequisite for growth, literacy acts as an important proxy for many key ingredients. Also, with the need for more skills in the present electronic and computer age, with increasing importance on competition and quality, education and literacy become even more important.

Vietnam, with a GNP per capita about the same as Pakistan's, had education statistics that would put many developed high income economies to shame, as would Sri Lanka. All the four poorest countries in our sample outperformed Pakistan very markedly. Even Bangladesh, which many in Pakistan saw as a country with few prospects, did far better than the much wealthier Pakistan. Some 91 per cent of Vietnamese, and 91 per cent of Sri Lankan women were literate, while only 29 per cent of Pakistani women could read or write. All Sri Lankan girls aged 5–9 were in school, while only half of Pakistani girls were in school, and even Bangladesh had a very impressive record in this area. Bangladesh and Pakistan were again, the worst performers when it came to labour force participation by women: only 8 per cent of Bangladesh, and 13 per cent of Pakistani women, were in the labour force, compared to 47 per cent for, the very poor, Vietnam.

The gender-related development index (GDI), an index created by UNDP, measures the inequalities between men and women, capturing differences of life expectancy; adult literacy; primary, secondary and tertiary enrolment rates; and a standard of living. The GDI in Table

12.3 shows that out of 175 countries, Pakistan and Nigeria performed the worst in our sample, while in Sri Lanka and China, the gender difference between men and women was less severe.

It is difficult to reach any definite conclusions from the myriad of data presented in Table 12.3. However, some general observations can be made:

1. Pakistan's economic and social and human profile over the period 1993–2003 looked increasingly like that of African countries, rather than that of South or East Asia.
2. Most countries in our sample saw their per capita income rise in the 1993–2003 period, except for two African countries — Nigeria and Ghana — *and Pakistan*. The GDP per capita rank of these three countries also fell.
3. Pakistan's literacy rate was abysmally low. With the exception of Bangladesh, all other countries, including Ghana and Nigeria both of which had lower per capita incomes, had better literacy rates.
4. Pakistan's performance was better in terms of health, although with one of the highest population growth rates in the world, problems may occur in the future.
5. Almost all indicators regarding women, showed Pakistan as the worst performer, revealing excessive and unacceptable levels of gender discrimination.

Although there are many contested explanations why this was the case, the decade of the 1990s was indeed the Lost Decade for Pakistan, with poor economic and social development, not just in absolute terms, but compared to many similar countries in the region and around the globe. Has the economic turnaround since 2002–03 resulted in an improvement of social and human development as well?

A Turnaround in Development?

At some point between 2002 and 2004, Pakistan entered the United Nations Development Programme's (UNDP) classification of those ninety or so countries that the Human Development Report (HDR) classifies as 'Medium Human Development'. Since 1990, when the UNDP initiated its annual HDRs, Pakistan was consistently classified as one of the forty or so countries in the 'Low Human Development' category. (As a comparison, both India and Bangladesh too, not surprisingly, were also originally considered in the Low Human Development category, but both moved into the Medium Human Development category well before Pakistan, somewhere towards the end of the 1990s). For many years considered to be a 'middle income country with low human development', perhaps Pakistan was now moving in to the category that better reflected its economic and social characteristics. The fact that this elevation to Medium Human Development came at the beginning of a so-far uninterrupted four year period of economic boom beginning in 2002, with per capita income almost doubling in this short period, implies that perhaps Pakistan's Human Development status and its ranking in 2004 (134/177) may have improved considerably since then.

In this section of the essay, we consider some recent trends in Pakistan's social development, dealing largely with data from the UNDP's HDRs, where some international comparisons can be made and where Pakistan's social and economic progress since at least the 1990s — when the HDR series was initiated — can be compared over the years using one consistent data set. Table 12.4 presents a series for Pakistan's HDI and shows its trend for a period of thirty years.

Table 12.4 shows a number of statistics related to Pakistan's economic and social performance over some decades. First, it shows that Pakistan's HDI value has risen over the last three decades between 1975–2004 by 47 per cent. As a comparison, India's value in the same period has risen by 48 per cent, Bangladesh by 53 per cent and Nepal by 76 per cent over the same period. In the 177 country sample, most countries show an increase in the value of the HDI over this period, some at a faster pace, some slower. In Pakistan's case, as well as many others, the value first rises, but then due to some shocks falls, but then rises again. Many of the poorer African countries in the 1980s and 1990s depict this trend probably due to the two-fold crises — that of structural adjustment and HIV/AIDs. Nevertheless, most developing countries do show overall progress over these three decades and Pakistan's record is no exception.

Between the period 1992–2004, Pakistan's rank fell from 128th in 1992 to 144th in 2001 and has only recently improved, although Pakistan is still below where it was in 1992. Per capita income in purchasing power parity terms also fell sharply between 1992–2001, and has risen again after 2001. From being the 100th country on the basis of per capita income in 1992, Pakistan's rank today is 130th,

Table 12.4: Pakistan's Human Development Index, 1975–2004

	1975	1980	1985	1990	1992	1994	1995	2000	2001	2004
HDI value	0.365	0.388	0.420	0.463	0.483	0.445	0.493	0.511	0.499	0.539
HDI rank					128/174	139/175			144/175	134/177
Per Capita (PC) income PPP ($)					2890	2154			1890	2225
PC income rank					100/174	120/175			137/175	130/177
PC GDP ($)					420	373			415	632

Source: UNDP, *Human Development Report 2006* (New York: Oxford University Press, 2006).

or the 47th poorest country in the world today. However, in terms of the overall size of the economy, Pakistan is the 44th largest economy in the world.

To summarize then, Table 12.4 suggests that in the 1992–2001 period, although there was an improvement in the HDI value by 12 per cent, other countries did far better than Pakistan (since its relative position — rank — deteriorated); Pakistan's per capita income fell as did its relative economic ranking in terms of per capita income. However, all these trends were reversed in the period 2001–04, where there has been considerable improvement. Moreover, given the fact that the period 2004–07 has seen higher growth than in the past, with per capita GDP reportedly having reached $847 by July 2006, one can safely assume that Pakistan's HDI value and rank would both have appreciated even further.

▨ Finally on Track?

What the evidence and data in the last section suggests, is that the 1990s — the Decade of Democracy in Pakistan — was the 'Lost Decade' in terms of social and economic development or the lack of it, and was the creation of underdevelopment, in relative terms — and that it was General Musharraf who gave back to Pakistan the high growth and development path to which Pakistan had been accustomed to for some years. Is this indeed the case?

Evidence from the period 1947–77 seems to show that the trajectory of economic growth was not translated into a corresponding trajectory for human and social development, and equally, low human and social development was still able to support high levels of economic growth. In fact, in the 1971–77 period, despite the low growth, we were able to see considerable reorientation in the delivery and expenditure on social development, which must have led to a marked improvement in outcomes. Between 1977–88, high economic growth did cause an improvement in human and social development indicators, most noticeably in causing poverty to decline, yet this improvement in human and social development did not carry through to the 1990s and sustain the economic growth trend, and in fact, an economic slowdown resulted in a severe deterioration of human development indicators in that decade. Despite the deterioration in human capital in the 1993–2002 period, the economy was able to pick up considerable speed following 9/11, a development that has led to an improvement in indicators in human development.

The high growth/high human development in the 1977–88 period was matched by high development expenditure, with the 1980s being the decade with the highest proportion of the GDP allocated to development. Similarly, the 1990s decade was the period when, as a consequence of poor economic growth and structural adjustment, a restricted fiscal space allowed only 4.7 per cent of the GDP to be spent on development. More interestingly, in the early Musharraf period where, as we show in Table 12.1 the economic slowdown from the 1990s continued, the development expenditure in the 1999–2005 period was a mere 2.6 per cent, amongst the lowest ever. What do these often contradictory and conflicting trends suggest?

The first main observation from our data and discussion suggests, that there are different patterns and processes at work in the period 1947–77 and 1977–2007. In the first, economic growth (either high or low) did not seem to reflect the same sort of trend in the social and human sectors. In the 1977–2007 period, there does seem to be a trend in human development which is reflected in trends in economic growth. A key difference in the model and structure of the type of social development delivery in the pre- and post-1977 period relates to the extent of state involvement and that of the privatization of services. Pakistan adopted a far more open and market-based delivery mechanism for social services after 1977, and perhaps that is why we see a closer relationship between growth and human development. In a market-based system in which the state plays a secondary role, people's incomes will determine their access to health and education services: private sector spending in health, for example, constitutes 76 per cent of the total health sector spending; at primary and secondary level education, one would expect similar trends. Hence, if social sector provision is market-based, one would expect incomes to govern access and hence, outcomes. This could be a possible reason why in the post-1977 period, one sees a closer relationship between economic growth and human development.

Linked with the argument above, perhaps, is the argument of the impact of development expenditure and public policy, more broadly. In the 1971–77 period, there was active intervention in the social sectors as well as increased spending, despite low growth. It is probable that human development outcomes improved as a consequence in this dominantly public sector delivery mechanism. In the 1999–2005 period, despite the fact that development expenditure was abysmally low, since private incomes were rising, the market-based model was more responsive to people's incomes than to development expenditure, resulting in improved human development indicators. This analysis shows that since 1977, private incomes determine human development outcomes, and increased development spending may not ensure better human development. Even if this conclusion is partially correct, it has major repercussions on strategy for development in Pakistan.

If human development outcomes are increasingly determined by the pace of economic growth and the rise in incomes, clearly, economic growth becomes critical for better human and social development. Hence, if economic growth falters, so does the human condition. And, herein lies the Achilles heel of Pakistan's economic and social 'success' and where the international relations and security dimension comes in, in a forceful manner.

Both in the 1980s under General Zia-ul-Haq and under General Musharraf since 1999, international powers — primarily, if not exclusively, the United States, along with international donors — have been more than generous in their support of military dictators in Pakistan when, on both occasions, Pakistan was fighting the US's war on its Afghanistan border as a front-line state. Under both military generals, Pakistan received financial and military aid, special privileges and grants, and political support for the two generals to perpetuate their undemocratic rule over the Pakistani people. Largely on account of this support and financial aid, Pakistan's growth rates in these two eras — as they were under General Ayub, another beneficiary of US largess — soared compared to other periods, particularly the democratic ones, in Pakistan's history. In this Age of Terror, General Musharraf far more than General Zia, has benefited immensely from the geopolitical events since 9/11.

Pakistan's economic growth and as a consequence, its human development improvement, is based on these weak and fragile foundations. If Atlas were to shrug, or Musharraf not to tow the Bush line, it is improbable that the growth seen in Pakistan in recent years would continue for much longer. As it is, trends related to Pakistan's economy suggest that the high growth of the last three years is slowing down, largely because Pakistan's recent growth has been built on a spurt of excess liquidity, mainly in the form of remittances and transfers, much of which have fuelled an artificial asset boom.

As this 'boom' slows down, the more fundamental issues of an un-manageable current account deficit and budget deficit, along with growing inflation, emerge and begin to undo the economic gains of the recent past.

In a market-based model of social development, with the state on the retreat, such a slowing down in the economy will have a deleterious impact on social and human development outcomes. In the context of Pakistan, we may have not seen the trend where increased human development increases economic growth — as in the East Asian model — hence only high economic growth can support improving human capital. Clearly, in the case of Pakistan, it is its international relations and regional and global security issues that determine human development outcomes through the linkages created by donor money and aid. Because of the precarious nature of the relationship between military dictatorship, compliance with US needs and demands in its War on Terror, and economic growth, Pakistan's model of social and human development, is not one to be recommended to other countries.

▓ Notes

1. Some of the historical narrative in this chapter is drawn from S. Akbar Zaidi, *Issues in Pakistan's Economy*, second edition (Karachi: Oxford University Press, 2005). For a more detailed history of the earlier years, see Rashid Amjad and Viqar Ahmad, *The Management of Pakistan's Economy 1947–82* (Karachi: Oxford University Press, 1984).

2. See some of the references in S. Akbar Zaidi, *Issues in Pakistan's Economy*, second edition (Karachi: Oxford University Press, 2005).

3. Despite the highest growth rates for any decade, the literacy rate rose from 18.4 per cent in 1961 to just 21.7 per cent in 1972, the lowest decadal rise between 1947 and 2007.

4. For a detailed analysis of the positive outcomes for the economy as a consequence of 9/11, see S. Akbar Zaidi, 'Pakistan's Economy After 9/11: Will the End be Different this Time Around?', Occasional Paper No. 6, Centre of South Asian Studies, University of Cambridge, May 2005.

5. This section makes use of S. Akbar Zaidi, *Pakistan's Economic and Social Development: The Domestic, Regional and Global Context* (New Delhi: Rupa and Co., 2004).

✳

Bibliography

Abbas, Hassan. *Pakistan's Drift Into Extremism: Allah, the Army, and America's War on Terror.* New Delhi: Pentagon Press, 2005.

Adeney, Katharine and Andrew Wyatt. 'Democracy in South Asia: Getting beyond the Structure–Agency Dichotomy'. *Political Studies,* vol. 52, no. 1 (2004), pp. 1–18.

Adeney, Katharine. 'What Comes After Musharraf?' *Brown Journal of World Affairs,* vol. 14, no. 1 (Fall–Winter 2007), pp. 41–52.

Ahmed, Ishtiaq. *The Concept of an Islamic State: An Analysis of the Ideological Controversy in Pakistan.* New York: St. Martin's Press, 1987.

———. *State, Nation and Ethnicity in Contemporary South Asia.* London and New York: Pinter Publishers, 1998.

———. 'South Asia'. In *Islam Outside the Arab World,* edited by David Westerlund and Ingvar Svanberg. Richmond, Surrey: Curzon, 1999.

———. 'The 1947 Partition of Punjab: Arguments Put Forth before the Punjab Boundary Commission by the Parties Involved'. In *Region and Partition: Bengal, Punjab and the Partition of the Subcontinent,* edited by Ian Talbot and Gurharpal Singh. Karachi: Oxford University Press, 1999.

———. 'The 1947 Partition of India: A Paradigm for Pathological Politics in India and Pakistan'. *Asian Ethnicity,* vol. 3, no. 1 (2002), pp. 9–28.

Alam, Shah. 'Iran–Pakistan Relations: Political and Strategic Dimensions'. *Strategic Analysis,* vol. 28, no. 4 (2004), pp. 526–44.

Alderman, H. 'Saving and Economic Shocks in Rural Pakistan'. *Journal of Development Economics,* vol. 51 (1996), pp. 343–65.

Ali, Ghulam. 'Fifty-Fifth Anniversary of Sino-Pakistan Relations: An Appraisal', http://cfcc.nthu.edu.tw/~chinastudies/fellowship-symposium/Ali's%20Paper%20CfCC.doc (accessed 4 August 2008).

Ali, Imran. *Malign Growth? Agricultural Colonization and the Roots of Backwardness in the Punjab, Past and Present,* no. 114, February 1987, Oxford University Press.

———. *The Punjab under Imperialism, 1885–1947.* Princeton, NJ: Princeton University Press, 1988.

———. 'The Punjab and the Retardation of Nationalism'. In *The Political Inheritance of Pakistan,* edited by D.A. Lowe. London: Macmillan, 1991.

———. 'Telecommunications Development in Pakistan'. In *Telecommunications in Western Asia and the Middle East,* edited by Eli M. Noam. New York and Oxford: Oxford University Press, 1997.

———. 'Business and Power in Pakistan'. In *Power and Civil Society in Pakistan,* edited by Anita M. Weiss and S. Zulfiqar Gilani. Karachi: Oxford University Press, 2001.

———. 'The Historical Lineages of Poverty and Exclusion in Pakistan'. *South Asia,* vol. 25, no. 2 (2002), pp. 33–60.

Ali, Imran. 'Past and Present: The making of the state in Pakistan', in Imran Ali et al. (eds), The Contours of State and Society (Karachi: Oxford University Press, 2002).

———. 'Historical Impacts on Political Economy in Pakistan'. *Asian Journal of Management Cases*, vol. 1, no. 2 (2004), pp. 129–46.

———. 'Business, Stakeholders and Strategic Responses in Pakistan'. Armidale: University of New England Asia Centre Paper No. 8, 2005.

———. 'Re-imagining Punjab: Shackled Potential'. *Seminar* (New Delhi), no. 567, November 2006, pp. 21–25.

———. 'Pakistan'. In *Regionalism and Trade: South Asian Perspectives 2006*. Singapore: Institute of South Asian Studies, National University of Singapore, 2007.

———. 'Power and Islamic Legitimacy in Pakistan'. In *Islamic Legitimacy in a Plural Asia*, edited by Anthony Reid and Michael Gilsenan. London: Routledge, 2007.

Ali, Imran and S. Mumtaz. 'Understanding Pakistan: The Impact of Global, Regional, National and Local Interactions'. In *Pakistan: The Contours of State and Society*, edited by Imran Ali et al. Karachi: Oxford University Press, 2002.

Ali, S. Mubashir and Faisal Bari. 'At the Millennium: Macro Economic Performance and Prospects'. In *Pakistan 2000* edited by Kennedy Charles H. and Baxter Craig. New York: Lexington Books, 2000.

Allana, G. *Pakistan Movement: Historic Documents*. Lahore: Islamic Book Service, 1977.

Amin, Tahir. 'Pakistan, Afghanistan and the Central Asian States'. In *The New Geopolitics of Central Asia and Its Borderlands*, edited by Ali Banuazizi and Myron Weiner. Bloomington, IN: Indiana University Press, 1994.

Amjad, R. 'Impact of Workers' Remittances from the Middle East on Pakistan's Economy: Some Selected Issues'. *The Pakistan Development Review*, vol. 25, no. 4 (1986), pp. 757–82.

Aneja, Urvashi. 'Pakistan–China Relations: Recent Developments (Jan–May 2006)'. IPCS Special Report no. 26 (June 2006), pp. 2–3, http://www.ipcs.org/IPCS-Special-Report_26.pdf (accessed 4 August 2008).

Ansari, Massoud. 'Between Tribe and Country: The Crisis of Balochistan'. *Himal South Asia*, vol. 20, no. 5 (2007), http://www.himalmag.com/2007/may/coverfeature_balochistan.htm (accessed 23 May 2007).

Anwar, Talat. 'Changes in Inequality of Consumption and Opportunities in Pakistan During 2001–02 and 2004–05', Research Report No. 3, Centre for Research on Poverty Reduction and Income Distribution, 2006.

Asma Jilani vs Government of Punjab. Criminal Appeal no. 19 of 1972, PLD *(Pakistan Legal Decisions)* 1972 Supreme Court 139, vol. XXIV, Lahore, n.d., p. 243.

Aziz, Mazhar. *Military Control in Pakistan: The Parallel State*. London and New York: Routledge, 2007.

Bailes, Alyson J. K. et al. *The Shanghai Cooperation Organization*. SIPRI Policy Paper No. 71 Stockholm: SIPRI, May 2007.

Bajpai, Kanti. 'Strategic Threats and Nuclear Weapons: India, China and Pakistan'. In *Prisoners of the Nuclear Dream*, edited by M.V. Ramana and C. Rammanohar Reddy. New Delhi: Orient Longman, 2003.

Bakshi, S. R. 'Resolution Adopted by Council of Action of the All-Parties Shia Conference', held at Poona, 25 December 1945. In *The Making of India and Pakistan: Ideology of the Hindu Mahasabha and Other Political Parties*, vol. 3. New Delhi: Deep & Deep Publications, 1997.

Baldauf, Scott. 'India–Pakistan Rivalry Reaches into Afghanistan'. *Christian Science Monitor* (12 September 2003).

'Balochis of Pakistan: On the Margins of History'. The Foreign Policy Centre Report. London, 2006 (http://fpc.org.uk/fsblob/817.pdf (accessed 31 July 2008).

Bandara, J. S. and Wusheng Yu. 'How Desirable is the South Asian Free Trade Area? A Quantitative Economic Assessment'. *The World Economy*, vol. 26, no. 9 (2003), pp. 1293–1323.

Baxter, Craig, ed. *Zia's Pakistan: Politics and Stability in a Frontline State*. Boulder, Colorado: Westview Press, 1985.

Baysan, T. et al. 'Preferential Trading in South Asia'. World Bank Policy Research Working Paper 3813 (January 2006).

Bhagwati, J. N. 'Immiserizing Growth: A Geometrical Note'. *Review of Economic Studies* (1958), pp. 201–05.

Bhagwati, Jagdish. 'U.S. Trade Policy: The Infatuation with Free Trade Areas'. In Jagdish Bhagwati and Anne O. Krueger, *The Dangerous Drift to Preferential Trade Agreements*. Washington, DC: The AEI Press, 1995.

Bhutto, Benazir. *Reconciliation, Islam, Democracy and the West*. London: Simon and Schuster, 2008.

Binder, Leonard. *Religion and Politics in Pakistan*. California: University of California Press, 1961.

Blank, Stephen. 'India's Rising Profile in Central Asia'. *Comparative Strategy*, vol. 22, no. 2 (April–June 2003), pp. 139–57.

———. 'Russian–Indian Row Over Tajik Base Suggests Moscow Caught in Diplomatic Vicious Cycle'. *Eurasia Net Insight* (1 January 2008), www.eurasianet.org/departments/insight/articles/eav011108f.shtml.

———. 'India: The New Central Asian Player'. *Eurasia Insight* (26 June 2006), http://www.eurasianet.org/departments/insight/articles/eav062606a.shtml (accessed 6 September 2008).

Blecker, R. and A. Razmi. 'The Fallacy of Composition and Contractionary Devaluations: Output Effects of Real Exchange Rate Shocks in Semi-Industrialised Countries'. *Cambridge Journal of Economics*, vol. 32, no. 1 (2008), pp. 83–109.

Borensztein, E. et al. 'How does foreign direct investment affect economic growth?'. *Journal of International Economics*, vol. 45, no. 1 (1998), pp. 115–35.

Burki, Shahid J. *Pakistan under Bhutto, 1971–1977*. London: Macmillan, 1980.

Calabrese, John. 'The Struggle for Security: New and Familiar Patterns in Iran–Pakistan Relations'. *Journal of South Asian and Middle Eastern Studies*, vol. 21, no. 1 (Fall 1997), pp. 61–80.

Carter, Lionel. *Punjab Politics, 1 January 1944 –3 March 1947: Last Years of the Ministries, Governors' Fortnightly Reports and Other Key Documents*. New Delhi: Manohar, 2006.

Chadda, Maya. *Building Democracy in South Asia*. London: Lynne Rienner, 2000.

Chami, R. et al. 'Are Immigrant Remittance Flows a Source of Capital for Development'. *IMF Staff Papers*, vol. 52, no. 1 (April 2005). Washington, DC

Chaudhary, S. N. 'Iran to India Natural Gas Pipeline: Implications for Conflict Resolution & Regionalism in India, Iran, and Pakistan'. *TED Case Studies: An Online Journal*, vol. 11, no. 1 (January 2001), http://www.american.edu/TED/iranpipeline.htm (accessed 6 September 2008).

Cheema, Zafar Iqbal. 'The Role of Nuclear Weapons in Pakistan's Defense Strategy'. *Islamabad Policy Research Institute (IPRI) Journal*, no. 4 (Summer 2004), pp. 59–80.

Cizre, Umit. 'Demythologizing the National Security Concept: The Case of Turkey'. *Middle East Journal*, vol. 57, no. 2 (Spring 2003), pp. 213–29.

Cohen, C. and D. Chollet. 'When $10 Billion is Not Enough: Rethinking U.S. Strategy toward Pakistan'. *The Washington Quarterly*, vol. 30, no. 2 (Spring 2007), pp. 7–19.

Cohen, Stephen P. *The Pakistan Army*. Berkley, CA and Los Angeles: University of California Press, 1984.

———. 'Policy Implication'. In *Nuclear Proliferation in South Asia: The Prospect of Arms Control* (Boulder, CO: Westview Press, 1991).

———. *The Idea of Pakistan*. Washington, DC: Brookings Institution Press, 2004.

Dahl, Robert. *A Preface to Democratic Theory*. Chicago: University of Chicago Press, 1961.

Daly, John C.K. 'The Baloch Insurgency and its Threat to Pakistan's Energy Sector'. *Global Terrorism Analysis*, The James Town Foundation, Terrorism Focus, vol. 3, no. 11 (21 March 2006), http://www.jamestown.org/terrorism/news/article.php?articleid=2369935 (accessed 3 August 2008).

Dreyfuss, Robert. *Devil's Game: How the United States Helped Unleash Fundamentalist Islam*. New York: Metropolitan Books, 2005.

Eichengreen, B. et al. 'The Impact of China on the Exports of Other Asian Countries'. Working paper no. 10768, National Bureau of Economic Research, Cambridge, MA, 2004.

'Ending the Rule of Punjab, by Punjab and for Punjab', Interview with Ataullah Khan Mengal. *Himal South Asia*, vol. 20, no. 5 (2007), http://

www.himalmag.com/2007/may/coverfeature_interview_sardar_ataullah_khan_mengal.htm (accessed 29 August 2007).

Faini, R. et al. 'The Fallacy of Composition Argument: Is it Relevant for LDCs' Manufactures Exports?' *European Economic Review*, vol. 36, no. 4 (1992), pp. 865–82.

Fair, C. Christine. *The Counterterror Coalitions: Cooperation with India and Pakistan.* Santa Monica, CA: RAND, 2004.

———. 'India–Iran Security Ties: Thicker Than Oil'. In *Gauging U.S.–Indian Strategic Cooperation,* edited by H. Carlisle Sokolski. PA: Strategic Studies Institute, 2007.

———. 'India and Iran: New Delhi's Balancing Act'. *The Washington Quarterly,* vol. 30, no. 3 (Summer 2007), pp. 145–59.

Faruki, Kemal. *The Evolution of Islamic Constitutional Theory and Practice.* Karachi: National Publishing House, 1971.

Faruqui, Zia-ul-Haq. *The Deoband School and the Demand for Pakistan.* Lahore: Progressive Books, 1980.

Finer, S. E. *The Man on Horseback.* Harmondsworth, Baltimore: Penguin, 1976.

Franks, Tommy. *American Soldier.* New York: Harper Collins, 2004.

Frazer, Jendayi. 'Conceptualizing Civil–Military Relations during Democratic Transition'. *Africa Today,* vol. 42, no. 1–2 (1995), http://elin.lub.lu.se/link2elin?genre=article&issn=00019887&year=1995&volume=42&issue=1-2&collection=ebsco&pages=39-49&resid=204415063fe08a588 7f240b99238ff30&lang=en (accessed 11 August 2008).

Fulcher, Ray. 'Baluchistan: Pakistan's Internal War'. *Green Left Weekly,* 8 December 2006, http://www.worldpress.org/Asia/2594.cfm (accessed 31 July 2008).

Furuoka, F. 'Japan and the "Flying Geese" Pattern of East Asian Integration'. *Eastasia.at,* vol. 4, no. 1, http://www.eastasia.at/vol4_1/article01.htm.

Ganguly, S. 'Will Kashmir Stop India's Rise?' *Foreign Affairs,* vol. 85, no. 4 (July/August 2006), pp. 45–57.

Gilmartin, David. *Empire and Islam: Punjab and the Making of Pakistan.* Delhi: Oxford University Press, 1989.

Government of India, Central Electricity Authority, http://www.cea.nic.in/hydro/status.

Government of India, Ministry of Defence. *Annual Report Year 2005–2006,* http://www.mod.nic.in/reports.

Government of Pakistan, Board of Investment. *Key Investment Indicators,* http://www.pakboi.gov.pk (accessed 19 August 2008).

Government of Pakistan, Ministry of Finance. *Accelerating Economic Growth and Reducing Poverty: The Road Ahead* (Poverty Reduction Strategy Paper). Islamabad, 2003.

Government of Pakistan, Ministry of Finance. *Economic Survey, 2005–2006.* Islamabad, 2006.

Government of Pakistan, Ministry of Foreign Affairs, Population Census Organization, Statistical Division. *Demographic Indicators in 1998.*

Government of Pakistan. 'President Musharraf's Address at the Inauguration of Gwadar Deep Seaport', http://www.presidentofpakistan.gov.pk/Files Speeches%5CAddresses%5C324200742225AMPreGwadar20Mar07. pdf (accessed 6 September 2008).

Government of Pakistan. *Census of Pakistan 1951*, Report and Tables, Karachi, n.d., vol. 1, pp. 19–23 and vol. 6, p. 65.

Government of Pakistan. *Census of Pakistan: Population 1961.* Karachi: Ministry of Home and Kashmir Affairs (1961), Statement 7-B, pp. iv–46.

Government of Pakistan. *Main Finding of 1981 Population Census.* Islamabad: Population Census Organization, Statistics Division, Government of Pakistan, 6 December 1983, p. 13, table 4(c).

Government of Pakistan. *The Constituent Assembly of Pakistan Debates*, vol. 5. Karachi, 1949.

Government of Pakistan. *The Constitution of the Islamic Republic of Pakistan.* Lahore: Government Printing Press, 1973.

Government of Pakistan. *The Journey to Pakistan: A Documentation on Refugees of 1947.* Islamabad: National Documentation Centre, Islamabad, 1993.

Government of Pakistan. *White Paper on Baluchistan.* Rawalpindi, 1974.

Grare, Frederic. *Pakistan: The Resurgence of Baluch Nationalism.* Carnegie Paper No. 65, Washington, DC: Carnegie Endowment for International Peace, January 2006.

———. *Pakistan–Afghanistan Relations in the Post-9/11 Era.* Carnegie Papers, No. 72. Washington, DC: Carnegie Endowment for Inter-national Peace, October 2006.

Guihong, Zhang. 'US Security Policy Towards South Asia After September 11 and Its Implications for China: A Chinese Perspective'. *Strategic Analysis*, vol. 27, no. 2 (April–June 2003), pp. 145–71.

Gul, Hamid. 'ECO, Strategic Significance in the Context of Islamic Resurgence and Geopolitical Environment'. In Tarik Jan et al. *Foreign Policy Debate: The Years Ahead.* Islamabad: Institute of Policy Studies, Islamabad, 1993.

Hagerty, Devin T. 'Kashmir and the Nuclear Question Revisited'. In *Pakistan 2000,* edited by Charles Kennedy and Craig Baxter. New York: Lexington Books, 2000.

Haider, Ziad. 'Baluchis, Beijing, and Pakistan's Gwadar Port'. *Georgetown Journal of International Affairs* (Winter/Spring 2005), pp. 95–103.

———. 'Sino-Pakistan Relations and Xinjiang's Uighurs: Politics, Trade, and Islam Along the Karakoram Highway'. *Asian Survey*, vol. 45, no. 4 (July–August 2005), pp. 522–45.

Halliday, Fred. 'Iran and the Middle East: Foreign Policy and Domestic Change'. *Middle East Report*, vol. 220 (Autumn 2001), pp. 42–47.

Hamilton, C.B., ed. *Textiles and Trade and the Developing Countries: Eliminating the Multi-Fibre Arrangement in the 1990s.* Washington, DC: The World Bank, 1990.

Haq, Noor-ul- and Sadia Nasir. *Pak-Afghan Relations.* Islamabad: Islamabad Policy Research Institute, August 2003.

Haqqani, Husain. *Pakistan: Between Mosque and Military.* Washington, DC: Carnegie Endowment for International Peace, 2005.

———. *Pakistan: Between Mosque and Military.* Lahore: Vanguard, 2005.

Harb, Imad. 'The Egyptian Military in Politics: Disengagement or Accommodation'. *Middle East Journal,* vol. 57, no. 2 (Spring 2003), pp. 269–90.

Harrison, G. W. et al. 'Quantifying the Uruguay Round'. *Economic Journal,* vol. 107 (1997), pp. 1405–30.

Harrison, Selig. *In Afghanistan's Shadow, Soviet Temptations and Baluch Nationalism.* New York: Carnegie Endowment for International Peace, 1981.

Hasan, Parvez. *Pakistan's Economy at the Crossroads: Past Policies and Present Imperatives.* Karachi: Oxford University Press, 1998.

Hate, V. 'India's Energy Dilemma'. *South Asia Monitor,* vol. 98 (7 September 2006). Washington, DC: Center for Strategic and International Studies.

Heller, Nathaniel et al. 'Pakistan's $4.2 Billion "Blank Check" for U.S. Military Aid'. New York: The Center for Public Integrity (27 March 2007).

Holsti, Ole R. 'A Widening Gap between the U. S. Military and Civilian Society?'. *International Security,* vol. 23, no. 3 (Winter 1998–99), pp. 5–42.

Human Rights Commission of Pakistan, Lahore. *State of Human Rights in Pakistan.*

Hunter, Shireen T. 'Religion, Politics, and Security in Central Asia'. *SAIS Review,* vol. 21, no. 2 (Summer–Fall 2001), pp. 65–90.

Hunter, Wendy. 'Continuity or Change? Civil–Military Relations in Democratic Argentina, Chile and Peru'. *Political Science Quarterly,* vol. 112, no. 3 (Autumn 1997), pp. 453–76.

Huntington, Samuel. 'Patterns of Violence in World Politics'. In *Changing Patterns of Military Politics* edited by S. Huntington. New York: Free Press of Glencoe, 1962.

———. *Political Order in Changing Societies.* New Haven, CT: Yale University Press, 1968.

Hussain, Akmal et al. *National Human Development Report for Pakistan.* Islamabad: UNDP, 2003.

Hussain, Asaf. *Elite Politics in an Ideological State.* Kent: Dawson and Sons, 1979.

Hussain, Mushahid and Akmal Hussain. *Pakistan: Problems of Governance*. Lahore: Vanguard, 1993.

Husain, Ishrat. *Pakistan: The Economy of an Elitist State*. Karachi: Oxford University Press, 1999.

———. *Economic Management in Pakistan 1999–2002*. Karachi: Oxford University Press, 2004.

Hussain, Zahid. *Frontline Pakistan: The Struggle with Militant Islam*. New Delhi: Penguin Books India, 2007.

Intergovernmental Panel on Climate Change. *Climate Change 2007: Impacts, Adaptation and Vulnerability*. Summary for Policymakers (13 April 2007), http://www.ipcc.ch.

International Crisis Group. *India, Pakistan and Kashmir: Stabilising a Cold Peace*. Asia Briefing No. 51. Islamabad/Brussels: International Crisis Group (15 June 2006).

International Crisis Group. *Pakistan: Karachi's Madrasas and Violent Extremism*. Asia Report No. 130. Islamabad/Brussels: International Crisis Group (29 March 2007).

International Crisis Group. *Pakistan's Tribal Areas: Appeasing the Militants*. Asia Report No. 125, Section A(2). Islamabad/Brussels: International Crisis Group (11 December 2006).

International Crisis Group. *The State of Sectarianism in Pakistan*. Asia Report No. 95. Islamabad/Brussels: International Crisis Group (18 April 2005).

Iqbal, Z. and A. Sattar. 'The Contribution of Workers' Remittances to Economic Growth in Pakistan'. Pakistan Institute of Development Economics Research Report No. 187 (2005).

Isard, P. *Globalization and the International Financial System: What's Wrong and What Can Be Done*. Cambridge, UK: Cambridge University Press, 2005.

Jaffrelot, Christopher, ed. *Pakistan: Nationalism Without a Nation*. New Delhi: Manohar, 2002.

———. ed. *A History of Pakistan and Its Origins*, translated by Gillian Berumont. London: Anthem Press, 2004.

Jahangir, Asma and Huma Jilani. *The Hudood Ordinances: A Divine Sanction?* Lahore: Sang-e-Meel Publications, 2003.

Jalal, Ayesha. *The State of Martial Rule: The Origins of Pakistan's Political Economy of Defence*. Cambridge: Cambridge University Press, 1990.

Janowitz, Morris. *The Professional Soldier: A Social and Political Portrait*. New York: The Free Press, 1965.

Jansson, Erland. *India, Pakistan or Pakhtunistan?* Uppsala, Sweden: Acta Universitatis Upsaliensis, 1981.

Jetly, Rajshree. 'Baluch Ethnicity and Nationalism (1971–1981): An Assessment'. *Asian Ethnicity*, vol. 5, no. 1 (February 2004), pp. 7–26.

Jetly, Rajshree. *Re-emergence of the Baluch Movement in Pakistan'*. ISAS Insights No.15, Institute of South Asian Studies, Singapore, October 2006, pp. 1–8.

Job, Brian L., ed. *The Insecurity Dilemma: National Security of Third World States*. Boulder, CO and London: Lynne Rienner, 1992.

Jones, Seth G. 'Pakistan's Dangerous Game'. *Survival*, vol. 49, no. 1 (Spring 2007), pp. 15–32.

Kapur, D. and K. Iyengar. 'The Limits of Integration in Improving South Asian Security'. In *Strategic Asia 2006-07: Trade, Interdependence, and Security*, edited by A.J. Tellis and M. Wills. Seattle, WA: The National Bureau of Asian Research, 2007.

Kasahara, S. 'The Flying Geese Paradigm: A Critical Study of its Application to East Asian Regional Development'. Discussion Paper no. 169. Geneva: United Nations Commission on Trade and Development, 2004.

Kennedy, Charles et al., eds. *Pakistan at the Millennium*. Karachi: Oxford University Press, 2003.

Kennedy, Charles H. 'Analysis of Pakistan's Devolution Plan'. Mimeographed paper, Islamabad 2001.

Kennedy, Charles. 'A User's Guide to Guided Democracy: Musharraf and the Pakistani Military Governance Paradigm'. In *Pakistan 2005*, edited by Charles Kennedy and Cynthia Botteron. Karachi: Oxford University Press, 2006.

Khan, Adnan Sarwar. 'Pakistan's Foreign Policy in the Changing International Scenario'. *The Muslim World*, vol. 96, no. 2 (April 2006), pp. 233–50.

Khan, Hamid. 'Military and Judiciary in Pakistan October 1999 Onwards'. *Journal of South Asian and Middle Eastern Studies*, vol. 26, no. 4 (Summer 2003), pp. 639–53.

Khan, Hamid. *Constitutional and Political History of Pakistan*. Karachi: Oxford University Press, 2001.

Khan, Wali. *Facts Are Facts: The Untold Story of India's Partition*. New Delhi: Vikas Publishing House, 1987.

Khawaja, Asma Shakir. *Pakistan and the 'New Great Game*. Islamabad: Islamabad Policy Research Institute, April 2003, www.ipripak.org/papers/pakandnewgame.shtml (accessed 6 September 2008).

Kim, Yong Cheol et al. 'Political Leadership and Civilian Supremacy in Third Wave Democracies: Comparing South Korea and Indonesia'. *Pacific Affairs*, vol. 79, no. 2 (Summer 2006), pp. 247–68.

Kona, Swapna. 'India in Central Asia: The Farkhor Airbase in Tajikitsan'. *ICPS Article no. 2347*, 4 August 2007, www.ipcs.org/whatsNewArticle11.jsp?action=showView&kValue=2363&status=article&mod=b (accessed 6 September 2008).

KPMG International. *India Energy Outlook 2006*, http://www.in.kpmg.com/pdf/India_Energy_Outlook_2006.pdf (accessed 6 September 2008).

Krepon, Michael. 'A Time of Trouble, A Time of Need'. In *Crisis Prevention, Confidence Building and Reconstruction in South Asia* edited by Michael Krepon and Amit Sevak. New York: St. Martin's Press, 1995.

Kucera, Joshua. 'Shanghai Cooperation Organization Summiteers Take Shot at US Presence in Central Asia'. *Eurasia Insight* (20 August 2007), http://www.eurasianet.org/departments/insight/articles/eav082007a_pr.shtml.

Kukreja, Veena and M.P. Singh, eds. *Pakistan: Democracy, Development and Security Issues.* New Delhi: Sage Publications, 2005.

Kux, Dennis. *Estranged Democracies: India and the United States, 1941–1991.* New Delhi: Sage Publications, 1994.

———. *The United States and Pakistan, 1947–2000: Disenchanted Allies.* Washington, DC: Woodrow Wilson Centre Press, 2001.

———. *India–Pakistan Negotiations: Is Past Still Prologue?* Washington, DC: United States Institute of Peace Press, 2006.

Lafitte, R. *Executive Summary: Baglihar Hydroelectric Plant-Expert Determination on Points of Difference Referred by the Government of Pakistan under the Provisions of the Indus Waters Treaty* (12 February 2007), http://www.pakistan.gov.pk/ministries (accessed 9 August 2008).

Levy, Adrian and Catherine Scott-Clark. *Deception: Pakistan, the United States, and the Global Nuclear Weapons Conspiracy.* New Delhi: Penguin Books India, 2007.

Lewis Jr., Stephen R. *Economic Policy and Industrial Growth in Pakistan.* Cambridge, MA: The MIT Press, 1969.

———. *Pakistan: Industrialization and Trade Policies.* London: Oxford University Press, 1970.

Lodhi, Iftikhar Ahmad. *Forthcoming Pakistani Elections: A Profile on the Islamic Parties.* ISAS Brief no. 39. Singapore: Institute of South Asian Studies, December 2007.

———. *The Grand Jirga Imperative: Is this the Solution to the Taliban Insurgency?* ISAS Brief no. 23. Singapore: Institute of South Asian Studies, September 2007.

Luft, G. 'Iran–Pakistan–India Pipeline: The Baloch Wildcard'. *Energy Security*, Institute for the Analysis of Global Security, 12 January 2005, http://www.iags.org/n0115042.htm (accessed 6 September 2008).

MacDonald, Juli A. 'South Asia'. In *Central Asia and the South Caucasus: Reorientations, Internal Transitions, and Strategic Dynamics.* Conference Report, National Intelligence Council October 2000, http://ftp.fas.org/irp/nic/central_asia.html (accessed 6 September 2008).

Malek, A. Abdel, ed. *Armée et Nations dans les Trios Continents*, Alger 1975 (Originally in English, mimeograph).

Maley, William. *The Afghanistan Wars.* London: Macmillan, 2002.

Malik, Afia. 'Demand for Textile and Clothing Exports of Pakistan'. Pakistan Institute of Development Economics, Research Report No. 180, 2001.

Malik, Hafeez. 'Iran's Relations with Pakistan'. *Journal of South Asian and Middle Eastern Studies* vol. 36, no. 1 (Fall 2002), pp. 56–71.

Mansergh, N. and P. Moon, eds. *The Transfer of Power 1942–47*, vol. 11 (May–July 1947). London: Her Majesty's Stationery Office, 1982.

Marty, Martin E. and R. Scott Appelby. *Fundamentalisms and the State: Remaking Polities, Economies, and Militance*. Illinois and London: University of Chicago Press, 1993.

Matinuddin, Kama. *The Taliban Phenomenon: Afghanistan 1994–1997*. Oxford: Oxford University Press, 1999.

Maududi, Syed Abul Ala. *The Islamic Law and Constitution*. Lahore: Islamic Publications, 1980.

———. *Al-Jihad Fi al-Islam*. Lahore: Idara Tarjuman-ul-Quran, 1981.

———. *Tehrik-i-Azadi-i-Hind Aur Musalman*, 2 vols. Lahore: Islamic Publications, 1981.

McCombie, J. S. L. and A. P. Thirlwall, eds. *Essays on Balance of Payments Constrained Growth: Theory and Evidence*. London: Routledge, 2004.

Mehdi, Rubya. *The Islamization of the Law in Pakistan*. Richmond, Surrey: Curzon Press, 1994.

Menon, Rajan. 'The New Great Game in Central Asia', *Survival*, vol. 45, no. 2 (Summer 2003), pp. 187–204.

Military Advisory Board. *National Security and the Threat of Climate Change*. Alexandria, VA: CNA Corporation, April 2007, http://.SecurityAndClimate. cna.org (accessed 6 September 2008).

Millison, Dan. 'Turkmenistan–Afghanistan–Pakistan–India Natural Gas Pipeline Project'. November 2006, http://www.meaindia.nic.in/srec/internalpages/ tapi.pdf (accessed 6 September 2008).

Minault, Gail. *The Khilafat Movement: Religious Symbolism and Political Mobilization in India*. New Delhi: Oxford University Press, 1999.

Mitra, P. 'Indian Diplomacy Energized by Search for Oil'. *Yale Global*, 14 March 2005, http://www.yaleglobal.yale.edu.

Mitra, Subrata K., ed. *The Postcolonial State in South Asia*. London and New York: Harvestor-Wheatsheaf, 1990.

Mohan, Malik J. 'The China Factor in the India-Pakistan Conflict'. *Parameters: U.S. Army War Quarterly [US]*, vol. 33, no.1 (Spring 2003), pp. 35–50.

Montville, Joseph V. *Conflict and Peacemaking in Multiethnic Societies*. Lexington, MA: Lexington Books, 1989.

Mueller, John. 'Is There Still a Terrorist Threat?' *Foreign Affairs*, vol. 85, no. 5, (September/October 2006), pp. 2–8.

Mumtaz, Khawar and Farida Shaheed. *Women of Pakistan: Two Steps Forward, One Step Back?* Lahore: Vanguard, 1987.

Munir, Muhammad. *From Jinnah to Zia*. Lahore: Vanguard, 1978.

Munro, Ross H. 'Security Implications of the Competition for Influence Among Neighboring States: China, India, and Central Asia'. In *After Empire: The Emerging Geopolitics of Central Asia*, edited by Jed C. Snyder. Washington, DC: National Defense University Press, 1999.

Muscatelli, V.A. et al. 'Intra-NIE Competition in Exports of Manufactures'. *Journal of International Economics*, vol. 37, no. 1 (1994), pp. 29–47.

Musharraf, Pervez. *In the Line of Fire: A Memoir*. New York: Free Press, 2006.

Mustafa, M. Qasim. 'Indo-US Civilian Nuclear Cooperation Agreement: Implications for International Nuclear Non-Proliferation Regime'. *Strategic Studies, Journal of the Institute of Strategic Studies*, Islamabad, vol. 26, no. 4 (Summer 2006), http://www.issi.org.pk/journal/2006_files/no_4/article/a6.htm (accessed 6 September 2008).

Nasr, Vali R. *Jamat Islami: Vanguard of Islamic Revolution*. London: I.B. Tauris, 1994.

———.'International Politics, Domestic Imperatives, and Identity Mobilization: Sectarianism in Pakistan, 1979–1998'. *Comparative Politic*, vol. 32, no. 2 (January 2000), pp. 171–90.

Niazi, T. 'Gwadar: China's Naval Outpost on the Indian Ocean'. *Association for Asian Research*, 28 February 2005, http://www.asianresearch.org/articles/2528.html (accessed 6 September 2008).

Noman, Omar. *The Political Economy of Pakistan*. London and New York: KPI, 1988.

Pakistan National Human Development Report 2003, UNDP, Pakistan, by Wasay Majid and Akmal Hussain, http://www.un.org.pk/nhdr/htm_pages/cp_1.htm (accessed 6 September 2008).

Pakistan Statistical Yearbook, 2006. Islamabad: Federal Bureau of Statistics, 2006.

Pakistan's Waters at Risk. Lahore: World Wildlife Foundation, 2007.

Palley, T. 'Export-led Growth: Evidence of Developing Country Crowding-out'. In *Globalization, Regionalism, and Economic Activity*, edited by P. Arestis et al. Northampton, MA: Edward Elgar, 2003.

Pan, Esther. 'China and Pakistan: A Deepening Bond'. Council on Foreign Relations, 8 March 2006, p. 4, http://www.cfr.org/publication/10070/china-and-pakistan.html (accessed 6 September 2008).

Papanek, Gustav F. *Pakistan's Development: Social Goals and Private Incentives*. Cambridge, MA: Harvard University Press, 1967.

PILDAT (Pakistan Institution of Legislative Development and Transparency). 'National Security Council: A Comparative Study of Pakistan and Other Selected Countries'. Background Paper, August 2005.

Qadri, Anwar Ahmad. *Islamic Jurisprudence in the Modern World*. Lahore: Sh. Muhammad Ashraf, 1981.

Rahman, Fazl-ur. 'Pakistan's Evolving Relations with China, Russia and Central Asia'. In *Eager Eyes Fixed on Eurasia: Russia and Its Neighbors in Crisis*, edited by Iwashita Akihiro. Sapporo: Slavic Research Center, Hokkaido 2007, http://src-h.slav.hokudai.ac.jp/coe21/publish/no16_1_ses/contents.html (accessed 6 September 2008).

Raman, B. *Dargai and Chenagai, Waiting to Hear Zawahiri's Version*. International Terrorism Monitor, Paper no. 152 (also Paper 2022),

13 November 2006. South Asia Analysis Group, http://www. southasiaanalysis.org/%5Cpapers21%5Cpaper2022.html (accessed 6 September 2008).

Ramana, M.V. and C. Rammanohar Reddy, eds. *Prisoners of the Nuclear Dream.* New Delhi: Orient Longman, 2003.

Rana, Muhammad Amir. *A to Z of Jehadi Organizations in Pakistan.* Lahore: Mashal Books, 2004.

Rashid, Ahmed. 'The Taliban: Exporting Terrorism', *Foreign Affairs*, vol. 78, no.1 (November–December 1999), pp. 22–35.

———. *Taliban: Militant Islam, Oil and Fundamentalism in Central Asia.* New Haven, CT: Yale University Press, 2000.

Rashid, Amjad and Viqar Ahmad. *The Management of Pakistan's Economy 1947–82.* Karachi: Oxford University Press, 1984.

Razmi, A. and Robert Blecker. 'Developing Country Exports of Manufacturers: Moving Up the Ladder to Escape the Fallacy of Composition?'. *Journal of Development Studies*, vol. 44, no. 1 (January 2008), pp. 21–48.

Reetz, Dietrich. 'Islamic Activism in Central Asia and the Pakistan Factor'. *Journal of South Asian and Middle Eastern Studies*, vol. 23, no. 1 (Fall 1999), pp. 1–37.

Rizvi, Hasan-Askari. *The Military and Politics in Pakistan 1947–86.* Lahore: Progressive Publishers, 1986.

———. *Military, State and Society in Pakistan.* London: Macmillan, 2000.

Rodriguez-Delgado, J. D. 'SAFTA: Living in a World of Regional Trade Agreements'. Working Paper Number WP/07/23, International Monetary Fund, 2007.

Rubin, Barnett R. 'Afghanistan Under the Taliban'. *Current History*, vol. 98, no. 625 (February 1999), pp. 79–91.

———. *The Fragmentation of Afghanistan: State Formation and Collapse in the International System.* New Haven, CT: Yale University Press, 2002.

Rubin, Barnett R. and Abubakar Siddique. 'Resolving the Pakistan–Afghanistan Stalemate'. Special Report 176, United States Institute of Peace. Washington: U.S. Institute of Peace, October 2006.

Sagan, Scott D. 'How to Keep the Bomb from Iran'. *Foreign Affairs*, vol. 85 (September–October 2006), pp. 45–59.

Saikal, Amin. 'The Role of Outside Actors in Afghanistan'. *The Middle East Policy*, vol. 7, no. 4 (October 2000), pp. 50–57.

———. *Modern Afghanistan: A History of Struggle and Survival.* London: I. B. Tauris, 2006.

———. *The Rise and Fall of the Shah: Iran from Autocracy to Religious Rule.* Princeton, NJ: Princeton University Press, 2009.

Samad, Yunas. *A Nation in Turmoil: Nationalism and Ethnicity in Pakistan 1937–1958.* New Delhi: Sage Publications, 1995.

Sethi, Harsh, ed. *State of Democracy in South Asia.* New Delhi: Centre for the Study of Developing Societies (CSDS), 2006.

Siddiqa, Ayesha. *Military Inc.: Inside Pakistan's Military Economy*. Karachi: Oxford University Press, 2007.

Siddiqi, A. R. *The Military in Pakistan: Image and Reality*. Lahore: Vanguard, 1996.

Siddiqi, T. A. and S. Tahir-Kheli, *Water Demand–Supply Gaps in South Asia and Approaches to Closing the Gaps*, vol. 1, Global Environment and Energy in the 21st Century, Honolulu, 2003.

Smith, David O., ed. *From Containment to Stability: Pakistan–United States Relations in the Post-Cold War Era*. Washington, DC: National Defense University, November 1993.

Smith, Dianne L. *Central Asia: A New Great Game?* Washington, DC: Strategic Studies Institute, U.S. Army War College, 1996.

Soros, George. *The Age of Fallibility: Consequences of the War on Terror*. New York: Public Affairs, 2006.

Speeches and Writings of Mr. Jinnah, vol. II. Lahore: Sh. Muhammad Ashraf, 1976.

Srinivasan, T.N. 'Regional Trading Arrangements and Beyond: Exploring Some Policy Options for South Asia'. *World Bank Report* no. IDP 42. Washington, DC: 1994.

Stanley, William Deane. 'El Salvador: State-Building before and after Democratisation: 1980–95'. *Third World Quarterly*, vol. 27, no. 1 (2006), pp. 101–14.

Stiftung, Bertelsmann. *Bertelsmann Transformation Index 2006: Toward Democracy and a Market Economy*. Bertelsmann Foundation (August 2006).

Stratchan, Hew. 'The Civil–Military "Gap" in Britain'. *The Journal of Strategic Studies*, vol. 26, no. 2 (June 2003), pp. 43–63.

Sullivan, Daniel P. 'Tinder, Spark, Oxygen, and Fuel: The Mysterious Rise of the Taliban'. *Journal of Peace Research*, vol. 44, no. 1 (2007), pp. 93–108.

Tahirkheli, Shirin. 'The Military in Contemporary Pakistan'. *Armed Forces and Society*, vol. 6, no. 4 (Summer 1980), pp. 639–53.

Talbot, Ian. *Khizr Tiwana, the Punjab Unionist Party and the Partition of India*. Richmond, Surrey: Curzon Press, 1996.

———. *Pakistan: A Modern History*. London: Hurst and Company, 1998.

Talbott, Strobe. *Engaging India: Diplomacy, Democracy, and the Bomb*. Washington, DC: Brookings Institution Press, 2004.

Tan, Tai Yong. 'Punjab and the Making of Pakistan, The Roots of a Civil Military State'. *South Asia, Journal of South Asian Studies*, vol. 18, supplement 1 (1995), pp. 177–92.

Taneja, Nisha. '*India-Pakistan Trade*'. Working Paper no. 182. New Delhi: Indian Council for Research on International Economic Relations/ ICRIER, June 2006.

Tapper, Richard. 'Tribal Society and its Enemies'. *RAIN*, no. 34, Royal Anthropological Institute of Great Britain and Ireland, London (October 1979), pp. 6–7.

Tellis, Ashley. 'US Strategy: Assisting Pakistan's Transformation'. *The Washington Quarterly*, vol. 28, no. 1 (Winter 2004–05), pp. 97–116.

Thakurta, P. G. 'Iran–Pakistan–India Gas Pipeline in Trouble'. *Counter Currents*, 14 February 2006, http://www.countercurrents.org/india-thakurta140206.htm (accessed 6 September 2008).

The Report of the Court of Inquiry Constituted under Punjab Act II of 1954 to Enquire into the Punjab Disturbances of 1953 (Munir Report). Lahore: Government Printing Press, 1954.

Thirlwall, A. P. and M. N. Hussain. 'The Balance of Payments Constraint, Capital Flows and Growth Rate Differences between Developing Countries'. *Oxford Economic Papers*, vol. 34 (November 1982), pp. 498–509.

Turner, Jefferson E. 'What's Driving India's and Pakistan's Interest in Joining the Shanghai Cooperation'. *Strategic Insights*, vol. 4, no. 8 (August 2005).

U.S. Central Intelligence Agency. *The World Factbook 2007* (last updated September 2007), www.cia.gov/library/publications/the-world-factbook (accessed 6 September 2008).

UBS Investment Research. *Asian Economic Perspectives, Pakistan Arrives.* Hong Kong: UBS, 2006.

UNCTAD. *Trade and Development Report.* United Nations Commission on Trade and Development 2003 (Geneva: UNCTAD, 2003).

———. *Trade and Development Report.* United Nations Commission on Trade and Development 2005 (Geneva: UNCTAD, 2005).

———. *World Economic Situation and Prospects,* United Nations Commission on Trade and Development 2007 (Geneva: UNCTAD, 2007).

Vennesson, Pascal. 'Civil–Military Relations in France: Is there a Gap?' *The Journal of Strategic Studies*, vol. 26, no. 2 (June 2003), pp. 29–42.

Viner, Jacob. *The Customs Union Issue.* New York: Carnegie Endowment for Peace, 1950.

Viola, Edward and Scot Mainwaring. 'Transitions to Democracy: Brazil and Argentina in the 1980s'. *Journal of International Affairs,* vol. 38, no. 2 (1985), pp. 193–210.

Waseem, Mohammad. *Politics and the State in Pakistan.* Islamabad: National Institute of Historical and Cultural Research, 1994.

———. 'Mohajirs in Pakistan: A Case of Nativization of Migrants'. In *Community, Empire and Migration,* edited by Crispin Bates. New York: Palgrave, 2000.

———. *Democratization in Pakistan: A Study of the 2002 Elections.* Karachi: Oxford University Press, 2006.

Weaver, Mary Ann. *Pakistan: In the Shadow of Jihad and Afghanistan.* New York: Farrar, Straus, and Giroux, 2002.

Weber, Max. 'Bureaucracy'. In *From Max Weber: Essays in Sociology* edited by H.H Gerth and Mills C. Wright. New York: Oxford University Press, 1958.

Weinbaum, Marvin G. and Jonathan B. Harder. 'Pakistan's Afghan Policies and Their Consequences'. *Contemporary South Asia*, vol. 16, no.1 (2008), pp. 25–38.

Weinbaum, Marvin. *Afghanistan and its Neighbors: An Ever Dangerous Neighborhood*. *USIP Special Report no.* 162. Washington, DC: United States Institute of Peace, June 2006.

Weinbaum, Marvin. G. 'Musharraf as Catalyst: Balancing Counterterrorism and Reforms'. Testimony before the Senate Foreign Relations Committee, 14 July 2004.

Whalley, John. 'The Post-MFA Performance of Developing Asia'. Working Paper no. 12178, National Bureau for Economic Research, Washington, DC, 2006.

Wirsing, Robert G. *The Baluchis and Pathans*. Minority Rights Group Report no. 48. London: Minority Rights Group, 1987.

———. *Kashmir in the Shadow of War: Regional Rivalries in a Nuclear Age*. Armonk, NY: M.E. Sharpe, 2003.

———. 'Hydro-Politics in South Asia: The Domestic Roots of Interstate River Rivalry'. *Asian Affairs*, vol. 34, no. 1 (Spring 2007), pp. 3–22.

Wirsing, Robert G. and C. Jasparro. 'River Rivalry: Water Disputes, Resource Insecurity, and Diplomatic Deadlock in South Asia'. *Water Policy*, vol. 9, no. 3 (April–May 2007), pp. 231–51.

Woodruff, Philip. *The Men Who Rule India: The Guardians*. London, 1954.

World Bank. Trade Policies in South Asia: An Overview. *World Bank Report* 29949. Washington, DC, 2004.

———. *Pakistan's Water Economy: Running Dry*. Islamabad: World Bank, 2005.

———. *Water Economy: Running Dry*. Report No. 34081-PK. Washington, DC: World Bank, 14 November 2005.

Zaheer, Syed Ali. 'Letter to Quaid-e-Azam by Syed Ali Zaheer, July 1944 and the Quaid's reply'. In G. Allana, *Pakistan Movement: Historic Documents*. Lahore: Islamic Book Service, 1977.

Zaidi, S. Akbar. *Pakistan's Economic and Social Development: The Domestic, Regional and Global Context*. New Delhi: Rupa and Co., 2004.

———. *Issues in Pakistan's Economy*, second edition. Karachi: Oxford University Press, 2005.

———. 'Pakistan's Economy After 9/11: Will the End be Different this Time Around?'. Occasional Paper No. 6, 2004, Centre of South Asian Studies, University of Cambridge, May 2005.

Zaman, Aly. 'India's Increased Involvement in Afghanistan and Central Asia: Implications for Pakistan'. *IPRI Journal* (Summer 2003), www.ipripak.org/journal/summer2003/indiaincreased.shtml (accessed 6 September 2008).

Zeb, Rizwan. 'Cross Border Terrorism Issues Plaguing Pakistan–Afghanistan Relations'. *China and Eurasia Forum Quarterly*, vol. 4, no. 2 (2006), pp. 69–74.

———. 'Pakistan and the Shanghai Cooperation Organization'. *China and Eurasian Forum Quarterly*, vol. 4, no. 4 (2006), http://www.silkroadstudies.org/new/docs/CEF/Quarterly/November_2006/Zeb.pdf (accessed 6 September 2008).

✳

About the Editor

Rajshree Jetly is Research Fellow, Institute of South Asian Studies, National University of Singapore, Singapore. Her general areas of expertise include ethnic conflicts and nation-building, as well as regional cooperation and confidence building in the South Asian region. Her present concerns focus on the domestic and international politics of Pakistan, and its impact on foreign policy and international relations, especially with respect to the United States, India and China. Her work has been widely published in books and international journals. Some of her articles include 'The Khalistan Movement in India: The Interplay of Politics and State Power' (2008); 'Tamil Nadu: Regional Politics and its bearing on Government Policies' (2007); 'Baluch Ethnicity and Nationalism (1971–81): An Assessment' (2004); 'Conflict Management Strategies in ASEAN: Perspectives for SAARC' (2003); and 'South Asian Association for Regional Co-operation (SAARC): Problems and Prospects' (1995). She has also written several policy papers and reports, newspaper articles, and has appeared in a number of media interviews on radio and television.

✳

Notes on Contributors

Ishtiaq Ahmed is Visiting Senior Research Fellow, Institute of South Asian Studies (ISAS) and Visiting Research Professor, South Asian Studies Programme, National University of Singapore and Professor of Political Science (on leave), Stockholm University. He has authored *The Concept of an Islamic State: An Analysis of the Ideological Controversy in Pakistan* (1987), as well as a major comparative study of separatism in South Asia entitled *State, Nation and Ethnicity in South Asia* (1996). He is the editor of *The Politics of Group Rights: The State and Multiculturalism* (2005). He has also contributed many chapters to academic books and articles to scholarly journals. At the ISAS, he has begun working on a research project 'The Pakistan Garrison State: Origins, Evolution and Future'. The aim of the study is to generate a comprehensive analysis of the reasons why the military came to play the dominant role in Pakistani politics. He is also in the process of completing a key study based on first-hand accounts of the partition of the Punjab in 1947. The research project has been funded by the Swedish Research Council (Vetenskapsrådet). In addition, he has written extensively on the politics of South Asia, especially on Pakistan, for academic books and journals. He is the chief editor of the electronic peer-reviewed journal, *Peace and Democracy in South Asia (PDSA)*. Apart from writing a weekly column in the Pakistan English-language newspaper, *The News International*, he is a frequent commentator on Pakistani politics in Singapore media.

Imran Ali is Professor of Economic History and Business Policy, Lahore University of Management Sciences. Previously, he has taught Economic History at the University of New South Wales and the University of Melbourne in Australia. He has been an Honorary Research Fellow, Institute of Commonwealth Studies, University of London; and a Visiting Scholar at the Harvard Business School, and at the School of Economics, University of Sydney, Australia. At LUMS, he has been Dean of Research, Head of the Department of Social Sciences, and Director of the Centre of Management and Economic Research. Professor Ali has several international publications on Pakistan and the Punjab, including *The Punjab under Imperialism, 1885–1947* (1988). He has published in international journals such as *Past and Present*, *The Asian Journal of Management Cases*, *Seminar* and *South Asia*. He has also served as consultant to several national and international organizations, most recently with the World Bank on Pakistan's water sector. Professor Ali has also been a member of various committees in both government and non-government sectors, including the Punjab Finance Commission, the Syndicate of Punjab University, the Institutional Review Board of the Shaukat Khanum Cancer Hospital and Research Centre, and the International Council of the Asia Society (USA). His research interests are in political economy, strategic management, agribusiness, and the history of agrarian and business development in Pakistan.

Kanti Bajpai is Headmaster, Doon School, Dehradun. He has taught at the School of International Studies, Jawaharlal Nehru University, and Maharajah Sayajirao University of Baroda. Amongst his publications are *Brasstacks and Beyond: Perception and Management of Crisis in South Asia* (1995) and *Roots of Terrorism* (2002). He specializes in India's foreign and security policy and South Asia.

Pervaiz Iqbal Cheema is President, Islamabad Policy Research Institute (IPRI). He was Professor of International Relations, Quaid-i-Azam University, Islamabad, Pakistan until July 1995. He has held various positions at both academic and administrative levels — he has been Director General, Academy of Educational Planning and Management, Ministry of Education, Government of Pakistan; Professorial Iqbal Fellow at South Asia Institute, Heidelberg University, Germany; Chairman, Department of International Relations and Department of Defence and Strategic Studies, Quaid-i-Azam University. Dr Cheema's articles have regularly appeared both in national as well as international academic journals, popular magazines and daily newspapers. He has published more than 100 research articles and over 500 other general articles and columns. In addition, Dr Cheema has authored many books and monographs, including *A Select Bibliography of Periodical Literature on India and Pakistan 1947–70*, in three volumes; *Quaid-i-Azam as a Strategist* (1977); *Restraints in Korean War* (1978); *Conflict and Cooperation in the Indian Ocean: Pakistan's Interests and Choice* (1980); and *Pakistan's Defence Policy 1947–58* (1990). He co-authored *Brasstacks and Beyond: Perceptions and Management of Crisis in South Asia* (1995). In addition, he co-edited *Nuclear Non-Proliferation in India and Pakistan:*

South Asian Perspectives (1996); *Perceptions, Politics and Security in South Asia: The Compound Crisis of 90* (2003); *Conflict Resolution and Regional Cooperation in South Asia* (2004); *Arms Race and Nuclear Developments in South Asia* (2004); *Tribal Areas of Pakistan: Challenges and Responses* (2005); *The Kashmir Imbroglio: Looking Towards the Future* (2005); *Problems and Politics of Federalism in Pakistan* (2006); and *Political Violence and Terrorism in South Asia* (2006).

C. Christine Fair is a senior political scientist with the RAND Corporation. Prior to rejoining RAND, she served as a political officer to the United Nations Assistance Mission to Afghanistan in Kabul and as a senior research associate in USIP's Center for Conflict Analysis and Prevention. Prior to joining USIP in April 2004, she was an associate political scientist at the RAND Corporation. Her research focuses upon the security competition between India and Pakistan, Pakistan's internal security, the causes of terrorism in South Asia, and US strategic relations with India and Pakistan. She has authored, co-authored and co-edited several books including *Treading Softly on Sacred Ground: Counterinsurgency Operations on Sacred Space* (2008); *The Madrassah Challenge: Militancy and Religious Education in Pakistan* (2008); *Fortifying Pakistan: The Role of U.S. Internal Security Assistance* (2006); *Securing Tyrants or Fostering Reform? U.S. Internal Security Assistance to Repressive and Transitioning Regimes* (2006); *The Counterterror Coalitions: Cooperation with Pakistan and India* (2004); *Urban Battle Fields of South Asia: Lessons Learned from Sri Lanka, India and Pakistan* (2004) and has written numerous peer-reviewed articles covering a range of security issues in Pakistan, India, Sri Lanka and Bangladesh. She is a member of the International Institute of Strategic Studies, London and is the Managing Editor of *India Review*.

Selig S. Harrison is currently a Senior Scholar of the Woodrow Wilson International Center for Scholars and Director of the Asia Programme at the Center for International Policy. He studied India, Pakistan and Afghanistan as an Associated Press correspondent (1951–54), South Asia Bureau Chief of The Washington Post (1962–65) and Senior Associate of the Carnegie Endowment for International Peace (1974–96). Dr Harrison is the author of four books relating in whole or in part to South Asia including *India: The Most Dangerous Decades* (1960); *The Widening Gulf: Asian Nationalism and American Policy* (1978); *In Afghanistan's Shadow:*

Baluch Nationalism and Soviet Temptations (1980); and *Out of Afghanistan: The Inside Story of the Soviet Withdrawal* (with Diego Cordovez) (1996). His numerous articles on South Asia have appeared in *Foreign Affairs*, *Foreign Policy*, *The Washington Post*, *The New York Times*, *The Los Angeles Times*, the *Financial Times* and other publications.

Arslan Razmi received his Doctorate in Economics from American University in Washington, DC, in August 2004 and has since been a faculty member at the University of Massachusetts at Amherst where he teaches graduate and undergraduate courses in international trade, macroeconomics, and international finance. His research examines issues related to international trade and finance, open economy macroeconomics, development, and political economy. Dr Razmi's recent work, which has focused on balance of payments-related constraints on the growth of developing countries, the distributional impacts of trade-related reforms, and the limitations of the export-led growth paradigm, borrows from diverse streams of economic theory. Other ongoing research includes an investigation of the effects of currency devaluations on developing economies. His work has recently been published or is forthcoming in the *Cambridge Journal of Economics*, *Journal of Development Studies*, *Journal of Post Keynesian Economics*, and *International Review of Applied Economics*.

Amin Saikal is Professor of Political Science and Director of the Centre for Arab and Islamic Studies (The Middle East and Central Asia) at the Australian National University. He is a specialist in the politics, history, political economy and international relations of the Middle East and Central Asia. He has been a Visiting Fellow at Princeton University, Cambridge University and the Institute of Development Studies (University of Sussex), as well as a Rockefeller Foundation Fellow in International Relations (1983–88). In April 2006, he was appointed Member of the Order of Australia for service to the international community and to education through the development of the Centre for Arab & Islamic Studies, and as an author and adviser. He is also a member of many national and international academic organizations, and has authored as well as edited numerous works on the Middle East, Central Asia, and Russia. He is the author of *The Rise and Fall of the Shah: Iran from Autocracy to Religious Rule* (2009); *Modern Afghanistan: A History of Struggle and Survival* (2006); *Islam and the West: Conflict or Cooperation?* (2003); and co-author of *Regime Change in Afghanistan: Foreign Intervention and the Politics of Legitimacy* (1991). He co-edited *The Soviet Withdrawal from Afghanistan* (1989); *Russia in Search of its Future* (1995); *Lebanon Beyond 2000* (1997); *Democratization in the Middle East: Experiences, Struggles, Challenges* (2003); and *Islamic Perspectives on the New Millennium* (2004). Professor Saikal has also published numerous articles in international journals, as well as many feature articles in major international newspapers, including the *International Herald Tribune*. He is also a frequent commentator on radio and television.

Mohammad Waseem is Professor of Political Science in Lahore University of Management Sciences (LUMS). He has written on ethnic, Islamic, constitutional, electoral and sectarian politics of Pakistan. His books include *Politics and the State in Pakistan* (1989); *The 1993 Elections in Pakistan* (1994); and *Democratization in Pakistan* (2006); and *Strengthening Democracy in Pakistan* (with S. J. Burki) (2002). He edited *Electoral Reform in Pakistan* (2002). Professor Waseem was Chairman of International Relations Department, Quaid-i-Azam University Islamabad from 2000 to 2006. He was Pakistan Chair at St Antony's College, Oxford from 1995 to 1999. He has been Visiting Professor in Sciences Po Paris; Visiting Scholar in International Programme for Advanced Studies MSH, Paris; Fulbright Fellow in New Century Scholars Programme at The Brookings Institution, Washington, DC; fellow of the Ford Foundation at Oxford; DAAD fellow at the University of Heidelberg; Fulbright Fellow at Columbia University, New York; fellow of the Indian Historical Research Council, New Delhi; fellow of the British Council in London; and fellow of the American Political Science Association in Washington, DC. Professor Waseem has been on the editorial boards of international academic journals *Ethnicities* (Bristol), *Contemporary South Asia* (Bradford) and *International Studies* (New Delhi). He was the team leader of research projects sponsored by DFID London and UNDP Islamabad. He was the country coordinator for Pakistan for a survey project on Democracy in South Asia sponsored by the Ford Foundation.

Robert G. Wirsing is currently Visiting Professor at Georgetown University's School of Foreign Service in Qatar. Previously, he was a member of the faculty of the Asia-Pacific Center for Security Studies in Honolulu (2000–08) and of the Department of Government and International Studies, University of South Carolina (1971–2000). A specialist on South Asian politics and international relations, he has made over 40 research trips to the South Asian region since 1965. His publications include *Pakistan's Security Under Zia, 1977–1988* (1991); *India, Pakistan, and the Kashmir Dispute* (1994); *Kashmir in the Shadow of War* (2002); he co-edited *Religious Radicalism & Security in South Asia* (2004); and *Ethnic Diasporas and Great Power Strategies in Asia* (2007). His recent research focuses primarily on the politics and diplomacy of river resource management in South Asia.

S. Akbar Zaidi is an independent Karachi-based social scientist. For around fourteen years he taught and researched at the Applied Economics Research Centre, University of Karachi, where he was Senior Research Economist/Associate Professor. Professor Zaidi undertakes research on social, economic and development issues. He has published in numerous international professional journals on themes as diverse as devolution, health sociology, local government, fiscal policy, and on international financial institutions. Professor Zaidi has also published eleven books, two of which, *Issues in Pakistan's Economy* (2005) and *The New Development Paradigm: Papers on Institutions, NGOs, Gender and Local Government* (1999), have become standard textbooks for graduate and postgraduate students of Pakistan's Economy and on Development Economics, in Universities in Pakistan and abroad. More recently, his books include *The Dismal State of the Social Sciences in Pakistan* (2002); *Continuity and Change: Socio-Political and Institutional Dynamics in Pakistan* (2003); and *Pakistan's Economic and Social Development* (2004).

✳

INDEX

Adeney, Katharine 192
Afghan jihad 166–67, 175,
Afghanistan 24–28, 35–42, 64–70,
  73–74, 76, 82, 125–39, 141–43,
  165–67, 225–26, 240–41; Akbar
  Ahmed on 371; anti-Taliban
  forces in 4; its civil war against
  Uzbek and Tajik ethnic groups
  141; and Pakistan's demand 11–
  12; Pakistan's goals for 135–38;
  and Pashtun identity 35–38;
  refusal to recognize Durand Line
  40; ties with New Delhi 1; US
  invasion of 52, 296
Agreement on Textiles and Clothing
  (ATC) 286
Ahmadinejad, Mahmoud 56, 140
Ahmed, Mushtaq, escape of 29
Aid-led growth and remittance
  295–300
Airborne Warning Control System
  (AWACS), China's supply of 86
Akbar, Mughal Emperor 154
Akram, Munir 58
Alavi, Hamza 188
Ali, Sardar Asif Ahmed 140
Al-Jihad Fi al-Islam, Maududi 160
Alliance for Restoration of Democracy (ARD) xv
Al-Qaeda xviii, 20–21, 25–27, 40,
  42, 52, 76, 89–91; action against
  34; attacks of 7; leaders captured
  by Pakistan 25; training facility
  39; Islamic radical movements
  linked to 27
anti-Ahmadiyya riots 160–61
anti-Bhutto movement 197, see also
  Bhutto, Benazir
anti-Indianism 194–95
anti-Shia *tanzeems* 132

anti-US sentiments xviii
Armitage, Richard 23
ASEAN (Asia, the emergence of
  Southeast Asian Nations) 68,
  103, 285–86, 290
Ataturk, Mustafa Kemal 6
Awami National Party (ANP) 181
Ayman al-Zawahiri 172
Aziz, Abdul xxiv
Aziz, Shaukat 56, 222; economic ma-
  nagement team headed by 252

Baba, Rahman 36
Babar, Naseerullah 127
Badawi, Abdullah of Malaysia 21
Bakhtiar, Nilofer 172
Baluch Liberation Army (BLA) 214,
  216, 224, 227, 230n2, see also
  Baluchistan
Baluchistan xxv, 213–22, 224–29;
  Akbar Khan Bugti as leader of
  xxv; Al-Qaeda/Taliban base
  shifting to xxv; Al-Qaeda–Baluch
  nexus 229; attack on Marri camps
  215; BLA guerrillas in 215;
  development 218; exploitation
  of natural resources 217; gas
  resources, Islamabad's utilization
  of 135; government perspective
  221; insurgency in 223–27, 214,
  227–30; marginalization of 218–
  23; Musharraf government's
  heavy-handedness 215; political
  representation level 220–21;
  Sardari system of 216; socio-
  economic underdevelopment
  216–18; violence in Gwadar and
  elsewhere 135
Bangladesh 31, 200, 242, 253,
  290–91, 324–27

Beg, Mirza Aslam 130
Bharatiya Janata Party (BJP) 48
Bhutto, Begum Nusrat 202
Bhutto, Benazir xxvii, 2, 66, 203;
   as alternated for power 66; assassination of 17, 90, 125–26,
   173, 184; crises in governance
   126; in exile 15; populism of
   315–16; formed coalition government 166; her PPP 16; as prime
   minister 203; pseudo-socialist
   model of 317; quasi-democracy
   under 2; returned to power 166;
   supporting Taliban 127
Bhutto, Zulfiqar Ali 162, 186; death
   sentence of 253; government of
   197–99; and nationalization 239
Bilateral and regional free trade
   agreements (BTAs and RTAs)
   288–89
bin al-Sheikh, Ramzi 25
bin Laden, Osama 23, 25, 71–72,
   128; Taliban's refusal to hand
   over 128; UN Security Council
   demanding 167; US officials
   about 74; World Trade Center
   killing 167
Binoria Town madrasa, see Jamia
   Binoria madrasa
Blasphemy laws 168
Brelawi Sunnis 175
Broad Economic Categories (BEC)
   systems 272–73
Brzezinski, Zbigniew 21
Bugti, Akbar Khan as Baluch nationalist leader xxv, 214–15; killing
   of xxv, 216; and Musharraf's
   government 221; received rent
   from Pakistani Petroleum Ltd
   (PPL) 232–33; his tribal territory attacked by Pakistani troops
   224
Burki, Shahid Javed 241

Bush, George and Manmohan
   Singh 53; Musharraf 7–16; visit
   to Pakistan 83; 'war on terror'
   7, 21

census of 1998 32
Central Asian Republics 140–43
Central Treaty Organization (CENTO)
   137, 237
Chashma nuclear plant, China's
   involvement in 59
China, as 'all-weather' friend 82;
   economic cooperation of 87–88;
   involvement with Pakistan's
   nuclear plants 59; its investments
   in Gwadar 142; missile technology
   to Pakistan 68; nuclear tests of
   46; ties with xviii–xix
Chowdhry, Iftikhar Chief Justice,
   dismissal of xxv–xxvi, 205, 253
civil society, role of xxvi–xxvii
civil–military 'gap' 182
Clinton's anti-terrorism policy
   with India 3; drive to punish
   Al-Qaeda 3
coalition government 181
Cohen, Stephen on army leadership 196
Cold War 67; US military aid 42;
   United States and China as
   allies 64; United States' criticism
   after 66
Comprehensive Test Ban Treaty
   (CTBT), pressure to sign 65
confidence building measures (CBMs)
   45

D-8 conference in Bali 56
Dar-ul-Islam, Islamic ideas of 160
Democracy, restoration of 166–67;
   under Structural Adjustment
   317–19
Deobandi, Jamiat Ulema-e-Islam
   165–66

Deobandis 155
development of 1958–68 313–15
Dosso Case 201
Durand Line 26–27, 35; recognition of 127
Durrani, Ahmad Shah 37
Durrani, Mahmud Ali 40

East Pakistan 212
East Turkestan Islamic Movement 85
Economic Cooperation Organization (ECO) 133
economy 240, 245; growth of 312
Egyptian Hassan Al-Banna 153
elections 17; of 2002 and fundamentalist gains 168–69
emergency 2007 16–17
Energy and Commerce 133–34
Enhanced Structural Adjustment Facility (ESAF) 319
ethnic conflict xxiv–xxv
European Union (EU) resolution to prevent export of nuclear materials 48
exports, cotton as main 87; diversification of 282–83; and Dutch disease factor 298, 301; and Imports 272–82; lack of diversification in 250–51
External Trade Regime 266–72; Exports Herfindahl–Hirschman index 282
Federally Administered Tribal Areas (FATA) xviii, 24, see also Baluchistan; in capturing Al-Qaeda operatives 25; Pakistani troops into xxiii–xxiv
Fissile Material Cut-off Treaty (FMCT) treaty 55

'flying geese' paradigm 292–93
Franks, Tommy 24

Frazer, Jendayi 184
Frontier Works Organization (FWO) 199
fundamentalism 151–52; Islamic 152–61
fundamentalist, ideology of 152–53; initiatives 159–60; politics 153; terrorism, proliferation of 169–70

Gall, Carlotta 27
Gates, Robert 27
Generals 200, see also specific names
Ghazi, Abdul Rashid xxiv
Gilani, Yusaf Raza as head of coalition government 181; and Zia-ul-Haq 185
governments under prime ministers 203
Gulf Cooperation Council (GCC) 5
Gulf, economic interests in 57
Gwadar deep sea port 117–19, 134, 219

Hamas 57
Harkat-ul-Mujahideen 28, 30, 128
Hazara Shias 138–39
Hekmatyar, Pashtun Gulbaddin 136; Pakistan's support to 166
Hezbollah 57
Hindus 123, 150–51, 154–55, 158, 164, 175
Hizb-e-Islami, by Gulbaddin Hekmatyar 127
Hudood Ordinance, imposition of 162, 168
human development 321–29
Human Rights Commission of Pakistan (HRCP) 215; and critics of Musharraf's government 31
Hussain, Mushahid of pro-Musharraf Muslim League 25

Hussain, Saddam removal of 52, see also Iraq invasion

Hussain, Zahid 27, 41

Hwan, Chun 186

Ikram, Tariq 87

income tax 242

India, Border Roads Organization of 132; granted Pakistan Most Favoured Nation (MFN) status 250; hydropower quest of 111–12; mishandling of Kashmir for extremism 76; relations with xx–xxiii; support to Karzai 40–41; with Tel Aviv and Washington 139

Indian National Congress 38

India–Pakistan, border, troops to mass up along 50, 168; dialogue xx–xxi, 48, 91; initiatives on Kashmir 120; military balance 41–42; peace process 54, 58–59, 115; trade 106

India–Sri Lanka Free Trade Agreement (ISLFTA) 290

Indo-Chinese, border war 4; relationship 89

Indo-Tibetan Police Force (ITPF) 146n29

Indo-US, Civil Nuclear Deal and Pakistan 53–58; nuclear deal xviii, xx; nuclear agreement 53, 80; relations 4, 67, 89

Indus Waters Treaty (IWT) 107–10

inequalities 239

International Atomic Energy Agency (IAEA) 53

International Institute for Strategic Studies (IISS) 49

Internationalization and sectarian terrorism 164–67

Inter-Services Intelligence (ISI) 2–3; linked Islamic groups 5; supported militant organizations xxi

intra-SAARC country trade 289, see also SAARC

IPI gas pipeline project with Iran 59

Iran 138–40; Tehran as antagonist to Washington 138

Iran's nuclearization and impact on Pakistan 56

Iran–Pakistan–India (IPI) natural gas pipeline 56, 115–16

Iran–UAE relations 6

Iraq invasion 21, 52

irrigation resources 246–47

Islam, Haroon 172

Islamic, extremism 2–3, 10, 13, 31, 66, 70, 82, 84–85; fundamentalism xxiii–xxiv, xxviii, xxx–xxxii 151–53, 167, 175; in Pakistan xxxii, 156, 159; militancy , xviii, xxiii, xxiv, 3; militants 15, 41, 66, 82; state in Pakistan 175

Islamic, Movement of Uzbekistan (IMU) 134

Islamist terrorists' as generation of American sponsorship 240; rise of 28–30

Jahangir, Asma 163

Jaish-e-Muhammad xxi, xxiii, 28–30, 41, 174

Jamaat-e-Islami (JI) 129, 165–66, 169, 198

Jamhoori Watan Party (JWP) 224

Jamia Abu Bakr Islamia Madrasa 29

Jamia Binoria madrasa 29; as 'fountainhead' of jihadi militancy nationwide 30

Jamiat Ulema-e-Islam (JUI) 129, 169, 198

Jemmah Islamiya of Indonesia 29

jihadi groups and growth of madrasas 29

Jilani, Hina 163

Jillani, Asma Case 201

Jinnah, Mohammad Ali 158, 175
Jintao, Hu 85

Kabul, see Afghanistan
Kalabagh Dam 246, 249
Kaluchak army camp, attack on xxi
Karakoram highway as links with China 86–87
Kargil conflict xx, 3, 48, 103, 195
Karimov, Uzbekistan's President 129
Karimov–Musharraf summit 142
Karzai, Hamid 129; proclaims India as ally 131

Kashmir 100–02; attack on Assembly of 168; Indian rule in xxi; Indo-Pakistan wars 195; Joseph E. Schwartzberg on 99; limits of cooperation 102–6; for Pakistan, xxii; policy in support of, Lashkar-e-Taiba and Harkat-ul-Ansar cum Harkat-ul-Mujahideen 3; Sumit Ganguly on 99–100; UN-sponsored ceasefire in 193; war of 1947–48 195
Kayani, Ashfaq as COAS General 16, 205
Kayani, Justice Rustam 161
Khan, A.Q. xviii, 10, 54, 65–66; nuclear arms bazaar 125; proliferation network to curb 79
Khan, Abdul Rahman 136
Khan, Ghaffar 38, 237; 'Red Shirts' of 38
Khan, Ghulam Ishaq 203
Khan, Liaqat Ali 158
Khan, Mohammad Ayub 195–96, 204, 239, 313–15; BD system of xiv, 159, 204–5; development under 312; economic policies

315; Harvard Advisory Group of 315; reign, agricultural growth increased 314
Khan, Wali 36, 38
Khattak, Khushal Khan 36
Khilafat Movement 155
Khomeini, Ayatollah 5; Islamic government of 6
Khushab, heavy-water plant at 80
Kissinger, Henry 64
Korean War 238; and mercantile class 313

labour demand 296
Lahore Summit 48,102
Lal Masjid, siege of xxiv
land distribution 236
Lashkar-e-Taiba xxi, xxiii, 28, 174; attack on Kashmir Assembly 41; runs madrasa, Jamia Darasitul Islamia 29
Line of Control in Kashmir 168
London terror attacks and Shehzad Tanweer 29

macro-economic evolution of Pakistan's economy 263–66
Madi, Ahmed as Gun Rusaman Gunawaji 29
Mahbub-ul-Haq Harvard Advisory Group of 315
Mahsud, Baitullah 174
Massoud, Ahmed Shah Northern Alliance commander 131, 166
Mazar-e-Sharif's fall to Taliban 139
Mengal, Ataullah 216
military, and economic aid for Pakistan 80–81; governments 316–17; mullah axis xxvii; politics 193–200; presidents 187
Mirza, Iskandar launched his coup 200
Muhajir commercial elite 198
mujahideen 69

Multifibre Arrangement (MFA) 286–87

Munir, Muhammad 161

Musharraf, Parvez, on Afghanistan 9; against 14–15; announced grants 222; anti-Taliban measures 12; Arab friends 5; attempt to kill 28–29; autobiography of 73, 75; as civilian president 16; coup of xiv; crackdown on heavily-armed Islamists xxiv; declaring emergency 16; demanding ethnic Pashtuns from Karzai 11; dictatorship 253; dismissal attempt of Chief Justice Iftikhar Ahmad 15; and economy 241; on extremism 75–76; on foreign militants in Afghanistan 76; handing Al-Qaeda operatives to US 10; on India 9, 10; and Indian Prime Minister Vajpayee xxi; and Islam Karimov agreement by Presidents 134; military operations against Taliban and Al-Qaeda 171; as moderate 73; National Security Council of Pakistan 9; Pakistan's GDP growth 9; plans for Kashmir 78; power through coup 2; Quran citations of 26; reforming religious education in madrasas 10; reforms of women 77; relation to Afghanistan 5; relations with India 12–13; as retired general 181; for right of Kashmiri people 6; rising to power xiv–xvi; subsidizing 21–25; support for US-backed Hamid Karzai government 10; support of Taliban 5, 26; suppressing radical Muslim group in Red Mosque 15; and Taliban–Al-Qaeda allies 7–8; trips to China 95n53; and Washington's partnership 8

Muslim state, demand for 155–58

Muslim World League 154

Muttahida Majlis-e-Amal (MMA) alliance 27–28; alliance xv, 169, 203

Muttahida Qaumi Movement (MQM) and Pakistan People's Party, confrontation between xxvi

National Awami Party 38

National Logistic Cell (NLC) 199

National Reconciliation Order (NRO) 253

National Security Council (NSC) 203

Nazir, Mullah as Ahmedzai Wazir militant commander 147n39

NGO 317

Niazi, Sher Afgan 226

9/11 Terrorist Attacks on WTC 20 167–68; impact of 40–42; and India's support to US's countering terrorism 41; and world 319–21

niqab-wearing armed women of Jamia Hafsa at Lal Masjid 171

Nizamuddin Shanzai 30

non-Muslims 163 sectarian killings 164–65

North Atlantic Treaty Organization (NATO) 58

North Korea 53, 68

North West Frontier Province (NWFP), Pashtun areas of Pakistan's 27

nuclear explosions of 1998 47–48

Nuclear Non-Proliferation Treaty (NPT) 45; pressure to sign 65

nuclear power 246; plants of civilian

Nuclear Proliferation 78–80

Nuclear Security Group (NSG) xix, xxx
Nuclear Suppliers Group (NSG) 55
Nuclear Weapons Free Zone (NWFZ) 58
nuclear-related US–Iran 'war of words' 56
N-Weapons Acquisition and Policies after 49–51

Omar, Mullah 130
Operation Parakaram for attack on Parliament 41
Operation Sunrise 172
Orakzai, Gen. 39
Organization of Islamic Conference (OIC) 78

Pak-Iran relations 57
Pakistan Army, radicalization of 165
Pakistan-based Islamist organizations 174; its credit to Kazakhstan, Kyrgyzstan and Tajikistan 141; declaring as terrorist state 72; economy of 242; fundamentalist parties in 165; as gateway to Muslim world 75; India rapprochement 58; as major non-NATO ally 59; military in xiii–xiv; its brand of Islam is to extremism 75; move with World Trade Organization (WTO) 250; policy of 52–53; problems of large provinces 249; Sunni Muslim status 13–14; support of radical Islamism 6; supported jihadi organizations 136; threats by Powell and Armitage 25; ties with Arab world 57; tribal areas of 142; moderate 75; for United States as non-NATO ally 70; US demands on 71–72; with Uzbekistan 141;

by Washington as major non-NATO ally 116
Pakistan Military Evacuation Organization (PMEO) 194
Pakistan Muslim League (Nawaz) or PML-N xxvii, 181
Pakistan Muslim League-Quaid-i-Azam or PML-Q 184
Pakistan National Assembly 183
Pakistan People's Party PPP xxvii, 90, 162
Pakistan–China relations 68, 89; since 9/11 82–88
Pakistan–US relations xvi, 64–67, 89
Pashtun, FATA into nationalist vision of 38–39
'Pashtunistan' 26, 31–35; Punjabi–Muhajir dominance 33; refugees into NWFP 35
Pickering, Thomas 3
Policies, domestic and foreign xvi, 7–17; and Musharraf xvii–xxiii
poverty, alleviation strategies 248; rates in xvi
Powell, Colin 25
Prime Minister Shaukat Aziz 244
proto-fundamentalism in Indian subcontinent 154
Punjab, tribes of 194

Qureshi, Moeen 241

Rabbani, Tajik Burhanuddin 166
Razmi and Blecker 293–94
reform under Musharraf regime 248–49
Regional Cooperation for Development (RCD) 133
regional economy and cooperation 249–50
Rice, Condoleeza 16
rivalry, natural resource 106–19; river resource 107–11; energy

(oil and natural gas) resource 114–15

Saudi Arabia 5; Iran's strategic rival, supported Afghan mujahideen and Taliban 138
Sayed, Mushahid Hussain 131–32
sea port development of Gwadar 244
SEATO and CENTO, Western military alliances of 165
Sepahe Sahaba 30
Shah, King Zahir 34
Shah, Zafar Ali Case 201
Shanghai Cooperation Organization (SCO) 84, 133–34
Sharif, Nawaz xxvii, 2, 102, 203; alternated in power 66; coup ousted civilian government of 235; dismissal on corruption 166; as elected prime minister 4–5; in exile 15; government passing 13th Amendment 202; overthrown by General Pervez Musharraf 167; overthrown by Musharraf 4; his Pakistan Muslim League (PML-N) 17, 90
Shen, Li 117
Sherpao 172
Shia, fielded Tehrik Nifaas-e-Fiqh Jafaria 169; Iran and Sunni Arab neighbours, rivalry between 164; mosques for attack 171; population of Pakistan 42; — Sunni terrorism 176
Shias 151
Siddiqa, Ayesha 193
Singh, Jaswant 67
Singh, Manmohan xxi
Sino-Pak friendship xviii–xx
Smith, Dianne 141
Social Development 312
social, development 315; sector spending 238

South Asia Free Trade Agreement (SAFTA) 103, 288–91
South Asia Preferential Trade Agreement (SAPTA), signing in 250
South Asian Association of Regional Cooperation (SAARC) 103, Afghanistan's entry into 14; Summit 12th 48; 14th at New Delhi 59; member countries and world trade 289–90
South Asian Customs Union (SACU) 288
Southeast Asia Treaty Organization (SEATO), inclusion in 237
Special Communications Organization (SCO) 199
Standard International Trade Classification (SITC) 272–73, 278–79, 303–4
state, clash with in 2007 171–73; constitution and law, westernized elite's views on 158–59; formation 189–93
structural adjustment program (SAP) signed with International Monetary Fund (IMF) 262
Sufi shrine of Bari Imam 171
suicide, blast at army officers' mess, near Tarbela Dam 173; bombers on Indian Parliament xxi
Sunni *tanzeems* 129

Tajikistan, India's airbases in 132–33
Talbott, Strobe 67
Taliban 2, 164; action against 34; Afghan government 76; Al-Qaeda nexus xxiii–xxiv; Al-Qaeda's support of Chechen separatists 3; and anti-Taliban forces conflict between 2; Islamic radical movements linked to 27; and Pakistan connection 25–28;

and Pashtun nationalism 38–40; terrorists xviii; US and NATO operations against 24

Tamizuddin Case 201

Taneja 103

Tapper, Richard 36

Tarar, Rafiq 203

terrorism networks, funding of 243, in Xinjiang 85; Pakistan links of 174

terrorist attack, on American embassies in Kenya and Tanzania 128; on Christians, Ahmadis, Shias and foreigners 170–71; on Christians, Hindus and Ahmadis 164; in Delhi during Diwali 174; in Srinagar and Delhi 168

textiles and clothing (T&C) sector 286; impact of WTO on 287

trade with India 250; through smuggling and via Gulf states 250; with SAARC Countries 249–50, 282–86

Treaty of Friendship, Cooperation, and Good-Neighbourly Relations, signing of 84

Turkmenistan–Afghanistan–Pakistan line (TAP) 60

United Arab Emirates (UAE) 5–6

United Nations Conference on Trade and Development (UNCTAD) 282

United Nations sanctions against militia 3

United States, and China 4; cost of Musharraf's cooperation 22, 125; declaration of a global war on terrorism xvi–xvii; demands for Pakistani 23–24; India dialogue 67; led war in Afghanistan 52, 56; nuclear relationship 78–79; its use of Pakistani territory coalition military 139–40; and Pakistan's backing of Taliban and Taliban–Al-Qaeda alliance 3; war on terrorism 129

UNSC, accepting Resolution of 58; India's case for permanent membership in 55

Uyghur problem in Xinjiang 69; restiveness 85; separatists in Xinjiang xx

Vajpayee, A. B. 47, 102

Vennesson, Pascal 182

Wahab, Shaikh Muhammad bin Abdul 154

Wahhabism, exporter of 139

water scarcity in South Asia 112–14

Waziristan peace accord 74

Weapons of Mass Destruction (WMD) 52

women 162–63, see also Musharraf, Parvez; and General Zia-ul-Haq 163; honour killings 163

World Trade Center attack, see 9/11 terrorist attack on WTC

Wyatt, Andrew 192

Yahya's military government 201–2

Zafrulla, Sir 161

Zia-ul-Haq, Muhammad 150, 240; coup of 201; death of 312; in power 175, 316; Islamization of Pakistan xiv, xxiii, 2, 7, 73, 76, 139, 150; martial law under 197, 312; relations with Arab states 164; toppled by 162

Zubaydah, Abu 25

For Product Safety Concerns and Information please contact our EU
representative GPSR@taylorandfrancis.com
Taylor & Francis Verlag GmbH, Kaufingerstraße 24, 80331 München, Germany

www.ingramcontent.com/pod-product-compliance
Lightning Source LLC
Chambersburg PA
CBHW070539270326
41926CB00013B/2146